LAND REFORM AND WORKING-CLASS EXPERIENCE IN
BRITAIN AND THE UNITED STATES, 1800–1862

Land Reform and Working-Class Experience in Britain and the United States, 1800-1862

Jamie L. Bronstein

STANFORD UNIVERSITY PRESS
STANFORD, CALIFORNIA

Stanford University Press
Stanford, California
© 1999 by the Board of Trustees of the
Leland Stanford Junior University
Printed in the United States of America

CIP data appear at the end of the book

For my parents

Acknowledgments

There are many people on both sides of the Atlantic to whom I owe credit and thanks. For their comments, words of encouragement, reactions to chapters presented as papers in various fora, and archival and bibliographic assistance, I would like to thank Owen Ashton, Jeremy Burchardt, James Alexander Chokey, Gregory Claeys, Carl Degler, Jonathan Earle, David Eastwood, George Fredrickson, Robert Fyson, Robert G. Hall, Andrew Harris, John Reeve Huston, Neville Kirk, Jim Knox, Mark Lause, Jodie Minor, Richard Price, Karen Sawislak, Dorothy Thompson, Ronald and Mary Zboray, and David Zonderman. I am especially indebted to Paul Gilje and James Epstein, who read the manuscript for Stanford University Press and provided me with extremely helpful suggestions. I am particularly grateful to Malcolm Chase, for his hospitality, assistance, and thought-provoking questions when this project was little more than a good idea; and to John L. Brooke, whose willingness to help at a key point in my research helped make this a much better project. A large share of appreciation is reserved for my advisor, mentor and friend Peter Stansky, who has seen me through every step from dissertation idea to published book with encouragement, boundless wisdom, and well-timed criticism.

I am indebted to the staffs at the following libraries and collections in Britain: the British Library and Newspaper Library at Colindale; Special Collections, Goldsmith's Library, University of London; Tameside Local History Library, Stalybridge; Chetham's Library, Manchester; Rochdale Public Library; Oldham Local Studies Library; Bolton Public Library; Working-Class Movement Library, Salford; Manchester Central Reference Library; Colne Public Library; Preston Public Library; The History Shop, Wigan; Wigan Archives, Leigh; National Museum of Labour History, Manchester; Stoke-on-Trent Public Library, Hanley; and the Keele University Library, Stoke-on-Trent.

On the other side of the Atlantic, I am indebted to the staffs at: Green Library, Stanford University—especially interlibrary loan librarian Sonia Moss and the changing staff at the reference desk; the American Antiquarian Society, Worcester, Mass.; Special Collections, Columbia University Library; Massachusetts Archives at Columbia Point, Boston; the Keyport, New Jersey, Historical Society; the Library of Congress, Washington, D.C.; the National Archives, Washington, D.C.; the Shaker Museum Library, Old Chatham, N.Y.; the Syracuse University Libraries; New York State Library, Albany; and the Rochester Public Library. This study was made possible in part by the generosity of the International Studies department at Stanford University, by the Stanford University History Department, and by the Mellon Foundation. I am particularly grateful to Norris Pope, John Feneron, and Paul Psoinos of Stanford University Press for their high level of care and concern in the transformation of this text from manuscript to book.

Parts of Chapter 6 appeared as Jamie Bronstein, "Land Reform, Community-Building and the Labor Press in Antebellum America and Britain," in Michael Harris and Tom O'Malley, eds., *Studies in Newspaper and Periodical History*, 1995 Annual, pp. 69–84, published by Greenwood Press, an imprint of Greenwood Publishing Group, Inc., Westport, Conn.

On a personal level, I would like to thank my parents, Ronald and Susan Bronstein, and my sister, Lori Gironda, for their encouragement, funding, and almost infinite patience when nothing was as interesting to me as working-class land reform. The pilgrimage to the grave of George Henry Evans was beyond the call of even familial duty. I thank my colleagues at New Mexico State University, for providing the friendly atmosphere necessary for serious thinking and writing. Finally, Mike Zigmond has added greatly both to this project and to my quality of life, with love, support, computer expertise, intellectual partnership, and timely interjections of common sense.

J.B.

Las Cruces, N.M.
April 1998

Contents

LAND REFORM AND WORKING-CLASS EXPERIENCE IN
BRITAIN AND THE UNITED STATES, 1800–1862

Introduction

Why Were There Working-Class Land-Reform Movements in Britain and America?

Give me a cottage low and neat
Decked out with modest flowers
A cool retreat in summer's heat
Snug in winter's hours. . . .
Give me a hearthstone free from spot
A cheerful fire at night
A shining grate, a bubbling pot
and all around me bright.[1]

Why were there working-class land-reform movements in Britain and America in the 1840's? Given that working people in Britain and the United States had divergent experiences of industrialization, and lived in countries with widely different definitions of political citizenship, how could these movements to claim the land for working people have been so similar? During a decade of reformist ferment with few precedents in either British or American history, working people on both sides of the Atlantic subscribed to the notion that society as a whole was deeply flawed because of the growing gap between the rich and the poor—but that it was also ready for change.[2] A fortuitous combination of circumstances in both countries—among them the experience of factory labor, transitions in the external environment, histories of failed political radicalism, the activities of experienced leaders committed to the notion of small proprietorship, and the widespread perception that farmers led particularly healthy and virtuous lives—combined to push this change in a new direction: the search for land for the laborers.[3] This study explores the way in which, in the face of material differences, an amazing confluence of ideas and organizational strategies convinced American and British workers to fight toward a common goal.[4]

Together, three working-class land-reform efforts, American National Reform, the Chartist Co-Operative Land Company, and the Potters' Joint-Stock Emigration Society, would transcend the then great physical distance between Britain and the United States, to craft an international movement to raise the economic, social, and moral status of workers everywhere. By opening a safety valve to the land, reformers in both countries sought to vouchsafe to factory workers and to artisans threatened by deskilling some of the pride and independence they had lost with the introduction of machinery and the decline of apprenticeship. Drawing their ideas on land redistribution from a common stock of turn-of-the-century philosophy, their leaders, including George Henry Evans, Feargus O'Connor, and William Evans, asserted that man had a natural right to a piece of the soil, the root of all life. They championed the laborer's right to equal protection and respect for his private property—the labor of his hands. Working in parallel, they conjured up elaborate visions of the healthfulness, beauty, and autonomous lifestyle awaiting workers in the countryside, and decried the burgeoning cities as dens of vice and decay. They argued that the cottage home would restore a natural family structure, bring wives and children back from the factories and into kitchens and schools where they belonged, and place breadwinning husbands back at the head of the table. They claimed that as labor markets rationalized with the siphoning off of excess labor, the wages of those left behind would rise, and the country would prosper. Through this combination of improvement in labor's condition and the restoration of "a stake in the hedge," respect for the "producer" would be assured.[5]

In the cotton towns of industrial Lancashire and across England, this message reached the ears of factory workers, unskilled laborers, and some artisans, whose experiences of industrialization both conformed with and reinforced the vision held out to them. Thus, disillusioned by years of ineffectual campaigning for the six points of the People's Charter, tens of thousands of British working people switched strategies, subscribing their pence to the Chartist Co-Operative Land Company in hopes of winning a cottage and agricultural land in a periodic lottery. Simultaneously, in the pottery districts of Staffordshire, Yorkshire, and Glasgow, disappointed former trade unionists bought shares in the Potters' Joint-Stock Emigration Society and dreamed of a home in faraway Wisconsin. In Massachusetts and across the industrial North, workingmen looked up from their lasts and forges or leaned on their hoes and decided that, despite the fact that they did have the right to vote, the landed independence promised by the frontier was the one factor saving them from the fate of the English worker. By the tens of thousands, they signed their names to petitions requesting land-reform measures, and sent them to Congress, hoping that, together with other pro-labor reforms, this "National Reform" would finally gain the producer his much-deserved equal rights. The land-reform movement in America was an obvious manifestation of cultural adjustment to the Market Revolution, the bundle of social and economic changes associated with the emergence of wage-labor capitalism and the introduction of markets in the Early Republic.[6]

The history of transatlantic working-class land reform adds complexity to three interlinked stories of workers' activity in the nineteenth century. It illustrates the way in which British workers' views of the United States shifted. At first, the United States seemed like a paradise of universal suffrage for British radicals, but when land monopoly came under the microscope, the United States appeared to be moving in the direction of less liberty rather than more.[7] It calls into question both traditional notions of "class" and historians' assumptions about the types of reforms in which workers should have been interested. The histories of the Chartist Co-Operative Land Company, the National Reform movement, and the Potters' Joint-Stock Emigration Society and the connections among them reveal that, throughout the 1840's, land reform was one of the main outlets for the energies of working-class leaders and a subject of great importance in the labor press.

Historians have until recently neglected the land-reform movements, finding the movements for family farms backward-looking, hard to reconcile with the rest of the romantic grand narrative of labor's struggle. In some cases, land reform has been dismissed as a middle-class movement which distracted workers from what should have been their primary interests.[8] But comparative examination of the land-reform movement shows that the quest for landed independence was a common reaction to capitalism and urbanization, and that the welfare of workers was always the central goal.[9] The

land-reform movement in fact crossed the class barriers which historians have rather arbitrarily drawn, linking factory workers and
owners of small businesses in a quest for the respect which only
landownership could provide.

This analysis of the transatlantic land-reform movements coheres
with the growing body of recent historical writing showing that working people had diverse goals during their period of adjustment to the
Market Revolution. Faced with palpable changes to social status and
physical environment, working men and women sought affirmation
of the right to property in labor; the right to be free of feudal tenures,
which smacked of aristocracy; the right to a clean, sturdy dwelling; or
the right to sufficient leisure to pursue moral and religious instruc-
tion.[10] Then as now, they measured their standard of living by where
and under what conditions they could afford to live, the roles which
the members of their families could afford to adopt, and the extent to
which society encouraged them to value their own contributions to
the community. Activist workers often had a higher moral vision
which cried out for a "regeneration" of society—a rethinking of basic
issues. Many were concerned with Christian social renewal of the
type the land reformers promised.[11] Others wished to restore "family
values"—even if these were wrongly remembered or completely invented.[12]

The quest for land for the workers does not seem anachronistic
when considered in light of the diversity of working peoples' goals
and the complexity of their values. Rather, there are elements of the
quest that were radical. American National Reformers would seek,
among their goals, the exemption of the homestead from distraint
for debt. This purposeful intervention into the free market would
have militated against what workers saw as the worst excesses of
capitalism, by making families the principal beneficiaries of state
paternalism, and giving women new property rights.[13] The Chartists' call for men to live and raise families on four acres of land
would have forced a radical reorganization of British society by reversing the trend toward consolidation of landholding among the
wealthy.[14] Workers in the 1840's saw society as fluid and changing;
they had no reason to expect that technology would make a world of
small family farms obsolete. Thus, rather than a quiescent pastoral-
ism, workers' land-reform movements attempted to achieve an organization of society which had not been seen before. Old ideas

about the sanctity and preferability of the land were being combined with new ideas about the value of labor, which had grown directly out of prior workers' movements.[15]

The story of the transatlantic working-class land-reform movement of the 1840's comprises three interlinked narratives, each with its own course and cast of characters. Although the approach of the rest of this book is thematic, Chapter 1 briefly narrates the course of each of these movements: the Chartist Co-Operative/National Land Company, the American National Reform movement, and the Potters' Joint-Stock Emigration Society. Taken separately, as historians have tended to take them, these movements seem different in their scope and effect—but the seeming differences have been allowed to disguise a wealth of similarities in the realm of ideas and organization.

These similarities were made possible in part because, no matter which particular version of land reform they espoused, the British and American land reformers drew their basic theories from a common stock of ideas. As Chapter 2 will illustrate, a wide spectrum of reformers and social thinkers, ranging from the politically central Thomas Jefferson to the politically marginal Thomas Spence, propounded land reform, setting forth a philosophic basis for the claim that man had a natural right to the soil. The second chapter of this study takes the measure of this discourse, and shows that the call for land reform increased in the 1830's and 1840's. Nor were labor leaders alone in claiming that an alternative mix of small farming and industry was possible; land reform was both a radical and a conservative prescription for the reorganization of society. The idea that man had a right to the soil would be a tenacious one, creating ripples of thought which lasted until the 1890's and after.

Despite the fact that the British and American land reformers operated in two very different environments, the arguments they used to make land reform appeal to their constituencies were surprisingly similar. Reformers conjured up a possibly exaggerated vision of the way in which the factory organization of labor perverted the working-class family and oppressed the individual. Land-reforming writers created pastoral visions of farm life, complete with abundant produce, and emphasized that a farmer's economic independence conferred political independence. Aware that some working people were intensely religious in this period of revivalism, leaders used Christian images and quoted from the Bible in an attempt to show that land redistribution was the will of God; but at the same time they appealed to freethinkers with a natural-rights argument. Patriotism was used in the service of land reform; owning land was said to be the right of the freeborn American as well as the freeborn Englishman. Chapter 3 explores these components of land-reform belief and examines the way in which these ideas were constructed on both sides of the Atlantic.

The producerist, labor-friendly character of the land-reform movements was obvious to contemporaries because each movement interacted with, and defined itself against, a movement with a more middle-class, "liberal" character. As Chapter 4 shows, in Britain, the Anti–Corn Law League served as the "other," while in the United States this role was occupied by the Abolitionist movement. While the Anti–Corn Law League and Abolitionists touted the moral responsibility of the individual, and emphasized that freedom meant the freedom of the individual to make his own contracts, the land-reform movements constantly emphasized the effect of environment on the formation of character. The land reformers used the contrast in basic beliefs between their movement and these other movements to advance their alternative, republican view that a humane society should provide for the social happiness and physical survival of its citizens. The contrast in principles was clear to other communitarian reformers, like the Owenites and Fourierites, who operated on the outer edges of land reform, occasionally aiding the land reformers with their experienced leadership.

The cultural and organizational similarities between land-plan Chartism and National Reform are particularly striking. As Chapter 5 illustrates, both movements shared similar leadership and revolved around major working-class newspapers; both sets of leaders understood the role of face-to-face contact in promoting transformation and commitment in a constituency. Even the fact that white American workingmen had the right to vote was de-emphasized, as the land-reform movements pursued a common organizational strategy.[16] Surprisingly, and in spite of rudimentary communications technologies, Chartism and National Reform traded advice and ideas through labor newspapers and even traded personnel, helping land reformers to feel as though they were part of an international movement to raise the living standard of the worker.

Although the ideology of land reform and leaders' organizational strategies were similar, the similarities between the movements break down when the constituencies for land reform are examined.[17] Although the sources to examine the audience for land reform have been available for some time now, only recently have historians begun to use statistics and the census to characterize individual National Reformers and Chartists.[18] Based on the examination of hundreds of petitions in the National Archives and thousands of names of Chartist Land Company subscribers, Chapter 6 reveals that National Reform appealed to a broader occupational base than did the Chartist Land Company. National Reformers tended to be mature, married men, some of them with property; they hailed from farms, small towns, and Fourierite communities as well as from factory districts. In contrast, about a quarter of the Chartist Land Company subscribers whom we can track down hailed from the environmentally oppressed and economically depressed cotton districts of Lancashire and Cheshire. The examination of land-reform membership bears out the theory that common languages of oppression overcame differences in experience to propel workers in the direction of the land.[19]

The most salient differences between the British and American land-reform movements emerged when the movements encountered the institutions of authority in each country—the presses and the governments. As Chapter 7 shows, enemies in the middle-class press, funded by the Free Trade movement, alerted the British government to the dangers inherent in the Chartist Land Company. Influential actors in the government, resentful of Feargus O'Connor's presence in the House of Commons, and fearful that the land company would lead to a resurgence of Chartist violence, acted to suppress the company through a Select Committee investigation.[20] All the while, the hierarchical nature of British society enabled opposition figures to claim that they were only interfering in the Chartist Land Company in order to protect the savings of British workmen who were too ill educated to protect themselves.

While the Chartist Co-Operative/National Land Company failed in part because it was suppressed by the government, National Reform ideas made a smooth transition into general acceptance because of political transformations taking place in the 1850's. Even as working men soldiered on for land reform through a number of different voluntary societies, the tribunes of the Republican Party picked up on National Reform measures and fused them with "Free Soil" for a wide, middle-class, antislavery appeal. Fears that National Reform was a leveling, "agrarian" measure were soon quelled, as "vote yourself a farm," the original motto of National Reform, became "homes for the homeless," a stirring call to domesticity for all. Any connections that National Reform had once had with the Chartist radicals or with the ideas of New York radical Thomas Skidmore were long forgotten by the time the Homestead Act was signed in 1862.

While working-class land reform never fully achieved the goals it set out for itself, in both Britain and America it revived the point of view that society should guarantee to its citizens some minimum standard of social happiness, without which the notion of political equality was a grim jest; in the words of the land reformers' favorite biblical verse, only under their own vine and their own fig tree could they be certain that none might make them afraid. Although the tree which the land reformers of the 1840's planted would not bear fruit in their lifetime, it would prove a tenacious plant for the rest of the century and even after, testifying to the continual appeal of social equality even in the midst of a capitalist revolution. [21]

1

Three Movements, One Goal

To secure the right of the soil to ALL, it is necessary to limit the possessions of families, corporations, and communities;—to prevent all further traffic in land by the Government, and to make the public lands free to actual settlers, that every man, woman and child in the Nation may have a home—a home, to which each one may retreat, and rest in safety, 'under his own vine and fig tree.'

—Industrial Congress, 1845[1]

Although the purpose of this study is to examine thematically the ideologies, organization, constituencies, and outcomes of the working-class land-reform movements of the 1840's, themes are of little use without an understanding of the basic narrative and cast of characters of each movement. A brief examination of the rise and fall of, respectively, the Chartist Co-Operative Land Company, the National Reform movement, and the Potters' Joint-Stock Emigration Society provides this schema. It also illustrates that land reform in both Britain and the United States grew out of existing working-class organizations. These groups sought land reform only when most other feasible options—petitioning, political organization, or trade unionism—had failed. In their elegance and simplicity, and in their claim to be able to solve working-class political and social problems with one simple economic equation, the land-reform movements quickly appealed to large constituencies—tens of thousands in the case of National Reform and Chartism; thousands in the case of the potters' society.

When the stories of the working-class land-reform movements are told, the differences among the movements also become immediately apparent. The Chartists' land scheme would be crushed by a combination of financial unwieldiness and harassment by the government, members of which claimed that the scheme would be detrimental to the interests of the working poor. In contrast, the same government never acknowledged the rather similar potters' scheme, except to grant it legal standing as a friendly society. Of the three movements, National Reform was nominally the most successful, winning land reform for American working people almost twenty years after the agitation had started.

What is not immediately apparent from telling these three sel-dom-told stories is how very interlinked the working-class land-reform movements were. Brief narratives cannot illustrate the common arguments used by British and American land reformers, or the common philosophers of the natural right to the soil whom each movement revered. Individual stories ignore the steady stream of land-reform news—printed in newspapers or carried by emissaries—which crossed the Atlantic on packet ships. Land was fodder for working-class hopes no matter how industrialization occurred; but as the remainder of this book will show, that only becomes clear if land reform is examined in an international context.

How did the Chartist movement transform itself from a political movement in the service of social ends to an economic movement in the service of political ends? The answer is, through desperation. The leaders of the Chartist movement found themselves in a bind in 1843. Nothing they had tried in their quest to win the six points of the People's Charter had seemed to work. Parliament had been petitioned, scattered armed uprisings had occurred, tracts had been written and conventions held, all to no avail. Universal male suffrage, equal electoral districts, payment of salaries to Members of Parliament, the elimination of property qualifications for MP's, secret ballot, and annual parliamentary elections seemed just as remote as they had at the inauguration of the movement in 1838. Even worse, the 1842 general strike in the North of England had plunged the government and the propertied classes into paranoia, and thus further discredited workers' legitimate political demands. It was therefore time to contemplate winning the vote, and achieving "social happiness" through the repeal of "class legislation" in some other way. Weighing his options, self-appointed tribune of the people Feargus O'Connor returned to a thread which he had been spinning out for almost a decade: that the land would fulfill working-class hopes. He began to fill the columns of his newspaper, the *Northern Star*, with explanations of the benefits to be reaped, in terms of economic satisfaction and work autonomy, from farming a small plot of land.[2]

Responding to the perceived need for new tactics, a Chartist Convention—a mere shadow of the Chartist "anti-Parliaments" which had once attracted such great attention—met in September 1843. The few delegates who attended reformulated Chartism as a species of labor party, with local branches and card-carrying members.[3] They also discussed the advisability of forming a cooperative land company, patterned after the familiar "friendly society" model, to collect and consolidate contributions from working-class shareholders, buy land, and parcel it out to them.

The plan for a Chartist Land Company could hardly have come at a better time. The idea of land for the laborers, whether in the form of small allotments or independent farms, had been bandied about for a long time; but the economic instability of the 1840's was beginning to convince workers that farming might be a more secure lifestyle than factory work or artisanal trades. Around the country, the slogan "the Charter and the Land" caught on, and the idea flourished. Through his newspaper and with the assistance of a band of traveling lecturers, O'Connor fomented interest in the land among workers, drawing their attention to its benefits in contrast with the factory system.

At first, the mechanism by which land would be redistributed was vague. But once the popular appetite had been whetted, and O'Connor's audience was familiar with the argument that small plots of land would improve the condition of the worker, O'Connor and a small group of close allies in April 1845 created a method for the redistribution of the land—the Chartist Co-Operative Land Company.[4] The company's executive panel consisted of O'Connor and several of his cronies, who were also veteran Chartist leaders with a lot of credibility in the industrial North: Christopher Doyle, Philip McGrath, Thomas Martin Wheeler, and Thomas Clark. Together, they formulated a plan for creating small allotments of land—each with its own snug cottage—on which participating working people would farm. A two-acre allotment might be secured for a reasonably priced £2 10s share in the company.

The land company appealed to subscribers in multiple and complex ways, but the major concept upon which its promoters relied was independence. Independence encompassed political independence underpinned by landownership, but it also connoted the freedom that the farmer supposedly had to use his time as he saw fit. Independence referred to the autonomy of the farming family, and the ability of women and children on family farms to take up roles which land-reforming rhetoric constructed as "traditional." As Thomas Martin Wheeler told his fellow land company directors,

The order of nature is at present entirely reversed. The mother, whose duty it is to attend to the affairs of her household, and the education of her children, is constrained to toil from twelve to fourteen hours a day in a nauseous and unearthly cotton mill. . . . the child of thirteen years of age is compelled to labour the same number of hours as the mother, while the father, who is destined by the Author of the universe to watch over and protect the interests of his family, is compelled to walk the streets an unwilling killer, living by the sacrifice of those whom he holds most dear.[5]

Finally, the land company's directors envisioned their efforts as an infrastructure through which the working classes could pool their resources and remove the surplus unemployed population from the labor market.

The Chartist Co-Operative Land Company moved next door to the printing office of the primary Chartist newspaper, O'Connor's *Northern Star*; their geographical proximity emphasized the close connection between the land scheme and the rest of the Chartist movement.[6] The company's central office encouraged the development of local branches, which remitted payment for the first shares.[7] Although it lacked the necessary legal registration, the company received so much money so quickly that it soon could afford to buy an estate, and in March 1846, the first patch of Chartist ground was purchased at Herringsgate (now Heronsgate), which was rechristened "O'Connorville" shortly afterward.[8] O'Connor and the directors elected to ignore the advice of their legal counsel, who recommended that allotments be distributed according to the order in which members had bought their shares. Instead, they chose a system of balloting, in part for its potential to keep excitement at fever pitch.[9] The estate was parceled out among 35 settlers, who, having been assigned allotments of two, three, and four acres, began to trickle onto the land and till it.

The lottery and successful settlement of O'Connorville only added to the flood of funds to the land company. Within two months, O'Connor had purchased a second estate at Lowbands, and

in December 1846, a Land and Labour Bank was established. The
Bank was intended to speed the purchase of estates by diverting
general depositors' funds to smoothing company cash flows. Four
more estates followed: Minster Lovell, later renamed Charterville,
Snig's End, Great Dodford, and Redmarley. These were colonized,
and a sixth estate, Mathon, was sold for a profit without being colonized. The land buying was part of what O'Connor called the "reproductive principle"—all estates, converted into investment prop-
erties by the addition of the rent-paying allottees, were meant to be
sold, thereby providing more money to purchase further estates. On
the strength of these actual purchases, and the construction of cottages and sowing of the first crops, the popularity of the land company zoomed. It reached its height in 1847, with 86 branches in the
North, 48 in the Midlands, 89 in the South, and 24 in London.[10] Riding this wave of popularity, Feargus O'Connor was elected to Parliament for Nottingham. In addition, in response to the influx of
shareholders, the original company was closed to new shareholders
and a second company opened.

Despite the appearance of prosperity and working-class energy
which the land company brought to areas where Chartism had apparently lapsed into quiescence, underneath the surface all was not
well. The company had at first sought to be recognized under the
Friendly Societies Act, but registration was denied. The next step
was to seek registration as a joint-stock company. The law required
that the company deposit with the government all papers enumerating the goals of the company, any advertisements, and a document
containing the signatures of holders of at least one-quarter of all
shares. Eventually the signatures of all shareholders would have to
be on file, and every page of this final document stamped with an
expensive stamp. Clearly, such registration was impracticable for a
company with tens of thousands of working-class shareholders,
scattered all over the country, many of whom, we must assume,
could not write. Nonetheless, in an effort at compliance, a monster
deed was prepared, and transported around the country, lying open
for signatures in the major population centers.[11] But the company
was running out of time—its period of provisional registration had
lapsed, and every monetary transaction made by the company
would be illegal until final registration was secured.

The legal tide was not the only one turning against the land company. While at first even the mainstream press reserved judgment about O'Connor's land experiment, by 1847–48 positive press reports about the Chartist colonies were becoming scarcer.[12] The allottees, certainly far from markets, were alleged to be destitute of agricultural knowledge, and many were unused to working outdoors in all weathers.[13] Whether or not the allottees were truly hopeless at holding body and soul together, they were effectively represented as being so by opponents of the land plan. The plight of the landed unfortunates was exploited in a sustained attack from the liberal press—a press with close connections to O'Connor's traditional enemies, the Free Traders. Partly in response to this public attention and partly as a political response to O'Connor's behavior as a loose cannon in Parliament, in the spring and summer of 1848 a Parliamentary Select Committee was chosen to investigate the land company. In short order, the Committee considered the practicality of the plan and found it wanting. Although O'Connor was not ordered to "wind up" (close down) his company at first, the doubt the Committee threw on the plan helped cut off the company's cash flow.

O'Connor offered to wind up his company and tried to restore the confidence of those who had paid up their shares. Unfortunately, to keep the company going, he was forced just at this time to collect the first rents from the allottees.[14] The allottees at the "People's First Estate," O'Connorville, had at first rallied around their benefactor, but when rents were requested they claimed they had been deceived, refused to pay, and joined the ranks of his detractors. O'Connor tried to cut his losses by sending bailiffs to evict some of the colonists who did not or could not pay their rents. He also worked to turn company members who had not yet been granted allotments against the allottees, calling the rent strikers "rascals."[15] Meanwhile, Tidd Pratt, the Registrar for Joint-Stock Companies, continued to refuse to register the floundering concern, and the Court of Queen's Bench upheld his refusal. Having no other choice, with his personal debts mounting, on July 9, 1850, O'Connor petitioned for leave to present a bill to dissolve the land company.

In May 1851, a faint hope glimmered for the Chartists' pastoral vision in a proposal for a National Loan Society to buy land company estates and parcel them out along the lines of a building society.[16] This plan was superseded, however, by the act for liquidation of the company in August of that year; all the lands which had not yet been bought would have to be sold. O'Connor finally threw up his hands and blamed the failure of the land company on the allottees for not having paid their rents.[17] Possibly affected by syphilis, O'Connor went mad, was institutionalized in 1852, and died a broken man in 1855, his land company thoroughly repudiated by Chartist leaders.[18]

When one of the allottees wrote a letter to the London *Times* pleading for justice, the government placed the National Land Company's estates under the supervision of a Master in Chancery, who was supposed to sort out all the competing claims. He was besieged by stockholders requesting the return of their money.[19] The allotments themselves were given over to the management of a man named Goodchap, who proposed that the original allottees might remain on their lands provided they paid back rents; but he had as much trouble collecting rents as O'Connor had had.[20] Because of this endemic inability to pay rent, most of the allotments changed hands within a few years, falling into the hands of market gardeners with more experience than the Chartist allotment holders possessed. While they never became the radical villages which O'Connor and his codirectors had had in mind, even today, the Chartist allotment cottages remain standing and occupied, albeit with architectural additions and modern conveniences. Although O'Connor's company failed, the Chartist cottages are a testament to his commitment to provide the poor with sturdy houses.[21]

The Chartist Co-Operative Land Company had risen and fallen meteorically; its trajectory was not mirrored by that of its American counterpart, the National Reform movement. The two movements did begin at approximately the same time. One crisp Sunday in February 1844, a year in which the *Northern Star* was seriously touting small farms as a safety valve for an overcrowded labor market, George Henry Evans, radical printer turned melon farmer, left his farm in New Jersey and made the journey into Manhattan, to his friend John Windt's print shop. There, he, Windt, and four other workingmen gathered to discuss what Evans called three "sliding measures," by which a complete reform of society, a so-called National Reform, might be achieved.[22]

Evans shared with the group a vision of the "freedom of the public lands," free homesteads for actual settlers; "homestead exemption," exemption of the family home from distraint for debt; and "land limitation"—a legal limitation on the number of acres any one man might possess. A reasonable, practical man who had been involved with the New York labor scene since 1829, Evans gave an explanation of the relationship between land and happiness which the other men found convincing; and once these goals had been decided on, it was a small thing for men with, variously, experience in the workingmen's movement, Chartism, and Owenite socialism to promulgate a constitution for the newly christened "National Reform Association." They declared that "the public lands of the States and of the United States shall be made *free to actual settlers*," and resolved "to take into consideration such other remedies for the distresses and embarrassments of the productive or working classes as may appear likely to be practically useful."[23]

From the ranks of reformers and workingmen who had participated in the trade union agitation of the 1830's, from Manhattan and Brooklyn, Jersey City, and Williamsburg, a National Reform central committee was culled. This committee set in motion a lobbying machine. They collected dues and donations, prepared memorials to Congress and the state legislatures, drafted legislation to eliminate public land monopoly, and oversaw deputations to wait upon lawmakers. Along with its lobbying mission, the National Reform central committee was to educate the public, through the press, tracts, and "the Missionary system by paid lecturers." It was empowered to book halls for meetings, and even to arrange for music and publish land-reform songs. The committee was also instructed to encourage women to attend National Reform meetings.[24] Armed with this comprehensive plan, the committee began to proselytize land reform.[25] The *Working Man's Advocate*, the labor newspaper Evans had run since 1829, but had been forced to give up in the wake of the 1837 depression, had already been resurrected to drive the movement forward.[26] Taking a page from temperance and capitalizing on the newly achieved widespread male suffrage, the National Reformers encouraged their followers to sign the "agrarian pledge." Workers were encouraged to "vote yourself a farm" by pledging to vote for no man unless he promised conformity with National Reform principles.

By 1845, the National Reform Association was sending representatives to the Industrial Congresses, the annual meetings of working people's groups which so characterized the reformism of that period.[27] These meetings would serve as the backbone of an organized, multi-city, Northern working-class activism until the mid-1850's.[28] National Reform articles and Industrial Congress proceedings alike were picked up and reprinted in a number of labor and general reform newspapers, from Maine to Wisconsin.

But National Reformers were also peripatetic. Traveling lecturers cultivated the Anti-Rent counties of New York state, cities such as Cincinnati, Chicago, and Philadelphia, and settlements of the Wisconsin frontier, preaching a moral economy, a producerist worldview, and a familiar scare story of the results of industrialization. They capped their expositions by distributing petition forms requesting that Congress comply with National Reform principles. National Reformers' local auxiliaries also sent homestead petitions to state legislatures, where they occasionally sparked great interest and elicited special reports and even the passage of legislation exempting a small homestead from distraint for debt.[29] In time, the words of the National Reformers made an impact; the signed petitions, at first a trickle, became a torrent.

In the 1850's, National Reform fragmented into several directions. The movement was troubled by its relationship with the "free soil" agitation, which attempted to exclude slavery from territories as they became states. Some National Reform leaders were ambivalent about the abolition of slavery, while others wholeheartedly favored it. Thus, while a core of New York–based lobbyists continued the campaign for free land, petitioning and speaking at mass meetings in the City Hall Park, workingmen in other cities sought free or inexpensive land through other means. They formed building societies, prayed for their deliverance, and directed their energies through the Brotherhood of the Union, a secret society dedicated to land reform. Meanwhile, in Congress, homestead bills were repeatedly proposed, and, as the Republican Party gained in strength with "Free Soil" as its motto, were increasingly well received.

By the time the Homestead Act was passed in 1862, providing the "free public lands" for which the National Reformers had so long campaigned, George Henry Evans had slipped from the scene and the moment of greatest grassroots pressure on the government had long passed. Nonetheless, National Reform was clearly responsible for publicizing the homestead issue. The popularity of land reform convinced the new Republican Party that to assume the mantle of land reform might attract workers to switch parties during the party disintegration of the 1850's. The measure that had been envisioned as an integral part of a campaign to raise the status of American workers, had been reconstituted as a plan to tie the West to the industrial North and to promote middle-class domesticity.

While the courses that National Reform and the Chartist Land Plan were to follow, and the fate of each, were different, the two movements shared great similarities in ideology, rhetorical presentation, and organizational structure, as the study that follows will show. Their leaders portrayed their own movements as part of an international working-class movement to gain land for the laborer. Although National Reform and the Chartist Land Plan were the two main movements of this type during their day, collectively calling on the loyalties of some 130,000 working people (and probably the imaginations of many more), the energy that they in particular produced, and the discourse of land reform in general, generated a host of regional building and allotment societies.

One of these, the Potters' Joint-Stock Emigration Society, participated in the discussion of the theoretical benefits of land for the laborers which was propagated by land-plan Chartism and National Reform. The society also bridged the transatlantic gap by proposing to release British workers from the clogged labor markets of the English potteries and send them to the "open" lands of the American West.[30] Again, the year 1843–44 was the turning point. In 1843, the threatening shadow of mechanization began to creep over the smog-obscured Staffordshire potteries. At their union meetings, in tones of unease, potters discussed a recently invented machine, the "jolly," which created standardized wares by combining the technology of the mold and the wheel. There was no way human hands, no matter how skilled, could keep up with the infernal creation. The revolution in potting would come, they feared—it was just a matter of when.[31]

Deskilling was not the potters' only fear. Their other grievances included masters who required pottery-baking ovens to be emptied before they had sufficiently cooled; being paid on the basis of what came out of the kiln in serviceable condition rather than what went in; and the "allowance" system, by which a man was pressured to allow, or give back, a percentage of his weekly wage to his employer. Apprentices also had a training allowance deducted from their already meager wages. Long hours and unhealthy work environments led to respiratory problems and short lives. The potters' discontent was long-standing; but what could they do? They had already suffered through one expensive and nonproductive strike in 1836–37. Like the Chartists, they needed another strategy.[32]

With dimmed hopes, therefore, the potters refounded the United Brotherhood of Operative Potters on September 6, 1843. In December, Owenite and Welshman William Evans initiated a newspaper, *The Potters' Examiner and Workman's Advocate*, to hold together the disparate trades which composed the potting industry by letting them understand their common interest.[33] The demands of the potters, as expressed in the newspaper, were at first the standard demands of nineteenth-century trade unionists: a twelve-, or even better an eight- or ten-hour day; a dwelling for every industrious man; and sufficient earnings to furnish his family with food, drink, clothing, and every comfort of life.[34] But before long, like George Henry Evans and Feargus O'Connor, William Evans had conceived a land plan. He proposed to relocate excess labor from the potteries onto farms in Wisconsin, using the same mechanism of collection of funds followed by a lottery which O'Connor and his deputies had chosen for their land company.

As Feargus O'Connor and his co-lecturers did, Evans gave lectures and supervised local meetings, edited the *Potters' Examiner*, conducted research, and traveled to the outlying potting districts, spreading the gospel of land reform.[35] Local branches of the company held meetings and collected payments, while Evans wrote to land officers in the United States to inquire about the possibility of buying tracts of land. When sufficient funds had been raised, three potters of good repute were handed £100 and loaded, with their families, into a second-class ship cabin to cross the Atlantic and find "Pottersville."[36]

Once the land had been purchased, the land officers and their families constructed the first buildings on the four miles' worth of purchased land, planting crops and sending back interim reports of their progress against ungiving nature. Meanwhile, lotteries chose the lucky paid-up potters who were to follow; 44 people were dispatched in early April 1847.[37] These settlers could claim 20-acre farms, with substantial "one up, one down" log dwellings and two years' credit on the company store, the lot to be paid off in installments of wheat. When the cash flow from the potteries slowed, Evans and his codirector broadened the scope of the society by offering farms to members of nonpotting trades. The Emigration Society also suggested tradespeople raise the price of passage by contributing to mutual assistance clubs. After a club had been established for six months, a ballot would be taken monthly from the names of all paid-up members. In a similar spirit to that of the American National Reformers, Evans and his group made farms available only to actual settlers; the "moral economy" applied to land as well as food.[38] Like the American National Reformers and, more implicitly, the Chartists, the potters hoped to exclude speculators from participating in their scheme.[39]

To an unbiased observer, the Potters' Joint-Stock Emigration Society might have seemed similar to the Chartist Co-Operative Land Company. Both operated on the same principle of mutual assistance. Both relied on lotteries to choose the lucky winners of allotments. Yet unlike the Chartist Land Company, the potters' society was quickly registered under the Friendly Societies Act, an act intended to encompass small, local efforts at working-class thrift. All that was necessary to register a friendly society was to submit a copy of the rules and a list of the officers, and have the rules signed by two county magistrates and the revising barrister, and the friendly society was on its way. There was no need to gather thousands of signatures or pay a stamp duty on each page of the deed of registration. The Emigration Society, partly because it was politically unobjectionable, cheaply became a legal operation and thus came under less official scrutiny than would the Chartist plan.[40]

Unlike the Chartist Co-Operative/National Land Company, the Potters' Society would crash under its own weight. At the height of its influence, in 1849–50, the Emigration Society had branches all over Britain, many bearing "inspirational" names.[41] The Crewe branch became the "Home in the West" branch; the Hull branch, "Slave's Hope"; the Enfield branch, "Good Intent."[42] But the 3,500 members of the company could not generate enough cash flow to support a transatlantic operation, and the allotments themselves were too far away to be easily controlled.[43] Reserved lands were being squatted upon but could not be preempted, as they had not been surveyed, and Evans urged the society to concentrate its efforts on securing a charter for the company in the Wisconsin legislature.[44]

Whatever efforts may have been carried out to salvage the potters' project on the American side are unclear. Evans had clearly failed in his educational mission; he had cultivated high expectations, but, out of ignorance of the American lifestyle himself, had left people without a clue regarding American farm life: life without potatoes, or life with Indian corn.[45] Certainly, the settlers vociferously condemned the conditions in America. In August 1850, a memorial from Wisconsin printed in the *Northern Star* complained that through the medium of the *Potters' Examiner*, the Potters' Emigration Society had led the working classes to believe that the society was offering tracts of good, black, easily cultivated soil, that stores had been purchased, and that ancillary employments were available both on the land and elsewhere. When they arrived, they found the land, unsurveyed by the government, was in the possession of Indians, and the settlers were looked upon as trespassers. The stores had hardly any common necessities, and commodities were so expensive that the squatters were reduced to buying on credit, in small and irregular quantities. The memorialists called for the British public to investigate this matter and put the company on a better footing.[46]

Soon after this cry from the wilderness, the *Potters' Examiner* folded. William Evans went back to Wales in 1850 a penniless man, leaving the Wisconsin emigrants to shift for themselves, which, ostensibly, they did. Evans's exile was temporary; he would be recalled to the potteries in 1854, and in 1864 began to edit the new *Potteries Examiner and Workman's Advocate*.[47] It was in the same year, 1864, that the government office responsible for tracking friendly societies received an unsigned purple envelope informing them that the Potters' Emigration Society had broken up.[48]

The National Reformers achieved their goal after much lobbying; the Chartist Co-Operative Land Company experienced dramatic public failure; and the Potters' Joint-Stock Emigration Company fizzled in a sea of transatlantic acrimony. On the surface, these were three very different movements. Yet all three movements shared organizational tactics, concern for the workingman, and several key concepts, the intellectual parentage of which deserves to be examined in greater detail. The leaders of all three movements inferred, from inequalities either visible or looming in society, that the balance between agriculture and manufactures in their areas needed to be readjusted. All three movements' rhetoric claimed that working people had a right to the land and a chance to reap political and social independence from the land. All looked to the land as a safety valve, claiming that once urban workers were released from wage competition to flood onto the land, urban wages would find a more natural and appropriate level. These similarities were far from coincidental. Rather, as the chapter which follows will show, they derived from a common discourse of land reform, a transatlantic discourse which, by spanning the ideological spectrum from radical to conservative, caused the land reformers to appear timely, if not practical.

2

The Intellectual Heritage of Working-Class Land Reform

Who can tell but the Millennium
May take its rise from my poor Cranium?
—Thomas Spence, *Constitution of Spensonia*

Although Feargus O'Connor's claimed in 1842 that land for the working classes was a "somewhat novel" idea, it was anything but.[1] In fact, there had been a steady stream of writing in both Britain and America on the topic since the turn of the nineteenth century. Both abstract thinkers on social questions and more pragmatic schemers considered the possibility of transferring allotments of land to the poor.[2] Reformers ranging from Thomas Paine to William Cobbett to the country gentlemen of the Labourer's Friend Society claimed that every man had a natural right or a birthright in the soil, and linked the distribution of land to the balance of political power or the existence of corruption in society. As this chapter will illustrate, two generations of writers on land reform created a discourse on the social and moral benefit of cultivation of land for the laborer. The first generation generated a series of natural-law propositions setting forth each man's right to the land, from which later reformers could and did draw at will. A second generation of social engineers attempted to translate these theories into practice, through programs ranging from home colonization to small-allotment farming to legislated redistribution of property. The working-class land-reform movements on both sides of the Atlantic were part of this discourse and drew from a common stock of ideas with a respectable pedigree.

If much that the reformers of the 1840's espoused had been suggested before, the working-class land reformers distinguished them-

selves from the conservatives by insisting that returning the laborer
to the land need not entail paternalistic social relationships, and
from the radicals by affirming the importance of private property.
Far from being utopian or even "backward-looking," their prescriptions, like many of the interventions in the land-reform debate, reflected the notion that society and the role of industry in it were
still malleable, and that a thriving agriculture was a sign of national
health rather than lack of progress. Examination of the invention of
the idea of land reform illustrates the "respectable" genesis of ideas
which would later be thought "radical." It also shows that the land
reformers were original—not in their theories, but in the way they
included or excluded concepts originated by previous reformers, in
order to build a rationale for land reform which would appeal to
their audience.

Where does the intellectual trail of modern land reform begin?
Along with Gerrard Winstanley's communistic Diggers, James Harrington is often identified as one of the first proponents of land reform in the Anglo-American tradition; it is certainly to him that the
eighteenth-century writers traced their roots and methods. Harrington's *Oceana*, written during Oliver Cromwell's tenure as Lord Pro-
tector, set out in minute detail the configuration of an ideal commonwealth, including among its most necessary elements an "agrarian law" to limit the amount of property which might be held by
any one person. Harrington was no democrat—his proposed constitution was intended expressly to preserve aristocracy—but the connection which he proposed between distribution of the land and political power rang true to eighteenth- and nineteenth-century thinkers of a wide range of political views.[3]

Writing more than a century after Harrington, Thomas Paine not
only played a seminal role in the chain of radical ideas which bound
the American and British radical movements to each other and to
their common history; he also linked citizenship to the land in a
way that all subsequent land reformers would also do. Paine's influence is incontrovertible—as a workingman turned political theorist
he was clearly popular among political radicals in both America and
Britain; some of those reformers who went on to call for small farms
had celebrated his birthday with toasts and feasts in the 1830's.[4] As
would the other proponents of land reform, Paine, in his little-
studied *Agrarian Justice*, bemoaned the chasm which had developed

between the rich and the poor. He felt it was unjust that man in a civilized state was worse off than man in a "natural" or prepolitical state. In a natural state, such as that among the Indians, although the land had been relatively unproductive, it was at least held in common.[5] Although in a civilized state men took land as private property and made it productive, Paine argued this should not be the end of the matter. Rather, landed men owed to society a form of rent in return for having their acquisitions protected against the claims of the nonlanded.

Paine's pragmatism and willingness to leave existing private-property relations alone made him a model for later working-class land reformers. But Paine would also differ from the land reformers of the 1840's because his plan stipulated that the landless would collect a stipend out of the national wealth in lieu of maintaining a continued connection to the land. Each man and woman would receive a lump sum at maturity, and would be entitled to an annual payment after age 50. The slush fund for such payments would be paid by landowners at the times in their lives when it would be least onerous.

Although they embraced Paine as an able rhetorician of land reform, the reformers of the 1840's did not accept the cash payments, centralization, and cradle-to-grave concerns of Paine's plan. The National Reformers and Land Company Chartists projected their plans as strategies for raising the condition of workers through their own efforts, rather than as charitable acts of government. They also emphasized that workers must have access to the land themselves, for farming generated economic, and therefore political, independence.[6] Replacing this direct connection to the land with a transfer payment denied the laborer the benefits of yeoman independence— in effect, it sold a man's right to the soil (something land reformers claimed was inalienable) for an annual fee.[7]

Another eighteenth-century social philosopher to take up the Harringtonian torch, Thomas Jefferson favored territorial acquisition designed to ensure that the United States encompassed enough land to maintain a landed and independent populace. He gave new rhetorical life to the equitable distribution of land in his *Notes on the State of Virginia*, later a popular source for quotation by land reformers:[8] "In Europe the lands are either cultivated, or locked up against the cultivator. Manufacture must therefore be resorted to of necessity, not of choice, to support the surplus of their people." As the working-class land reformers would later do, Jefferson favored a strong agricultural sector because it was in the best economic interests of the nation. But Jefferson's concerns were also moral. He asserted that "those who labour in the earth are the chosen people of God, if ever he had a chosen people, whose breasts he has made his particular deposit for substantial and genuine virtue."[9] This connection between farming and superior morality cohered well with environmental explanations of the formation of human character.

According to Jefferson, the husbandman was moral because he was independent, and therefore free from the economic pressure that might force political compliance. Such independent civic actors were the stuff of which republics absolutely had to be made. As Jefferson noted, "Generally speaking, the proportion which the aggregate of other classes of citizens bears in any state to that of its husbandmen, is the proportion of its unsound to its healthy parts, and is a good-enough barometer whereby to measure its degree of corruption." When the Jeffersonian legacy was interpreted by the labor newspapers of the 1840's, their editors deliberately chose not to reprint Jefferson's more intemperate comments about the immorality of mechanics. He advised his readers to be content with letting Europe pursue manufactures, noting that "the mobs of great cities add just so much to the support of pure government, as sores do to the strength of the human body."[10] Nonetheless, Jefferson was too important an intellectual progenitor for the land reformers to reject him on the basis of his elitism.

While Jefferson railed against the cities because he was a republican, back in Britain, William Ogilvie, chair of humanities at the University of Aberdeen, promoted land reform for the opposite reason—because it had the potential of retaining healthy social hierarchies.[11] Ogilvie proposed a plan for purchasing estates up for sale at a reasonable value, and dividing them into small farms. While on its face this would seem similar to the Chartist Land Plan, in Ogilvie's vision every person who acquired an allotment of land in this way would have to pay feudal aids and services to the lord of the manor. This was intended to produce "that degree of connexion and dependence which may be expedient for preserving order, and subordination in the country, without danger of giving rise to oppression and abuse."[12] Like Jefferson, Ogilvie argued that farming made men of superior morals. "English land-holders and English farmers are superior in all respects to the same class of men in other countries; in their manly vigour, their plain good sense, their humane virtues, consists the true basis of our national pre-eminence," he wrote.[13] A more poignant contrast with the landed independence that Jefferson emphasized could hardly be found.

If Ogilvie's goal was the maintenance of social hierarchy, in other ways his reasoning resembled that of Jefferson and Paine. Ogilvie justified an expansion of the English agricultural sector on the grounds that every man had a natural right to an equal share of the soil. This right, like all natural rights, was inalienable, and it was the task of government to ensure that it was protected, so that any man might till the land should he choose to do so. An equitable distribution of land could be justified on the grounds of social expediency as well as moral and natural right; the farming lifestyle, Ogilvie argued, was conducive to physical and moral health for the country as well as the individual. Not only was farming one of the most productive industries, promoting individual excellence, temperance, strength, physical beauty, and good health, but farm families also quickly increased, providing workers for other sectors of the economy.

The idea that abundant agricultural land could act as a "safety valve" to siphon excess workers from overcrowded urban labor markets would prove one of the most tenacious concepts in the land-reform movements of the nineteenth century. Ogilvie captured one facet of the "safety valve" with his suggestion that new land-holders would serve as a market for even more manufactured goods. "The progress of agriculture will more readily excite the activity of manufactures and carry that branch of national industry to its proper pitch, when the progress of manufactures will carry agriculture to its most prosperous state."[14] Ogilvie contrasts with Jefferson, who feared that commerce bred corruption; but the two men shared a fear that burgeoning cities threatened the moral health of the nation, and a belief that a more equitable distribution of land was the best solution.

Like Ogilvie, Jefferson, and Paine, physician and economic writer Charles Hall was disturbed by the existence of poverty in a land of relative plenty. Like them, Hall concluded that too few people were employed in agriculture; but his critique went a step further, as he believed those employed in industry were producing un-necessary items for the consumption of the rich.[15] Hall agreed with those who argued for man's natural right to the soil; he argued that God would not create humanity without due provision for humans to sustain themselves. Yet he also blamed misuse of power for the juxtaposition of patrician and plebeian he saw around him. As the working-class land reformers of the 1840's would, Hall arrayed him-self confidently against the pessimism of Malthus; he believed that if man's misuse of power were stopped and people returned to the soil, it could provide bountifully for all who were in need. "The Be-ing who made the earth and all the living creatures on it, so consti-tuted the earth that it produces the things necessary for the subsis-tence of those creatures; and he so constituted those creatures that their existence should depend on those things which the earth pro-duces." Hall's confidence in God's logic led him to argue that all men must be entitled not only to use the land, but also to possess a portion; "no creature ought to be cut off from the possession of some part or other of the earth, and that in such quantity as to furnish him with the necessaries of life."[16] Working-class land reformers in par-ticular would seize upon Hall's suggestion that the state grant land "in small quantities, gratis, to all such persons as would form set-tlements on them." In America, this concept was transformed into the homestead on the public lands.

Hall reiterated Harrington's argument that real property had a symbolic value in the realm of political legitimacy which tran-scended its monetary value. Having found themselves in a civilized state with control of the legislative arm, those with landed property made strong and secure laws to protect their hegemony over all property; they enshrined property as the highest value in the state, while virtues like compassion and mercy went begging. This con-cept was particularly appealing to the Chartists, who would contend that property owners used their property to monopolize political power, and from the seat of power passed "class legislation," which further oppressed the unpropertied. Feargus O'Connor would call for the "Charter and the Land" because these two concepts were mutu-ally reinforcing.

If Hall provided the land reformers with a valuable theoretical basis, he also made some controversial suggestions which land reformers chose to ignore. Like Jefferson, Hall hoped that small farms would provide an environment which would transform the human character. Society would be enriched by the fact that each person was economically independent and self-supporting.[17] Only a few people need be trapped in manufactures, and they would be there for the public good.[18] Hall went beyond even Jefferson and Paine by proposing something like an equality of property, on the grounds that civil society would be much more secure, without expensive militias and the theater of the law, if everyone were in a "middling state." As he noted concisely, "All strife about meum and tuum would nearly be at an end."[19] In order to achieve an equality of possessions, Hall was willing, on the grounds of social good, to allow the state to determine which manufactures were luxury items.[20] He made the startling suggestion that the state prevent the exploitation of labor by either prohibiting the manufacture of these luxury goods or imposing steep taxes upon them to discourage their sale.[21] Like Jefferson's remarks about corrupt mobs, Charles Hall's prescriptions for a command economy would conveniently be left behind as the land reformers of the 1840's constructed their belief systems.

While Ogilvie, Paine, and Jefferson would propose redistribution and systems of taxation to promote more widespread possession of land, another early reformer, Thomas Hodgskin, focused on legal measures. Like the other theorists, Hodgskin argued for a natural right of property proceeding from the fact that man was impelled by nature to work to satisfy his basic wants, and should therefore own whatever he produced—especially that which he produced on the soil.[22] Hodgskin further argued that the law, which should protect this natural right of property, protected only the artificial right of property; laws came into existence not to create new practices, but rather to codify present habits. The linkage Hodgskin proposed between legal reform and a natural right to the land could be used to justify reform of the inheritance laws; by the end of the 1840's, the elimination of primogeniture, expected to lead eventually to a wider distribution of landed property, would become a popular demand among middle-class land reformers.

The writings of the first generation of land-reform theorists were motivated by the same concerns which gripped later land reformers: disappointment and pessimism about social and economic condi-

tions; fear of the moral effects of mass manufacturing; optimism regarding the possibility of a more equitable distribution of property;
and a belief in the moral health of the small farmer. Their insistence
that man's natural right to the soil could be inferred from God's
creation of man would give land reformers of the 1840's a powerful
basis from which to argue. Moreover, all of the members of this first
generation of reformers were respectable; it could not be argued that
their insistence on man's right to the soil was motivated by a poor
man's desire to rob the rich. The same could not, however, be said of
Thomas Spence.

Working-class land reform in the 1840's had a problematic intellectual ancestor in common-property advocate Thomas Spence. As
James Epstein has pointed out, Spence's natural-rights rhetoric differentiated him from the "constitutionalist" idiom which pervaded
much other radical thought on landownership, rights, and obligations.[23] Along with his disciples, Spence fused agrarian thinking
with political radicalism in a way which forever compromised the
respectability of suggestions for more equitable distribution.[24]

Born to a Newcastle netmaker, Spence was raised in poverty although surrounded by intellectual stimulation. Upon reaching
adulthood, he moved to London, where he opened a bookstall and
cultivated a coterie of radicals like himself. Spence refused to adopt
the deferential attitude and careful dress that might have marked
him as a striver for respectability. The fact that he was a short and
palsied man would have made him stand out in any case, but he cultivated difference by refusing to lose his northern burr and by going
about in ragged clothes. As Francis Place noted, "he was rather en-
dured than tolerated by those whose circumstances were above his
own, who came occasionally in contact with him."[25] Spence's failure to conform to the requirements of respectability was exacerbated by his querulous, irritable disposition, and bizarre manners—
he believed the world was out to get him (which at times it was).
Spence's dogmatism, and his impatience with those to whom his
ideas remained unclear, made him hard to get along with:

Like most other men who believed they had made discoveries for the advantage of mankind, and had devoted themselves to this service, he held
those who dissented from his doctrines in the utmost contempt, and his
words as well as his manner were frequently expressive of the contempt
he felt. . . . he spoke his thoughts freely without regard to the words he
used or the person to whom he addressed them.[26]

Spence's redeeming personal virtue was his sincere concern for the future of mankind, and this altruism must have been visible (or else it is impossible to understand how Spence attracted any disciples).[27] Although he may have been a personally unpleasant, irascible, self-professed prophet, he was also a completely committed publicist for more equitable landownership; his passion and vision still impress the modern reader.

Like Ogilvie and Hall, Spence both was influenced by Harrington and invoked the concept of "natural right" to explain his focus on the soil.[28] Among man's natural or self-evident rights he numbered equality, liberty, safety, and natural and acquired property. Since all men were equal by nature and before the law, they collectively had an equal, continual, and inalienable property in the earth and its natural productions.[29] To transform this theory into practice, Spence took a page from Harrington and drew up a constitution for an invented island utopia, called Spensonia. All the residents of a hypothetical Spensonian parish would meet on a particular day, and take the joint ownership of the parish land from its present proprietors, simply by consensus, without bloodshed. Each of the parish residents over 21 years of age, male and female alike, would then become a fully voting member of the community, responsible for the rental of the repossessed lands and the disposition of the new rents, which were now the parish funds. Spence was no proponent of equal property; only the rents of land were expropriated in his scheme, and movable property remained untouched.[30] He explained the distinction he was making in verse:

> The rents throughout that happy state
> Each parish deals so fair
> That every householder therein
> Does get an Equal Share.

> Of equal shares of land or goods
> They never once do dream;
> But in each parish, *part the rents*
> Which better far they deem.[31]

Lest one wonder why Spence proposed that property be held in common, thus contravening so much Anglo-American tradition and inviting controversy, it must be noted that his decision was not random. Thinking farther along the line than most of his fellow land-reform proponents, Spence feared that even if landed property were at some point divided equally, inequalities would eventually grow just as they originally had.[32]

Unlike Charles Hall, Thomas Spence was suspicious of the centralizing state; his land-reform plan therefore invested much power in his invented local government. The parish was to be responsible for its own maintenance and improvement, remitting a small sum to the county and state. Local regulations would also govern the strength and comfort of farm buildings that Spensonian residents erected, and local governments would provide low-cost housing for tradespeople and cottagers who did not require much land. A focus on local problems would transform the citizens of Spensonia from "mere spectators in the world" to actors for their own benefit.[33] Like all the first-generation land reformers, Spence was suspicious of industry, and preferred that most of the residents of his utopia be employed in agriculture. When manufactured products were required, Spence favored the small-producer system of manufacture and where possible wanted to vest parishes with manufacturing responsibilities.[34]

Spence repeated many of the land-reform nostrums of more "respectable" thinkers; but more important than Spence's prescriptions were his abilities as a creative communicator who provided a template for disseminating radical information to the working classes.[35] His ideas reached the public not only through his penny periodicals, Pigs' Meat or Lessons for the Swinish Multitude (1793–1795) and Giant-Killer, or Anti-Landlord (1814), and tracts on land, but also through methods which required a lower standard of literacy: graffiti, writing slogans on money and then distributing it, composing songs, and distributing tokens emblazoned with various antigovernment mottoes. As a result of his often seditious irreverence, he was arrested several times and spent time in jail before his death in 1814.

All later working-class land reformers would resemble Spence in the diversity of their methods, which helped to create a culture of land reform. Both the National Reformers and the Chartists appropriated Spencean buzzwords as propaganda tools.[36] "Let the People Go and Cultivate the People's Farm," the Working Man's Advocate demanded.[37] George Henry Evans also printed a long gloss on Spence which noted the indebtedness of both the Chartist Land Plan and National Reform to Spence; he noted that

One, at least, of Spence's publications found its way to America and, in all probability, led to the movement of the Working Men of New York in 1829, of which the present movement is a second edition, "revised and corrected.". . . For several years past in England there appeared symptoms of a revival of Spence's principles, though perhaps the men now professing them may not perceive the chain of circumstances connecting their opinions with those of the bold reformer; and now we see principles identical with those of Spence, openly and fearlessly promulgated by an O'Brien and an O'Connor, without hindrance by Acts of Parliament.[38]

As Spence had, the Chartists and National Reformers would rely on a number of forms, not all of them literary, to promote their ideas about land redistribution. All would espouse varying degrees of decentralization, participation, and mutuality. All considered the safety-valve merits of turning to the land, and all used the natural-rights argument to justify a move which might also have been justified on the basis of economic well-being alone. While these treasures came from a common trove, Spence, as a workingman, might have been a more acceptable prophet than was the cadre of "respectable" social theorists (if, of course, working-class readers could procure Spence's works, many of which were not reprinted until the twentieth century).[39]

British and American land reformers would depart from Spence on one important point: they categorically refused to collectivize private property. Although their enemies would try, and often succeeded, to tar them with the brush of common property, both sets of land reformers in the 1840's believed in the sanctity of private property, insisting only that it be sanctified for labor as well as capital. As early as 1838, Chartists who favored land reform advocated land purchase rather than redistribution by violence.[40] Years later, Feargus O'Connor would try to achieve legislative protection of the poor man's property rather than menace the property already owned by the rich. Although one observer compared the Chartist Land Plan "to the Socialist system of Mr. Owen in England and America, and to the Fourier system on the continent," it was clear even to onlookers that "those systems were co-operative and co-proprietary; whereas, under Mr. O'Connor's adaptation of the plan, each individual is independent of his own allotment, and has nothing to do with his neighbours."[41] The Gloucester Chartist Samuel Bowly would ask rhetorically, "Is not then, I ask, the industrious workingman interested in the inviolability of property like the greatest lord in the state?"[42]

Similar sentiments in favor of private property obtained among land reformers on the other side of the Atlantic. Chartist–turned–National Reformer John Campbell and others felt that it was no more acceptable to appropriate the private property of landowners than it was to countenance unjust taxation or manufacturers' combination in restraint of wages.[43] Although the National Reformers would seek to define "citizenship" in terms of an economic competency as well as the vote, their attitude toward the use of extra-legal methods to redistribute property was fixed. They remained publicly devoted to private property even though (since some of the main land-reform advocates had a history of participation in associationist or Owenite movements) their own feelings on the question of private property might have been slightly qualified.[44] They never contemplated redistribution of lands which were already owned, but rather looked to federal public lands, which they argued belonged equally to all. Even the plank in their platform which would have contravened capitalism by limiting the amount of land that any one man could own would only have referred to future, not present, landownership.

The legacy of Spence for later land reformers is even more complicated because "Spenceanism"—the ideas of Spence culled, changed, and disseminated by his followers after his premature death—was a different phenomenon from Spence himself. It forms yet another part of the intellectual heritage of land reform, although an even less respectable part. After Spence's death, the Spenceans went underground; and in 1820 they were discredited, and Spence's name was further blackened, by the abortive Cato Street Conspiracy to overthrow the British government. Various members of the group did survive the government repression, to resurface in the late 1820's and 1830's and keep the nexus between land redistribution and political radicalism alive at the grassroots level. Richard Carlile, editor of the *Republican*, was a Spencean who consistently opposed agrarian monopoly and espoused a single tax on land.[45] Robert Wedderburn, a charismatic West Indian mulatto, fused Spence's land-redistribution schemes with anticlerical and antislavery views.[46]

The land-reform ideas inherent in Spenceanism were best expressed by reformer Allen Davenport, an early physical-force Chartist.[47] Davenport had become a soldier at an early age for lack of other opportunities, served during the Napoleonic wars, then became a shoemaker. In 1805, he was introduced to a work by Thomas Spence, the *Spencean System*, and was instantly converted to the cause. Over the clap of hammer against shoe leather, he evangelized Spenceanism to his shopmates, but they laughed at him and called him a visionary.[48] Davenport fused belief in Spence's theories of landownership with Robert Owen's plan for socialist communities.[49] Davenport saw Robert Owen not as a competitor with Spence, but as a fellow eschewer of private property. He saw both Owen's and Spence's plans as alternative superstructures, either of which might be achieved once the base, the equal right of all men to the soil, was put into place.

As would the land reformers of the 1840's, Davenport felt that all past working-class reform efforts had failed because of the inequality of land distribution.[50] Davenport thought land reform would restore to working people a belief that they had something worth fighting for.[51] He also emphasized that land redistribution would provide each man with a vote, and allow him to legislate "for peace, prosperity, and the happiness of the whole people."[52] But Davenport and his ideas were always on the margins in the 1840's because of his close connection to socialism. As late as 1846, Davenport was evangelizing in favor of more equitable land distribution, spurred by the popularity of the Chartist Land Plan into warning fellow socialists:

Do not let the Chartists outstrip you in the Agrarian Reform, and snatch from you forty years' growth, while you are yielding to despair, the Chartists with a zeal and perseverance that does honour to their cause, have commenced the Agrarian revolution by purchasing more than 100 acres of land to be distributed by lot to the members in the shape of small farms with a cottage attached to each. This is the way to gain the Charter; make the land the foundation of your reform and the superstructure will be as enduring as the pyramids of Egypt, or the rocks of Gibraltar.[53]

If Alan Davenport represents an economic trajectory of Spenceanism, George Julian Harney, a prominent Chartist, represents a political trajectory. Harney kept Spence's impact alive by mentioning him in public in the 1840's, and by doing so became the crux of a historical claim that Spenceanism continued to be influential among English radicals for several decades after Spence's death.[54] Speaking at a London meeting to commemorate the release of

O'Connor from York Castle, Harney said he was a first-principle man. "His creed was—and Thomas Spence had taught it him—that 'the land is the People's Farm' and that it belongs to the entire nation, not to individuals or classes."[55] Of all the major Chartists, Harney seems to have had a special interest in Spence; Spencean tracts were found in his possession at the time of his death.[56]

Besides avowing the impact of Spence on his life, Harney, while involved with the East London Democratic Association, adopted Spence's specific plan for management and rental of socially confiscated land. He propounded his ideas in the short-lived penny *London Democrat*, a pocket-sized newspaper that called for social as well as political equality. While political equality meant the right to vote and to hold any office, social equality signified "that all shall have a good house to live in with a garden at the back or front . . . good clothing to keep him warm, and to make him look respectable, and plenty of good food and drink to make him look and *feel* happy."[57] Harney continued his criticism of private property throughout the 1840's, peppering his *Democratic Review* with his ideas on the land. He also, however, remained staunchly opposed to the peasant proprietorship O'Connor espoused, noting that "Those who had money to buy land would become landlords, and every such landlord, whether lord of five or fifty thousand acres, would become a conservative—the sworn enemy to further changes."[58]

The Spenceanism represented by Davenport and Harney was too opposed to private property to have much of an impact on the Chartist Land Company. As the discussion below will show, the impact on O'Connor of more conservative intellectual influences—William Cobbett and Tory writers on allotments for the poor—is much more evident. Nor were the links between Spencean ideas and the American land-reform movement as close as historians have repeatedly asserted.[59] Nonetheless, the ideas of Spence were alive in the 1830's and 1840's, and cherished by workmen like Davenport and Harney; their interventions into the land reform added weight to the contention that land could solve the problems of laboring people.

Examination of the ideas of Paine, Jefferson, Hall, Ogilvie, Hodgskin, and Spence and his followers reveals that the turn of the nineteenth century produced an influential corpus of social-scientific writing about land redistribution as a solution to social and political inequality. For all of these writers, as for Harrington, the distribution of land and the distribution of power in society were inextricably intertwined. The methods which they suggested for implementing land redistribution diverged widely, and while none of the methods was adopted wholesale by the working-class land reformers of the 1840's, the writings provided propositions from which practical solutions might be deduced. And practical solutions were generated—not only by the emigrant potters, land-hungry Chartists, and American homesteaders, but also by a host of other thinkers who grappled with the issue between the turn of the nineteenth century and the 1840's. It was this second generation of social "engineers"—among them William Cobbett, Thomas Skidmore, the Labourer's Friend Society, and other writers on "home colonization"—responding with the knowledge born of local experience to the discourse on land redistribution, which directly influenced the working-class land reformers of the 1840's.

THE SOCIAL ENGINEERS

Thomas Skidmore, the main American publicist for land reform during the late 1820's and early 1830's, represented a significant departure from Jefferson and the yeoman ideal.[60] Because Skidmore's radicalism helped taint the American land-reform movement with "agrarianism," by proposing institutionalized confiscation of property, it is necessary to look at his contribution to the heritage of land reform in detail. Having spent his early, peripatetic years as a teacher and manufacturer of chemicals, he had settled down in New York by the late 1820's. He was a major force there in the opening moments of the Working Men's movement, but his leadership did not last long—his caustic and overbearing personality soon alienated his projected constituency. Like Thomas Spence, he was dogmatic, especially intolerant of his fellow reformers who did not espouse his favorite reform.[61]

Skidmore detailed his prescriptions for social reform in a sprawling, 405-page tract whose very title, *The Rights of Man to Property!*, was a rejoinder to Paine's attempt to separate man from the land.[62] Like Spence and Paine, Skidmore began with the premise that all the "property" on the earth belonged in common to all the people of the earth, but, flying in the face of John Locke, he also insisted it continued to belong to everyone despite any man's attempt to turn it into private property by mixing labor with it. Rather than acquiring any part of the earth or its fruits through industry and skill, humans, placed upon the earth by a necessity they did not understand, were impelled to fulfill certain wants in order to survive.[63] Further, Skidmore claimed, man's very fulfillment was inseparable from satisfaction of his basic human needs, including property. "If ... Mr. Jefferson had made use of the word *property*, instead of *the pursuit of happiness*, I should have agreed with him. ... In the pursuit of happiness, is property of no consequence? Can any one be as happy without property of any kind, as with it? Is even life and liberty to be preserved without it?"[64] Like his theoretical forerunners, Skidmore confronted the imagery of Thomas Malthus, who had painted a picture of Nature's Feast with no empty seats at the table; "it reminds me of a large party of gentlemen, who should have a common right to dine at one and the same public table; a part of whom should arrive first, sit down and eat what they chose; and then, because the remaining part came later to dinner, should undertake to monopolize the whole, dictating the terms on which the latecomers should have any."[65]

Skidmore believed that man's right to property ceased upon his death, thus making the laws of inheritance positively illogical. Translating an end to inheritance into practice in New York was the most radical part of Skidmore's plan. He called for a state convention to draw up a new constitution which would abolish all debts and renounce all property outside the state owned by New York citizens, while confiscating all property within its boundaries. Next, a census would be taken, at which time every person was bound to provide an inventory of all personal and real property. The worth of all this property would be calculated and divided, and the dividend credited to each male or female over 18 years. All the confiscated property would then be sold to the highest bidder, the bidders using the previously mentioned dividend to buy a portion of the confiscated wares. After this original division had been made, those reaching maturity could benefit from a dividend on the property of all those who had died during the year, and use it to purchase new property. In short, everyone started out their adult lives with equal opportunities and equal means, and Skidmore expected this would prevent any person from amassing an undesirable fortune.[66]

Much more radical in Skidmore's plan than its premises or the actual operation of the division of property was the governmental expansion required to enforce equality of property until such time as public opinion alone was sufficient enforcement. Since a continued balance of property depended on the operation of the cash nexus in every transaction, charity and gift giving were prohibited, and penalties were in store for those who ignored the laws or secreted goods away during the general census. Men of the 1830's who might have agreed in theory that more equality in property was desirable would have railed at the enormous centralized power Skidmore envisaged.

The hints of Jacobinism in Skidmore's proposals would also alienate from him the land reformers of the 1840's. Skidmore anticipated resistance to his plan, and if the rich did resist, it could be claimed that "the government has suddenly ceased to exist; that it has expired, as it were, in a fit of apoplexy; and it will then be incumbent on the people to organize a temporary committee of public safety" until a convention could be called to reorganize society around the rights of man.[67] These echoes of the French Revolution might send chills up the spine of even the best Republican! Thus, where both Skidmore and Spence were willing to subvert the existing order, the land reformers of the 1840's would not be.[68]

Skidmore would also differ from later land reformers in his denial that labor was a form of property. Apparently he felt that there was no way to secure the equal protection of labor as a form of property, given the existing distribution of property and thus power, and the increasing introduction of labor-saving machinery. In contrast, the National Reformers, realizing that not all mechanics would immediately be able to settle on the land, continued to value labor as private property. Skidmore had been more willing than the National Reformers would later be to acknowledge that, given an equitable system of property distribution, machinery could raise the general standard of living. Finally, the land reformers of the 1840's would reject Skidmore's proposal that the state play a continuing role to ensure ongoing equality of property. Evans would not share Skidmore's antipathy to the inheritance of property, but rather envisaged several generations of a family on the same or adjoining parcels of land. The extended family, he felt, was a community of interest stronger and more logical than any group of strangers forced together in an Owenite utopia.[69]

Skidmore and his controversial program played a role in practical politics during the short tenure of the New York Working Men's

Party.[70] On April 23, 1829, a group of self-described mechanics had met at a New York hotel to protest the proposed extension of their workday from ten to eleven hours.[71] Within days, they had selected a committee of representatives to discuss the issue (although they chose not to heed Robert Dale Owen's suggestion that they form an independent labor party). Then, on October 19, this committee produced its resolutions for change, some of which embodied Skidmore's agrarian theories. The committee also resolved to nominate candidates for state assembly and senate, and thus the Working Men's Party was born. A full "Workie" ticket was chosen at random from the list of nominees, and at the next election, of 21,000 votes cast, the Workies got 6,090. An impressive result for a first election, this indicates that the Committee of Fifty's resolutions—including those on land reform—probably resonated with their constituency.[72]

Along with an equal distribution of property, the Working Men called for equal access to public education, abolition of imprisonment for debt, reform of the militia and of the legal system, direct election of the mayor, salaries for public offices, and an end to the ticket system of nomination, which perpetuated a machinelike grip on city power. As Walter Hugins has pointed out, all these grievances opposed some type of monopoly on power.[73] Working Men's issues were crises of defining citizenship—of dispelling fears about slipping in the social and economic order. Thus, the state guardianship educational plan which was the panacea of one faction among the Working Men was meant to promote equality and stifle the trend toward the burgeoning of an aristocracy. Most of the grievances were of fairly long standing, but the movement was also catalyzed by the arrival in America of Robert Owen and Frances "Fanny" Wright, British radicals with the organizational pedigree to make such a movement work.[74]

Between the November election and December, the Working Men divided into two camps. One, led by Skidmore, favored agrarian resolutions. The other, led by Robert Dale Owen and George Evans, sought a less centralized plan of organization, and formed its own executive committee. Skidmore's ideas soon came under attack by the new group, which went so far as to prevent Skidmore from speaking at meetings.[75] George Henry Evans worried that the Working Men's movement was becoming undemocratic, and urged his fellows not to reject Skidmore's proposals out of hand. "If they are wrong they can be shown to be so and discarded; if they are absurd, the sooner will they be so discarded. If, on the contrary, they are right, they ought to be adopted, or any part of them that is so."[76] Some other participants did sympathize with land-reforming notions. "Bush Hook," writing in the movement's newspaper, saw the public lands as an important source of independence:

I am no Skidmorite, Mr. Editor, but really it appears to me that, while some of my acquaintance are possessed of from one to fifteen thousand acres, and Uncle Sam a hundred millions, I, who am conscious of never having done any thing to forfeit my rights, ought to have as much, at least, as would suffice for a *potato patch*, or the profits of it if sold.[77]

The land reformers of the 1840's saw Skidmore's influence as a problem not only because he had proposed an equality of property, but also because he had considered the interests of masters and men to be completely antagonistic. In late March 1830, Skidmore was involved in discussions to define who was eligible for membership in the Working Men's Party. George Evans and his cohorts opposed the exclusion of hardworking masters from their ranks (Evans was an employer himself); the irascible Skidmore, evidently with a sharper definition of class boundaries, proposed that the interests of the mechanics and other workingmen were essentially different from those of persons not engaged in any useful occupation. In his view, employers belonged among the scrounging classes, along with lawyers, bankers, and brokers. Although one might have expected Skidmore's attempt to redefine the movement in terms of producerism to be popular, it was not adopted, partly because it was proposed by Skidmore, who had made himself disagreeable to everyone.[78] By July, any direct influence Skidmore had once possessed had dwindled to nothing.[79]

As Edward Pessen noted, Thomas Skidmore's role in helping to define the ideology of the Working Men's movement remains controversial. He made influential enemies by expressing his antipathy to the middle-class elements—including Fanny Wright and Robert Owen—which he felt were perverting the power of the workingmen to achieve their own ends. These reformers were quick to characterize Skidmore's suggestions as both too radical and so complex as to be beyond the grasp of the workers who had originally supported him. Historians who have wanted to agree, seeing Skidmore's plans as more chimerical than were state education or a ten-hour day, have accepted this analysis.[80] Whether the majority of workingmen had fully understood and supported Skidmore's proposal at the beginning or not, it is clear that their leaders soon recognized the danger in being associated with his ideas and vociferously began to distance themselves. The Philadelphia *Mechanics Free Press* noted that the newspapers had called the New York Working Men "*agrarians* and in this city, also, the same word has been applied reproachfully to us. No doubt many honest and simple people have thought that this word contained some horrible meaning, something like robber, incendiary, anarchist, or perhaps, cannibal." The *Free Press* provided its readers with a short history of the Roman agrarian law and then declared, "We, in this city, have declared over and over again, that we only want to be secured in our labor, and have no more intention of taking what does not belong to us, than we have of taking arsenic."[81]

Despite all the name-calling and acrimony, one leader, George Henry Evans, had clearly imbibed Skidmore's key notion—that land was a natural right, not a privilege, and that the incorporation of the *sale* of land into the American legal framework was a major mistake. Like Skidmore, Evans would espouse legislative intervention rather than either the use of force or marketplace operations to achieve his social readjustments. Evans would badger Congress to provide free homesteads; Skidmore had proposed conventions and rewriting state constitutions to incorporate his grand plan.[82] While pointing out his differences from Skidmore, Evans clearly still admired the man after his death. "Skidmore was grossly misrepresented and cried down, as every Radical Reformer is almost sure to be, during his lifetime; but his work, though now nearly suppressed, contains more truths than any ten books that have since been published."[83]

Skidmore was an important local thinker, polemicist, and politician who managed to link the traditional program of workers' grievances with a call for land redistribution. While the Working Men's movement in which he participated was a short-lived and geographically limited phenomenon, his involvement in it did have one major impact—the conversion of George Henry Evans to land reform. Without Skidmore's influence, it is doubtful that Evans would have begun to think about land reform as a potential solution to the problems of American workingmen. Furthermore, while Evans would eventually acknowledge other intellectual progenitors also, the image of Skidmore and his social martyrdom in pursuit of one idea remained with him, becoming a pattern for his own behavior.[84]

IMAGINING RURAL ENGLAND: WORKERS
AND THE ALLOTMENT SYSTEM

While George Henry Evans's intellectual ancestor was known for has radicalism, the immediate discourse on which Feargus O'Connor drew, the second generation of land-reform thought in England, was much more conservative, emphasizing "home colonization." Writers in favor of home colonization suggested that providing allotments of land for poor workers would counteract the emigration to the colonies and elsewhere that was sapping Great Britain of one of its greatest natural resources—labor. In addition, allotment farming which kept workers close to the land would halt the steady flow of impoverished laborers to the cities, and help keep political power and sentiment on the side of the landed gentry.[85] In contrast with the situation in America, in Britain, land for the laborers could be a Tory as well as a radical demand. The writers on small farms whose prescriptions the Chartist Land Plan would most resemble all came from the conservative end of the spectrum.

One great source of inspiration to O'Connor in his preparation of a land plan was William Cobbett, who so effusively supported the basic human rights of the agricultural laborer.[86] Cobbett considered his practical writings, especially *Cottage Economy*, to be a manual in independence for such laborers. It instructed peasants in the skills which would render each family self-supporting and possibly even market contributors: building, brewing, baking, animal husbandry, and straw plaiting. O'Connor would attempt to be similarly practical in his agricultural tract, noting that he had written a practical work on the management of small farms so that each farmer "may be independent of every other man in the world for his daily bread; so that the prosperity of the country shall consist in an aggregate of happy individuals, rather than in a community of a few owners of aggregate wealth."[87] Cobbett was not a democrat or a leveler; like O'Connor, he thought of himself as a tribune of the people.[88] He did, however, set a theoretical standard of living below which freeborn Englishmen should not suffer to be degraded. Like O'Connor,

Cobbett thought activism among workers was a knife-and-fork question, and seemed to expect that it would go away with the achievement of equal protection and fair remuneration for workers.[89] Cobbett and O'Connor saw land as the salvation of the masses and set themselves up as ombudsmen for the working classes.[90]

William Blacker's treatise on small farms also must have influenced O'Connor. Not only are the titles of his and O'Connor's works similar; the practical ground they cover is almost identical, covering such mundane topics as the growing of green crops, pen feeding of cows, and composting of manure in detail. Like O'Connor, Blacker was a proponent of spade farming rather than farming using draft animals. While O'Connor espoused such cultivation because it was labor-intensive, thus helping to employ lots of otherwise idle hands, Blacker favored it for reasons of efficiency.[91] Like O'Connor, Blacker addressed the workingman directly. Putting in one green crop straight after the other is a lot of work, he averred in one place; "but is not want of employment your constant complaint, and if the crop pays you, are you not better off working for yourselves on your own farms, than working for Lord Gosford or Colonel Close?"[92] Finally, just like O'Connor, Blacker used as his illustrative example a small farm with four acres and a cow.

William Allen of Stoke Newington, affected by the poverty he had seen while in Ireland, wrote in a similar vein, and also may have provided O'Connor with the practical background needed to seem like an authority on farming. Allen claimed that a family might be supported for a year on the corn and potatoes grown on a single acre of land under spade cultivation and properly manured. Another acre could feed two cows for a full year, and a third acre might be profitably cultivated partly in flax and buckwheat with the rest as a kitchen garden. Partly prefiguring O'Connor's plan, Allen suggested families club their funds together to buy cows. Yet unlike O'Connor, Allen was not a proponent of working-class independence except as a side effect; his priority was to provide the poor with allotments of land in order to wean them from dependence on the parish, enable them to educate their children, and raise moral feeling in them. Tenants of the home colonies of Allen's devising would have to agree to observe moral conduct, receive neither alms nor charity, cultivate the land in the prescribed manner, send their children to school, pay the rent on time, and prohibit spirituous liquors from being sold in their neighborhoods.[93] If O'Connor was reading William Allen's work to get ideas, he could not have escaped from a persistently patronizing picture of the peasant.

The idea of land redistribution as the key to social amelioration never disappeared in England, but through the writings of Blacker, Allen, and Cobbett metamorphosed into a remedy for poverty which did not menace existing ideas of property right.[94] Far from ushering in some new social order, these writers showed that turning the attention of the working classes to the land could help maintain Tory political hegemony by increasing the scope of the "agricultural interest." The practical applications of this idea were so tempting that a group of clerics and gentry, acting from a combination of philanthropic inclinations and financial self-interest, formed the Labourer's Friend Society in the early 1830's to promote the idea of allotments for the poor.[95] They accomplished this through a monthly periodical aimed at the landholding classes and a series of public meetings held throughout the southern agricultural districts. The Labourer's Friend Society sought to "print, in cheap form, and distribute, Communications of Facts, on the advantages of small farms, and the important benefits which have been, and may still be derived by labourers, from possessing small portions of land."[96] Their constant theme: the soil was the natural outlet for the employment of the "unoccupied population."

John Ilderton Burn, author of tracts favoring home colonization over emigration, was one of the motive forces behind the society.[97] Like O'Connor, Burn felt the strength of a country lay with its population, and that working people especially had important ties to the regions where they were born—ties which enhanced their perceived quality of life.[98] Like the first-generation social thinkers, Burn disparaged Thomas Malthus for daring to outguess Providence on the amount of land necessary to feed the people. An advocate of labor, Burn argued that the labor market should never be allowed to become glutted. Making sure there was enough to go around should be the first and last duty of government, Burn noted, while recommending a program of public works to accomplish it.

The Labourer's Friend Society in which Burn was so active took as its main task explaining how allotments could benefit the poor,

while still maintaining, and even enhancing, a hierarchical system
of social relations. If a laborer were allowed to rent, directly from
the landowner rather than through the farmer, a small amount of
land which he and his family cultivated in their leisure time, the
benefits would be legion. First, the crop would ensure the family
emergency rations all year round (the cultivation was to be for their
sustenance rather than for sale in the market). The poor rate would
decrease, a clear benefit for the local gentry.[99] Furthermore, land cultivation was thought to be a more morally improving occupation
than the dissipated ways in which the working poor currently spent
their time—especially drinking.[100] At the Society's third annual
meeting, Lord Morpeth contrasted the industrial and the agricultural worker in a manner which O'Connor's land-plan rhetoric
would later echo:

only mark the contrast between labourers who had small allotments and
those who had not, and who lived partially on parochial aid; this you
might see spending his last penny at some beer-shop, in vice and idleness,
and afterwards going home and acting brutally towards his wife and family, thus raising bad blood, and generating deeds of violence throughout
the country. Behold the other, in the sunset of a summer's day, with the
spade in his hand, his wife and children in happiness beside him, enjoying
the gratifying luxury of a well-cultivated garden, stocked with a variety of
vegetables.[101]

Because rents were to be charged for the allotments proposed by the
Labourer's Friend Society, the plots were less objectionable than
unmitigated charity. In addition, wasteland cultivation brought environmental and aesthetic improvement. "The little nooks and apparent waste corners of our soil will, by degrees, be brought into a
state of cultivation, and glow with all the beauty incident to a well-
kept garden."[102]

   The benefits of allotments would not end there. If the poor had a
stake in society, they would be more tractable, it was thought, more
likely to submit to governance—and this was why it was especially
important for the land to be rented directly from the elite landowner
rather than from some middling farmer. The rental for the small
plot of land should be reasonable, the same rate paid by the farmer
who rented from the landowner. But the working poor should never,
under any circumstances, be allowed to rent enough land under this
system to render themselves completely self-sufficient, or give
them delusions of being market gardeners.[103]

The tenets of the Labourer's Friend Society were disseminated in two ways. In addition to its magazine aimed at landowners, clergymen, and others who could put the allotment plan into practice in their localities, the Society also issued tracts for the laborer, inculcating the values of thrift, sobriety, and deference. Members of the Society warned laborers to save money by forgoing liquor and by avoiding ostentation in dress, and to avoid having large, expensive families. They barely disguised their moral lessons in fictional dialogues or resorted to outright commands. When reading these tracts, it is hard to repress the specter of some bloated squire, squinting through his spectacles, one leg propped up on the ottoman and inflamed with gout, warning the laborer that "riches are far from being the best gift of God. The poor partake often in a larger share than the rich of the blessings of health, contentment, and the affection of friends and relatives. ... when the poor man is unwise enough to look with envy on those who enjoy more of the luxuries of life than he does himself, it is very probable an exchange would teach him how very much he was deceived in thinking their lot preferable to his own."[104]

The tone of much of the Labourer's Friend Society rhetoric, as well as its undisguisedly conservative underpinning, might have alienated later Chartists (although perhaps not O'Connor, who seems to have fancied himself a vicarious lord of the manor).[105] Despite the possible dissonance between these paternalistic land solutions and the Enlightenment-individualistic radicalism that usually characterized the Chartists, the Chartist land scheme would share many elements with the Labourer's Friend Society. Both were based on the principle that the land could be a safety valve for overpopulation. Further, representatives of both claimed that laborers had a right to the produce of the land simply by virtue of being freeborn Englishmen.[106] Both saw a redistribution of land as a necessary forerunner of social peace. Like the Chartists, the editors of the *Labourer's Friend* opposed plans for emigration, on the grounds that it was tantamount to "transporting" the working population. In contrast with the colonization of America and New South Wales, "home colonization" would add to the national defense and not cultivate enemies abroad.[107] Opposition to emigration would later be a popular subject for the *Northern Star's* polemical pens, and even for O'Connor on the platform; at the mass demonstration in Birmingham celebrating

his liberation from York Castle, O'Connor said he was a great friend
of emigration, but that he would not send the laborers far—only to
the fields of Warwickshire.[108]

The *Labourer's Friend* and O'Connor concurred on many practical details as well.[109] O'Connor claimed he put a lot of thought into
his design for the allottees' houses; the *Labourer's Friend* often ran
blueprints of proposed model homes for agricultural allotment
holders, many of them remarkably similar to O'Connor's final design. Perhaps most significant, both O'Connor and the *Labourer's
Friend* Tories were staunch proponents of spade husbandry, which
came to be a symbol both of contented poverty, and of hand labor
against the encroachments of mechanical improvement.[110] Cultivation of the land by spade rather than the plow not only employed
more hands, but also was said to yield a greater crop and enrich the
soil, adding to its value.[111] In addition to these similarities of principle and detail, which suggest a great deal of philosophical overlap
between O'Connor and the conservative proponents of allotments
for the poor, there was a direct connection—the *Northern Star* in
1842 promoted the Labourer's Friend Society.[112] Clearly, O'Connor
either read the *Labourer's Friend* or at the very least read and was
influenced by the same authors who inspired that magazine's correspondents.

Clearly, land reform was being touted as a conservative reform in
the 1830's; and given the conservative nature of British society, one
would have expected land reform to have been relatively noncon-
troversial. But O'Connor would have had another reason to believe
that his land company would be supported rather than thwarted—
the British government endorsed home colonization. In 1843, as the
land plan was taking on a concrete shape, the British government
joined the discourse on allotments and gave them its ideological
sanction.[113] Sixteen members of a Parliamentary Select Committee
concluded that "the tenancy of land under the garden allotment system is a powerful means to bettering the condition of those classes
who depend for livelihood upon their manual labour, whether in
manufacturing or agricultural employment; and it has this peculiar
merit, that its benefits are not obtained at the expense of any other
class, nor accompanied by any corresponding disadvantage." The
committee members also found that working people hungered for
land. "The desire of obtaining the tenancy of land appears to be uni-

versal among the mechanics and artisans of manufacturing towns and villages, as well as among the inhabitants of rural districts," although the paucity of land had frustrated many a laborer's desire.[114] The Select Committee report revealed that workers' affinity for the land was so intense in some places that they attempted to obtain it themselves. When one former stocking weaver organized the dispersal of allotments in his area of Leicestershire, more than a hundred applicants immediately sought land on the 37.5 available acres. Although the men were employed at their regular jobs four and a half days a week, and were barred from working their allotments on Sundays, they were still eager to spend all remaining leisure time tilling the soil.[115] With facts like these emerging, it was impossible for the land plan not to be popular.

The tone of the Select Committee hearings celebrated the power of land to shape the moral and economic life of the laborer for the better, illustrating that all the rhetoric of the 1830's had paid off in a prevailing viewpoint. Committee members regaled each other with tales of success on the land, and witnesses gave overwhelmingly optimistic evidence which would only have reinforced O'Connor's determination to put forward a land plan. Land allotments were credited with the power to employ the displaced handloom weaver, to make the poor sober, and to create impulses for family planning among the rural poor.[116] Allotment farming improved morality and bound landowners and rural or "domestic system" workers in a bond of common interest.

Testimony before the Select Committee emphasized that land-ownership made workingmen more politically and socially conservative. James Brooks reported to the committee that a Chartist lecturer had visited Leicester a week or two since, "and made a great noise, but none of the allotment tenants visited him; instead of going to the meeting, they went with their spades on their shoulders to their gardens."[117] Sets of allotment-scheme rules submitted to the Committee emphasized antiradical values; "industry, education, temperance and morality," were encouraged by work in these gardens. Autonomy and independence were not prized values, however, as the type of crop to be grown might be dictated, and harsh penalties set, for those who dared to work on a Sunday.[118] When it came time to issue recommendations, the Parliamentary Select Committee reflected its conservative leanings by recommending

small allotments for leisure-time cultivation—allotments not calculated to make workers financially independent. The committee
also gave its approval to spade husbandry, noting that it provided
sound industrial training for children, and helped to reclaim disso-
lute working people, preventing them from applying for parochial
relief.[119]

Although the Chartist Land Company had little in common with
the prescriptions of the Select Committee, which were clearly paternalistic and not geared toward self-sufficiency, both O'Connor's
scheme and the government's report reflected the triumph of a discourse on the benefits of land cultivation for the laborer and for society. The Select Committee hearings, the work of the Labourer's
Friend Society, and the popularity of Cobbett's ideas created an
awareness, in Britain, that land reform was a possible solution—and
not necessarily a radical or Spencean solution—for unemployment
and poverty.

Both British and American land reformers benefited from an entire spectrum of ideas, from the radical to the conservative, the paternalistic to the fiercely independent, centering on land as a solution to poverty and overpopulation. The theoretical writings of such
thinkers as Ogilvie, Hall, Jefferson, Spence, and Paine, produced at
the turn of the nineteenth century, introduced later writers to the
notions of land as a natural right and to the relationship between its
redistribution and political power. A second generation of thought
on land reform, which ranged from the politically dangerous "agrarianism" of Thomas Skidmore to the smug paternalism of allotment
schemes, flourished in the 1830's, providing the working-class land
reformers with a language of land reform and a repertoire of ideas for
putting theory into practice. While none of these prescriptions
would be adopted without reservation by the British and American
land reformers of the 1840's, who rejected the extremes of confiscation and paternalistic dependence, the very fact that such a lively
discourse existed lent a practical weight to schemes which historians have often derogated as "utopian." Rather than seeming to their
contemporaries to be backward-looking visionaries, the land reformers of the 1840's were in the company of a number of others
who, because they believed working the land to be a social good for a

number of different reasons, looked forward to a new balance of agriculture and manufactures.

Although the heritage of land reform was a common legacy upon which both British and American land reformers drew, they added their own rationales for their brand of land reform. They based these rationales on shared ideas about the drawbacks of city life, the benefits of landed independence, the feasibility of the "safety valve," and, especially, fears about the power of factory production to transform working-class life and working families. As the next chapter will illustrate, despite the differential pace of industrialization between and within Britain and the United States, and despite the distance and difficulty of communicating, the rationales which did evolve to explain the importance of land reform were both very similar to each other and substantially different from what had come before.

3

Land-Reform Rhetoric and the Currents of Reform

When the war is over, and our freedom won, the people must make a new declaration; they must declare the rights of man, the individual, sacred above all craft or priesthood or governments—they must, at one blow, put an end to all the trickeries of English law, which garnered up in the charnels of ages, bind the heart and will with lies. They must perpetuate republican truth, by making the HOME-STEAD of man a holy thing, which no law can touch, no juggler wrest from his wife and children. Until this is done, the Revolution will have been fought in vain.

       —George Lippard, *Washington and the Generals*[1]

The intellectual heritage of land reform, ranging as it did from the radical Spencean to the pragmatically Cobettian, provided land-reform leaders with a reasonable basis of authority from which to contest orthodox political economy. Reasoning from the experience of work and life, invoking both natural rights and a Christian moral economy, the philosophers of land reform shaped their arguments in a way which they ostensibly felt would appeal to a large audience. Although the pace of both industrialization and the growth of cities was uneven within and between Britain and America, the leaders of the land-reform movements produced similar arguments to support their promotion of land redistribution. The land-reforming ideology was generated by leaders whose social and occupational positions allowed them the time to craft those rhetorical elements which would have the widest appeal for their constituencies.

While the constituencies to which British and American land reformers appealed had different experiences of industrialization and of radicalism, the rhetoric which these leaders developed to justify land reform to workers was remarkably similar. Although the volume of writing on the land is vast—testifying to the importance of print culture for workers' movements at this time—and although land-reform leaders used many different appeals and mixed appeals within each work, five aspects of rhetoric stand out as having appeared regularly in both Britain and America. The overarching theme connecting the British and American movements was the fear of the degradation of labor. The symbol of labor's degradation in both places was the factory system, despite the fact that factory production did not occupy the energies of a majority of workers in either country. Even in the United States, where factory production in the 1840's was largely limited to the textile towns of industrializing Massachusetts, fear of the large-scale introduction of British-style mechanized production elicited some wistful glances in the direction of the land. As this chapter will show, on both sides of the Atlantic, land-reform leaders constructed "the factory" in such a way that only a free flow of workers to the land—a safety valve—could offset gluts of workers in the cities who might otherwise be forced into the factories.

But fear of the factory and the attendant safety-valve solution were not the only concepts which would unite British and American land reformers in common cause. The much-touted virtue of the independent property holder, an idea usually associated with early American politics, surfaced in Britain as well, as land-reform leaders justified a redistribution of property on patriotic grounds. Although many land reformers were freethinkers, they appealed to a constituency which was in many cases Christian, and thus cast the question in terms of Christian morality. The Bible was an authoritative source militating against exploitation of the poor and against land monopoly; land reformers borrowed the authority of the Christian preacher as they stood in their own makeshift pulpits.

For the land reformers, the land had inherent attractions, exerting a pull to match the factory's push. In contrast with the vices imputed to the cities, the countryside was portrayed as a unique repository of health and even of aesthetic charm. Other elements of a landed life appealed to workers' goals of an economic competency and a happy home. Life on the land could satisfy all natural wants without forcing the small farmer to rely on anyone else. Land reformers, influenced by the Fourierites and Owenites, devised spatial arrangements for small farms which accommodated both increased space and workers' habits of sociability and mutuality. Finally, land reformers worked with normative gender and age roles by describing ways in which a movement to the land would restore "normal" hierarchies of power within the home. On the land, women could conduct their productive activities within the home instead of in the factory, and children could attend school, thus delaying the wage earning that unduly raised their status in the household.

THE SAFETY VALVE AND THE FACTORY BELL

Historians in the 1930's used statistics to disprove the notion that some safety valve made the development of American labor exceptional. They correctly denied that "free public lands" drew surplus American industrial workers away from the cities in times of depression, thus keeping that discontent which might manifest itself in class ways to a minimum.[2] Yet this debate also unfortunately, if inadvertently, dismissed the idea that no matter what the statistics said, the idea of free land might have played a role in raising working-class hopes. In fact, the idea that land might be a safety valve to release the pressures of a clogged labor market was central to the reasoning not only of working-class land reformers, but also of contemporary social commentators.[3] As this study illustrates, even if an insufficiently large proportion of American workers managed actually to go west, the idea of free homesteads remained viable to the antebellum worker looking for a solution to an overcrowded labor market. In fact, the inability of many workers to find the means to go west before the Civil War may have increased the call for migration as a solution; land reform could not be cried down when it had not even been tried.

Nor was the presence of vast tracts of "unoccupied" land in the United States a factor which greatly differentiated the British and the American land-reform movements. The National Reform movement appeared on the scene three years after preemption laws supposedly made the public lands cheaper and more accessible; the Americans would still agitate for free homesteads. Likewise, discussion of the land as a safety valve in Britain illustrates that the concept could exist even in the absence of currently unoccupied public lands.[4] John Campbell reasoned from the American example that the land could serve as a safety valve for British workers. "If the soil of Great Britain belonged to the people, no employer could cheat

them, because the moment that wages fell too low, that moment
the workman could fall back upon his rights, and go and occupy his
quota of the land."[5] What united American and British workers behind this call for a safety valve was the specter, or image, of the factory, as it was then making inroads in Britain.

In both Britain and the United States, the penetration of a particular idea of "the factory" was more important than the presence
of actual factories in making a safety valve seem urgent. Both sets of
land reformers feared that the factory system would degrade the
worker rather than increase his wages. National Reformers were
"uncommon Jacksonians" in part because they constantly invoked
the declining standard of living of the British worker, and warned of
a widening economic chasm in America during a period of supposedly growing democracy. They feared widespread poverty; like
many artisans of their time, spoke of labor disrespected; and postu-
lated a connection between economic and political power. Edward
Pessen diagnosed these reformers as suffering from a bad case of
false consciousness: "The political and social landscape they drew
of America bears a remarkable resemblance to the dismal English
social landscape painted by William Cobbett and their radical English socialist contemporaries in Old England."[6] Yet while their tone
was melodramatic, their rhetoric without question embodied fears
which were present in American society and should not be mini-
mized. Admittedly, Robert Dale Owen and Fanny Wright, of the
Workingmen's Movement, and George Henry Evans and Thomas
Devyr, of National Reform and the Anti-Rent movement, were British; yet their prognostications appealed to native workers precisely
because they warned that labor would soon be degraded. American
workers knew that, unlike the British, they still had something to
lose, and factory labor soon became a shorthand for a whole way of
life, the extinguishing of equal rights and artisan independence.

For Americans, Britain, and the North of England in particular,
was, rather distortedly, the land of a degraded factory proletariat,
whose workers had blazed a path along which Americans were
quickly following. Workingmen in Charlestown, Massachusetts,
warned in 1840, "We are aided by the discoveries of science, and the
introduction of machinery which gives to our labour a thousand fold
additional power of production; and yet our condition relative to the
capitalist does by no means become better."[7] Although George Hen-

ry Evans had not yet introduced ideas of land reform to his readership, these Massachusetts laborers longed for the land:

Lands are monopolized; the whole earth is foreclosed. However well disposed the laborer might be to cultivate the soil, he has not the means of
becoming its owner. He has no spot on which to erect him a cabin, or on
which he may raise a few potatoes to feed his wife and little ones; for the
broad hands of the few cover it all over.[8]

Workers' fears of worsening conditions in America were not
wholly imaginary. By the mid-1840's, British radicals warned that,
because of land monopoly, America was no longer the utopia it once
seemed. Although the editors of the *Northern Star* originally suggested emigration to America as the solution for political exclusion
and economic marginality, sentiments turned against emigration by
1842. The turnaround was, in part, a reaction to worsening conditions in America. One Chartist emigrant from Leeds described how
thousands of Americans were out of work and relying on alms-
houses for food.[9] Chartist Lawrence Pitkeithley, whose tour of
America received extensive coverage in the *Northern Star*, warned
that "no one should depart their native land, unless under complete
arrangements for entering upon THE LAND at the place of their intended destination." Because of the immense numbers that had
flocked to the United States during the past year and the two previous years, there was a "great 'redundancy of hands' in every department of labour," so that when labor was obtained, it was uniformly
followed by a wage cut.[10] If even the British turned their noses up at
emigration to America, complete degradation of the American
worker could not be far behind.

American and British land reformers borrowed their objections
to "the factory" from the factory-reform movement of the 1830's.[11]
The factory reformers had complained that machinery perverted
family roles, sending children and sometimes mothers out to work
at unskilled jobs while men moped around the house, eking out a
few pennies a week on a handloom.[12] Joseph Rayner Stephens, the
factory and Poor Law reformer who captivated huge crowds in the
late 1830's with his melodramatic and moral bombast, conjured up
gothic tales of pregnant women who bled to death because they had
gone into labor while at the factory.[13] It would be specious to contend that women did not normally contribute to household incomes
before the advent of the factory.[14] Nonetheless, factory critics were

helping to define a male breadwinner and female housekeeper as normal during this period.

Land reformers in the 1840's adopted this tradition and built on it. Like their British counterparts, National Reformers constructed the family as be the natural unit of survival. Independent wage-earning women, like the working girls in Lowell, were an unnatural result of the factory system, and of poverty on Northern farms which made families send their girls out to work. Poverty in the cities further complicated the picture. Men who could not get a competency could not afford to marry, leaving armies of disappointed young women to scratch out their own livings, perhaps pursuing the most economically debased of all occupations (not prostitution, but dressmaking). Girls who worked in factories or in the parlors of an uncaring upper class were no longer under the supervision of the parental roof. They were thus thought to be subject to the dual evils of moral temptation and economic exploitation. *Young America* hinted at sexual dangers, warning that sewing shops were little more than "dens of procuration,"

mere marble brothels, inhabited by the most corrupt, profligate, and pampered sons of luxury, who are armed with obscene books, prints, money, impudence and every venal instrument of treachery and seduction. Now all prudent parents know, if their daughters possess beauty, grace, and attractive charms, that the snares and allurements laid for them by these cruel, heartless and educated spoilers are almost certain to consign them to ruin.[15]

Land reform would reverse this insidious trend. Relieving the economic pressure would allow young men to marry sooner; reformers assumed that young women would prefer to marry and live as farmers' wives on the frontier than earn precarious livings in the city.

Along with its perversion of family roles and the economic and social degradation of the worker, the factory was criticized for the unpredictability of employment—a natural result of dependence on one's employer and on a boom-and-bust business cycle.[16] In the factory, man was slave to machine, permitted to work only as long as he could keep up. On the land—at least in the romantic view—man, beast of burden, and nature cooperated.[17] In contrast with the stereotype of the "factory slave," yoked to his master the machine, Fergus O'Connor conjured up a rural Eden—a vision of a farm wife enabled to sleep in of a morning, and happy children spending their morning watching their father dig a field. The children rush in from among the new-sprouting plants to wake their mother, who has slept late. They greet her with the news, "Here's posies for baby, Tom and me picked in land; get up, mammy, we's so hungry, and faither has dug, oh, so much, and the taties and cabbage and all the things look so nice. Faither says he'll have baby out with him in wheel barrow while he digs. Oh, mammy, all the little children look so happy. Mammy, sure you won't let us go back to Stockport and factory any more to be whipped."[18] Here sex and gender roles have been restored to "normal," with the mother cooking meals, the father doing the heavy labor (although also, surprisingly, minding the children), and the children enjoying the childhoods which they had been denied at the evil factory in Stockport. The reference to the factory at the end of the passage serves to emphasize how close their collective escape from family disaster has been.

The effects of the factory on one's independence and one's internal environment were not all the land reformers found objectionable. The factory also reshaped the built environment, creating haphazard agglomerations of people, unsanitary conditions, and, possibly, crime. By the 1840's, workers in both countries were beginning to see the results of the failure to plan the allocation of urban spaces. Developers bought land wherever it was available, and especially in textile and pottery areas, workers' housing jostled together with smoking chimneys and overflowing earth closets. Middle-class sanitary voyeurs were not the only ones who saw a problem in this. A mass meeting of the Jubilee Association, an American land-reform grouping, drew connections between land monopoly and crowded city housing, indicating the existence of environmental classism: "We are living over cesspools that impregnate with corruption and disease the waters under the earth, as well as the air above the earth. No trees are planted to absorb this corruption; the earth is covered for miles square with stones, bricks, and mortar."[19] The Jubilee Association members feared that trapped pollution resulted in higher rates of disease, especially among women and children.

Criticism of the environmental consequences of British factories was common. In England, the editor of the *Ashton Chronicle* noted that "when the more than forty [factory] chimneys are pouring out their blackening fumes, like as many small volcanoes, the atmosphere is filled and darkened to so great a degree that we cannot properly distinguish objects on the other side of the town." Even the gardens and fields of nearby Stalybridge were sooty and dingy, lacking the freshness and cleanliness of the "real" countryside.[20] Although American factories were often located in more rural areas and did not belch up as much smoke, being largely dependent on water power, the factory as mental construct overrode the reality.

Reformers constructed the factory as a particularly dangerous place compared to the farm. Although farm equipment can be dangerous, the factory was more so, as anyone who worked around machinery would have agreed. Boiler explosions and roof collapses occurred intermittently. Machine makers failed to build housings around gears, and workers owned nothing but street clothes to wear in the factory; as a result, clothes wrapped around gears, and workers' limbs were torn off. Local newspapers often ran titillatingly gruesome stories of industrial incursions against the body; industrial machinery seemed to have an endless appetite.[21]

Although occasionally admitting that the advent of the factory had made more consumer goods available to more people, land reformers found almost nothing good to say about factory work. When they described the effect that the factory system had on families, on individual health, on morals, and on the environment, reformers were implicitly comparing the factory to the freedom of the farm. And the more the factory was cast into the part of the "evil" in the binary opposition of good and evil—a binary opposition borrowed from evangelical Christian modes of thinking—the more the farm became "good."[22] The evil was made even more powerful by the existence of an alternative, a social good lying just beyond the fingers' ends. That "good" was a life on the land, with its aesthetic, moral, and sanitary benefits.[23]

Farming families, it was argued, especially women and children, would grow up healthier and stronger in the country air, eating fresh food. At a time when outdoor work of whatever stripe was healthier than indoor work, it was argued that gardening provided needed exercise for workmen trapped indoors, especially tailors and shoemakers. "Here may be seen eight or ten men crowded into a small, dirty shop, with less space for the whole number than is often allowed for a respectable horse in his stable." Gardening would also enable workmen to raise fruit and vegetables in the name of nutritional variety.[24] *Potters' Examiner* editor William Evans, beginning to gravitate toward a land-based solution for the Staffordshire potters in

1844, gave his tribute to the land, which mixed aesthetic appreciation with a paean to the independence of the farmer: "to breathe, for
once, the pure breath of heaven; to gaze on that broad expanse of
earth and sky; to feel that health and liberty is yours; that you are
free from the pent-up prison work-bell!"[25]

Evans expressly contrasted the "villainous factory system" with

scenes, where homesteads and barns are filled with golden grain and thriving cattle; where natural beauties spread themselves around, in fields of
waving corn, dells of secluded beauty and flowery sweetness, orchards of
many coloured fruit, streams and rivulets of pellucid water, filled with
every variety of the finny tribes, and all free, *free*, FREE from the smoke,
sulphur, toil, dust, turmoil and early graves of the factory system.[26]

National Reform newspapers and tracts also contrasted the nox-
ious sights and sounds of the city with an exaggeratedly pastoral and
pure vision of the country, and emphasized the independence from
want and from supervision that was inherent in farming. As John
Campbell wrote:

It is not for me to feebly direct the working man's attention to the independence of an agricultural life. The free air of heaven, the clear stream,
the neat farm house, the well stocked barn, the fresh milk, butter and
eggs, the poultry, the sheep, the goats, the horses, the milk cows, the fat
hogs, the fields yellow with corn, the garden full of good vegetables, the
snug orchard, the free earth under the farmer's foot, the broad blue sky
over his head, all prove, all are evidences that his is the most independent
life of the whole community![27]

Farm life was thought to improve the human constitution morally
as well as physically. Washington, D.C., land reformers thought the
homestead measure would free laborers from "useless and even injurious occupations" and redirect them to the more natural and
beneficial project of "replenishing the earth and subduing it."[28]
While Crèvecoeur had linked morality with the American soil long
before, what was new here was the feeling of urgency—that the
United States was actually in danger of losing the Jeffersonian vision.[29]

The grittiness of American frontier existence—cold winters,
failed crops, having to slaughter animals, fend off Indians, and perhaps combat loneliness in the absence of the city culture—was not
often publicized, and not only because such an exposé would not
have aided the National Reform cause.[30] The only National Reformer who had farmed as an adult was Evans, who had spent seven

years on his own farm in New Jersey—but even then, melon grower Evans was close to major markets and to sources of information about farming. Granville, New Jersey, near modern-day Keyport and practically within shouting distance of Staten Island, was a far cry from the wild Wisconsin woods.[31]

If the aesthetic benefits of farming may have led to an exaggerated picture, British and American land reformers attempted to buttress their romantic instincts with Ricardian economics. They argued that the removal of surplus labor from the cities and onto small farms would raise the wage rate for those artisans who ignored the siren call to come till their own land. This connection between migration and rising urban wages was especially important in the American movement, whose participants were more ambivalent than the British about farming. Many of them probably clung to the hope that when homestead became law other workers would go, and the ensuing labor shortage would eliminate the threat of factory organization. In time, if enough workers were convinced to leave, those they left behind might even become masters.

British land-reform leaders, while they lauded the independence and health of a life on the land, clearly did not think all their constituents would drop everything to take up the spade. William Evans calculated the exact number of workers who would have to leave the potteries in order to raise the wages of the rest to an acceptable level.[32] Of the three main land-reform leaders, Feargus O'Connor was the most committed to settling as many of the "Chartist children" on the land as possible. As O'Connor constantly pointed out, a factory operative could never even be sure of survival through steady work—not when his wage was dependent on such slippery elements as the size of the labor market, the progress of machinery, and the state of trade. The farmer's return, in contrast, was consistent, year after year (there was apparently no weather in the O'Connor cosmos).[33] Yet committed to freedom through the land as he was, even O'Connor described the land as a safety valve.[34]

Land reformers also used economic discourse to illustrate the abundance of the farm. O'Connor in particular liked to back up his assertions with the authority of numbers. His own experiments and those of other small farmers provided evidence of the bounteous possibilities of a very few acres of land. In his *Essay on the Management of Small Farms*, he estimated that, with the help of his wife and children, after 180 days' labor a workman on his own four acres could produce one 280-pound bacon pig, 14 pounds per week of flour, 16 pounds of potatoes per day, three quarts of milk or butter made from it, and as much eggs, poultry, vegetables, and honey as the family could consume. Beyond this, there would be enough left over that, even if sold in the wholesale market, a profit of £100 could be expected.[35] Perhaps because he was appealing to a constituency used to nutritional deprivation, he often listed the probable produce of a small farm in such a way as to make the mouth water. "Think of such a difficulty as working men having more of the produce of their own labour—beef and mutton, and milk, and butter, and cheese, and poultry, and eggs, and vegetables, and honey, and clothing, and fruit, and pigs—than they know what to do with!"[36]

How effective might these arguments, aesthetic, moral, social, and economic, pitting the idea of the factory against the idea of the farm, have been? British immigrants from working-class backgrounds who settled in America represented both sides of the equation, combining experience of industrialization with the opportunities of the frontier. Their letters illustrate that, independently of any National Reform or Chartist propaganda, these immigrants expressed their desire to become farmers for the stability and even for the leisure which they thought such a living promised.[37] The presence of pro-land sentiments among immigrants seems to indicate that the Chartists and National Reformers were appealing to a land hunger which was already present among the working people. As one such emigrant wrote in 1830,

Dont you think farming the best and surest way of getting a living? Manufacturing is a very unsteady business, sometimes up, and somtimes down, some few gets Rich, and thousands are ruined by it. . . . In Short no honnest man can live by it. A Factory too, is liable to be burnt down, but a Farm cannot easily be burnt up. Manufactoring breeds lords and Aristocrats, Poor men and slaves. But the Farmer, the American farmer, he, and he alone can be independent, he can be industrious, Healthy and Happy. . . . I cannot bear the idea that I or my children . . . should be shut up for 16 or 18 hours every day all our life time like Slaves and that too for a bare subsistence! No, God forbid. If I had the chance to morrow of either a Factory worth 10,000 dollars, or a farm worth 5,000 dollars, I would take the farm.[38]

The Morris family, formerly of Lancashire and latterly of the textile mills of Manayunk, Pennsylvania, were hit hard by the 1837–38 depression, at which time the brothers moved out to Ohio to look for farms. William Morris wrote to his Lancashire friends on June 4, 1837, to report that some of the cotton mills had stopped entirely, throwing manufacturers and employees alike out of employment. "We think it most suitable for such folks as us to get a piece of land and live upon it for this houlds out a permenent and encourageing prospect."[39] By July 1841, Morris had completely imbibed the safety-valve principle. "Their is one advantage in this countrey and that is in such times their are a number of mecanics moves back to the land where their is plenty for them to do and this gives more room for the others."[40] In both Britain and America, land-reform leaders who prided themselves on being responsive to the popular will crystallized latent sentiment against the factory and its moral, economic, and environmental effects. The farm was a logical reverse side of the coin, enhanced by hyperbolic literary description in the romantic vein. The farm as safety valve and fear of the factory system were inseparable.[41]

RELIGION AND NATURAL RIGHTS

Although rooted in daily experiences, reform arguments based on rejection of "the factory" and appreciation of "the farm" as a whole way of life had a strong religious and moral component, the binary opposition of farm and factory echoing the dichotomy between good and evil proposed by evangelistic preachers. Just as the land reformers benefited from the content of the factory movement, so they adopted the process—its voice of religious redemption. Of course, millennialism was not unique to the factory or Poor Law reforms—it was also characteristic of Robert Owen's colonizing experiments and Thomas Spence's forceful proposals. Not limited to believers, redemptionism was manifested as a joyousness about the future, a brighter future to be earned through positive alteration of man's environment.[42] Thus, in tune with the spirit of the age, Chartists and National Reform leaders, whose own backgrounds ranged from "freethinking" to religious, used the common cultural inheritance of Old Testament biblical language to express both their hopefulness and the righteousness of the land-reform cause.[43]

Opportunistically, land reformers latched on to the Old Testament, with its many direct references to land, and to the concept of Jubilee.[44] Chapter 25 of Leviticus describes the jubilee, by which once every 50 years landholdings reverted to their original arrangement and all slaves were freed:

And ye shall hallow the fiftieth year, and PROCLAIM LIBERTY THROUGHOUT ALL THE LAND, UNTO ALL THE INHABITANTS THEREOF; It shall be a JUBILEE unto you. AND YE SHALL RETURN EVERY MAN UNTO HIS POSSESSION, and you shall return every man unto his family. . . . The land SHALL NOT be sold FOR EVER; for the land is mine; and ye are strangers and sojourners with me.[45]

As noted above, the jubilee was a powerful image both for redemption of the land and as a sign of the end of wage slavery, and the chapter provided some oft-quoted lines, especially "the land shall not be sold for ever."[46] Thomas Spence, wedding millenarianism with concerns about inequality, had been a proponent of the jubilee:

> Hark! How the trumpet's sound
> Proclaims the land around
> The Jubilee
> Tells all the poor oppress'd
> No more they shall be cess'd
> Nor landlords more molest
> Their property.[47]

As Iain McCalman has explained, the use of the jubilee image by Spence and other "Enlightenment" figures can be explained in other terms than simply cynical exploitation of a religious audience.[48] In Spence's mind, and perhaps in the minds of later proponents of land reform, "millenarianism, political radicalism and freethought were intertwined, if not synonymous"—an Enlightenment goal of equality was held in mind, but it would be reached with divine dispensation.[49] Similarly, "One of the Turn Outs" in the Staffordshire potteries responded to William Evans's invitation to go onto the land in Wisconsin with, "If your readers are believers in Divine Revelation, and I believe they are, and if they hold the doctrine of the Millennium, which no doubt they do, let me ask them, if the land is not a very essential part of the blessings promised in that era?"[50] Land reformers alluded to the jubilee throughout the entire period.[51]

Another fruitful biblical field for land reformers lay in the prophesies of Micah, chapter 4.[52] That chapter concerned the future glories of Jerusalem: "Sword they will fashion into ploughshare and spear into pruning-hook; no room shall there be for nation to levy war against nation, and train itself at arm. At rest you shall sit, each of you with his own vine, his own fig-tree to give him shade, and none to raise the alarm."[53] All this was to occur when God redeemed his chosen nation. This passage seems to have had special appeal for the land reformers, as it was quoted constantly. The National Reformers' memorial to Congress prophesied that when land limitation was enforced, the millennium would arrive, and "that promised day, spoken of in Scripture, would arrive, when 'they shall sit, every man under his vine and his fig tree, and none shall make them afraid.'" The example of the United States would reach other nations and be instrumental in the regeneration and enfranchisement of the entire earth, a direct fulfillment of John Winthrop's hopes for the New World.[54]

The allusion to vine and fig tree was also popular in Britain among land company leaders and subscribers writing letters to the *Northern Star*.[55] In 1850, as O'Connor's land empire was disintegrating around him, it was this evocative verse which sprang from his lips: "However I may be attempted to be put down by government, I am determined to go on until I have placed every surplus labourer in the market in his own vineyard and under his own fig-tree, none daring to make him afraid."[56] It appeared in other Chartist land-reform organs as well. John Barker, an English emigrant to Ohio, wrote Joseph Barker's newspaper, the *People*, "I have been out feeding my stock, and I feel a pleasure that I cannot describe in being under my own vine and fig tree. . . . Dear Stephen, I would advise you to escape for your life. Come here and secure a portion of the land."[57] It is interesting that this verse and its connection to land reform had a longer history in radicalism. In May 1839, Anti–Poor Law crusader Joseph Rayner Stephens gave a sermon before a London audience in which he encouraged his listeners to lay claim to the land of England. Although Stephens claimed he was no friend of revolution in the abstract, if the rich continued to deny the poor wherewithal even to eat, he advised the poor to march onward: "The God of Mercy will very soon enable them to lay down the sword and take up the olive branch of peace, every man sitting under his own vine and fig tree, none daring to make him afraid."[58] Stephens was not a political, but rather a moral radical, and the same tone of righteous indignation about the abuse of the poor for which he was so famous would characterize later land-reform rhetoric also.[59]

The constant use of the "vine and fig tree" verse is revealing on several levels. The vine and the fig tree are part of the appeal, conjuring up a relaxed, pastoral idyll, complete with perennial supplies of food and drink. But the second half of the verse is also important, as it encompasses the power of landownership to eliminate two types of fear: the anxiety about earning a living, and the fear of lack of power and respect. A biblical verse could not have been more appealing to workers afraid of deskilling and in search of equal rights. In addition, in the original passage, the subjects of the verse were specifically to be unafraid of foreign aggression. Land reformers would base part of their appeal to authorities, government, and the press on the idea that new landholders, people with a stake in the hedge, would be more willing than nonlandholders to defend their country with arms.[60]

When spreading the gospel of land reform through speeches, land reformers accompanied their use of key biblical verses with familiar pulpit-style delivery—something which might have made unfamiliar arguments seem less jarring to the open but unradicalized ear. Here is Ernest Jones, celebrating the opening of the first land company estate:

We have recently celebrated the birthday of renewed Chartism in the north—I think we may call this its christening. Her Majesty's children are baptized with holy water from the river Jordan. . . . at the great christening we baptise with earth instead of water—and this indeed is holy earth, since it is the land devoted to the purpose for which God designed it, the maintenance of those who till it by the sweat of their brow. . . . I have come from the land of slavery, to the land of liberty—from the land of poverty to the land of plenty—from the land of the Whigs, to the great land of the Charter! This is the promised land.[61]

Similarly, in America in the early 1850's, a group of associated working women and men would actually gather in a Philadelphia grove to hear sermons on land reform. At one, given by one Fleming, land monopoly assumed the role of Satan, becoming the motive force of evil: "Who fills our insane hospitals? LAND MONOPOLY. Who robs the poor of year after year's toil? LAND MONOPOLY. Who steals the dearest rights of the unborn generation? LAND MONOPOLY."[62] Even printed National Reform tracts shared with evangelical delivery stylistic choices like repetition and exhortation.[63]

Why did land reformers in Britain and America use religious texts and delivery? In one sense, the answer is obvious—Christianity had a wide appeal, especially in America, where enthusiasm had so recently cast all of upstate New York into apprehension of sin.[64] Religion was the basis of a moral economy, which contrasted with the amoral political economy of cotton lords and land monopolists. Looking beyond the laws of the nation, the National Reformers appealed to a higher authority; they contrasted a biblical injunction, from "THE Lord," "In the *sweat of thy face* shalt thou eat bread," with an injunction from "Land Lord," "Thou shalt not till the ground unless thou payest rent."[65] In the worldview of working-class land reformers and many workingmen alike, unlimited acquisition of wealth was un-Christian, whereas working to obtain enough to make one's family comfortable—a competency—was appropriate.

Religion was also inseparable from the nonreligious argument that man had a natural right to the soil. By the natural-rights argument, it was incontrovertible that all men had similar needs, which had to be fulfilled in order for them to survive. Thirst, hunger, and sensation required drink, food, and clothing and shelter, and the genesis of all these was the soil; therefore, all men had an equal right to the soil. As the National Reformers resolved in convention, "the right of mankind to the SOIL is evident from the Scriptures, from the nature of man, from his inability to exist without it, and from the deleterious effects which eighteen centuries of wrong have shown to be the result of societies which do not recognize this right."[66] The strongest American proponent of a natural-rights argument for man's access to the soil was Thomas Devyr, who had written a pamphlet on the subject, titled *Our Natural Rights*, while still in Ireland in 1836; it was reprinted in 1842.[67] The natural-rights argument for the land made its way into National Reform newspapers and pamphlets.[68]

The natural-rights argument linking mankind with the soil was refined in the corridors of freethought, where many of the American land reformers had received their intellectual training. Freethinkers in cities had formed enclaves of activity throughout the 1820's and 1830's, toasting Tom Paine and discussing natural rights.[69] They were accustomed to public speaking, to organizing meetings, and to thinking critically. Their theoretical position against the institutionalization of religion naturally led to the desire to change the social and economic systems which they thought resulted from religion. Gilbert Vale, who emigrated to America from England in the late 1820's and had edited the freethought *Beacon* since 1836, participated in the National Reform movement in New York.[70] Vale's journey to England in 1848, where he met with prominent Chartists, helped to cement the transatlantic connections in land reform. Boston freethinkers Josiah P. Mendum and Horace Seaver published the *Boston Investigator*, which supported the National Reform movement, and they also participated in conferences of the New England Labor Reform League, avowing solidarity with Evans and his cause. One of the two land-reform petitions to originate from Boston bears both their signatures.[71] Jeremiah Hacker's infidel paper, the *Pleasure Boat*, supported land reform and was excerpted in the labor newspaper the *Voice of Industry*, and Aaron Hinchman of Goshen, Ohio, was publisher of both the infidel *Self-Examiner* and later the *Homestead Journal*, a National Reform newspaper. Finally and perhaps most important, George Henry Evans was privately an avowed freethinker, and publicly promoted infidel publications and materials in the *Working Man's Advocate*. As a printer, he printed antireligious tracts and books.[72]

The natural-rights argument also appeared in England, more often among abstract thinkers on the land, but occasionally among land-reform planners.[73] William Evans argued that, since life was the gift of God and all people must live from the fruits of the earth, anyone who interfered in that process was stepping between man and his Maker. "The few have monopolized the land of the many, and God's laws are violated. . . . They have made a seizure of the sustenance of life, and have told the poor that they have no right to live."[74] Similarly, O'Connor reasoned from nature. "The wild beast of the forest, the fish of the sea, and the bird of the air, all, all have their resting place, and an ample provision from nature's store; *while man, poor man* is alone an outcast in the land which the Lord his God told him to subdue for his own use."[75] A nonreligious natural-rights argument was less controversial in America, where it was linked to Enlightenment opposition to unnatural social hierarchies, and where natural rights undergirded the theory of governance. Nonetheless, in both countries, it was used to balance the millennial religious content of the quest for the land. Together, these political languages helped land reformers reach an audience with diverse religious views.

PATRIOTISM

Along with opposition to factory labor and invocation of a Christian moral economy tempered by natural rights, patriotism was a common field of force binding American and British land reformers. Labor historians have long identified a strain of "equal-rights ideology" among American artisans, expressed through the claim "the laborer is worthy of his hire" and other like sentiments. They have noted that the ideology was precipitated by the perception that the road from journeyman to laborer was becoming increasingly difficult to travel.[76] Land-reform propagandists expanded this critique by presenting artisans with the specter of an unfinished American Revolution, unfinished because there was as yet no social equality. As George Lippard wrote, "the next Half Century will witness a peaceful Revolution, which will give to every man the fruits of Labor; and develop the American Union into that perfect Brotherhood, of which the fathers of the Revolution intended it should be the visible symbol."[77]

Abolitionist land reformer Gerrit Smith adopted the National Reform version of history, which connected land reform and the Working Men with the Revolution: "The inalienable right to the soil was a truth recognized and asserted by the far-seeing patriot, the great and good Jefferson." While Jefferson had hinted at the evils that would result from land monopoly, "It was not, however, until the year 1829 that the landless clearly perceived the predicament into which they had been gradually led."[78] Without land reform, the chasm between rich and poor would increase, an aristocracy would burgeon, and even political rights would be endangered. The "Dorr War," over the extent of political representation in Rhode Island, was "evidence" of the relentless march into tyranny: when George Henry Evans was asked how the National Reformers were connected with the Dorr conflict, he replied, "What the landed aristocracy of Rhode Island and of England were now doing to withhold the right of suffrage, the same aristocracy elsewhere would do if they could get the power."[79]

Speaking before an audience of upstate New York farmers, National Reformer Thomas Devyr painted the American revolution as an unceasing battle fought in each generation. The great design the forefathers had dreamed for America was nothing less than the "earthly redemption of the human race." But it would be frustrated if land reform were not pursued to the bitter end: "Progress, Liberty, Independence, would be impossible if Land Monopoly were allowed to fasten itself upon the Republic."[80] National Reformers appealed to their constituency as a group of citizens, and a call for a landed democracy as the goal of the unfinished American revolution, to "scatter the fundamental capital of the country—the soil—among the greatest possible number of persons, thus counteracting the tendency of the aristocratic principle, which is to concentrate all property in the hands of a few."[81] Surprisingly, the rhetoric about a landed democracy was not limited to the United States. Ashton-Under-Lyne's William Aitken toasted at a Chartist function in 1848: "A landed democracy, and may the plan proposed by F. O'Connor, esq. and the Chartist executive lead to the destruction of the law of primogeniture, a better cultivated native land, and a greater state of happiness for the Industrious of these Islands."[82]

The National Reformers appealed to their white-male audience as a group of powerful voters. Their popular pamphlet, exhorting "Vote yourself a farm!" provided the group's main slogan, and the slogan in turn became shorthand for the group—the "vote yourself a farm party." A closer examination of this pamphlet illustrates the way National Reform publicists combined their concepts for the strongest possible presentation. "Are you an American citizen? Then you are a joint owner of the public lands. Why not take enough of your property to provide yourself a home? Why not vote yourself a farm?" Poor white males could make an impact by voting, if not in any other way.[83] The pamphlet reached out to cultivate the workman's pride, making equal treatment a priority at a time when class divisiveness belied the supposed egalitarianism of the Revolution. "If a man has a house and a home of his own, though it be a thousand miles off, he is well received in other people's houses; while the homeless wretch is turned away." A series of rhetorical questions followed, slowly sketching out the author's idea of his audience, and what image of themselves he expected would appeal to them. For each identity, there was a reason to vote oneself a farm. "Are you a party follower?" "Are you tired of slavery?" "Are you endowed with reason?" "Are you a believer in the scriptures?" Those who answered yes to the last question, for example, were urged to "assert that the land is the Lord's because he made it. Resist then the blasphemers who exact money for his work, even as you would resist them should they claim to be worshipped for his holiness. Emancipate the poor from the necessity of encouraging such blasphemy—vote the freedom of the public lands." The pamphlet ends with an appeal to free the country from an "aristocracy of avarice"—harking back again to the unachieved goals of the Revolution and fears of an invasion by European traditions—by voting for the measures of the National Reformers.[84]

When the National Reformers memorialized Congress they couched their demands in a political form suitable for popular and official consumption. The language of the preamble to their memorial echoed the Declaration of Independence, and spoke of the need to maintain a republican citizenry. The National Reformers argued that freeing the public lands for actual settlers and establishing a limitation on the number of acres held would increase the number of freeholders, the best type of republicans, and decrease the number of those who were economically dependent on others. Clearly, the project of the National Reformers could be presented as a patriotic one, identical with preservation of the republic.[85]

National Reformer John Campbell's work echoed eighteenth-century American radicalism by tying machinery to the old critique that corruption was caused by commerce run out of control. He dedicated his 1848 work to the French revolutionaries, and his Rousseau-like turns of phrase and allusions to Locke and Paine let the reader know he was influenced by the Enlightenment.[86] Campbell disapproved of the centralized institutions of tariffs and banking, designed to cheat the workingman out of his small savings. But financial instruments were not the only harbingers of monopoly—machinery was also to blame. Like other land reformers, Campbell evoked the yeoman farmer as Jefferson might have, calling cities the "putrid cesspools of a nation," and factory hands "wage slaves."[87]

Because machinery held large numbers of people completely in its thrall, Campbell argued, it was inextricably linked to land monopoly. As the nation's more technologically skilled individuals learned how to accumulate and cultivate the soil, they gained a monopoly of the production of the earth, and a monopoly of money, education, and government.[88] Campbell listed classes of men who unfairly forced the productive members of society to maintain them: lawyers, bankers, landlords, merchants, brokers, legislators,

soldiers, judges, doctors, shopkeepers, and those manufacturing useless or injurious articles.[89] Campbell's rhetoric, with its Jeffersonian
and Revolution-era overtones, warned that to leave landownership
unregulated was to send the fledgling Republic into the corrupt
footsteps of its progenitor, England.

Like John Campbell, Cincinnati's John Pickering was a land reformer suspicious of any government which threatened to buttress a
moneyed aristocracy in America. He produced a book intended to
expose society's false principles and support the claims of the working classes, particularly to the land. Pickering blended an older language critical of aristocracies with the language of capital and labor.
While capital in itself was not an evil, being nothing more than surplus labor, "this surplus past labor might, and in justice ought, to be
employed in promoting the prosperity of the people; but it is not; on
the contrary, it is made use of as a terrible agent of oppression."[90] Reformers like Pickering and Campbell made clear connections between saving the Republic and preventing the unlimited acquisition
of wealth.

The patriotic appeal to land reform was not confined to the
United States. Margot Finn has identified nationalism as a key facet
of British radicalism in the late 1840's, and the land reformers were
no exception.[91] British land reformers argued that as freeborn Englishmen, they had right to a portion of the soil of the land where
they were born. Thomas Spence had argued that those too lazy to
claim their patriotic right to property should not be granted the right
to vote.[92] In a dialect pamphlet that featured a dialogue among three
village workers, O'Connor made the case that worker landownership was a long-standing tradition, an integral facet of Englishness.
At the end, two of the men, Smith and old Robin, drink to "the restoration of old English times, old English fare, old English justice,
and every man live on the sweat of his brow ... when her hardy,
honest peasantry were their country's pride, when the weaver
worked at his own loom, and stretched his limbs in his own field."[93]

Patriotism motivated O'Connor's opposition to emigration.
Home colonization, in contrast with emigration, strengthened the
country by preventing the sapping away of human resources and by
increasing home markets. Another possible benefit of land reform,
income equity, aided the nation by building up national markets.
Such equity, O'Connor suggested, would also cheapen government

by removing the need for Poor Laws and a rural police. Finally, income equity would make benefit clubs, unions, and other such working-class societies, whose existence might make the middle classes nervous, unnecessary.[94]

The argument was often made that working people with land could become valuable defenders of the nation; but this could cut both ways. In 1846, the *Northern Star* began a "no vote, no musket" campaign as newspapers discussed war with the United States over the Oregon boundary question. Chartists, O'Connor asserted, patriots although they might be, could not in good conscience defend a country which refused to enfranchise them. The staff of *Young America* got wind of this campaign after it had been running for about four months, and responded with a "No Land, No Rifle!" campaign of their own. They refused to take up arms against the British both on the basis of universal brotherhood and because the government which refused to give them land on which to live did not deserve their support as cannon fodder.[95] But if patriotism could be internationalist, as in this example, it could also take a more parochial form. Philadelphia land reformer John Sidney Jones, in the spirit of Washington's farewell address, conjured up the specter of European powers designing to infringe on the freedom of American labor by speculating in American land.[96] Thus, whether they were internationalist or nationalistic, by appealing to their audiences on the ground of patriotism, American and British land reformers appealed to a strain of popular conservatism the extent of which historians are just beginning to discover.[97] Their appeal was also strategic, however, as it made it more difficult for state and the press to dismiss the "patriotic" land movements as nationally disruptive.

THE INVENTION OF THE AGRICULTURAL
SUBURB

Like the socialists of their time, the land reformers believed the human character was formed by the environment in which it was nurtured. On both sides of the Atlantic, therefore, land reformers concerned themselves with not simply returning the individual to the land, and providing him with autonomy, but also configuring communities on the land to enhance character formation. Examination of their plans for the distribution of public and private space and for the configuration of neighborhoods reveals they intended to provide working families with increased space, but still allow them the face-to-face interaction which made sociability possible. Plans for land-reform colonies also provided more "public space" than working people normally had access to.

The Chartists and the National Reformers both sought to impose some of the city's artificial order on the countryside, to settle workers close together on the land. To the modern eye, maps of the Chartist allotments resemble nothing so much as maps of American suburban subdivisions dating from the 1960's and 1970's. Each Chartist estate was cut through by private roads, which were built by the company, and the houses all fronted onto the roads, with yards stretching out behind (although the "yards" of the allotments were intended to be completely cultivated with vegetables). The layout of each development depended on the size and shape of the tract, but the houses were arranged so as to minimize the necessity for road construction. They were also meant to maximize neighborliness, each house along the street facing another. In the case of Rickmansworth, the houses attached to the three- and four-acre allotments were semidetached, but this style was unpopular and was eliminated on the rest of the estates.

One notes a chronological progression in the layout of the estates. At Herringsgate, the simplest, there are only two parallel roads and one perpendicular, with the two-acre cottages relegated to a less desirable position behind their wealthier neighbors' holdings. This layout was eliminated at the more complex and much larger Minster Lovell. By some creative boundary drawing, all except four of the allotments were arranged so that each house faced another house or houses, and there were no parallel roads. A semicircular court was added in one area, cutting awkwardly through nine lots. The map of Lowbands shows the most closely packed arrangement, a series of roads curving out from the central gathering point at Forty Green, where the schoolhouse was located. Each house at Lowbands, again opposite a neighbor, was provided with its own driveway.[98]

Chartist suburbs were a design before their time. Just as, in a Whig and Tory world, Chartists were neither one thing nor the other, so the Chartist estates were a permanent, and possibly threatening, geographical testimony to difference. They resembled neither cities nor villages, and the tininess of the allotments was a marked contrast with the broad swaths of individually owned land which abutted the estates. That the allotments were both small and completely at the whim of working-class tenants may have threatened the rural "natives" politically. Would the Chartists outnumber them in local elections, and perhaps elect radical vestrymen for these areas? Neighboring squires might also have feared the scenario that Poor Law inspector John Revans would warn of in 1848 while testifying before the Select Committee on the National Land Company. He thought successive waves of poor Northern factory workers would settle on the Chartist allotments for just enough time to claim a settlement under the Poor Laws. After having lost all their money, they would leave the land and become a permanent drain on the local rates, only to be replaced by another set of unfortunates.[99]

Neighbors' distrust was probably fueled by the presence of public spaces on the allotments, intended to keep Chartism, or at least politics, alive on the estates. Each estate was provided with a school, which would double as a lecture hall, suitable for entertaining roving Chartist lecturers; allottees were a captive audience. Although the "public space" was automatically provided, however (whereas Chartists ordinarily had to contest for the right to use public spaces), other public spaces were missing from the estates. In the towns, working people had been famed for spilling out onto their stoops in the evenings, chatting and obstructing the paths of passersby. Children played in the streets and courts, and women gossiped as they hung up their laundry. There was a world of difference between the proximity to which town-dwellers were accustomed and that experienced on the estates. In purpose-built suburbs of workers' row housing, so many families were crammed together that, although moving from one "two up, two down" to another such was commonplace, kin and friends, known to be reliable, always remained nearby.[100] In contrast, on an allotment, town-bred women and men who were used to meeting their friends during the working day would have to start afresh making friends—usually with allottees from far-flung areas of the country—and would now find they had only their own families to depend upon.

Although in an age before public transportation the commute to work was usually less than half a mile, the factory provided a clear separation between work and home.[101] Those working in the home during factory hours did not have their factory-employed relatives around all day, getting underfoot; in an allotment, families would be thrown together more. Allotment life would also have added to the responsibilities of the women in the house; home baking and brewing, two tasks familiar and essential to the countrywoman, were less necessary in towns, and some allottees would have to learn them for the first time. Furthermore, on a small allotment, all members of the family would have been needed to till the soil, and even to handle fairly heavy jobs like digging, in the absence of a horse and plow. Nonetheless, if the rhetoric of land-plan advertising is any reflection of working-class attitudes, the gains perceived—increased independence, the reversion of the family unit to its more "natural" form, and the opportunity to send children to school rather than the factory—may have compensated for this sacrifice of sociability.[102]

Because no National Reform townships were ever constructed, proposed layouts for these remain more general, but they do give an indication of the principles held by their designers. In 1852, when the Homestead Act had passed the House of Representatives but not the Senate, the latter body received a copy of the National Reform sketches, along with a neat etching of a National Reform village. The etching shows a large, federal-style civic building in the center of a bare octagonal plaza, from which radiate a series of straight roads. Each road contains a row of boxy, two-story houses, flush up against the road, but each with its own spacious back lawn.[103] Taking a page from the U.S. Rectangular Survey System, the National Reformers proposed that townships be laid out six miles square, bisected horizontally, vertically, and diagonally by major roads. Each township would contain 140 farming families, each farm a neat 160-acre square within the larger square. In an innovation on the government's plan, which had set aside one section for school land but nothing for public life, the center of the National Reform township was reserved for 5-acre village lots, intended for craftspeople, and for a park and public edifices.[104] The village was laid out on a plan resembling a spiderweb—a series of concentric octagons, with the main streets running out from a 30-acre park in the center, which might contain the public buildings.[105] The main streets were to be built wide enough to accommodate railroad lines.

The National Reformers' six-mile-square townships, each of

which should have a town hall and a college, might, under pressure of population, be further divided into homesteads of no less than 10 acres each. (This was the size tract which one family required to support itself.) Homesteads would trade, the local economy facilitated by marts in the central village, running on the principle of equitable exchange for each item "according to the cost of labor in their production with the value of material added." A sense of community was vital to the National Reform village project, since many of the land reformers had backgrounds in or ties to Fourier's Associationist movement.[106] Community in National Reform townships would be promoted by a phonetic newspaper, its novel system of spelling testifying to the inauguration of a new social era on the American plains.

National Reformer Lewis Masquerier hoped that a minutely planned, tightly settled frontier would promote community.[107] A former Owenite, Masquerier had been the motive force behind securing a charter for the New York branch of the Owenites in 1840.[108] Masquerier claimed that no matter what one's views on Association, tight settlement along the National Reform plan would ensure each homesteader had "the sublime power of self-direction and self-employment," and would "be stimulated to duty by the example of neighbors."[109] George Henry Evans added his own reasons for wanting to see the West tightly settled: it kept large-tract speculators away, provided a market for locally produced goods, decreased required expenditures on infrastructure, and gave greater facilities for education.[110] Tight settlement was not likely to appeal only to East Coast mechanics used to the sociability of cities. As Charlotte Erickson has noted, those already in the West encouraged tight settlement, to improve their own infrastructure and access to goods.[111]

Although the amount of public land available for settlement in America far outstripped the amount likely to come up for sale in England, both National Reformers and Chartists pursued their own quest for order and responded to what they perceived as working people's desires for sociability and security.[112] Both groups designed tightly settled compromises between city and farm—thereby pioneering agricultural suburbs. Both groups also attempted to promote and maintain upward mobility, a sense of community, and political involvement, by building schools and town centers and providing opportunities for economic exchange on their own terms.

LAND REFORM, WOMEN, AND THE FAMILY

Like the proponents of factory reform before them, both the Chartists and the National Reformers used gender to advance land reform by claiming that the factory system perverted normal family roles.[113] In doing this, leaders appealed to men's paternalistic instincts and emphasized the injustices which land monopoly wreaked on women and the family by removing women and children from their proper sphere.[114] As in the factory movement, within the land-reform movement such rhetoric about gender could be used to forge understandings between workingmen who were committed to a patriarchal system, and men with similar beliefs in other classes. This is not to state, however, that women served land reform only as rhetorical objects; rather, they were encouraged to participate in both movements as auxiliaries, thus imbuing the movements with moral weight originating in women's assumed moral superiority. Where women and children were visible participants in land-reform activities, they helped to transform these activities from the strictly political to the more broadly cultural.[115]

Whether the rhetoric of domesticity was used to sway middle-class audiences using their own arguments, as Anna Clark has suggested, or because it authentically resonated with working people, the Chartist Land Company and other reform efforts sentimentally invoked the "proper role" of women.[116] "The Mother never should leave the house except upon business or pleasure. Little children unable to take care of themselves are not infrequently scalded to death, while the poor mother is making money for her employer—At home is her proper place," O'Connor wrote.[117] He accepted the argument that a mother's proper role was education of the children, but also called the woman the "greatest ornament" of the house, echoing many a middle-class writer. He felt strongly that there were "natural positions" for man and wife within the household context, and provided horrific examples of the subversion of the natural order.

Chartist supporters of the land company claimed that the factory system leveled these natural gender and age differences by forcing all members of a family to awaken before sunrise, and compelled children to trundle sleepily to work or be ferried on the shoulders of their unemployed fathers while grasping crusts of bread they could barely muster the energy to eat. In contrast, the farm system made the "natural" gradations within the family possible again. The man who worked independently got up and went to bed when he wanted to. He would go out to the fields during the day, and when he came home, his eyes would shine at the sight of a clean wife and children waiting for him in the doorway. "All are straight, erect, and healthy, because each has been trained according to their strength. . . . he is master of himself and of his time. . . . he seeks no refuge for wounded feelings in the beer shop or the gin palace," O'Connor said in one speech; and in another, "This is a portion of a great feature of my plan to give the fond wife back to her husband, and the innocent babe back to its fond mother."[118]

The National Reformers also argued land monopoly perverted many natural relationships, crowding trades with rotating shifts of apprentices, threatening small farmers with losing their farms, and also leading to the degradation of women. "But for Land Monopoly, every female in a factory would have a parental roof to retreat to from the oppression of capital," George Henry Evans, sure that women did not want to work, wrote to a delegate from the Lowell Female Labor Reform Association.[119] Protection of the homestead from distraint by creditors could be supported on the grounds that it protected women: "There is no reason, neither in nature and justice, why [women] should sink their identity in the husband and father, and be made to feel the full force of all his faults, errors and misfortunes."[120] Even the degradation of women through the social evil of prostitution had an environmental cause linked to land reform. "I believe many of America's fair daughters abandon themselves to crime—many abandoned ones, I believe, would gladly return to a life of virtue if they could have plenty of employment at good wages. Alas! how much there is to compel us to be criminals," despaired Massachusetts land reformer J. E. Thompson.[121]

Land reformers' rhetoric not only proposed an idealized vision of the farming family, but also was meant to appeal to men who had no inkling of the unrelenting labor required of small-farming wives. A false contrast, between a romanticized version of women's work in a farming home, and a harsh version of women's work in a factory town, was deliberately heightened. In the end, the women who did settle on the Chartist allotments were compromised by the failure of their leaders fully to disclose what they were in for—they were terrifically hampered by their lack of knowledge of country arts of self-sufficiency, especially bread making. Nor did the kin networks, on which women relied for sociability, support in sickness, and assistance in child care, exist on the allotments.

Despite its less than optimal practical effects, the paternalistic rhetoric linking land reform with restoration of traditional family roles was not meant to exclude real women. Both National Reform and Chartist leaders appealed to women directly on the podium and through the press. Although women could not sign the agrarian pledge or vote, National Reform measures were calculated to benefit women as well as men. The constitution of the Industrial Congress, promulgated in 1845, permitted women to be represented at that body.[122] On behalf of the New Jersey National Reformers, Henry Smith petitioned the U.S. Senate to allow any landless adult person, male or female, rich or poor, to locate a lot on a quarter-section. This did not really mark a departure from prevailing ideas of women's property, because "in case of the marriage of two persons holding lots, the possession of one of the lots [was] to be sold, or otherwise transferred, by the parties, to a landless person."[123] Based on the fact that their prescriptions could be helpful to women, land-reform leaders urged women to compel their men to join the movement and sign the Agrarian Pledge. "How often, at the death of the husband, is the widow turned out of house and home to seek a precarious existence, without even the cold charities of a cold world to comfort her?"[124] Another article waxed, "When woman—lovely, disinterested, warm-hearted, sympathetic woman—throws by her distaff, and espouses the cause of suffering humanity, where is the faint-hearted man . . . who will not gird on his armor and press forward to the rescue?"[125]

The National Reformers realized that the presence of women among their ranks could be salutary, because of the perception current in society that, since women were more moral than men, nothing truly underhanded could go on if women were present.[126] Women did participate in some of the labor meetings at which National Reform was discussed. At a regular meeting of the National Reformers, Michael T. O'Connor, editor of the *Irish Volunteer*, "alluded handsomely to the presence of the ladies, and hoped they would continue to attend the meetings, for the cause demanded the consideration of every man and woman."[127] At one meeting of the New England Working Men's Association at Tremont Chapel in Boston, the company present included the Ladies' Labor Reform Association, which brought a banner, "Union for the sake of power, and power to bless humanity." Sarah Bagley addressed those present, noting that, like the women of the American Revolution, the female labor reformers did not "expect to enter the field as soldiers in the great warfare; but we would . . . be permitted to furnish the soldiers with a blanket or replenish their knapsacks from our pantries."[128]

National Reformers failed to use women's strength as much as they could have. As Ronald and Mary Zboray have shown, antebellum women did take an interest in politics, including the politics of Free Soil.[129] Ostensibly, National Reformers in places like Lowell could have exerted themselves to court women's signatures on homestead petitions.[130] Large numbers of working women had signed antislavery petitions, and John Cluer demonstrated how such workers could become a moral force for action in the ten-hour debate.[131] Huldah J. Stone, on behalf of the Lowell Female Labor Reform Association, had invited the National Reformers to cultivate her group in 1845, and personally supported National Reform.[132] Yet in an open letter to the Lowell Female Labor Reform Association, George Henry Evans noted that if he had his way, women would not be working in factories at all, but rather administering their homes; it was attitudes like these which distracted workingmen leaders from employing the moral force of female operatives.[133] Such ideas, combined with the rhetorical force of "Vote yourself a farm," excluded rank-and-file women, who could not vote, from participating.

Thus, the presence of women in the National Reform movement was generally auxiliary, and women leaders were discouraged. Martha Hollingworth, offered a position on the Executive Committee of the Industrial Congress, declined on the grounds that to accept this position would put her in a higher position than her husband—an idea which she thought preposterous.[134] Besides Hollingworth, only one woman appears in the existing record of National Reform who can be considered a leader, and through her actions she became more sui generis than a representative of "womanhood."[135] Fannie Lee Townsend made her first foray into the National Reform cause as an honorary member at the 1847 Industrial Congress. She started a controversy there by proposing a resolution which would have advised clerics to take the side of labor rather than capital.[136] The strongest opposition to Townsend's resolution, and that which pre-

vailed, came from George Henry Evans, who said without intentional irony that he "thought the resolution greatly impolitic, for an
attack on the clergy would be considered an attack on religion, one
effect of which would be to deprive us of the support of women, over
whom the clergy had influence."[137] As Fanny Wright, the radical
Owenite, had been in the 1830's, Townsend was a liminal figure,
but she attempted to amass authority for her opinions based on the
fact that she spoke for the women. Townsend pointed out that
Evans "wished to obtain the influence of women, and yet, when a
woman had entered into the reform movement with all her heart,
had come from Rhode Island purposely to attend this Congress, had
offered a single resolution, he opposed it. This seemed to her very illogical and inexplicable."[138]

Townsend, born Fannie Lee Drew, was unlike other women labor
activists in that she was middle-class and educated. After her marriage
to Solomon Townsend, Esq., a ship's master in the American East India
service, she worked as lecturer on science, philosophy, and land reform
before being chosen to represent New England at the Fourth Industrial
Congress in Cincinnati.[139] The reason for her conversion to the labor
cause is unknown, but it may relate to her enthusiastic Baptist faith.
Townsend started up her own religion-saturated labor newspaper, the
Philadelphia *Monthly Jubilee*, partly financed by the textile workshop
of her second husband, "General" John Sidney Jones, whom she had
met in the course of her working-class advocacy.[140]

Townsend's monthly magazine, which she claimed reached a
circulation of 10,000 in 1853, would combine a very personal mix of
theology and reformism, its truth predicated on the moral superiority of woman. She produced a "Jubilee catechism," which mixed
land-reform rhetoric, religion, and peculiar health issues.[141] Her
original contribution to the theory of land reform was her bizarre
linkage of land monopoly with a societal sanction against a man's
growing his beard long. For her, refusal to crop the beard was a form
of social rebellion, a visible marker that one refused to succumb to
the land monopolists:

The subjugation of the beard to false usages of society tallies with the
subjugation of the soil, to Land Speculation and Land Monopoly; the same
principle destroys the strength and vitality of both man and the soil. Man
has in a proper state of society, power to maintain the freedom of the
Beard and the freedom of the Land, through his birth right to Free Speech,
Free Inquiry and Free Discussion.[142]

Townsend attempted to be more than a token woman and a rab-ble rouser. At her first Industrial Congress, she was elected to the Executive Committee, and also registered her opposition to the pro-posed Constitution of the Industrial Congress because it failed to give women the right to vote.[143] In Philadelphia, Townsend spoke from the podium numerous times, not only as an advocate of women's rights, but also as an advocate of human rights, comparing herself to Jesus and Thomas Paine.[144] Townsend accumulated a per-sonal following in Philadelphia, but her interactions on the Na-tional Reform scene were never as successful. Her presence as a lone woman in a male forum, and the reception of her suggestions in the Industrial Congresses, seems to indicate she was tolerated but that other reformers were afraid to take her suggestions—especially for woman suffrage—seriously. Although they may personally have supported increased rights for women in theory, they were by defini-tion more concerned with increasing economic freedom for both sexes. To that end, land reformers' rhetorical construction of the family was more useful than the full inclusion of any particular woman in the decision-making process.

Although women subscribed to the Chartist Land Company and emigrated with the Potters' Joint-Stock Emigration Company, there is no evidence of individual women promoting the plan on either the national or the local level.[145] Because the land company was a company, propagation of its tenets was carried out through the company directors, all of whom were men. It is probable, however, that women, if they had a voice regarding any discretionary income in their homes, were central in encouraging the purchase of family shares. O'Connor liked to tell the story of a man who came up to him exceedingly eager to purchase a share in the land plan. When asked why he was in such a rush, the man replied that his wife kept pinching him at night and said he should have no peace, or sleep, or rest, till he purchased his freedom by buying shares. O'Connor would then turn to his mixed audience and say, "Now, I implore every wife to do the same; pinch your husbands and bite them, till they take you out of bondage."[146] At a public meeting at the Chartist allotment at Lowbands, a Mr. Wild counseled the young women present never to take husbands unless the young men agreed to be-come Chartists.[147]

American women were encouraged to use their supposedly

scolding tongues for the same political means. "Teach your children to lisp that this is not right, and ask your husbands if they are *men*, supinely to sink under the growing evil? ... Can't you coax your husbands and sons to join this association?"[148] American women since the Revolution had been taught to use their seductive charms, and other aspects of their womanly nature, to coerce their husbands and sweethearts into virtuous republicanism; now they were asked to become shrews in the service of a better future for themselves and their families.

Both Chartist and National Reform rhetoric constructed a return to family farms as that social system most able to rescue women and the family from dangerous brushes with the public sphere. A life in the countryside removed women and children from sexual danger, from other forms of temptation, and, perhaps most appealingly for working-class men, from the labor market, where their lower wages pushed men aside. Even in their invitations for women to participate, male land-reform leaders presented stereotypical images of women, as moral guardians, eager helpmeets urging husbands, or scolding shrews. Yet given the participation of women within the movements, occasionally as leaders, more often as shareholders or emigrants, it would be rash to conclude that working-class women rejected the popular presentation of themselves as in need of protection or wishing to remain in the home. After all, when they could do so by the middle and end of the nineteenth century, working-class wives stayed home and cared for their families in droves—just as the early land reformers wished their wives could.

Despite differences in experiences between countries and among regions, American and British land-reform leaders used many of the same basic appeals. On both sides of the Atlantic, the land was portrayed as a safety valve to release the pressure on overfilled labor markets—a construction of the operation of land reform which rendered it a particularly wide-ranging solution. Combined with labor-intensive spade husbandry, a controlled flow of workers to the land would raise wages for those left behind and create new markets of home colonists for manufactured goods.[149] Examination of the safety-valve process as described by land reformers shows them to have been surprisingly scientific, imbued with the realization that while machinery could not be eliminated, the market for labor might be manipulated.[150]

The use which land reformers made of the cultural inheritance available to them reflects their assumptions about the working-class mindset. The factory was the most powerful image for land reformers, conjuring up as it did a whole undesirable way of life. The factory connoted a working class trapped in the cities, choking on smoke, exposed to vice and crime, and at the mercy of factory owners. Still, while factory owners were cast as the human enemy, the land reformers only rarely referred to the capitalist or capitalism. Rather, land reformers on both sides of the Atlantic created their own enemy class, the "land monopolists," including anyone who speculated in, and thereby foreclosed workers from a brighter future on, the land.

Land reformers used the language of the Old Testament, looking with millennial fervor for a transformation as complete as that of the Levitical jubilee. Use of such language built on enthusiasm for recent evangelical movements in Britain and in the American Northeast, and on the popularity of the movement to regulate factory work hours.[151] Even as they appealed to their constituents with religious language and fervor-filled podium thumping, land-reform leaders, many of them freethinkers, devised Enlightenment notions of the natural rights of man, including the right to a living from the land.

Anticipating the wishes of working-class audiences for more space and better physical environments, the land reformers crafted elaborate plans for the distribution of space, promoting tight settlement of the frontier in America and small-farm suburbia in the Chartist Land colonies. Planned public spaces, including schools, trading marts, and spaces for political use, would have allowed working people forums for discussion and interaction from which they were otherwise foreclosed. Finally, detecting the concerns of their audiences for the future of their children and the conservation of their family structures, they drew strong conceptual links between the farm lifestyle and "normal" gender roles. Women were encouraged to participate in these movements to the extent to which their individual participation did not dilute the strength of this collective message.

Although the messages of both sets of land reformers, the British and the American, were similar, multifaceted, and rooted in working people's real experiences and fears, these messages were heard through the wall of reformist background noise that characterized the 1840's. In addition to the land reformers, whose actions, as well as their words, demonstrated a concern for working people's welfare, a variety of other reformers, some of whom had a more middle-class orientation, competed for popular attention and support. One of the major challenges that land-reform leaders faced in the search for their constituencies was that of distinguishing their prescriptions, in both content and relative urgency, from those of the Anti-Corn Law League, the Abolitionists, the Owenites, and other reform movements. Both British and American land-reform leaders were able to contrast their prescriptions against those of other contemporary movements to their own advantage; the interplay of these reform movements is the subject of the next chapter.

4

The Competition for Reforming
Attentions in the 1840's

I need not say how deeply I feel that every person needs to be the admitted owner of a parcel of land. This every person should be, without having to pay for it. But if a free ownership be withheld, still let there by an ownership whenever it can be bought, if for no other reason than that the more who are the admitted owners of land, the sooner will that ownership be acknowledged to be a natural, universal and inalienable right.

—Abolitionist Gerrit Smith[1]

As the previous chapter showed, the concepts developed in concert by British and American land-reform leaders constituted an ideology—"the system of beliefs, values, fears, prejudices, reflexes and commitments" of a social group.[2] Land reform was not just an instrumental reform to be achieved—it was an outgrowth of support for producerism and distrust of rampant industrialization. Land reformers' vision of how the world worked also hinged on a more equitable distribution of property, argued for the strong impact of environment on the formation of character, and claimed that the only correct role for industrial activity in a healthy state was a diminished role. But this worldview was not created in a vacuum. In both Britain and the United States, the 1840's marked a decade of moral reform enlivened by evangelicalism and the belief in progress.[3] This being the case, land reformers in Britain and America developed their ideas and arguments in a lively process, by differentiating themselves from other active reforming groups historically described as having had a more "middle-class" character—the abolitionist movement and the Anti–Corn Law League.

As this chapter will illustrate, American National Reformers occupied a variety of positions on slavery, but were forced to exaggerate the arguments against abolition in an attempt to prioritize the plight of the white workingman. Similarly, in Britain, land-reforming Chartists, struggling to be heard against the well-financed clamor of Free Trade, exaggerated their opposition to Free Trade and adopted a land plan which Free Traders would claim was protectionist and backward-looking (but would later adopt—with revisions—for themselves). In both cases, as land reformers attempted to present land reform as a holistic solution to all social problems, and to differentiate themselves from other reforming efforts, their prescriptions took on a more worker-centered, "producerist" character. Although the land-reforming ideology in Britain and America was in part a reaction to the vitality of "middle-class" reform movements, which tended to ignore (or to give only lip service to) the social plight of the worker, leaders in neither country took land reform to its farthest possible conclusion—elimination of private property. While benefiting from the rhetorical support of the Fourierite Associationists in America and the Owenite remainder in Britain, land-reform leaders continued to emphasize the importance of private property and the necessity to accomplish their goals in a lawful fashion. On the British side, this led to attacks on the Chartist Land Company by "Chartist schoolmaster" Bronterre O'Brien, an intellectual heir of Spence and proponent of nationalization. There was no comparably important figure in American radicalism, but National Reformers carefully distanced themselves from the claims of social revolution occasionally leveled by the press. By thus skirting the dangers of "agrarianism" while claiming that the right to life was nothing without the right to property ownership, the land reformers constructed an ideological middle ground, which on the basis of its flexibility and inclusiveness would have wide popular appeal.

SLAVERY, ABOLITION, AND LAND REFORM

In the 1840's, antislavery sentiment had a useful rhetorical function for British proponents of the equal rights of labor. By parading their charges before the middle classes as victims of "wage slavery," leaders of British working-class movements could claim the moral high ground. Which was more important, they had long asked, the plight of black workingmen in faraway colonies, or the plight of fellow supposedly freeborn Britons? The abolition of black slavery from the British colonies in 1833 made the argument against wage slavery even more potent. As labor's tribunes never tired of pointing out, the Emancipation Act had freed the poor black workingman, so where was the justice in his white brother's continued subjection to the factory system, driven to his work as he was by the lash of poverty rather than by free choice?[4] Even Feargus O'Connor invoked the shadow of slavery in support of opening up the land as a field for endeavor: "When one man employs another and makes profit of his labour, let others call it what they will, I call it slavery. That is, provided the man employed is compelled to work for another, because he has not the means of working for himself."[5]

In America, in contrast, the issue of slavery involved more than rhetoric in the 1840's. Land reformers faced, in the person of the abolitionist movement, a well-organized and vocal group of middle-class and working-class activists who—in the land reformers' view—denied the importance of wage workers' oppression, and refused to recognize that freeing the slave would bring grave consequences for the white workingman. Forecasting wholesale economic doom if their suggestions were not attended to, American land reformers demanded that the situation of whites be ameliorated even before blacks were granted personal liberty. As Noel Ignatiev has pointed out, white workers were steered in this direction by the Democratic Party, which sought to consolidate its political power by making whiteness the "big umbrella" under which all citizens, including the poor and the Irish, might unite.[6]

Understanding the importance of morality in American reform, American working-class land reformers confronted the abolitionists by elevating the land question to the status of a moral dilemma. If land were a gift from God, they demanded, who in good conscience could sell it? Rebelling against the commercialization of every aspect of human life, land reformers referred to land sales as "traffic," conjuring up visions of traffic in slaves which the abolitionists so opposed. As Thomas Spence had once commented, "I contend that many things are too sacred and of too great importance to the Happiness and Dignity of the Human Race to be trafficked in, and in order to put a stop to all illicit trade I begin with prohibiting all Commerce in Land, for that is the root of all the other branches of injurious trade."[7]

While the abolitionists paid little attention to the land reformers, the land reformers attempted to capitalize on the burgeoning success of the abolitionists by laying claim to the vocabulary of that movement. They broadened the definition of "slavery" to encompass landlessness or any relation in which a man was forced to work without choice of employer.[8] Frederick Robinson, a state senator in Massachusetts and author of an 1851 report favoring exemption of family homesteads from seizure for debt, made the link between slavery and land monopoly clear when he claimed that "slavery is the end to which excessive accumulations always tend."[9] Horace Greeley, editor of the *New York Tribune*, defined slavery as that economic and social inequality which trapped men into feeling inferior to other men:

Wherever certain human beings, devote their time and thoughts mainly to obeying and serving other human beings, and this not because they choose to do so, but because they *must*, there (I think) is slavery. . . . Wherever the ownership of the soil is so engrossed by a small part of the community that the far larger number are compelled to pay whatever the few may see fit to exact for the privilege of occupying and cultivating the earth, there is something very like slavery.[10]

In Horace Greeley's formulation, wage work under pressure was slavery because it denied equal rights.

With its philanthropic societies, petitioning activities, and newspapers, the abolition industry became an "other" against which National Reformers could insurgently define their own movement.[11] For the American land reformers, abolitionism served the same purpose that the Anti–Corn Law agitation would serve in the British case. Both abolitionism and Corn Law reform had fairly revolutionary implications for traditional hierarchies and values, helping to pave the way for a reconsideration of social certainties. Yet while some workingmen participated in antislavery activities and signed abolition petitions, both Abolitionism and Corn Law repeal were middle-class-driven agitations.[12] Both Abolitionism and Corn Law repeal had such coherent ideological arguments that working-class land reformers tried to strengthen their positions by playing off these arguments, appropriating the language and the pathos but twisting them to serve their particular ends.[13]

While the National Reformers constantly attempted to broaden the definition of slavery and thereby prioritize land reform, individual land reformers' views of black slavery occupied a continuum. Jonathan Halperin Earle has recently illustrated a strong strain of antislavery feeling among antimonopolistic Democratic leaders of the 1830's and 1840's—leaders who espoused the producerist rhetoric which appealed to working-class land reformers.[14] George Henry Evans was a public opponent of slavery.[15] Another National Reformer, Benjamin Timms, came to American land reform from a background as a British abolitionist.[16] On the other end of the scale, to the end of his life Thomas Devyr considered black slavery a red herring; land reform was the central question dividing North from South.[17] Hermann Kriege, the liaison between the English-speaking National Reformers and like-minded German workingmen, also opposed wasting time on abolition. As he wrote in a New York newspaper in 1846, "We could not improve the lot of our 'black brothers' by abolition under the conditions prevailing in modern society, but make infinitely worse the lot of our 'white brothers.' . . . we feel constrained, therefore, to oppose Abolition with all our might, despite all the importunities of sentimental philistines and despite all the poetical effusions of liberty-intoxicated ladies."[18]

If George Henry Evans's disapproval of slavery occupied one end of the spectrum, Philadelphia land reformer John Campbell's views occupied the other.[19] After leaving the organized land-reform movement because of its soft line on slavery, Campbell published *Negro-Mania*, a rambling compilation of scientific-racist musings.[20] Finding blacks inferior to whites in almost every way, Campbell thought that the black man and the white would never be equal and thus it was extremely dangerous to contemplate freeing the black at all. Slavery was the best status for the black man. But even while Campbell's racism was predicated on insistence that blacks were inferior, his statement of the problem of freeing the slaves resembled that of the land reformers most opposed to slavery: all felt the two labor markets, black and white, should be kept separate. Campbell was more explicit than most land reformers, specifying that the blacks should continue to labor under the hot Southern sun at tasks unfit for free white men. But even if antislavery land reformers did not phrase their concerns in quite that way, both they and the proslavery land reformers worried about the economic consequences of freeing the slaves. "Will any one dare to say that were the whole slave population thrown into the great white labor market at once that the results would not be most disastrous to our mechanics and working men?" Campbell asked; it was a question which vexed even the mild and accommodating Evans.[21]

Campbell's inferiority-based arguments did not characterize the majority of visible land-reform leaders. They were enlightened individuals who did not question that slavery was wrong; they simply argued that wage slavery was worse than chattel slavery.[22] At least in the latter variety the slaveholder felt some responsibility for his slaves. He owned them, after all, and to starve them or mistreat them was to decrease his own capital investment, while wage workers—especially women and child operatives who required little training—were plentiful. Thomas Spence would echo one of the more extreme apologists for the Southern regime when he suggested that "all our landless people had better live in slavery, under humane masters that would provide them with the necessities of life, than be turned out of their rights as outcasts upon the face of the earth whereon they must neither feed nor rest."[23] Caught in an eddy between Northern wage slavery and Southern chattel slavery, National Reformers looked to the West as the channel in which a new moral era could be inaugurated.[24]

The distinctions between wage and chattel slavery were too nice for most abolitionists, who, when they paid attention to them at all, classed National Reformers with the enemy.[25] They were able to sense that their quarrel over the meaning of slavery hinted at a more profound issue—a disagreement over the meaning of freedom.[26] In his work on Reconstruction, Eric Foner has distinguished between a white, liberal, middle-class version of "freedom," and a definition shared by the four million freed slaves. While white liberals defined freedom as political citizenship and ownership of one's own body, to freed blacks, these elements were necessary but not sufficient. The true test of freedom was economic, and was best embodied in ownership of one's own land, because of all possible economic relationships, only independent farming did not painfully recall the relationship of master and slave.[27] The "black" view of freedom was not limited to or original with the freedmen, but rather was a tenacious republican discourse advanced by National Reformers.

Twenty years before Reconstruction, when George Henry Evans and his brothers-in-arms had objected to abolition of "slavery" as defined in white-liberal terms, their allegation that it was too narrow a definition was motivated by the same belief that freedom had an economic component. "What is slavery but the deprivation of freedom? Names do not alter things. If a human being is *compelled*, it matters not by laws written in Statute Books, and enforced by the lash of a driver, or by the stern law of necessity, imprinted on the organization of a false society, to toil for another to whom he must resign a portion of the products of that toil, that human being remains a slave."[28] If the government denied black and white workingmen access to the land, chattel slavery might disappear, but wage slavery would be worse than ever, and a wage slave, because he was under the economic thrall of another, could be easily pressured politically. As the voices of abolitionism became more insistent, so the land reformers became more anxious and thus more strident—unable to understand, perhaps, why the abolitionists were ignoring the perfectly self-evident role of land monopoly in creating a master-slave mentality among whites.

Far from being ready to reject the opinions of possible allies outright, however, American land reformers engaged with the slavery question personally, taking great pains to illustrate the completeness of their own moral vision. The conversion of New York philanthropist and abolitionist Gerrit Smith to National Reform illustrates this process. George Henry Evans had begun the controversy by writing to convince Smith that wage slavery was a more pressing problem than Negro slavery. Smith, in turn, was disheartened by Evans's seeming equation of black slavery and white poverty. He disapproved of the term "wage slavery" and accused the workingmen of having no understanding of the essential brotherhood of man.[29] Smith thought Evans was callous because he did not dedicate his reform energies to freeing the black slaves.[30] Evans's reply on the question of the brotherhood of man showed a discomfort with race which was typical of his time:

I believe that all men have equal natural and political rights; and I harbor no prejudice against color; still, there is a prejudice against color, which it would take ages to remove; and for *their* sakes, and not from any prejudice of my own, did I *suggest*, that if the public lands were made free, a portion of them might be set apart for their voluntary settlement. Although I know thousands of whites who contend that the blacks have equal political rights, I have yet to be acquainted with one who would like to be placed on terms of *social* equality with them.[31]

Unless Evans was deliberately hedging here, his views on civil versus social equality matched those of all but a small number of abolitionists.

After exchanging a few more angry letters with Evans in the

Working Man's Advocate, Smith eventually came around to the position that freedom for the blacks had to mean something more than just the freedom to participate politically.[32] Without a suitable economic base, he reasoned, the freed blacks would lapse into economic dependence, and from there into political dependence. Smith's reasoning illustrates that an argument for economic competence could proceed from a "liberal" argument for political inclusion.

The National Reformers jumped at the chance to use Smith's conversion as a propaganda weapon. A letter Smith wrote to J. K. Ingalls, editor of the National Reform *Landmark,* was reprinted as a broadside. Smith explained that while he could vote for no man for president who was not an opponent of slavery, neither could he vote for any man who did not oppose land monopoly. "Abolitionist though I am, I regard Land-Monopoly . . . as a far more abundant source of suffering and debasement, than is Slavery. . . . while to abolish chattel-slavery is not to abolish land-monopoly, to abolish land monopoly is to abolish chattel slavery."[33] Smith's writings illustrate the theoretical connection which was possible between the Free Soil and Free Land philosophies. As Smith went on to explain, breaking the West into family farms of 50 or 100 acres each would leave little room for the employment of slaves.[34]

Smith became a template for land reform as well as a National Reform propagandist. In 1846, he decided to donate some of his unused land in upstate New York—ranging from the cultivable to the nearly worthless—to deserving landless blacks. Smith had heretofore given tracts of land to public institutions, and a few small parcels to individuals, but now wanted to make large donations of land to the poor, in the shape of a total of 3,000 deeds, most of them conveying 40 to 60 acres of land each. After some soul-searching, Smith decided to confine his gifts to poor black men, on the grounds that, while all white men could vote, blacks were precluded from voting unless they owned $250 worth of property.[35] Landholding would secure the political and economic participation of a number of particular black men, and give encouragement to the enslaved remainder.[36]

Smith asked three black churchmen to search 12 counties and compile a list of free colored men, neither younger than 21, nor older than 60, who owned no other land, and were not drunkards. By September, Smith had translated the judgment of these three churchmen into action, drawn up 2,000 of the deeds, and prepaid the taxes on and delivered the lands, along with a dose of paternalism and moral reproach. According to Smith's biographer, the churchmen prepared an address to the new landholders, urging them to act in such a way as to make Smith proud: "to practice system, economy, self-reliance, mutual assistance, temperance, and [hail] the promise of a new career on the continent for their oppressed and discouraged race."[37]

Smith's first experiment was evidently successful enough in the short run for him to consider a second try. In 1849, Smith explained to George Henry Evans and others that he now intended to give tax-free land to 1,000 poor white men and women.[38] As with his former beneficiaries, these were to hail from New York state, and be between 21 and 60; virtuous, landless, poor, and sober.[39] Unfortunately, Smith had run out of good land, and some of what was left would serve for neither farming nor timber, nor might his title to the land hold up in all cases. Nonetheless, even at the risk of plunging a thousand poor people into a legal morass, Smith would express his dedication to the idea of free land for the landless. If there were not enough land to go around, he promised that those selected would receive $50, with which they could buy some government land. As Smith proclaimed, "One of my deepest convictions is that every person who can, should make himself the acknowledged owner of a piece of land. His doing so would hasten the day when the right to the soil shall be everywhere acknowledged to be as absolute, universal and equal as the right to the light and the air."[40] Although Smith's second attempt at land distribution ended in economic failure because of the nature of the land he was giving away, some of his poor white beneficiaries eventually embodied the morally uplifting properties of landownership by forming themselves into the New York Temperance Land Society.[41]

Although Smith took a high moral tone in his philanthropy, and insisted that land should only be a reward for respectability, he was in sympathy with the transatlantic working-class land-reform movement. He hoped that by increasing the proportion of small landholders in the overall social mix, a small-proprietor interest in government would be created. In turn, this interest could then provide for the rest of the landless.[42] Smith supported the National Reformers through public speeches, writings, and philanthropy, and for a time he was a fine example of the possibilities of middle-class leadership for the movement. Yet his contribution to National Reform was short-lived. By the early 1850's, he had drifted away from land reform and toward abolition again.[43] National Reformer Thomas Devyr pleaded with Smith to act on his own conviction and not be dragged aside by Garrisons and Phillipses; his repeated pleas fell on deaf ears.[44] Nonetheless, for a short time, land-reform arguments had romanced Gerrit Smith into giving away 200,000 acres of land; the arguments set forth in the *Working Man's Advocate* and *Young America* had appealed even to an ardent abolitionist.[45]

While individual National Reformers occupied a continuum of opinion on slavery, for land reformers as a collectivity the abolitionist movement served as an "other" against which they defined their own concerns. Land reformers also appropriated some of the passionate language and sentiment that abolitionists used to tug middle-class heartstrings, and applied it to white workers instead of blacks. The National Reformers' concern with the slavery issue helped define their movement as one which sought to make land monopoly a moral priority, redefine "liberty" in a positive sense to include economic welfare, and redefine "slavery" to include coercive work relationships where the coercive force was poverty instead of the law. As the brief National Reform career of Gerrit Smith illustrates, this process of redefinition was in part successful.

THE ANTI–CORN LAW LEAGUE AND O'CONNORITE POLITICAL ECONOMY

The Chartists were watching as the National Reformers battled the abolitionists, and they sent the Americans their good wishes and moral support.[46] They knew what it was like to try to create a mass movement even as another, more powerful, mass movement held center stage—in their case, the adversary was the Anti–Corn Law League. The adversarial relationship between working-class and middle-class reformism in Britain was a legacy of the O'Connorite wing of the Chartist movement. When the strategy of seeking political inclusion by petitioning, and then by insurrection, failed, Chartist leaders sought other fronts on which to challenge their Establishment. Some, like William Lovett and John Collins, embarked on the "New Move," seeking to broaden the front of agitation to include household suffrage, or elevation through education. Because these strategies were appealing to the middle class, O'Connor and his followers rejected them, categorizing them as a desertion in favor of middle-class values. (O'Connor, who might have been labeled middle-class, called himself "a member of the aristocracy who had been promoted to the democracy.")[47]

As the Chartist leadership splintered into various enthusiasms, the *Northern Star* began reflect a general dropping off of mass interest in the Chartist movement. Reacting to the deadly combination of mass inertia and a challenge to his popularity in the form of the New Move, O'Connor began to bring forth some theoretical notions about the value of the land for the laborer.[48] O'Connor's source of strength had always been the industrial North, yet it was here that the Manchester-based Anti–Corn Law League, already incredibly well organized, had begun to display its own alternative culture—a culture based on industrialism and the Anti–Corn Law League.[49]

The Anti–Corn Law League, or "Free Traders," were a group of lobbyists for the rising English industrial class. Their goal was to strip English agriculturalists of the protection which had long been granted them by the Corn Laws. These were sliding restrictions on imported grain which Free Traders claimed kept the price of bread artificially high. The Free Traders were an extremely visible organization, with ready money to stage elaborate public-relations events.[50] On the grassroots level, they challenged the Chartists both by being everywhere and by claiming that Corn Law repeal would bring cheap bread to the worker, providing a kind of immediate amelioration that the Chartists could not promise.[51]

When the Anti–Corn Law League emerged as a powerful rival for the attentions of Northern working people, Chartists fought back, especially in Lancashire, where the League's petition-tables were set up on almost every street corner.[52] They penetrated meetings, posed irreverent questions to the industrialists who took the platform, and introduced their own resolutions in favor of the Charter.[53] This pattern had begun as a Chartist strategy to capture major venues, like town halls, for their own meetings. To hold a public meeting, local householders had to petition the town police constables to convene a public meeting; Chartists were sometimes among the petitioners. When, given the notoriety of the Chartists, their requests were sometimes denied, they took their revenge by taking over other public meetings and thereby demonstrating their power.[54] Gratifyingly for the Chartists, such coups were invariably reported in the newspaper; Free Trade newspapers had to report Free Trade meetings, and conservative papers, siding with the agricultural interests, enjoyed reporting such Chartist takeovers to annoy local Free Traders. Coups also made economic sense, since the League, and not the Chartists, paid for these halls, in which the Chartists could continue passing their own resolutions after Free Traders had given up and gone home.

When Chartists in the field took over these meetings they expounded their own political economy in rivalry to that of the Free Traders. Chartist views on the Corn Laws as expressed in these meetings spanned a continuum of antagonism. A Chartist speaker might opine that, while Corn Law repeal was a good thing, it was but a trifle compared to the great changes the Charter might achieve. Or he might deny that the miseries of the working classes had anything to do with cheap bread as the Free Traders claimed; rather, the profusion of machinery pressed workers into destructively underbidding each other. Chartist orators buttressed their probably rehearsed interruptions with "authoritative" facts and figures, showing that, as machinery increased, the output of workers increased and their wages decreased. Moving along on the continuum, it was relatively rare but not unprecedented for a Chartist orator in mixed company (that is, workmen and employers) to malign the very motives of industrialists in opposing the Corn Laws.[55] If the Corn Laws were repealed, the orator would argue, and the price of food did drop, industrialists would cut the wages of working people in response, all in the pursuit of higher profits.[56] In other words, in the strongest formulation, Corn Law repeal was an industrialist conspiracy.

John Campbell, the English emigrant who became both an American land reformer and a virulent racist, had explored the question of land for the working classes and its relation to the Anti–Corn Law League before leaving England, while still a Chartist. He alleged that the League was an industrially motivated class movement meant to cheapen labor.[57] Viewing the effects of industrialization in Salford, Campbell wrote that he wanted to see the plowshare pass through Manchester and Birmingham, through London, Liverpool, Newcastle, Glasgow, Edinburgh, and all other great towns, "and to see the people return to where nature and Nature's God intended they should be placed, viz., on the land; every man cultivating his own farm, living free, contented and happy."[58]

Why didn't the Chartists favor Corn Law repeal and instant gratification on the cheap-bread issue? The Chartists wanted to show that they differed from the Free Traders on a central question of political economy—the Chartists believed freedom included some basic level of economic comfort.[59] If a workers' political economy was predicated on notions of entitlement, then some authority (be it government or the private sector; what agency was to do the intervening was a negotiable question) had to be prescriptive and interventionist rather than laissez-faire as the Free Traders wanted. In England—as they had in America—land reformers hit upon a definition of liberty that included not just freedom from constraint but also the freedom to live reasonably well.[60]

Of course, Anti–Corn Law Leaguers ignored this nuance and charged that O'Connor was a Tory paternalist in fustian clothing, trying to create an outdated world of small farms. He countered by emphasizing the symbiotic relationship between the Land and the Charter. The land was only valuable to the extent that it would strengthen the political power of working people; political power was worthless without land-based social power to back it up. "I would not give a fig for the Charter if we were not prepared with a solid social system to take the place of the artificial one we mean to destroy. . . . The Charter and the Land!"[61] The Charter was already familiar, having been repeatedly described to audiences as a stepping-stone to the resolution of inequity. Landed property, besides guaranteeing economic independence, was the key to political power, which protected this economic independence. "So long as one man's property constitutes another man's title to vote, so long will the landowners take care to leave their land as to preserve a monopoly of votes, which constitutes a monopoly of legislation."[62]

Even in Chartist fiction, the political economy of land reform—forging the connection between political power and the economic wherewithal to protect it—was manifest. As the fictional allottee "Will" told his wife, in a story in the *Labourer*, the land was "Charter all the time, for only for Charter the land would never come up, and I'de never know aught about it; Charter is the means and land is the end; as old general says, 'Charter is spit, and Land is

leg of mutton.'"[63] Clearly, the Anti–Corn Law League, with its Free
Trade views, gave O'Connor a palpable political economy to criti-
cize. If Free Trade was black, home colonization and land for the laborers were, in O'Connor's way of looking at the world, white. But
there was more—when under attack, O'Connor could explain away
any waning of working-class interest for his own land scheme by
blaming it on the Anti–Corn Law League's organization and brain-
washing propaganda.[64]

Nor was the relationship between the Chartist and the Free
Traders unidirectional. While Free Trader and League celebrity
Richard Cobden professed to despise O'Connor and his demagoguery, the Chartist land scheme did influence the activities of his Free
Traders. In 1846, the Anti–Corn Law League achieved its presumed
goal of Corn Law repeal. Keen to increase the electoral power of Free
Trade, Anti–Corn Law leaders moved into the organizational realm,
introducing their own Freehold Land Societies. With organizational
help to coordinate large land purchases, thrifty mechanics could
combine their pence to buy enough freehold land to qualify for a 40-
shilling freehold. These new voters would not only take more pride
and interest in their country's affairs—something O'Connor had
been repeating all along—they would also naturally express their
gratitude for enfranchisement by supporting Free Trade.[65] In an interesting inversion of the American National Reformers' "vote
yourself a farm," subscribers to the Freehold Land Societies might
farm themselves a vote—although the allotments were not really
meant to be used for agricultural subsistence.[66] Despite this departure from the Chartist Land Plan on the question of a farming lifestyle, the Freehold Land Society's promoters did follow the Chartists by exploiting the perceived environmental benefits of country
living, using some of the same language as the Chartists.[67] Chartists
in turn decried the Freehold Land scheme as an attempt to steal
O'Connor's thunder.[68]

The Chartist Land Company originally benefited from its oppositional relationship to the Anti–Corn Law League, which forced local leaders countering League power to formulate their own oppositional theories of economics. Feargus O'Connor was then able to
use these theories to propose his own organization of society based
on the "natural" market for labor on the land. At the same time, by
showing political power to be inextricable from landholding,

O'Connor made his land scheme appear to proceed naturally from the previous agitation for the Charter, rather than as a defensive reaction to the popularity of the League. By the end of the 1840's, however, the Chartist relationship with the former Leaguers had become much less beneficial. The National Land Company's uniqueness was undermined by the League's willingness to adopt its methods, not only destroying the land company but also attracting less combative and more prosperous working people into the ranks of the Freeholders it had made. The Free Traders' land scheme, similar schemes, benefit building societies, and even a "Home Colonization Company" reaped the enthusiasm for space and the countryside which O'Connor had so assiduously cultivated.[69]

ASSOCIATION AND COOPERATION:
LAND-REFORM ALTERNATIVES

Both the Chartists and the National Reformers operated alongside and defined themselves against an "other"—middle-class reforming organizations whose stands on certain issues spurred the land reformers to a measure of extremism. Just as important as these adversarial relationships, however, were the relationships of the transatlantic land reformers with groups which had similar goals— namely, the proponents of Association and community living.[70] The trajectories of the groups were not completely similar. O'Connor and both Evanses, William and George Henry, preached the importance of independence for the worker. In contrast, Cooperation and Association, even in their most empowering forms, forced a reliance on an organic community. Nonetheless, Associationists and communitists participated to varying extents in the land-reform movements—especially in America, where Associationists' pessimistic view of the state of society and of the impact of the environment on the formation of human character prepared the ground for working-class land reform. As one Associationist wrote, "everywhere in competitive society the tendency of existing institutions is to sink all classes of worker to an equilibrium. We can no more keep off the pauperism and corruption of English factory labor from our land, than we can keep off the pestilence, which travels in the air."[71] George Henry Evans could not have put it better.

Although they thought land reform insufficient to achieve full social change, American Associationists, or followers of Charles Fourier, generally viewed it as a first step toward building communities. As their official organ, the *Harbinger*, noted, "this movement [National Reform] is far deeper than any that has ever before been undertaken by the Working Classes, and it is a gratifying sign of the increase of intelligence among them with regard to the importance of true and organic Reform."[72] Fourierite and National Reform thinking did, however, diverge on two points: private property and practicality. Rather than approve a general right to private property in land, Fourier's followers acknowledged the right of each person to a portion of the usufruct of the earth.[73] And although American Fourierites were the more practical subset of Fourier's followers, National Reformers generally shunned all theory and derided grand plans in favor of a self-professed practicality—a practicality which they did not think the Associationists shared.[74]

The relationship between National Reformers and Associationists was strained by the fact that editors of the Associationist *Harbinger* portrayed the National Reformers as naive, if well-meaning. They considered that redistribution of the public lands, although a necessary change, was not a sufficient one. "They should not desire that those who are laboring for a Social Reform should throw down their arms, abandon their work, and run to their camp. They must know that when the public lands are made free, and the people settle upon them, Industrial Association, upon some plan, must be established. Isolation, free competition, anarchical commerce, which absorbs half the profits of the producing classes, . . . cannot be suffered to exist."[75] By 1847, however, Associationists acknowledged in their own newspaper that the National Reform movement was not only more popular than Association, it was also more realistic about the possibilities of enlisting capitalists in the cause of reform.[76]

Although the Fourierites considered the National Reformers ideologically unsophisticated, many of them turned to National Reform because their original pet ideology had several fatal flaws. Association was elitist—Fourier's own work spoke of preserving class relations intact in Associationist communities so that the rich would not have to socialize with the coarse.[77] Associationism was authoritarian, specifying human interactions and behaviors and even modes of clothing for its adherents. It was also cynical; Fourier's plan for getting people to enjoy work more and thereby work harder was based on exploiting some of the baser human instincts. Associationists were not required to regenerate themselves morally—the environment would do that for them. Some utopians also had suspect practices when it came to sex and marriage.[78]

Despite these differences in tone, the Associationist movement and the National Reform movement shared personnel.[79] Those doing double duty included Parke Godwin, L. A. Hine, Horace Greeley, W. H. Channing, and Charles Sears, but most notably speakers Lewis Ryckman, H. H. van Amringe, and Albert Brisbane.[80] Ryckman, a shoemaker, had lived at the Brook Farm collective before beginning a career as a National Reform lecturer.[81] As early as May 1845, he presided over a meeting of the New England Working Men's Association, and helped guide the gathering toward approval of the plan, set forth by the National Reformers, to hold annual Industrial Congresses. He continued to lecture for National Reform throughout the 1840's.[82] Harry Hamlin van Amringe, a Pittsburgh lawyer and author of a book attempting to give Association a Christian theoretical basis, wrote letters to the Associationist *Harbinger*.[83] He was also the National Reformers' main emissary to the frontier, and a popular speaker at many National Reform and Association meetings.[84] While van Amringe was willing to admit that machinery had done much good, by making the accoutrements of a comfortable life available to all, his anti-technological rhetoric was strong; machinery, he claimed, "expels man's service for woman's service—it reduces the child to the rank of a mere cog or attendant upon a wheel, and drags, and mangles, and grinds the poor, defenseless thing, until you cannot recognize it as the form of a human being." According to van Amringe, Association and National Reform were two solutions to the perversion of society caused by technological change.[85]

Like Lewis Ryckman and H. H. van Amringe, Albert Brisbane came to land reform through Fourierite Associationism.[86] Brisbane was born into a wealthy family in the Holland Purchase of western New York. (He would inherit a fortune of half a million dollars upon his father's death in 1851.) Taking advantage of his situation, he matriculated at the Sorbonne and then the University of Berlin (where he studied with Hegel), and communed with a host of famous intellectuals, among them Fourier.[87] Brisbane assimilated Fourier's doctrine of Association into a mental picture already sympathetic to the labor movement; he shared the workingman's distaste for the abolitionist cavalierness about wage slavery, asking, "Why should not the strong philanthropic feeling, which exists for a few negroes of the South, be extended to the white laboring populations of civilized countries, which are so much more numerous?"[88] Brisbane blamed the condition of slavery, wherever it occurred, on indigence; and indigence, in turn, on competition for jobs. Brisbane was particularly conversant with the ideas of Fourier, having in 1843 published a tract translating and publicizing them.

Associationists like Brisbane adopted Fourier's contention that alienation was inherent in the organization of society—but blamed this alienation on isolation rather than work.[89] According to Fourier, alienation could be overcome if man's work activities were arranged according to his natural tastes and proclivities. All workers, in an Associative community, would work alongside others whose characters most harmonized with their own, and in fields of labor which appealed to them. The hours of labor would be short and pleasant, with "groups" and "series'" of workers—each representing a minute subfield of production—spurred on to higher levels of industry by friendly competition and by the desire to show off in front of attractive members of the opposite sex.[90] It is easy to understand why such a retheorization of work would have appealed to people who worked 12-hour days. Furthermore, Fourierite Associationism as Brisbane explained it clung to an individual right of property. Religion and marriage were also to be preserved, making Fourierism more palatable to contemporaries than was Owenism.[91]

Like National Reformers, Fourierites thought the economic system led to mass degradation; they therefore focused primarily on economic relations.[92] They differed from National Reformers, however, in their belief that large farms enjoyed economies of scale and were more ecologically harmonious than smallholdings. Fourierites thought it unnatural to forgo increasing production simply to preserve individual decision making. Brisbane ridiculed the sight of the land when "cut up into little farms, and subjected to the caprice of three hundred families. Here one family makes a meadow of a sloping piece of land, which Nature destined to the vine; there another sows wheat where grass should grow; a third, to avoid buying grain, clears a declivity which the rains will strip of its soil the following year."[93] Fourierites derided individualism, but their appreciation for the alienation workers were beginning to feel at their jobs made them, in general, good allies to have.

Brisbane in particular was popular in National Reform circles because he could bring sophisticated sociological analysis to bear on contemporary problems but did not couch everything in Fourierite jargon. Society had been corrupted by the unnatural separation of capital and labor by class legislation, he argued. Working people had to associate and to acquire possession of the land and the machinery. Corrupt politics had to be replaced with a truthful and wise system of legislation, which could be achieved through the ballot box and the presses. When it was necessary, Brisbane even denied he was a Fourierite: "He repudiated the name, he was an advocate of universal unity, and came to the Convention as a man, earnestly desirous of advancing the cause of humanity, and not as the representative and exponent of any particular doctrine or principle."[94]

Such careful politicking made Brisbane popular enough to be chosen National Reform candidate to the New England Industrial Convention at Lowell.[95] He also had the honor of being the subject of an entire editorial in *Young America*, "for his ardent and devoted exertions recently in the Free Soil cause. He handles the wrongs of Labor in exactly the right spirit, goes to the very root of the matter, and points clearly to the true remedy."[96] Brisbane's charisma was legendary. On one occasion at a National Reform meeting, an argument broke out between physical-force proponent William West and moral reformer Lewis Ryckman. The bickering ceased when Brisbane entered the hall and strode up to the podium, silencing all with his presence.[97]

As the examples of Brisbane, Ryckman, and van Amringe show, the National Reformers benefited from their connection with Fourierite communitarianism. Both groups were among the healthiest of a number of communal efforts dotting the antebellum American landscape. While National Reformers were willing to open their movement to middle-class leaders like Brisbane or Gerrit Smith who were willing to advance the land-reform cause, they did so on their own terms. Their coalition politics spoke a common language of producerism so clearly that even the Chartists, observing the actions of the communitists from overseas, were able to perceive the interconnections, while understanding the nuances, between the Associationists and the National Reformers.[98]

While American Fourierism, both in the person of Brisbane and other leaders and at the level of mass participation, had a great positive impact on National Reform, English socialism played less of a role in the cultivation of the Chartist Land Company. Like American Fourierism, English Owenite socialism was in decline by the mid- to late 1840's, its experimental communities proving to be ungovernable as well as financially unmanageable.[99] Nonetheless, unconvinced that communal-living schemes were bound to fail, socialist thinkers continued to hatch new ones. A "Trades' Association for the Employment of Surplus Labour in Agriculture and Manufactures" would have bought and divided large estates into small farms and erected worker-owned dwellings and workshops using subscribed capital and reinvesting any earnings. Trades could then lease or purchase from the Association such lands and buildings as they needed to employ their surplus members. *Potter's Examiner* editor William Evans briefly took out 100 shares in the new organization on behalf of his union.[100] Another scheme, John Minter Morgan's Christian Commonwealth, attempted to bolster communitarianism with organized religion.[101] The Leeds Redemption Society, founded in 1845, enjoyed some limited success at the end of the decade, drawing energy from the attention to the land which the Chartist Land Company had encouraged.[102]

Because these post-Owenite movements had a limited reach and appeal, there was little opportunity for the same kind of public relationship to develop that developed between the American National Reformers and Fourierite Associationists.[103] The English communitists who did react publicly to the land plan tended not to condemn it, but rather to see it as part of a larger movement toward moral regeneration through the regeneration of the environment.[104] The impact that Owenism had on the land company was indirect and intellectual; as Gregory Claeys notes, the land company absorbed some of the ideas and rhetorical tropes of the Owenites without crediting them to their source. For example, John Francis Bray, a social reformer whose main nostrum was joint-stock companies for ownership of industry, suggested that working people club their funds together to buy land as early as the 1830's.[105] The Owenite socialists shared several other fundamental tenets with O'Connor: they believed Britain might still be agriculturally self-supporting; they doubted Free Trade was a panacea; they shared a preference for the agricultural life, and were vague about the hardships farming might entail.[106] The land plan would have been a logical place for former socialists to direct their energies, since the land plan allowed them to be (landholding) citizens without having to be socialist saints.[107] Yet O'Connor rebuffed their aid because of a fundamental disagreement over private property, saying, "I tell you that my plan has no more to do with Socialism than it has to do with the comet."[108]

After Owenism, Bronterre O'Brien's land-nationalization movement was another option for Chartist interest in land reform. O'Brien set forth his own scheme for government purchase of all land and then redistribution of the land by rental. This helped to advertise the potential importance of the land to workers' well-being, and isolated the O'Connorite Chartists as a separate, more conservative land-reforming phenomenon. O'Brien portrayed land nationalization as the only politically correct land-reform option. Thus, even though land nationalization never got anywhere, it became easier for Chartist leaders in hindsight to belittle O'Connor's plan as a conservative and backward-looking sellout scheme, because there seemed to have been a more progressive road not taken. O'Brien was also poised to capture some of the international movement for land reform, as his own newspaper often considered the progress of the American National Reform movement and attempted to engage the movement's leaders in transatlantic debate.

O'Brien could also claim to have given the land matter deeper thought than had O'Connor. A lawyer and an editor, the intellectual of the Chartist movement, James Bronterre O'Brien indicated an interest in the disposition of the land early in his career. By the 1840's even the National Reformers considered him an authority on the land question.[109] Like the Enlightenment writers, O'Brien distinguished between a natural right of property, which stemmed from creating the property, and a conventional right, which existed only to protect the natural right.[110] Given O'Brien's vision of the natural right to the use of the soil, he was naturally interested in securing its redistribution, and for philosophical and personal reasons opposed O'Connor and the land plan. O'Brien feared that under O'Connor's supervision, satisfaction among the now-landed poor would lead to stability for the rich: "The government is cunningly making the working classes a party to the maintenance of the very system which has crushed them to the earth. ... Every man who joins in these Land Societies is practically enlisting himself on the side of the Government against his own order."[111]

O'Brien's plan to redistribute land without creating peasant proprietors (who would be natural Tories) thus had fine theoretical credentials, but was impractical.[112] Because state-owned rental plots would be distributed by bidding, just as in the private market, O'Brien could not promise that each workingman could secure a plot of land. O'Connor was willing to make that (empty) promise. O'Brien's plan also called for the growth of government power at a time when working people felt ambivalent about government. He acknowledged this as a weakness: "This still savors a little of the present system of the alienation of rights," he wrote. "It makes a kind of landlordy and tenure, and supposes a government separate from the people, consisting of a separate interest and a class of non-producers."[113] O'Brien's plan further ignored working people's reverence for private ownership.

The appeal of O'Brien's land scheme was also limited by his poverty and lack of access to any organizational infrastructure—and this helps to explain the personal animosity between O'Brien and O'Connor. O'Brien blamed O'Connor for depriving him of influence and funds to publicize his views or even feed his family. After O'Brien and O'Connor parted company on bad terms, O'Brien was left to canvass his friends for jobs. "My hope is that either through [Manchester bookseller Abel] Heywood or anybody else you may know, you may be able to get me placed in the position to use my faculties fully for the next twelve months," O'Brien begged a friend, "a thing I have been debarred from for now seven or eight years, mainly through O'Connor."[114] Furthermore, although it may have been out of envy of O'Connor's popularity, O'Brien expressed ambivalence about courting the public at all.[115]

Shut out of the *Northern Star* and the main Chartist organization through his estrangement from O'Connor, O'Brien attempted to promote his ideas about the land through speaking engagements. Between 1845 and 1847, he visited Birmingham, Sheffield, Rochdale, and Glasgow, promoting his own land scheme and taking shots at O'Connor's.[116] Probably more effective was his newspaper, the *National Reformer*, inaugurated in 1846.[117] The *National Reformer* became O'Brien's entree into an international dialogue on land reform which drew land nationalization and American National Reform into a common discussion. In his first issue, he mentioned the existence of a parallel land-reform movement in America with its own newspapers, including *Young America*.[118] O'Brien mentioned the National Reformers for the purposes of international solidarity. In O'Brien's view, National Reform was "the Great Democratic Movement in America for the Freedom of the Public Lands, and other Social Reforms in Favour of the Working Classes." He introduced to his audience the names and various talents of American land reformers—not only Devyr and Evans, but also Brisbane and Channing, John Commerford, Mike Walsh, Hermann Kriege, and Michael Thomas O'Connor.[119] He shared with his British audiences not only the mechanism of the agrarian pledge, but also many of the other measures, including debt reform and judicial restructuring, for which American proponents of "equal rights" contended.

O'Brien thought the Americans might be fine collaborators if they would just rethink the individualism inherent in their plan, and consider state ownership.[120] Convinced as he was that the American movement might be a worthy one with a little direction, O'Brien addressed a series of open letters on policy in his *National Reformer* to George Henry Evans.[121] Over time, as Evans failed to tailor his land scheme to O'Brien's specifications, O'Brien's opposition to National Reform sharpened. He decried the National Reformers' views on private property, and wondered in print how the system of land redistribution they proposed would "operate upon the next generation or two, or upon the millions of immigrants who may hereafter desire to settle there."[122]

As the self-appointed expert on working-class land reform, O'Brien lavished criticism on the Chartist Land Company as well. His *National Reformer* printed letters from readers casting doubt on the success of the Chartists' plan.[123] O'Brien also used his editorial space to deride O'Connor as a political cynic, using the Land Scheme "to enable himself and his co-directors to live like gentlemen, and half-gentlemen, at the public expense, and to swell their importance by patronizing printers, card makers, stationers, secretaries, reporters, etc. At the lowest calculation, Feargus sells 4000 copies extra of the *Northern Star* solely through the Land Scheme."[124] He poked fun at O'Connor's rhetoric and tried to sow the seed of doubt by outlining his main objections to O'Connor's plan.[125]

Although O'Connor paid little attention to the land schemes of Bronterre O'Brien while promoting his own land scheme, Bronterre O'Brien's newspaper and speaking tours helped define the difference between two very distinct programs: nationalization and private ownership. The Chartist Land Company certainly emerged from this process looking like a scheme more sympathetic to private property, and probably more feasible, than O'Brien's nationalization.[126] The one benefit that O'Brien brought to the Chartist Land Company was his focus on the land as a credible outlet for workers' energies. Together, O'Connor's and O'Brien's emphases on the importance of working-class landownership helped to shift Chartism from a political movement with social and economic goals to a social and economic movement with political consequences.

This chapter has discussed the reforming milieu in which the proponents of land reform operated. Propositions for social amelioration and moral regeneration were on every hand in the 1840's, putting the land reformers right in tune with the critics of their age. Leaders of the British and American land-reform movements used other movements for contrast, to distinguish themselves from the general discourse of reform. Middle-class-driven reform movements, like the abolitionists and the Anti–Corn Law League, impelled working-class leaders to form new arguments using an old vocabulary. National Reformers used abolitionist rhetoric as a springboard from which to argue that the degradation of all workers, black and white, was on the horizon. Chartists used Anti–Corn Law League meetings as schoolrooms, in which they practiced public speaking and sharpened their ideas about political economy.

More friendly interactions, with Associationist and socialist movements, helped swell the numbers of land reformers through membership crossover. While the Fourierites in America provided valuable leadership and a mass base for the National Reformers, however, English Owenites were much less visible in the Chartist Land Plan. Bronterre O'Brien helped to foment an international discussion of the value of land redistribution, and to bring the American National Reformers to the attention of his limited Chartist audience. Discussions among Associationists and National Reformers, socialists and Chartists, helped to distinguish working-class land reformers from those who questioned the propriety of individual private property. All these interactions mapped out a theoretical space in which American and British land reformers might develop their own ideologies of land reform.

As the last two chapters have shown, land-reform leaders appealed to what they thought people wanted to hear. If the fit between the concepts they had chosen and popular belief were strong enough, the land-reform movement would create disciples easily. But creating a message was only a small part of generating enough momentum to force change; to do that required organizational strategies. Newspapers had to be written, halls rented and regular meetings conducted, lecturers hired, pamphlets printed, petitions drafted, signatures sought, local chapters supported, funds collected, lotteries held. Ideas and people had to cross and recross large areas to maintain a critical mass of excitement, without which the land-reform movement would die. The next chapter will examine the organizational dynamos of leadership, lecturing, print culture, and international influence which drove land reform into the minds of thousands.

5

Making Working-Class Activism: Anglo-American Organizational Strategies

They were in the last stage of the agitation. The first stage was the creation of public opinion; the second was the organization of public opinion; the third was the direction of public opinion.
—Feargus O'Connor, in the *Northern Star*[1]

The Chartists of Great Britain, the Repealers of Ireland, the Republicans and Associationists of France, and the Communists of Germany—Noble pioneers of a 'good time coming' when National Reform for a Free Soil shall be triumphant throughout the world."[2] So George Henry Evans, stalwart of American National Reform, raised his glass and toasted his fellow workers in the cause of international land reform at a ball held in his honor. Although the newspaper which chronicled this toast does not record the response of his fellow revelers, his words probably met with cheers, the ring of glass upon glass, and the stomping of approving feet. Evans was not alone in viewing land reform as a transatlantic effort requiring the cooperation and coordination of workers in both Britain and the United States. Rather, as this chapter will show, internationalism was a common sentiment among land reformers, and had a strong impact on the creation and maintenance of common organizational strategies: newspapers, public meetings, and the cultivation of leadership.[3]

Once the ideology of land reform and its relationship to a particular solution were conceived, leaders faced the monumental task of disseminating their messages to the widest possible audience on a shoestring budget and in the face of press or governmental hostility. The obstacles that each group faced differed, and the previous forms of activism which working-class reformers had used set parameters within which organizers were accustomed to operate—eliminating the option of armed rebellion, for example. Still, despite substantial differences in state structures in Britain and America, land reformers used many of the same organizational tactics. Both the organizational structures and the tone of each movement were heavily influenced by their common construction as part of an international effort; international communication, by newspaper and personal interview, made this cross-fertilization possible.

In illustration of the richness of the land-reform organization which leaders on both sides of the Atlantic managed to construct, this chapter will explore the leadership, the press, and the culture of land reform.[4] In all three of the movements discussed here, the most prominent national leaders were set apart from the masses they strove to reach, through middle-class or employer status and histories of involvement as advocates of the working classes. Each considered himself able to determine the ills of society and construct a comprehensive plan for their amelioration. Thus, while some land reformers were more ready to compromise points of their plans than were others, leaders of working-class land-reform movements resembled the Owenite and Fourierite leaders with their dictatorial preferences for minutely planned communities.[5]

The second key facet of working-class organization was the printed word; in each case examined here, land-reform leaders were also proprietors of their own newspapers. These newspapers, the *Northern Star*, *Working Man's Advocate/Young America*, and the *Potter's Examiner*, all professed to advocate the cause of working people foremost, building broad bases by mixing substantial doses of land-reform ideology with examination of other issues: workplace grievances, ten hours, Chartism, or the constitutional crisis in Rhode Island. In addition to disseminating ideology, these newspapers reported on the activities of local branches and reprinted speeches at local meetings, creating at least an illusion of both community and momentum. Each newspaper had a substantial circulation—if not directly, then through the then current custom of copying articles into newspapers printed elsewhere. As the success of each newspaper encouraged leaders to explore other forms of printed expression, direct advertisement, pamphlets, books, and almanacs were all pressed into the service of land reform.

Despite the triumph of the printed word even among the working classes, the "organization of public opinion" to which Feargus

O'Connor referred would not have been possible without new cultural forms, encompassing meetings, recreational activities, and even the mapping out of specific spaces in which working-class land-reforming politics could take place.[6] In the United States, National Reformers conducted meetings outdoors to attract casual passersby, and then integrated interested workingmen into a network of ward meetings and weekly meetings at the Croton Hall. In Britain, Chartist celebrities crossed the country capitalizing on guaranteed audiences. They also made use of the new, wholly Chartist spaces—the allotments at Herringsgate, Lowbands, and Redmarley—which became tourist attractions and centers of leisure. The Potters' Joint-Stock Emigration Society fostered local interest with imaginatively named local branches led by local men, and occasional visits from William Evans or his American superintendent, Thomas Twigg. All three groups held land-reform gala events, enticing the wives and children of land reformers to join in the fun. Through the rituals of signing the agrarian pledge or the deed of the National Land Company; through handing over, and seeing recorded, a weekly share payment for a Chartist allotment or twenty acres' worth of Wisconsin; through shouting and stomping in approval at meetings, or joining in songs about the land set to rousing and familiar folk tunes, workingmen were transformed into land reformers.

Although the goals of British and American working people were sometimes different, the similarities among their organizational methods buttress the assertion that working Americans were not exceptionally quiescent compared with other groups of workers. In addition, similarities in modes of organization helped land reformers of both nationalities to sense that they were part of an international movement. Just as American and British land reform shared a common intellectual heritage and shaped the membership of their movements through juxtaposition with "middle-class" abolitionism and Free Trade, so they reinforced the idea of participation in a common cause by trading and reprinting newspaper articles, through emigration of activists, and through visits by some temporary emissaries. For a short moment in the 1840's, the movements transcended structural and economic differences and constructed a vision which professed to address working people transatlantically.

As Feargus O'Connor's brainchild, the Chartist Co-Operative Land Company owed its success in part to a guaranteed audience which had been attracted to Chartism by O'Connor's charisma; but it also owed its downfall in part to his paranoia, puffery, and refusal to admit he did not have entire grasp of the complexities involved in legalizing his company.[7] Beyond the relentless search for love and approval which drove him from childhood, O'Connor's personality was a mass of contradictions, exacerbated from the end of the 1840's until his death by what may have been syphilitic madness.[8] During his decline he would come under frequent attack for being an undemocratic megalomaniac; the land scheme, with its almost exclusive focus on himself, was necessary as a political move to neutralize the effect of his poor relations with other Chartist leaders.[9] One who knew him struggled to make sense of him: "O'Connor was the most impetuous and most patient of all the tribunes who ever led the English Chartists. In the *Northern Star* he let every rival speak. . . . Logic was not his strong point and he had colossal incoherence."[10]

How did such a man become the tribune of the working classes? Tall, broad, and considered good-looking, O'Connor was physically cut out to be a symbol of the strength of the toiling millions.[11] Thus, he offered up his own portrait as a premium for subscription to the *Northern Star*; it was also engraved on medals, to be purchased and worn around the neck by other Chartists.[12] One portrait, in his magazine the *Labourer*, depicts him against a backdrop of a richly appointed study, with a large hardwood chair and an apothecary's cabinet full of leather-bound books.[13] He wears a dark suit and shiny black boots, a white shirt, and a black stock around his neck, and a gold watch dangles down from the pocket of his vest. He is clean-shaven except for muttonchop whiskers, and his short hair curls tightly all around his head. His round, wide face, large forehead, large eyes, and heavy brows would be serious were it not for the mouth, set in an ambiguous, perhaps mirthful, expression. One hand stretches out to the side as if in a gesture of demonstration, and the other is tucked into his breast, Napoleon-style. The caption reads, "Feargus O'Connor, Esq. MP for Nottingham." O'Connor's portraits showed he was not of the class which he deputed himself to represent; the working classes could have a representative in Parliament and a soldier for their cause who was both respectable and imposing.

Lionized by his friends, denigrated by his many foes, O'Connor transcended his position as leader of one sector of the Chartists to become something of a demigod, a martyr to the people's cause, as his uncle had been before him.[14] His attempts to liken himself to Christ attracted rather than alienated a large sector of the working population. W. E. Adams characterized O'Connor as the "idol of the day," noting that "when he addressed in the rich brogue of his native country 'the blistered hands and unshorn chins of the working classes,' he appeared to touch a chord which vibrated from one end of the kingdom to the other."[15] His personal popularity instantly invested his land company with a certain cachet. Although O'Connor's decision to urge land on the English people has often been attributed to his ancestry, even more important was his belief in the merits of an organic society, in which the rich would offer the poor protection, and the poor would offer the rich respect.[16]

O'Connor's affinity for traditional social responsibility intersected with his messianic self-esteem; he expected devotion from his own reading public, the members of which he referred to as his "Chartist Children."[17] As he boasted, "my children—my family—my land family—now numbers nearly half a million—that is, a hundred thousand heads of families, to whom their wives and children are rendered more dear, since I have shown them the way out of the house of bondage to the Labour castle."[18] Despite the fact that O'Connor's planned social program for Chartism had its roots at least in part in his own vision of himself as the lord of the manor, he was far from being the only Chartist leader who saw a need for a social program to accompany the Chartist political program. Since the whole tenor of Chartism had moved toward seeking social benefits by 1848, with his land plan, O'Connor was both riding and creating a wave.

An untiring speaker and a consummate showman, O'Connor had a famously stentorian voice and a knack for humor.[19] As Richard Oastler had done during the factory agitation, Feargus O'Connor combined these speaking skills with the assumed mantle of kindly governor, transforming his audience into loving subjects. While O'Connor told audiences at the town hall in Cheltenham that they must do for themselves, he said he would take the credit for making their independence possible; "he should never be satisfied until he had located on the land and in a house of his own all who were willing to be located, and when he walked from villa to villa, and saw the fruits growing up around him, he should have the proud satisfaction of saying, 'This is my work.'"[20]

Feargus O'Connor was clearly the motive ideological and physical force behind the land plan, but he was not the only Chartist celebrity to be linked with the scheme. Ernest Jones, the highly presentable young barrister and successful writer who had joined the Chartist cause in 1845, coedited the *Labourer*, a land-reform magazine, with O'Connor, and accompanied him at major meetings.[21] Like O'Connor, Jones was descended from people of quality. Raised abroad, he was able to speak German from babyhood. A prodigy, he attended a selective school, and had his first poems published when still a child. When he grew to young adulthood, his life was a happy whirl of social engagements—paying and receiving calls, eating the statutory number of dinners at the Temple in order to become a barrister, promenading in gardens, and taking dancing lessons. Perhaps his most serious effort prior to his involvement with Chartism had been an abortive attempt to establish a foreign affairs journal in the early 1840's.[22] All the jollity was pulled up short, however, by a traumatic bankruptcy proceeding, after which Jones suddenly plunged into political activity with the same enthusiasm he had previously reserved for his social life.[23]

Although he first appeared at a Chartist meeting in April 1845, Jones was soon presiding over meetings and finding himself elected to committees, probably a result of natural talent for public speaking and a palpable nobility of bearing. Just months after becoming a fully fledged Chartist, he was asked to stand as the Chartist delegate for Limehouse, and turned down the invitation only when the Chartist executive disapproved.[24] By January 1846, Jones had become an insider; by May, O'Connor and Jones were meeting regularly. Appointed secretary to the second section of the Chartist Co-Operative Land Company in September 1846, Jones remained among its officers until his arrest. He was most effective in a nonbureaucratic position—standing at the podium of a provincial town hall or addressing the masses from a hastily constructed hustings.[25] There, he shared the youthful enthusiasm which had made him write joyfully in his diary:

I am pouring the tide of my songs over England, forming the tone of the
mighty mind of the people. Wonderful! Vicissitudes of life. rebuffs and
disappointments countless in literature, in toil, in business! loss of legal
and social struggles, poverty, domestic bickerings, almost destitution—
hunger—labour of mind and body—have left me through a wonderful
providence of God as enthusiastic of mind—as ardent of temper—as fresh
of heart, and as strong of frame as ever! Thank God, I am prepared to rush,
fresh and strong, into the strife and struggle of a nation, to ride the torrent
or to guide the rills as God permits![26]

The daily schedule to which land company leaders were subjected required youth and enthusiasm. On one stump-speaking tour,
Jones left London for Manchester by the government-standardized
cheap train, arriving at 11 at night on August 1 in the midst of an
awful thunderstorm. The next day dawned "glorious," and Jones,
O'Connor, and Chartist Peter McDouall spoke at Blackstone Edge.
Jones later recorded the meeting in a poem: "waved the wind on
Blackstone Edge / a standard of the broad sunlight / and sung that
morn with trumpet might / a sounding song of liberty! ... Though
hunger stamped each forehead spare / and eyes were dim with factory glare / Loud swelled the nation's battle-prayer / death to Class-
monopoly!"[27] That evening, McDouall and Jones "addressed the
People in their Hall at Manchester," after which Jones, O'Connor,
and McDouall joined William Prowting Roberts, treasurer of the
land company, for a late dinner. The following day, August 3, 1846,
the group proceeded to the Chartist Convention in Leeds, where
Jones was responsible for the expulsion of Thomas Cooper, O'Connor's vehement critic. On succeeding days, Jones found himself in
Barnsley and Nottingham, lecturing during the day and sleeping two
to a bed with other Chartist lecturers at night. Not until August 10
did Jones finally return to London.[28] Clearly such a routine—made
necessary by financial constraints—was exhausting, but O'Connor
and Jones realized their presence could electrify audiences as no
others could.

While promoting the land company often severed Jones from
home and his evidently beloved wife, it also had its psychological
rewards, chief among them fame. On one journey from the land
company convention in Leeds to Burnley, Jones saw walls placarded
with bills featuring his name in letters a foot long. At another place
he spoke before 3,000 people out of a total population of 13,000 in-

habitants. Invitations flooded in from York, Newark, Sheffield, Birmingham, and Leicester so quickly that he was forced to turn some down.[29] Within a few months in 1846, Jones had visited London, the cotton districts, Ely and Lynn, Birmingham and Brighton—this last, in January 1847, although his wife, Jane Atherley Jones, had just given birth four days previously.[30] By this time, Jones had ingratiated himself so much among the Chartist rank and file that at least one Chartist begged him to become the icon of the land plan, the key figure uniting all the disparate Chartist energies: "Come forth, dear Sir, and bless our land. Your demeanor and talents would ensure a triumph and then right, not might, would be the law of our country—and thousands would hail you with Duncombe-O'Connor as the deliverer of a generous people."[31]

The platform partnership of Jones and O'Connor was powerful, combining one of the oldest hands in the Chartist movement with skilled and rising talent, and giving Chartists hope that even the loss of O'Connor might not mean the end of their movement. Yet like everything in the Chartist Land Company, the partnership was short-lived, as Jones became a sacrifice to O'Connor's leadership style. Arrested for sedition and unlawful assembly and jailed, Jones was forced to focus more attention on his family's financial situation, and to depend upon the unreliable charity of O'Connor to get by.[32] While in jail, he received very negative reports of the progress of Chartism and the land plan.[33] Finally, upon his release, he instructed his wife that the family was to have nothing more to do with O'Connor, and the partnership was dissolved.[34]

While neither the Potters' Emigration Society nor the American National Reform movement could boast charismatic leaders on the order of O'Connor or Jones, each movement did acknowledge a single person as the "father" of its plan. George Henry Evans has been called "the heart, soul and voice" of National Reform.[35] Born in Worcestershire in 1805, the first child among four in a manufacturing and farming family, Evans emigrated to America at age 15 with his twin uncles, his father, and his younger brother Frederick, who was later to become a prominent Shaker elder.[36] Together, the emigrant family founded a flourishing copper-, tin-, and sheet iron–importing company in Broome County, New York. Having received a classical education in Britain, George was apprenticed to printer and publisher Augustus P. Searing in 1821. Searing principally printed almanacs, including special ones for some of the reform movements.

By 1824, young George understood the mysteries of printing sufficiently to publish his own newspaper, the *Museum and Independent Corrector*, which "sandwiched reform, mild freethought items and short political comment, casting a shadow before of the George Henry Evans to come." While Evans had yet to find his grievances in labor issues, he was already championing the vision of political equality that Jefferson and company had written into the Declaration of Independence.[37] Evans's biographer has theorized that, although Evans's newspaper was one of six similar papers reacting to revivalism in the burnt-over district, his reformism was partly formed before he left England, in reaction to that country's tithe-exacting state church and its land-aggrandizing aristocracy.[38]

After several years of publishing the *Museum and Independent Corrector*, Evans moved to New York and by March 1827 was printing George Houston's *Correspondent* from his own printing office, which his parents had probably helped to finance (at least in his youth, he did not suffer from the economic inequities he came to condemn).[39] Shortly afterward, the freethinking Evans printed the *Free Enquirer*, which introduced him to controversial English radicals Robert Owen and Fanny Wright, and the following year—1829—he set up the *Working Man's Advocate* and became involved in the Working Men's movement.[40]

The *Working Man's Advocate*, later titled *Young America*, flourished under Evans's proprietorship between 1829 and 1837, and then again from 1844 to at least 1849. Although one historian doubts the circulation of that newspaper ever passed the 2,000 mark, it enjoyed incredible longevity for a labor paper, providing workingmen in New York and—because of the possibilities for newspaper exchange and copying out of articles—across the nation, with long-standing advocacy of what were presented as their interests.[41] At first, Evans tried to build a consensus among workingmen, by mediating between Thomas Skidmore's suggestions for an equality of property and less radical views.[42] After Skidmore's decline, Evans still mentioned the importance of the public lands as a safety valve for workers from time to time, but until 1837 discussion of land reform was largely displaced from the paper in favor of other goals, all outgrowths of Evans's opposition to monopolies and special privileges.[43]

The same depression-linked financial difficulties which cooled the ardor of the 1830's trade unionists got the better of Evans, and, $6,000 in debt, he gave up printing in New York. At first he moved to Rahway, New Jersey, where the rents were cheaper, and commuted the 20 miles to New York, but in the depths of the depression of 1837 relocated to a farm in Keyport, New Jersey, overlooking Raritan Bay.[44] Just as bankruptcy had changed Ernest Jones's life, so financial hardship redirected Evans; the leisure time available to him as a market-gardening farmer allowed him to study Thomas Paine's *Agrarian Justice* and the works of Thomas Spence, St. Simon, and Fourier.[45] Evans's thought would also be influenced by the work of English socialist John Francis Bray, with whom he may have forged a personal connection.[46]

When he reemerged onto the journalistic scene in the early 1840's as both printer and editor, land reform would be at the center of Evans's prescriptions for improvement of working-class lives. It was a topic he never relinquished until the day he died. He has been accused of having had a one-track mind—yet it is easy to believe that the track was built by altruism rather than ego. Unlike O'Connor, Evans was no Stentor, no seeker of the limelight. He was physically unobtrusive, more effective as a writer than as a speaker; but he was also the leader of a much more decentralized movement. "He possessed great evenness of temper, he was mild and courteous in his intercourse with others, he made no parade of oratory, but spoke in a plain and clear manner—direct to the point. He was patient in argument, and never allowed himself to arise to a passion."[47]

Evans worked well with others, exerting a moderating influence over his more quixotic colleagues. When sociological pioneer Lewis Masquerier concocted a whole classification of rights and wrongs based on Blackstone's *Commentaries* and tried to link this system to Evans's proposal for land reform, Evans rejected it because "he thought it would frighten and repulse public sentiment to feed it with more new doctrine than it would digest at one time."[48] His patience and self-effacement were notable. While at first sanguine about the prospect of achieving National Reform during his lifetime, "when he came to understand the ignorance of the people, and that all the institutions of government and society were founded upon the laws of alienation, he realized that all he could do would be to start a new era of reform, and trust in an enlightened posterity for its consummation."[49] Evans took his role extremely seriously, always harboring hopes that his movement would usher in a new era. In 1849, he encouraged readers of *Young America* to buy back volumes of the newspaper on the grounds that "they will be invaluable to historians and public libraries, as it would be impossible even now to obtain so complete a history of the Land Reform movement, the greatest movement of the age, from any other source, and time will increase the difficulty."[50] Evans became so identified with the plight of the working classes that he had become a mythic hero to local radicals by the mid-1840's, eliciting eulogies in print.[51]

While Evans was never a charismatic leader, National Reform had other men who were popular speakers, among them Thomas Devyr, whose long career in land reform spanned both sides of the Atlantic.[52] Born in County Donegal to poor parents, Devyr, bright and a great reader, barely escaped a clerical life.[53] As one might guess from his extremely eccentric memoirs, subtitled *Chivalry in Modern Days*, his favorite novels had been chivalric romances, which he credited with inflating his pride and enhancing an already pugilistic personality.[54] At 16 he boarded a boat for Liverpool, full of high hopes for a life in a new place. They did not last long. After a harrowing passage (he was nailed in below decks when a storm hit and he and 14 other passengers nearly suffocated), he could find no work in Liverpool and had to come home. Other jobs followed: on a local fishing boat, as a yarn merchant's clerk.

Feeling stunted, young Devyr hit upon land reform as the panacea for all Ireland's evils. "Was a criminal executed, was a young girl seduced, did a merchant fail in business, were ten thousand men left on the battle-field, others might refer the causes to what they pleased, I regarded them as the effects sprung, either directly or remotely, from the absolute monopoly of the soil."[55] Devyr had read Thomas Spence's work, but professed to disagree with Spence on private property. "Many things may be on the land that were produced by human industry. Such things do not belong equally to the inhabitants living on the land. What the Creator made belongs in usufruct to all. What man's work produced belongs to the producer."[56] In this vein, Devyr produced a pamphlet, *Our Natural Rights*, published in Belfast in 1836.[57] It sold few copies. Undaunted, Devyr traveled to London to embark on a journalistic career. He worked for a daily paper, and while collating and commenting on Irish affairs, put forth a prescription for the poor to work on farms constructed from reclaimed government land.[58] His belligerence about the evil Poor Laws helped him out of this job, and he struggled along, trying to support his family through penny-a-line journalism. He drifted through various jobs before finally finding a niche in radical politics in Newcastle, where he was elected corresponding secretary of the Northern Political Union.[59]

During the days of Chartist agitation, Devyr was a constant presence on the Newcastle scene and may have met Feargus O'Connor as early as 1838.[60] By 1839, he had taken on a greater role, traveling to local meetings, speaking on the platform with other Chartists, and once interrupting an Anti–Corn Law lecture at Newcastle in favor of universal suffrage.[61] A proponent of physical force, he insisted on the right of the people to bear arms and use them.[62] When he was not rabble-rousing, Devyr worked on the *Northern Liberator*, a weekly four-page broadsheet chronicling democratic movements.[63] Nor had he given up on the land question—but his attempts to bring the subject forward were cut short by leaders who said the land would be taken care of with the first democratically elected English government after the Charter was gained. Devyr pointed to the example of America, where democracy was hindered by land monopoly, to refute their optimism.[64]

By August 1839, Devyr had been arrested, his position on physical force catching up with him.[65] His arrest set the stage for a midnight flight to America and a new career. Having jumped bail, leaving the two men who had provided securities for his good behavior in the lurch, he and his wife arrived in New York penniless. They pawned their possessions, rented unheated rooms, and scraped by on a diet of Indian meal and molasses.[66] Devyr began to work on a Democratic newspaper in Williamsburg in 1840, railing against land monopoly and speculation in natural resources. As usual, he could not restrain himself from participating in other party squabbles, and at one point was jailed over a libel suit.[67] Having tossed around aimlessly for so many years, with land reform echoing like a leitmotif in the background, Devyr finally found stability in the fledgling Anti-Rent movement, organized to protest the long-standing and semifeudal system of rents which carried over from the time of the Dutch settlements in several upstate New York counties.[68]

Under Devyr's influence, the Anti-Rent farmers undertook civil disobedience, refused summonses, demanded recognition of their right to own land outright, organized into "cells," each bound by a secret oath and knowing only its own business, and even dressed up as Indians in imitation of the Boston Tea Party to terrorize landlords.[69] According to Devyr, on the basis of this experience, early in 1844, John Windt and George Evans came to Devyr's printing office and enlisted him in the National Reform movement, the movement which Devyr felt "led to the Great Civil War."[70] With two years of agitation behind him, and experience as both a British and an American organizer, Devyr was just the man to act as liaison between the Anti-Renters and the National Reformers. "I threw myself right into the ranks of the Anti-Rent farmers," Devyr explained. "During nearly five years I aided them with my voice and pen—made many a pilgrimage to their hills when I could ill afford to spare either the time or the expense. Made the first speech ever was made in The 'National Reform' movement—drew out the Report of facts and grievances on which that movement was founded, joined the good and virtuous Evans in conducting the *Workingman's Advocate*."[71]

Devyr was an energetic leader who understood the power of both the press and the personal appearance. He launched his own Anti-Rent newspaper, the *Freeholder*, which defended the National Reformers against charges that they were confiscators of property.[72] He lectured throughout the countryside, and went to New York City as the Anti-Rent delegate to the National Reform convention. When his personality caused his removal from the *Freeholder*'s editorial board, he attempted to found two more newspapers, the *Anti-Renter* and the *Albany Workman*. Of the $2,000 he had upon leaving Williamsburg, Devyr lost all but $500 of interest in a house on the *Anti-Renter* experiment, leaving there only when he could no longer feed his children.[73] Although financial problems and his tendency to pick fights prevented Devyr's involvement with National Reform from being continuous, he proved valuable both for his Chartist organizational experience and his speaking and writing abilities. A template for the "workingman-activist" rather than the object of any particular loyalty himself, Devyr—and the other National Reform speakers like him who visited regions outside the New York metropolitan area—encouraged local men to take up the mantle of National Reform.

Of the three movements studied here, the leadership of the Potters' Joint-Stock Emigration Society was the most centralized; its leader, like O'Connor, brought the movement to the people through lecturing as well as the press. William Evans was an editor, a publisher, and the proprietor of a shop in Brunswick Street, Shelton, one of the five towns which together compose "the Potteries." A Welshman with Owenite sympathies who had grown up in Worcester and moved to the Potteries in his early teens, Evans had been blacklisted from the industry after participation in the 1836 potteries strike, and was knowledgeable enough about potting methods to write a primer on every aspect of the trade.[74] In 1843, in the service of a revived potters' union movement, he initiated *The Potters' Examiner and Workman's Advocate*.[75] But more than a radical potter, he also maintained a typical radical newsstand—carrying Feargus O'Connor's work on small farms, William Lovett and John Collins's *Chartism*, Johannes Etzler's utopian plans, and portraits of Chartists and sympathizers like John Collins, Peter Murray McDouall, O'Connor, Robert Emmett, John Frost, Richard Oastler, and J. R. Stephens.[76]

Like George Henry Evans, William Evans was primarily a working printer who formulated a single idea which he hoped could act as the main lever to raise the men around him, for whom he felt unaccountably responsible. He claimed:

a sincere desire to advance the intelligence and skill of those amongst whom my life has been cast; to add to their societarian, social, and political power; to assist them to remove, if possible, all difference, that may exist between them and their employers; to establish a just appreciation of the rights of labour, and a due respect for the interest and safety of capital.[77]

William Evans considered the potters a "them," not an "us." Like the product of a potter's mold, his life had been "cast" among them by no design of his own. Finding himself among the potters, however, with the unique gift of being able to see "what God and nature intended," William Evans addressed the potters' flaws. He was protective and proprietorial of the potters in the same way that O'Connor worried about his Chartist children.

A certain paternalism was not the only similarity between the leader of the Chartist land scheme and the leader of the potters' scheme. Even as Evans took an instant dislike to O'Connor and Chartism, seeing the movement as his competition, he also seems to have modeled his leadership style on O'Connor's.[78] Like the Chartist Land Plan, the Potters' Joint-Stock Emigration Society professed the interests of English workers first and proposed to carve out a space peculiar to them. Thus the name of their new town in Wisconsin, "Pottersville," echoed the Chartists' "O'Connorville." As O'Connor had a vision of balance between the "natural" market for wages on the land and the "artificial" market in the factory, so Evans similarly proposed that the Emigration Society would enable those potters who did not emigrate to wring concessions from their employers without a strike. Evans expressed the goals of the potters' society in the form of six points, symbolically replacing the six points of the Charter: to purchase 12,000 acres of land; to remove the surplus labor of the business thereonto; to oppose the introduction of machinery into the trade, and ensure success in case of a strike; to shorten the duration of the hours of labor; and to establish a new town, the property of working potters.[79]

Given Evans's and O'Connor's similarities, it was not long before the land plan and the Emigration Society fought an all-out war for local influence. Land-plan missionaries and William Evans disputed openly, in public meetings in the Potteries and in the pages of the *Potters' Examiner*. Thomas Clark, a member of the Board of Directors of the Chartist Land Company, publicly criticized the Emigration Society during a visit to the Potteries.[80] In response, angry letters trickled in to the *Potter's Examiner* over the next few weeks, and the local workmen divided into Chartist and emigrationist factions. A Hanley branch of the Chartist Co-Operative Land Company was soon formed, and its representatives interrupted Potters' Emigration Society meetings, just as four years earlier Chartists had interrupted Anti–Corn Law League meetings—with arguments and ad hominem attacks.[81] Evans, in self-defense, used the flaws he perceived in O'Connor's scheme to illustrate the benefits of his own.[82] Why, Evans repeatedly asked his audiences, would anyone pay £50 per acre for English soil, when good American land could be had for a relative pittance? One hundred families, he reasoned, could be located on 2,000 acres of freehold land for less money than O'Connor had paid for 170 acres of British ground.[83] Evans argued that his scheme was better than O'Connor's because emigrating potters would be escaping from the British labor market entirely. While Evans's main focus was on the opportunity for increased wages, he noted that the American farmer was also free from rent, tithes, poor rates, church rates, taxes, and tyranny—all the bugbears which oppressed the British workingman.[84]

The infighting which plagued the British land-reform movement should not be allowed to disguise the important similarities which characterized the leaders of working-class land-reform movements. Each of these men chose to set himself apart from the working-class rank and file, adopting an attitude of otherness which enabled him to assume a position of authority, and from there to suggest a coherent solution to society's ills.[85] Each leader operated within the familiar Anglo-American intellectual tradition of land reform: George Henry Evans's exposure to land-reforming ideas had come from books and exposure to Painites, freethought, and socialism; William Evans received a similar education in radicalism as he ran his print shop, and Feargus O'Connor also read widely. Each leader was an outsider, and so perhaps less invested in maintenance of the status quo: O'Connor and Devyr, both pugilistic and popular, hailed from Ireland, where rents and tenantry were explosive issues; William Evans had come to the crowded Potteries from more bucolic Wales; George Henry Evans, to the United States from England; Ernest Jones had grown up in Germany and come to Chartism from a bourgeois milieu which had isolated him from the problems of poverty. Finally, one other essential thread united all these men, and, in terms of explaining the success of each as a leader, outweighs all the other common aspects—access to the printed word. If other similarities are coincidental, that each of the men described here either ran or contributed to a land-reform newspaper or magazine was not.

SELLING THE LAND PLANS: NEWSPAPERS

AND TRACTS

James Vernon has described political culture in early Victorian England as increasingly exclusionary, based in part on a transition from a more "democratic" and inclusionary oral political culture to a more individualistic and closed politics based on the printed word and constituting the individual reading subject as the political actor.[86] His attempt to revise the history of English political culture ignores the key role that the working-class press and the reading subject played in political and social movements that were avowedly working-class. The transatlantic movement for land reform in the 1840's serves as a case study in which the impact of the press on reading and nonreading subjects alike is palpable. Examination of the newspapers which helped to promote a move back to the land by working people in either Britain or the United States reveals that the pro-labor press was essential in furthering the spread of ideas, information, and solidarity.

Alexander Saxton has suggested that the period between 1833 and 1853 saw the optimal convergence of two trends in American newspaper printing. While new technology was increasing the cost of starting up a newspaper, this same technology was bringing down the price of producing newspapers, and making it easier to provide newspapers for an expanding literate public.[87] That 20-year window saw artisans inaugurate the era of the popular newspaper, becoming involved with some of the largest-circulating dailies before finally being relegated to the world of the labor press.[88] At the same time this was occurring, Americans estranged from each other by technology attempted to forge bonds of community through print media.[89] Fortuitously, the proliferation of print coincided with the attempt to create a land-reforming culture, an alternative political framework which included oral and participatory activities, and encompassed women and children along with men. Without access to publication this "imagined community" of land reformers would never have been possible.[90]

Land-reform leaders were also proprietors of their own newspapers. These newspapers, the *Northern Star*, *Working Man's Advocate*, and the *Potter's Examiner*, all professed to advocate the cause of working people foremost. They built broad bases by mixing substantial doses of land-reform ideology with examination of other issues: workplace grievances, the ten-hour day, Chartism, or the constitutional crisis in Rhode Island. The juxtaposition of these issues against news about land-reforming efforts might even revive the fortunes of the linked movements, as in the case of Chartism. In addition to disseminating ideology, these newspapers reported on the activities of local branches and reprinted speeches made at meetings, creating at least an illusion of both community and momentum. Each of these newspapers had a substantial circulation; if not directly, then through the then current custom of copying articles into newspapers printed elsewhere. Finally, the success of each of the newspapers encouraged leaders to explore other forms of printed expression; direct advertisement, pamphlets, books, and almanacs were all pressed into the service of land reform.

Workingmen in both countries understood the power of the press and of public education in stirring up excitement for their causes. "The ballot box is a primary means, and then we must establish presses," Albert Brisbane, the "apostle of Association," boomed from the rostrum of the National Reform convention. "The press of this country is almost omnipotent, and we must endeavour to secure such an influence in it as will enable us to disseminate effectively our principles."[91] Thomas Devyr told an early National Reform meeting in New York that he had once been one of only a few people engaged in a political movement (Chartism) "yet in a few months, by writing down and publishing *facts*, in pamphlets, handbills, and newspapers, the people were aroused till they assembled in a mass meeting, with 25 bands and 500 banners, *eighty thousand strong.*" Devyr speculated that if the National Reformers pursued the same publicity tactics, "we should be enabled to assemble the greatest concourse in the Park that ever were assembled on one occasion in this city."[92] This awareness of the importance of print culture led to the creation of a primary newspaper in each movement, creating opportunities for the exchange of articles and ideas with other like-minded organs, and thus spreading information in a way no other method of the time could match. Even in "enemy" papers, long extracts of National Reform or Chartist propaganda might be reprinted—with hostile comments, perhaps, but the very presence of such extracts angled for the sympathy of those unfamiliar with the working-class press.

The *Northern Star* was a unique asset, a national organ already enjoying a large following when the land plan was conceived. It had a following which well outnumbered its official circulation, because reading O'Connor's weekly letter was a group activity, a Chartist bonding ritual. In W. E. Adams's boyhood home, a crippled shoemaker named Larry would make an appearance for the communal reading of Feargus O'Connor's letter, "interjecting occasional chuckles of approval as some particularly emphatic sentiment was read aloud."[93] Similarly, in Ben Brierley's Lancashire home, the *Northern Star* was shared among five men.[94]

The land plan—and Chartism itself—evolved under the manipulation of the *Northern Star*. When the *Northern Star* was the only paper that many working people read or had read to them, O'Connor had the opportunity to shape public opinion by playing up the successes of the plan and downplaying public criticism of its dubious legal position. On a regular basis from 1846 to 1848, the *Northern Star* published the returns of the funds flooding in to the land company, reported on local land-company meetings, especially in the continuing hotbed of Lancashire, and reprinted O'Connor's speeches promoting the company, even when the speeches became repetitive.

The *Northern Star* created public awareness of the land as a solution to working-class problems. James Rogers of Devonport, a man whose life had been changed by his transition to peasant proprietorship, wrote a letter to O'Connor, whom he addressed as "most honoured parent." He explained that he had given up a job as a hairdresser in 1844 in response to O'Connor's book on small farms, and letters promoting landownership in the *Northern Star*. Rogers had bought eight acres of land and planted them with potatoes, and although he had experienced some adversity in his new role as farmer, "the pleasure to me is inexpressible as, using your words, every day to me is a laughing holiday."[95] By printing such letters, O'Connor showed that he understood the power of the testimonial.

When the Chartist allotments were the site of any celebration or harvest home, or when communities sent off their lucky allotment-winners with gala parties, reporters were on the scene. The *Star*'s editors might also refuse to print discussion of plans, such as those of the Potters' Emigration Society or the ideas of Bronterre O'Brien, that conflicted with O'Connor's own scheme. William Evans wrote two letters to the *Northern Star* begging O'Connor to print refutations of charges against the Potters' Emigration Society; he was refused.[96] Of course, once the land plan became popular, it had an impact on the *Northern Star* as well, helping to resuscitate the flagging circulation of that newspaper.

When, because of size constraints, the *Northern Star* alone was an insufficient organ of publicity for the land plan, O'Connor used it to advertise the existence of more focused propaganda tools, aimed at various audiences. His *Notes on the Management of Small Farms*, which appeared in installments at sixpence apiece, targeted the practical-minded workingman and the Cobbett devotee with its long instructions on agriculture and animal husbandry.[97] O'Connor and Ernest Jones also combined their efforts in 1847 to bring out the *Labourer*, a new monthly literary periodical, evidently aimed at a more upscale, perhaps autodidact, working audience. The magazine, largely written by Jones, featured inspirational poetry, political updates, straight exhortatory pieces in favor of the land scheme, and even allegorical fiction.[98]

Taking advantage of his network of *Northern Star* distribution agents, Feargus O'Connor also printed tracts—general pamphlets detailing the benefits of the land, tracts aimed at answering specific criticism, and advertisements for the National Land Company.[99] He had penned his first tract on land, a recommendation to the Irish landlords, from his cell at York Castle in 1841.[100] During the depression of 1842, another tract presented the land as the natural solution to economic problems.[101] Of course, turnabout was fair play, and tract wars might ensue. One critic called the land scheme nothing more than O'Connor's personal hobbyhorse disguised as a benefit society. O'Connor and a supporter of his responded with their own pamphlets. "I am a Chartist, sir, and I would not give you three straws for the Charter tomorrow, were it not for the certainty that it would lead to an agricultural life."[102]

John Sillett's *A Practical System of Fork and Spade Husbandry*, which was bound with the 1847 issue of O'Connor's *Labourer*, described the epiphany which had led to his conversion from grocer, draper, and haberdasher to small farmer. Sillett, like many urban working people, had a natural taste for rural life. When his mother died, and he acquired two acres of land, he educated himself in farming by reading first Cobbett's *Cottage Economy* and then O'Connor's *Management of Small Farms*. "I was so delighted with the contents of this work that I determined at once to give up my business and devote the whole of my time to the cultivation of my land." Sillett's neighbors teased him for breaking up a nice piece of pastureland to grow crops, but he was determined to be self-sufficient. "Since I have given my attention to the cultivation of the soil, I find I have no competition to fear, I have nothing to apprehend from the success of my neighbour, and I owe no thanks for the purchase of my commodities. Possessing on my land all the necessaries of life, I am under no anxiety regarding my daily subsistence."[103]

Regular advertisements for the National Land Company, cheaper and produced in greater quantity, detailed the immense possible

produce of three acres of land.[104] One circular targeted at those with
a republican bent was said to claim that the land was the people's
inheritance; and that kings, princes, peers, nobles, clergy, and com-
moners, who had stolen it from them, held it upon the title of popular ignorance, rather than upon any right, human or divine. Another
quoted the Bible: "Embark in our ship; she has good berths for passengers; the fare is but £2 10s; her destination is the promised land
where, on debarkation, each passenger can sit down under his own
vine and fig tree, none daring to make him afraid."[105] Another, promoting the land company as a kind of benefit building society,
noted that "the Object of the Company is to enable Working Men,
for a trifling sum, to obtain possession of Land and Dwellings, upon
such terms that, by honourable and independent labour, they may
maintain themselves and families in comfort and respectability."[106]
Focused advertising of this kind could appeal to every demographic.

The case of the Potters' Joint-Stock Emigration Society also supports the notion that, far from being marginalized by the need for
literacy, working people used print to their own benefit. The newspaper of the Emigration Society, the *Potters' Examiner and Workman's Advocate*, later the *Potters' Examiner and Emigrants' Advocate*, began as the official organ of a revived potters' union. Within
the pages of the eight-page tabloid, correspondents demanded a
twelve-, or even better an eight- or ten-hour day, a dwelling for every
industrious man, and sufficient earnings to furnish his family with
food, drink, clothing, and every comfort of life.[107] At first, the *Potters' Examiner* served as simply a forum for grievances, but after a
few months of publication, William Evans set out his plan to drain
excess workers from the potting trades and send them to Wisconsin.

The idea of relocating surplus workers to the land was brought to
his immediate attention by a letter to the editor—illustrating that
within land reform, the formation of ideology could be a democratic
process.[108] In the following issue Evans responded keenly to this
suggestion, altering it by suggesting that potters buy land in America rather than renting it in England. Emigration was already on
Evans's mind, since the *Potters' Examiner* had begun to print letters—almost every week—from emigrants reporting favorably on
life in the United States. He calculated that if only 600 potters were
removed from the potteries, unemployment would be eliminated, at
least temporarily. To this end, he proposed a joint-stock emigration

company, in hopes that over the course of twenty weeks, this company could purchase half a township and clear the migrating expenses of 100 families.[109] Like the *Northern Star*, William Evans's newspaper cultivated the land-reform movement through editorials on the benefits of the land, schedules of the funds that had accumulated at the company from the localities, and testimonial letters from satisfied parties. As with other movements, the newspaper helped unite far-flung regions.[110] Reports of land-reform galas, with food and entertainment, leavened the reportorial mix.

The development of a working-class press in Britain was not exceptional. Land-reform printed propaganda was just as ubiquitous in the United States as it was in Britain. Like their British counterparts, the main American promoters of land reform were also printers. George Henry Evans, a printer and editor with a long pedigree in labor advocacy, was a familiar supplier of the works of Thomas Paine, Seth Luther, and William Cobbett, among others. When after a hiatus from printing he began to promote land reform in his new newspaper the *Radical*, he softened the impact of his new ideas by combining them with long-considered reforms, including universal freedom, universal suffrage for "all free citizens" (women included), secret ballots, direct taxation, demilitarization, gradual repudiation of state debts, the repeal of all bank charters, and the simplification of existing laws. Evans produced between 1,250 and 2,500 copies of each issue of the *Radical*, and those he did not sell he gave away.

After the *Radical* had been in publication for a couple of years, Evans and several other reformers collaborated to bring back the *Working Man's Advocate*, that venerable labor newspaper which had been around since the late 1820's.[111] A solid, good-looking product, the *Working Man's Advocate* became a source for articles which other editors might copy, and eventually over 600 of the 2,000 newspapers then extant in the United States endorsed the idea of free homesteads.[112] The *Working Man's Advocate* impelled workingmen in most states north of what would later be the Mason-Dixon line to sign petitions asking the federal legislature for a homestead act. At least one workingman prized the newspaper enough to bring it west with him in 1870—the most complete run of the newspaper was found in a private collection in Council Grove, Kansas.[113] The newspaper certainly attracted able agitators to the movement. Joshua King Ingalls described his discovery of the newspaper, "a working man's paper, which drew my attention to the question of Private Landownership with great force, and at once convinced me, of what I had inferred, after the discussion on interest, that usury of land (rent) was the basic usury, on which that of money, and of other property chiefly rested."[114]

Sold at a price the workingman could afford ($1.50 a year, or 4¢ a single copy), Evans's newspaper had an avowedly educational and political mission, and contained few of the jokes, puns, minstrel routines, and sentimental tales which riddled other American papers of the same period. Its grave aims were emphasized by the banner engraving of a nude man sitting atop the world, supported by the earth in the most fundamental way. He pointed at the earth with one hand and in the other wielded a banner reading, "For me for thee for all." Besides illustrating the notion that man was inseparable from the soil and its produce, this image indicated that the reformer, while vulnerable, occupied a privileged position in society.[115]

While the *Working Man's Advocate* was the primary source of information about National Reform, it was just one of a diverse group of propaganda weapons. Just as O'Connor had done to reach the Chartist reading public, so Evans printed a series of cheap tracts which provided a summary of land-reform arguments and often testimonials from respected figures on the necessity for such reforms. A National Reform Almanac for 1848 was also produced—a pocket-sized book which bore the motto "Free Soil for a Free People!"—and was sent free to all subscribers of Evans's newspaper. The first few pages of the almanac contained the expected tables of eclipses, sunrises, and sunsets, but this was followed by full reportage on the 1848 Industrial Congress, and reprintings of tracts on land monopoly, and on the homestead.[116] Special features of the almanac the following year included engravings of peacenik Elihu Burritt and of "the Mormons, with the Prophet's autograph"—enticements aimed at an audience of reformers and idealists.[117]

National Reform tracts like the *Jubilee, Young America!* and especially the one-page sheet *Vote Yourself a Farm!* could be printed up cheaply by the thousands and sold or given away by peripatetic lecturers like Lewis Ryckman, who asked for "5,000 YA and 300 Jubilees" to be sent to him via canal as he perambulated upstate New York.[118] They also, predictably, cited multiple authorities on the injustice of land monopoly, and reprinted supportive citations from friendly newspapers. By autumn of 1845, the pamphlet *Young America* was in print to the tune of 4,000 copies, and the goal was to circulate 100,000.[119]

While none of the land-reform movements was an unqualified success, none of them can be said to have lacked adherents. Supporters of the National Land Company and American National Reform numbered in the tens of thousands. Thus, the cases of the Chartist Co-Operative/National Land Company, the Potters' Joint-Stock Emigration Society, and American National Reform suggest that in the 1840's on both sides of the Atlantic a working-class movement required a major newspaper. While it is true that historians have often based their judgments on what constituted a major movement—and much of their research—on these very newspapers, surely contemporaries would have come to some of the same conclusions. Newspapers chronicling the activities of workman-activists first exerted a powerful attraction, and then promoted a sense of belonging and of power.

Besides their impact on individuals, the most impressive achievement of the British and American working-class land-reform newspapers was to create the appearance of one international movement seeking to return workers to the land. The three newspapers mentioned here, along with Bronterre O'Brien's *National Reformer*, engaged each other in debate through open letters, discussed ideology, and reported each other's successes and failures. Newspapers, which enjoyed reduced postage rates, held this transatlantic movement together much more effectively than transfer of personnel ever could have.

In each of the movements studied here, the formation of a centralized newspaper was the first step toward organization. Once a single organ had been founded to disseminate information from the center, communication through letters and editorials became a multidirectional process, giving at least the illusion of democratic process in decision making. Newspapers served to demonstrate the strength of the movements they represented, and to integrate regional activities. Finally, leaders of the land-reform movements targeted more than a single audience by using a wide variety of printed forms. At a time when almost no sector of society could command a weapon more impressive than the printed word, these tribunes of the people, despite financial constraints, were able to assert notable power.

LAND-REFORM CULTURE IN
BRITAIN AND AMERICA

The impact of working-class printed matter, while central to the popularity of these movements, was not a sufficient condition for activism. Face-to-face contact helped make land reform something more than just an interesting idea for the individual workingman or woman, and the need for personal interaction was appreciated and catered to similarly on both sides of the Atlantic. Land-reform culture appropriated a number of cultural forms which had been seen before: public meetings, indoors and outdoors; festive occasions, with toasts, the singing of songs, and dancing; and conventions of working-class delegates. One new addition to the repertoire, a practice made possible by the focus on land, was the transformation of a particular tract of land into a professedly working-class space and also into a tourist attraction; this was a powerful tool of acculturation in the case of the Chartist Land Company.[120]

One may reasonably surmise that Chartist Land Company meetings were interesting breaks in a dull routine. A Manchester resident wishing to hear details of the land scheme, perhaps having seen a printed poster or been handed a handbill on the way to work, proceeded to the Carpenter's Hall, Garratt Street, at 6 P.M. on a Sunday. Moneytakers were stationed on the stairs, and a penny dropped into the box purchased admission into the hall. Meetings almost never started on time, and it would be an hour before the whole audience had assembled; nor would the start of the meeting stem the tide of people swelling indoors. As the evening advanced, the crush and the heat in the hall might impel the speaker to call out for water, but the audience had nothing to fortify them save their own interest.[121]

One of O'Connor's lieutenants usually spoke first, to warm up the audience. O'Connor was kept from making his grand entrance until his deputy had finished, perhaps to ensure that the human tendency to gape at celebrity would not distract everyone from listening to the warm-up speaker. Then O'Connor would enter the hall, his voice perhaps a bit hoarse, if he had come directly from another meeting, but still able to "out-Stentor Stentor." He would be relentlessly positive and self-assured, rebutting objections already raised about the scheme. The land plan was unique, and should not be likened to the failed socialist experiments of recent years, he would argue. Previous agrarian plans to remake society had failed because their people loved pleasure too much and were not concerned enough with practical details, he would claim. No one could accuse O'Connor, author of a book which instructed readers in the preparation of fertilizer and the feeding of cows, of inattention to mundane details. Once the land plan had been promoted through every conceivable argument and with a good deal of bombast and wit, it was over. The meeting might end with a charitable subscription for a Chartist down on his luck, and then several degrees more tired, several pennies lighter, the Manchester man or woman, lad or girl, and hundreds of other working people in clogs and shawls, would filter back through the darkened streets to crowded homes.

Like other Chartist meetings, meetings to promote the land company were often held outdoors in fine weather. South Lancashire Chartists gathered one Sunday afternoon in August 1847 at a racecourse halfway between Manchester and Liverpool. Throughout the morning, day-trippers disembarked from third-class trains from these termini. By the start of the meeting at half past one, the crowd was estimated at between 6,000 and 8,000 men, with a good sprinkling of women, "and from the groups scattered about the common, partaking of refreshments and enjoying themselves by strolling across the country, it was evident that many had come as gipsy or picnic parties." Outdoor meetings were often gathering places for working-class entrepreneurs, who mixed up beverages and brought along jugs and a glass to sell refreshments, or prepared snacks and erected impromptu food stalls.[122] Speakers stood on carts which had been drawn together, the journalists enjoying pride of place by the wheels.[123] The admixture of business with pleasure in this way ensured a wider exposure of land-reform ideas than meetings held in pubs, and also helped moderate the previous connection that had been made between outdoor meetings with flaming torches and threats of violence.[124]

As one might expect given the long history of local workers' organization in many of the land-plan strongholds, localities strove for autonomy and individuality in their local meetings. The company

sent out lecturers and materials from the center, but the dictates
from above were not accepted without question. Preston land company members resolved that members should be chosen for holdings
in rotation according to the number on their certificates, rather than
by lottery, contravening the land company's rules.[125] The Holbeck
chapter resolved that the board of directors should not be able to use
money from the land fund for any other purpose but land and buildings, and also sought to close the society to further membership after December 31, 1845.[126] Individuals could make influential suggestions; the *Star*'s correspondence column recognized "a member of
the land society" who "suggests that a portion of land be set apart,
in each colony, for the erection of a school-room and play-ground for
the children of the occupants."[127] In the event, this criticism was
heeded—the school buildings were the largest, most handsome
structures in the allotment villages.

Chartist land-reform culture was inculcated at the level of regional public meetings and at the quarterly or weekly local meetings at which money was collected and administrative arrangement
discussed. There was, however, a third important space for the in-
culcation of culture, and one which the other land movements
lacked: the allotments themselves. The purchase of the "Chartists'
first estate" at Herringsgate in 1846 marked the designation of a plot
of ground in England that could be classed as a purely Chartist site, a
new, rural space where a working-class culture could be celebrated
on a grand scale without outside interference. Constant visits to the
area by Chartist leaders and the Chartist-curious even seeped into
the local consciousness. As O'Connor himself professed, "When he
first came to Herringsgate Chartism was unknown; now every labourer called himself a 'Charterer' [laughter], and when their mis-
tresses asked them what they meant by 'Charterer,' they responded,
'House and Land, if you please, marm.'"[128]

The allotments were cannily exploited as tourist attractions
meant to spur on further interest in the land plan. The grand opening of "O'Connorville" (as Herringsgate came to be known), on
August 17, 1846, provides a good illustration of the type of communal cultural activity the land plan could support. An estimated more
than 20,000 visitors began to arrive at the allotment by 7 A.M., supplemented by a large, banner-bedecked convoy from London.[129] Passing through the gates of O'Connorville, each of these visitors was

treated to a feast for the senses: he heard a band play the "Chartist Land March," saw tricolored "O'Connorville" banners and streamers hung from trees, saw Rebecca, the Chartist cow, dressed in the Chartist colors, and perhaps even sampled some of the 28 quarts of milk a day she was rumored to produce.

The usual elements of the English fair were present—dancing, singing, donkey races, ninepins, wandering minstrels, eating and drinking. The main entertainment for visitors, however, was to walk all over the allotments, marveling at the size of four acres— surely many of them had never seen such an empty expanse before—and inspecting the crops already poking up from the ground. Revelers crammed Herringsgate's nine-foot-wide roads, and toured the tough little cottages of stucco-covered brick, each cottage with its tiled kitchen, iron oven-grate, and boiler for hot water. The rooms were neatly boarded and papered, with windows that actually opened, and even the privy and pigsties, woodshed, and fowl shed were built impressively of brick with slate roofs.[130] In the afternoon, jubilant speeches by O'Connor and Ernest Jones punctuated the festive atmosphere. Shortly before 6:30 in the evening, the wagon train pulled out again, its occupants singing "Those Beautiful Villas" and "The People's First Estate." At dusk, those who were left enjoyed in a monster bonfire lit on either side of the estate. "Skyrockets, blue-fire, catharine-wheels, roman candles, and all the different descriptions of fireworks brightened the atmosphere till twelve o'clock at night, the cannons still keeping up a continuous peal until the same hour."[131]

Ernest Jones's poem "O'Connorville" illustrates the meaning which land-plan leaders hoped their followers would invest in this and other occasions on the Chartist allotments. The poem recounts the special day through the eyes of a wan factory operative who travels to O'Connorville through the English countryside:

> There wheaten lea and clovery field unfold
> Nature's rich blazonry of green and gold
> There wooded lanes, with undulating rise
> Lift their long-murmuring phalanx to the skies
> There winds the river like a silvery band
> To bind the scattered glories of the land.

Upon arriving at O'Connorville, the speaker in the poem and his wife see the tents and pennons of the festival waving in the breeze, and hear music, and think of an army—but it is an army of their fellows, and they have won their first battle. The man cries out ecstatically: `

> See there the cottage! Labour's own abode,
> The pleasant doorway on the cheerful road
> The airy floor, the roof from storm secure
> The merry fireside and the shelter sure
> And dearest charm of all.—The grateful soil
> That bears its produce for the hands that toil.[132]

Evidently the sentiment Jones's poem describes—that O'Connorville was a powerful symbol of achievement—did permeate both the O'Connorville tourists and those who could not afford to make a visit. The estate became so popular that a tea-tray engraved with its likeness was raffled off, the proceeds to benefit the Chartist political prisoners. In addition, an engraving of O'Connorville was commissioned for reproduction—just as portraits of Oastler, Stephens, and O'Connor had been commissioned in the early days of the *Northern Star*.[133]

   O'Connorville was not the only Chartist tourist attraction.[134] The *Gloucester Journal* reported in August 1847 that several thousand visitors were at Redmarley, another of the allotments, daily. Thousands of people turned out for one demonstration despite the rain that began pelting down at 10 A.M. The women were there in their holiday garb, cheerful despite being inundated with water and mud. The reporter mentioned a "tolerably full and efficient band of music," some banners which had recently seen service at the Nottingham election, and many people with Northern accents. These Chartist tourists would have seen the most imposing building at Redmarley, an elevated schoolhouse, whose two rooms on the ground floor were ample enough for political meetings, religious services, or village fetes. In the shadow of the schoolhouse spire, cottages perched at the heads of their allotments, with carpets of ridged, potato-cropped soil stretching out beyond. A little wheat had nosed up out of the ground in one area, but generally, the trees and hedgerows having been grubbed up "there [was] an air of nakedness about the settlement almost amounting to desolation, which appeared to us to be calculated to have a depressing effect on the mind." Nonetheless, the Malvern Hills were a few miles away, and the intermediate space was undulating, and well wooded, with brooks and streams.[135] Such scenes might well have been Arcadian for people used to the closeness and sameness of the city and workshop. And all of it belonged to working men and women.

The Chartist allotments were natural locations in which to celebrate the antiholidays which had become part of the English radical tradition. Thus, when O'Connor issued an open invitation to all working people to celebrate the settlement of allottees at Lowbands, he planned the visit to coincide with the anniversary of Peterloo, the armed government attack on radicals in 1819. A ten-acre swath of uncultivated land was set aside for the festivities, and festival parking was arranged with a neighboring landowner. William Dixon and Lowbands occupants volunteered to supply tea and cold provisions, to fortify revelers for the music, bonfire, dancing, and public meeting that would occupy their day. It rained, but there was still a good showing of Chartists—whose presence was said to petrify the local gentry.[136] Nor were radical anniversaries the only cause for celebration on the Chartist allotments. Unlike many urban working-class neighborhoods, the allotments had space to hold communitywide celebrations for those who lived there. At O'Connorville, where homeowners literally flew the Chartist flag, May Day was celebrated with dinner, tea, and a concert and ball at the schoolhouse. The local schoolmaster-cum-artist painted a mural facing the entrance to the hall, depicting O'Connor's presentation of the third petition to the House of Commons, and farm laborers doing their work above the motto "Speed the Spade." Later that year, harvest home was also celebrated at O'Connorville.[137]

Just as the allotments were sites of cultural activity, so they spawned cultural activities in the localities. It was customary for local branches to give their lucky allottees a big send-off. Thomas Acklam departed his hometown of Barnsley in an open carriage decorated with Chartist evergreen rosettes and ribbons, with four grays leading and two postillions looking ceremonious behind. The church bells pealed as the carriage pulled out, followed by a procession of about 8,000 people, with Chartist representatives and a brass band. Even when allottees were not so wealthy, some sort of "soiree" would be held.[138] The round of feasting surrounding these occasions no doubt increased local subscriptions.

The Chartist Land Company was clearly associated with a number of activities intended to attract followers and inculcate them, in an entertaining manner, with its ideals. Its cultural activities attracted women and children as well as men; in addition, by the very nature of its program, the land company provided these working people with an alternative public sphere. In contrast, the National Reform movement, by virtue of its goals, did not set up a permanent alternative political space of the same magnitude as the Chartist allotments (it was limited to a reading room and office space at 13 Chambers St. in Manhattan).[139] Nonetheless, National Reform meetings did create a temporary cultural space which symbolically asserted that American workingmen's concerns were on a par with other reforming concerns aired in the same meeting rooms and public streets.

At the beginning of the National Reform movement's existence, weekly meetings were held at the movement's "headquarters," Croton Hall. By 1845, attendance had grown sufficiently for weekly ward meetings to be held in participants' houses throughout the city.[140] Like the Chartists, the National Reformers strove from the first to entertain as well as inform. Taking a page from a popular Victorian entertainment—the magic-lantern show—an artistic land reformer converted the iconic figure from the front page of the *Working Man's Advocate* into a transparency to project onto the podium during meetings.[141] Similarly, when Albert Brisbane lectured on a new organization of society in Massachusetts, he carried with him illustrative paintings on 140 feet of canvas.[142]

Realizing that indoor meetings would only appeal to the already committed, the National Reformers began to lecture in the open air from the first days of their movement. They announced their gatherings by posters, handbills, newspaper advertisements, and word of mouth. Some handbills included illustrations, symbols of the movement, such as a wheat sheaf and the implements of husbandry drawn upside down, and might contain even several hundred signatures of men calling the meeting.[143] The National Reformers' handbills even reached out to Nativist sentiment, despite the high proportion of English emigrants among the National Reform leadership, announcing "a Public Meeting of the Mechanics and other Working Men of New York and its vicinity; the Members of the National Reform Association and all who are in favor of rescuing the Public Lands from the grasp of British Capitalists and Speculators and of preserving them for the free and exclusive use of actual set-tlers."[144] Outdoor meetings were the venue for both Devyr's wild-eyed oratory (swinging pendulumlike from praise of nature's bounty to vehemence against the oppression of the system) and Evans's simply worded, evangelistically repetitive sincerity.[145] Nor was the harangue limited to the English language; once German-speaking immigrants became interested in National Reform, some speeches were given in German, and multiple speakers were positioned on the platform if audiences became very large.[146]

Sometimes the National Reformers confrontationally infiltrated middle-class spaces, like St. John's Park. This little greensward, a privately owned four-acre square with gravel walks, flower borders, grass plots, and ornamental trees, all enclosed by an eight-foot-high iron railing, was a favorite spot in which black and white baby nurses perambulated their little charges. It must have been shock-ing to see there a podium erected with an American flag and a ban-ner reading, "The only efficient remedy for hard times is to make the public lands free to actual settlers," and to hear the land-reforming perorations of veteran trades unionist John Commerford. The intrusion of the public sphere, into a park which was normally an extension of the home, would have been palpable. A reporter noted that from time to time a gentleman with a lady on his arm would approach the railing, listen to the speaker for a few moments, and then strut off. The spectacle reportedly lasted several hours, un-til by 10 at night the crowd "almost filled the broad street and side-walk, the sea of faces and the foliage of the Park forming a novel scene as viewed by the light of a single taper on the stand."[147]

Perhaps because of budgetary constraints, or perhaps out of a concern to increase their constituency, the National Reformers oc-casionally interrupted meetings of their competitors, just as the Chartists interrupted those of the Anti–Corn Law League. Joshua King Ingalls described a meeting of capitalists at the Broadway Tab-ernacle. The meeting had been called to elicit pledges of public lands for the Pacific Railroad, but Lewis Ryckman stood up during the question-and-answer portion. He wondered aloud why the peo-ple should be "doomed to lose their birth right in the Earth, and be made tenants and serfs, or helpless wage workers to the end of time, for the benefit of titled, or untitled lords, and soulless corporations."

Stunned by the wave of applause this loaded question received, the railroad promoters sneaked out of the hall, leaving it to the land reformers to pass resolutions against the railroad scheme.[148]

Within New York those interested in land reform could be sure of meeting the movement's leaders at the weekly central and ward meetings. New members would go to their local meetings to pay a 25-cent initiation fee and begin on their 2-cents-a-month dues, to sign the agrarian pledge and the National Reform Association constitution, and to receive a membership card and a diploma.[149] Although many of the same issues were addressed every week, the meetings, like the newspaper, went through fads, sometimes concentrating more intensely on issues like the Dorr War or Anti-Rent in order to bring less committed groups into the National Reform ranks.[150] National Reform meetings transacted little business, but served as a forum for speeches and sometimes altercations. There was also the occasional burst of comic relief, as when John Windt proposed to lay upon the table resolutions deploring the violent actions of the Anti-Renters:

> Mr. WINDT – I propose to lay them on the table, as I am prepared to put an amendment.
> A VOICE – There is no motion before this house ["Yes, there is" —question and confusion].
> A MEMBER – I move that the amendment be laid on the table [Interruption].
> ANOTHER – I move that it be laid under the table. [Laughter, fresh tumult, and cries of "Put it out of the window into the street."]
> ANOTHER MEMBER – And I move that it be given to Van Rensselaer as an equivalent in full for all arrears. [Loud laughter].[151]

Meetings often ended with a song. Like Chartist songs, National Reform songs were set to familiar tunes, to promote the rank and file joining in the chorus.[152] Although it had negative connotations, in song the word "agrarian" served as an easy shorthand for National Reform goals; the image of the "agrarian ball" rolling on over all obstacles was a popular one. As one song, set to the ubiquitous tune of "Rosin the Beau," declared:

> Come, all ye true friends of the nation;
> attend to humanity's call
> Come, aid the domain's liberation
> And roll on the Agrarian ball.[153]

> The agrarian hosts are advancing
> The freedom of land they declare
> The down-trodden millions are crying
> come, break up our gloom of despair.

The same song emphasized the nonpartisan nature of National Reform measures:

> Ye Democrats come to the rescue
> And aid in the agrarian cause
> And millions will rise up and bless you
> With heart-cheering songs of applause.
>
> Let Whiggery forsake its minions
> and boldly step into our ranks
> We care not for party opinions
> But invite all the friends of the Banks.

This song, written before 1848, shows that the term "free soil," later appropriated by the Free Soil Party, had originated with the homestead movement:

> The question of test is now turning
> And free soil or monopoly must fall
> While hope in the bosom is burning
> We'll roll on the Agrarian ball.

Finally, the last verse of the ditty elevated National Reform participants and their mission, voting, by linking voting with the state of being a freeman:

> Ye freemen, attend to your voting;
> your ballots will answer the call
> While others attend to log-rolling
> We'll roll on the Agrarian ball.

Other songs expressed the National Reformers' sense of fun and triumph. In one such, set to the tune of "Old Dan Tucker," the chorus ran, "Get out of the way, you speculators, / You shall no longer be dictators."[154] Some of the choruses—and new ones were no doubt invented at meetings—included:

> Time was, once, when honest workers
> were put upon a par with porkers (swinish multitude)
> But now a new reform's beginning
> Selling land is now a sinning.[155]

Like Methodist hymns, National Reform songs were full of images of gladness, freedom, and bells tolling a new order. Although in his *Working Man's Political Economy* John Pickering reprinted one strikingly gory short anthem, most songs were positive and exhortatory in tone. They predicted the "good time coming" rather than harping on the depressing aspects of the prevailing order. These were songs meant to lift the spirits of ambivalent participants and bind the movement together, much in the same way as singing "The Lion of Freedom" would have bound Chartists together in common cause; there is no arguing with a song.[156]

Reading and writing poetry was important to both Chartists and National Reformers. As Ernest Jones was poet laureate for the Chartists, so National Reform had its own poet, A. J. H. Duganne. His poetry appeared in labor newspapers, in response to the clamoring requests of readers. "The Unsold Lands" is one example:

> Those millions of acres belong to Man!
> And his claim is, that he *Needs!*
> And his title is signed by the hand of God—
> Our God, who the raven feeds
> And the starving soul of each famished man
> At the throne of justice pleads!
>
> Ye may not heed it, ye haughty men,
> Whose hearts as rocks are cold
> But the time shall come when the fiat of God
> in thunder shall be told!
> For the voice of the great I AM hath said
> that the "land shall not be sold."[157]

Meetings at which songs were sung and poetry was recited were surely social events; grand fetes were also held to bring in the partially committed. The first National Reform Ball, held in January 1846 at Tammany Hall, boasted all the accoutrements of a New York occasion, including invitation cards which labor editor William F. Young called "a little the nicest thing, of the kind, our admiring eyes ever beheld."[158] The following year, at the same location, William Lloyd Garrison, H. H. van Amringe, Ryckman, Parke Godwin, Albert Brisbane, and other prominent men came again to dance and mingle. Nor was business far from pleasure; representatives passed around gold-printed Free Soil memorials to Congress— for signature by the ladies as well as the men. Attendees feasted on supper, and then, like the radicals of old, toasted their cause. The Declaration of Independence, the Four Measures of the National Reformers, a Free Press, the Will of the Majority, the Industrial Congress, and the English Chartists—"may they speedily gain their 'six points'"—were among the notions meriting particular approbation. George H. Evans was the only person singled out for a toast, as "the Father, Guardian, and self-sacrificing Pioneer of National Reform."[159]

National Reformers were invited to a ball in honor of George Henry Evans. When half the planned dances had been performed by "Dingle's excellent band," Ryckman presided over a ceremony at which Evans was toasted; then Evans was invited to give his own speech. His comment, "already has a history of the 'American Agrarian Movement' appeared in the best paper in Europe," illustrated his internationalism and sympathy with the Chartists. Nothing reveals the various sympathies of the National Reformers as well as do their toasts. After toasting the international workingmen's effort in the cause of land reform, Evans appealed to the women: "There is no word in the English language so pregnant with delightful associations as that little word Home. I doubt not that the ladies will agree to this with a single exception."[160]

The tradition of radical toasting was also evident at a great National Reform banquet in Cincinnati which reportedly attracted a thousand attendees for sentiments and speakers, refreshments, and dancing. Each toast given was followed by piece of appropriate music: the Marseillaise was meant to illustrate "the rights of man and the defenders of his rights," "Speed the Plow" to illustrate land limitation, and "Haste to the Wedding" to emphasize the cooperation of reformers.[161] A Fourth of July celebration in western New York state featured similar toasting. One attendant was even moved to write a land-reform poem and share it with the audience. The last stanza managed to incorporate two National Reform mottoes—the "vine and fig tree" and "homes for all":

> Be this the rallying watchword
> The man-ennobling call
> No longer room for Landlords
> But homes, sweet homes, for all
> Nor cease the cry till each is free
> To sit beneath his vine and tree.[162]

Although cultural occasions occupied much more of the National Reformers' energy than did more traditional politics, the group was dedicated to political change and did attempt at first to work through the party system—not surprising in the party-charged antebellum atmosphere which Jean H. Baker has described.[163] In 1844, the National Reformers listed their first slate of candidates. The nominees for Congress and for state senate were Commerford, Windt, Masquerier, Parke Godwin, Ely Moore, and J. E. Thompson, while the lesser state assembly slots were populated by the less celebrated but equally active footsoldiers of National Reform, mostly shoemakers, metalworkers, printers, and woodworkers.[164] Nothing came of this first attempt. In 1845, the same year an entire National Reform ticket was reportedly elected at charter election in Birmingham, Pennsylvania, National Reform was still inconsequential in New York politics.[165] Although the National Reform vote grew from 89 in the fall of 1844 to 124 in the spring of 1845 to 547 in the autumn of 1845, this was a drop in the bucket compared with 9,059 votes for the Native American Party, 12,137 for the Whigs, and 16,846 for the Tammany Democrats.[166] Robert Taylor, a union officer for the New York Journeymen Coopers' Benevolent Society, recorded in his diary that the National Reformers had garnered 712 votes for their mayoral candidate, Ransom Smith, in 1846, compared with 22,238 votes for the winning Democrat and 8,372 for the Native American candidate.[167] Significant here is not the National Reform vote totals but rather that the National Reformers had come to Taylor's notice at all.

Because it was impossible to get elected as a third party, the National Reformers changed their electoral strategy, and began to exert their influence on traditional-party candidates. In this way, they had some success; a correspondent to the *Harbinger* reported that "the National Reformers are much elated by the result of our municipal election, their influence having elected our Mayor and Alms-House Commissioner, the former nominated by the Whigs and the latter by the Democrats." Without running independent candidates, it was much easier to claim substantial influence on the campaign.[168] Similar attempted intervention in the presidential race was less effective. Joshua King Ingalls described how the 1848 Industrial Congress in Philadelphia, "mislcd by the political spirit . . . resolved itself into a nominating convention." Land reformers wanted to make a clean ticket, with Judge William S. Wait for president and Senator Walker or Andrew Johnson for vice-president, but because Evans, Windt, van Amringe, and some of the others were antislavery men, Gerrit Smith was chosen. "This did not suit some of the Land Reformers especially those with party proclivities. John Campbell of Philadelphia bolted outright, and went with the Democratic Party." After the congress ended, some worked for the chosen ticket, some for abolition, and more for Free Soilers. "I suspect that most of the Land reformers, were seduced to vote for Van Buren and Adams, cajoled by the false cry of 'Free Soil, Free Men,' and other designing catch words," Ingalls mused.[169]

Thus, while National Reform workingmen were clearly political animals, socialized to believe in the importance of party, early and repeated defeats at the polls ensured that the organization turned from politicking to petitioning in an attempt to sway the people's representatives. Although their motto, "Vote Yourself a Farm," suggested that the vote was central to their plan to achieve the National Reform platform, their small numbers, compared with the electorate as a whole, pushed them toward the realm of public relations. Their minority status put them on a political par with disenfranchised Chartists.

Compared with the volume of information which exists concerning meetings of Chartist Land Plan adherents and National Reformers, little is known about meetings of Potters' Emigration Society branches. As soon as the Potters' Emigration Society graduated from the planning to the implementation stage, however, it also developed a cultural arm. To see off its estate committee on their journey to Wisconsin, the Emigration Society held a gala event in March 1847. Like the celebrations at O'Connorville, it was calculated to raise future local interest as much as to commemorate the event at hand. The great concert and party was held in the Hanley town hall. Eight hundred representatives of the Potteries turned up in their best attire, to listen to the glee singers, who sang hymns and union songs. Lest anyone doubt the millennial hopes present at this occasion, William Evans recorded that "'The Good Time Coming' was loudly echoed, the audience joining in the chorus of the latter, at the end of every verse, and making the whole hall reverberate to the sentiment, 'That Right, not Might, may be the Lord, in the Good Time Coming!'"[170] As in the other land-reform organizations, such events would have performed an important function by drawing in women and children as organizers and participants. They marked off and displayed a new, voluntary community of emigrationists—especially important once the society was opened to nonpotting trades in 1849.

In both Britain and America, land-reform leaders, raised to their heights by the exertions of their audiences as well as themselves, used a combination of print and participatory culture to interest working people in their ideological wares. While much of the interaction between leaders and led was from the top down, letter writing and local meetings also encouraged leaders to adjust their plans to local desires. Although, appropriately, these reformers held indoor and outdoor meetings and created working-class tourist attractions in a struggle to claim back the public sphere, the inclusion of songs, poetry, galas, and fairs widened the definition of this sphere, creating something between public and private in which even women and children participated. In this way, land reform could truly become a part of life rather than simply a political profession.

INTERNATIONAL CONNECTIONS

Working-class land reformers on both sides of the Atlantic quickly learned that they shared similar ideologies, press traditions, and cultures with groups across the ocean. The editors of the *Working Man's Advocate*, while they denied that the National Reform movement was the brainchild of expatriate Chartists, admitted that "one of the things which cheered us on, when preparing to embark in this movement, was to learn that Feargus O'Connor was engaged, by lectures and by his papers, in promulgating the doctrine that 'The land makes the man.'"[171] Similarly, National Reformer Alvan Bovay likened the two movements in a New York speech:

After manifold Chartist insurrections the people of England are now fast coming to the conclusion that nothing short of an outlet to the land will answer, and they are calling aloud for the restoration of the common lands, stolen heretofore by a partridge-shooting aristocracy. In this country, we, the National Reform Association, turning away from the cultivated and appropriated earth, take our stand on the Public Lands.[172]

The *Working Man's Advocate* even took credit for the success of its English counterpart, noting that the *Northern Star* "has nearly a whole page respecting the National Reform and Anti-Rent movements, including some of our most radical proceedings. If our movement has had no other effect than that of laying so much essential truth before the working men of Great Britain, I should consider that we had done well."[173] Feargus O'Connor, in turn, took credit for building the American land-reform movement: "Thank God a poor Irish demagogue had forced the land question on the press of the country, and done something towards leading Republican America on to an examination of the all-important question."[174]

Although the land reformers themselves testified to their international connections, the few historians who have considered the land-reform movements have underestimated this tie.[175] "Despite mutual sympathy and the work of certain Chartist immigrants, it is difficult to establish a direct influence between the two movements," Helene Zahler wrote.[176] Dennis Hardy agreed, positing that the abundant land on the American frontier differentiated the American land-reform movement from its English counterpart, in which land was a struggle between the proprietors and those who sought to gain their land. "For those who identified a return to the land with greater freedom, America—a republic of small, independent farms—was an attractive model, but the land movements of the two countries followed their own paths."[177]

The so-called open frontier which Hardy claimed differentiated the land-reform movements has been overrated. While unoccupied public lands did exist in America, they were hardly "free" in the collective imagination of the National Reformers. Even if unoccupied land actually existed, even if the price per acre were affordable by a workingman with the habit of saving, even if pre-emption made lands beyond the rectangular survey accessible to a man wishing to farm, the land reformers perceived that none of this was the case. It was their perception that was important, since it drove them to draw links of sympathy between their own movement and that of the bottled-up British. On the other side of the equation, had the Chartists not been such creatures of habit, they might have considered such colonizable areas as Australia, New Zealand, India, or even North America to constitute a free British "frontier." Instead, Chartists, like the National Reformers, portrayed themselves as victims of land monopoly and resulting class legislation. Given these shared perceptions, the "mutual sympathy" between the movements—the internationalist discourse shared in land-reform newspapers, and the exchange of personnel—must move to the forefront of our investigation.[178] Analysis of these factors reveals clear links between the movements.

The American and British land-reform movements began communicating early, and communicated often. Thomas Devyr, the emigrant Chartist, linked the *Northern Star* to the *Working Man's Advocate* and later to *Young America*.[179] "Send over your *Albany Freeholder*, Mr. Devyr, in exchange for the *Northern Star*, and we will take care that the Workies of England and Scotland shall know the real truth of who the Anti-Renters are, and what they want. . . . Hurrah, for a free soil! Hurrah, for the people's right to the land, wherever the land is, wherever the people are!"[180] Evans and his compatriots later used the front page of the *Working Man's Advocate* to declare, "the people of England will be astonished to learn, that, although it is ten weeks since we commenced our movement, we have only hundreds instead of thousands of names to our *Pledge*, and only thousands instead of hundreds of thousands taking a lively interest in our movement."[181] Such progress reports assumed a continued interest on the part of the Chartists.

The *Northern Star* began to report on the American land-reform movement in April 1844, because National Reform supported O'Connor's preoccupation with the land. Even in the United States, where men had the vote, corruption's tree—land monopoly—was growing.[182] A *Northern Star* editorial, noting the deteriorating position of American workers, urged every Chartist to read about the American workingmen. "It will . . . show our readers that their American brethren are, like themselves, fast learning the secret of their deliverance; *that it is to THE LAND they look as Nature's resource, to which they must betake themselves as a refuge from man's oppression*, and that the Land they are determined to have." The *Northern Star* explained that the Americans felt a responsibility to their descendants and knew that this was a crucial moment for the forging of their institutions, and chided, "when our posterity look back to the opportunity that we are now losing, they will not bless our memory if we leave nothing but a heritage of toil and dependence."[183] Feargus O'Connor also urged Chartists to correspond with the National Reformers. Not only would such a connection facilitate understanding of each other's principles, but it also might solicit money for the Chartist cause and increase the respect shown by the British government.[184]

The editors of the *Northern Star* assumed responsibility for what they called the "Movement Party." They reprinted material from *Young America* until the demise of that newspaper in the early 1850's. One particularly comprehensive *Northern Star* account of the origins and progress of the National Reform movement ensured loyal Chartists would know more about National Reform than would most middle-class Americans.[185] These excerpts presented National Reform as an object lesson in unity in a common cause, since, according to the *Northern Star*, the movement united Reformers, Socialists, Fourierites, and Anti-Renters.[186] It was easy for O'Connor to explain American land reform to his English reading public since, in addition to familiar concepts, American land reform involved familiar personalities. Devyr, if somewhat disliked for having jumped bail, was still remembered for his connections with Northern Chartism and the *Northern Liberator*. The Canadian patriot William MacKenzie, a fan of O'Connor's, also spoke at early National Reform meetings.[187]

National Reform and Chartist leaders addressed open letters to each other, and encouraged individual members of their respective movements to do so.[188] Chartist Abram Tucker addressed the National Reformers in the *Spirit of the Age* as a soldier in a common cause. The writer noted that the laborers in England were at a relative disadvantage, since they had less control over the press than did their American counterparts: "I trust you have commenced the free soil agitation in America ere it is too late. With us the power is so consolidated that, by the possession of all the land and these feudal rights, they have, through their legislative power, thrown off all duties of maintenance and protection."[189] Tucker went on to suggest that Evans's plan for fee-simple possession of land would not work well in a densely populated country like England; rather, land rents should be taken by the state to answer the common expenditures. Despite the fact that Tucker felt the solutions proposed in each country were incompatible, his letter illustrates that the U.S. and British workers could see common problems and feel part of a common dialogue.[190]

American activists latched on to any news they could glean of

the Chartist Land Company—and not because the National Reformers were mostly Chartists themselves, as American newspapers
liked to allege.[191] Rather, representing land reform as an international movement increased the ostensible authority of its proponents—akin to quoting copiously from "authoritative" writers or
citing names of newspapers which supported land-reform views.
From the center and the periphery—through George Henry Evans's
open letters to O'Connor in the *Northern Star* and through letters to
England from land reformers in Mineral Point, Wisconsin—an international connection was constructed.[192] The 1848 Industrial Congress created a committee to address the Chartists and Repealers of
Great Britain and Ireland, the National Assembly and citizens of
France, and the republicans and liberals of Europe generally, giving a
statement of its principles and inviting attention to land reform.[193]
At one 1852 land-reform mass meeting in Philadelphia, veteran
trades unionist John Ferral inquired if Mr. Feargus O'Connor was
present in the audience; O'Connor had in fact been invited, although he failed to attend.[194] At the same meeting, General Sidney
Jones appealed to the audience to call to their English brethren to
unite with them in contending for land freedom.[195] American interest in the continued success of the Chartist movement continued
throughout the years *Young America* was printed.[196]

The Potters' Emigration Society also inaugurated an international relationship with the American National Reform movement.
In the summer of 1845, George Henry Evans reprinted a letter from
the *Potters' Examiner* signed "One of the Turn-Outs." Perhaps
through this early connection, William Evans acquired a copy of one
of the National Reform pamphlets, which he published in parts
throughout 1846 and 1847.[197] From then on, potters could read about
the National Reform tenets of free land, inalienable homesteads,
and land limitation; study Masquerier's map of a hypothetical
township in the West; or read a memorial which the National Reformers had sent to Congress in the 1844–45 session.[198] The *Potters'
Examiner* never made clear to its readers that National Reform was
a workers' movement, so that to some extent the similarities between the movements remained hidden. Since William Evans did
not include any commentary or context for National Reform theories, these, along with the overwhelmingly positive emigrants' letters reprinted each week in the *Potters' Examiner*, were simply

meant to illustrate that America was a land of progress, plenty, and, possibly, free land for the workingman.

Both newspaper-based communications and the volume of traffic of Chartists emigrating to America made personal connections across the Atlantic possible.[199] The first transatlantic visit which seems to have directly affected the course of land reform was Albert Brisbane's 1844 sojourn to England, in the midst of the first Chartist discussions of a practical plan for going onto the land. "In traversing England I was powerfully impressed, and in a practical and palpable manner, with the truth of a Principle which I have long felt and long advocated in theory, to wit, the necessity of securing to the laboring classes the Right of Labor and the Right to the Soil," he reported. Reflecting on the aristocratic monopoly of the land in England, Brisbane mused: "This monopoly of the soil may take place in the United States, although it will be effected in quite another way, but the same result—the exclusion of the mass from the right to the soil—will follow. . . . The Right to the soil is of a hundred fold more importance to the people than the Right to vote, and the other rights which the Constitution guarantees to them; it is of all rights, the fundamental one."[200] Nor was Brisbane the only National Reformer to visit England during the critical period. Gilbert Vale was nominated to the National Reform constitutional convention in late February 1846.[201] In October 1847, Vale was in England, meeting cooperative reformer G. J. Holyoake on several occasions and attending his lectures.[202]

Transatlantic agitation was carried out in both directions. An English joiner named James Alexander migrated to Texas in 1849 as a member of the Texas Colonization Society, professing himself thoroughly wedded to the principles of National Reform, which he had learned about through the Chartist press.[203] Meetings in favor of the Charter were held in Boston, co-led by émigré John Cluer, who had become an agitator in the American ten-hours movement.[204] Speaking as a Chartist authority, Cluer had addressed New York audiences on the dangers of land monopoly several times, and later addressed at least one Boston meeting on National Reform.[205] Cluer also awakened New England radicals to the importance of the *Northern Star*, by announcing that if a resolution made by a convention of U.S. working people were printed in the *Northern Star*, it would be read by thousands in a few weeks.[206] Another Englishman,

"Mr. Bussy," drew upon personal knowledge to paint "a picture of the condition of the working classes in England, and said he could see the same cause gradually but surely producing the same results here. The equal right to the soil, which belongs to man as truly as the air, the water or the glorious sun-light, was the only thing that could save our people from England's degradation and misery."[207] This speaker was surely Peter Bussey, the Bradford Chartist who had been implicated in the abortive Yorkshire rising of 1839 and then unceremoniously fled to New York.[208]

Trowbridge Chartist John Stevens emigrated to Philadelphia, and wrote to his friends back home that while he still believed in "the Charter and something more" he had also become a member of "the Young American or National Reform Party." He told his English connections that land reform was society's greatest evil, but had high hopes that "before long some of the states, if not all, will adopt the National Reformers' plan and make the land free to actual settlers."[209] Yorkshire land reformer Joseph Barker learned of the doings of the National Reformers while visiting his brother in the United States. He told his newspaper readers that he planned to present his views on land reform to Horace Greeley and the American public, and, rejoicing that Americans were declaring themselves in opposition to land monopoly, pledged them his aid.[210]

Broadening the transatlantic connection, two Germans also operated in both the English and the American radical milieus of the mid-1840's. Wilhelm Weitling, the German utopian communist and social reformer, came to London in 1844 and was there for almost a year and a half. Although, according to his biographer, Weitling did not involve himself with the Chartists while in England, he did speak at a "Festival of the Nations" commemorating the birth of the French Republic, at which Thomas Cooper and Feargus O'Connor also spoke. When Weitling came to in America in 1847, he helped organize *Arbeitervereine*, organizations of German workers, in Philadelphia and New York, Milwaukee, Cincinnati, Boston, Newark, Chicago, and St. Louis. These supported National Reform principles as well as free public education, a mechanics' lien law, and abolition of banks.[211] Weitling's activities in the service of labor reform paralleled those of the National Reformers. Besides publishing *Der Republik der Arbeiter*, his labor-reform newspaper, Weitling toured the country lecturing to German groups, attended the 1850

Industrial Congress, encouraged the formation of between 1,000 and
5,000 members of auxiliary societies into a *Bund*, and supported co-
operative efforts which culminated in his personally nurturing the
utopian community at Communia, Iowa. Even as the ranks of
American National Reform had thinned, the *Arbeiterbund* was still
protesting land speculation and black and white slavery in connection with the Nebraska bill in 1854.[212]

Weitling's colleague whom he had met in London, Hermann
Kriege, ended up in America as a National Reformer and editor of
the *Volkstribun*, a land-reform newspaper which had European and
German American circulation. Kriege also founded a *Deutsche
Jung-Amerika Gemeinde* (German Young America Community),
which championed the demands of the American land reformers. He
wrote, "if once the soil is free, then every honest workingman"
would be welcomed as a "blessing to our republic." Kriege and his
Gemeinde formed their own Social Reform Association, which,
while favoring communal ownership of property, was able to em-
brace the freedom of the public lands as a contribution to its larger
goals.[213]

Although much cross-fertilization between the American and
the German land reformers was impossible because of language
constraints, some did occur. The *Northern Star* reported that "Her-
man [sic] Kriege, Editor of the *Tribune of the People*," was one of the
main speakers at National Reform meetings in New York in 1846.[214]
In one of the more amusing episodes in the history of land reform,
Young America sent a reporter to cover one of the German National
Reform meetings at the National Hall. Unfortunately for him, it
was conducted entirely in German, a language with which the reporter was totally unfamiliar. He compensated by using his imagination and poetic sensibilities: "I could discover a most eloquent
portrayal of the wrongs of Labor through the monopoly of the soil,
illustrated by the aristocracy and licentiousness of the pampered
Land-Lords and capitalists of Europe."[215]

The three-way transatlantic working-class land-reform relationship among the Chartists, the National Reformers, and the Potters'
Joint-Stock Emigration Society was not always a smooth one. The
extremely slow pace of the exchanges in the dialogue exacerbated
small misunderstandings.[216] O'Connor bridled at any suggestion that
the American movement, despite its decentralization, was moving

faster than the British movement: "Here, in less than two years and a half, I have erected 300 homesteads ... while, in free America, where you have the Charter, I have not heard of one home being erected for the wanderer."[217]

Despite occasional rough patches, the international connection among the three movements studied here was clearly important to the rhetorical and ideological development of these movements. Émigré Chartists played active roles in the American land-reform movement; while they did not introduce new methods of organization, they injected their own political experience and oratorical skills into a movement already under way. The Chartist Land Plan and Potters' Emigration Society showed fewer signs of having directly absorbed American methods, but exploited the American example to spur on adherents and to illustrate that the franchise was an insufficient guarantee of their liberty. On both sides of the Atlantic, land reform was portrayed as an international movement of the industrious classes; Chartists and National Reformers had a responsibility to make land reform succeed, not just to benefit their own families or their own nations but because they were in the forefront of a movement which could benefit working people everywhere.

This chapter has shown that working-class land reformers, despite their original connection with the frightening epithet "agrarian," innovated little—rather, they used traditional organizational strategies which were already in play on both sides of the Atlantic. Although leadership styles differed, and only the Chartist Land Company had what might be termed a charismatic leader, leaders who claimed to have developed a unique vision of the problems of working-class existence were common to the Chartist Co-Operative/National Land Company, the Potters' Joint-Stock Emigration Society, and the National Reform Association. In each land-reform movement, leaders shared their ideas and created a feeling of community and common interest through newspapers identified with their movements, and benefited from the willingness of other editors to copy out their articles. Where funds were available, the working-class reading public was also targeted through tracts, books, handbills, and broadsheets.

Although the print media were indispensable because of the complexity of some of the economic arguments for land reform, leaders also brought a wide variety of cultural experiences to bear in the service of land reform—in which women, youths, and the illiterate also participated. Indoor and outdoor meetings, sing-alongs, galas, and outings to the Chartist allotments occurred frequently, giving potential adherents the chance to socialize with other land reformers and incorporate "land reformer" as a component of identity. "Land reformer" had an international ring to it; similarities in intellectual background, ideology, organization, and even exchange of personnel supported American and British land-reform leaders' assertions that they were engaged in a movement of international significance.

One might reasonably argue that newspapers and statements of leaders, while they represent the richest sources of information about these movements, illuminate little about either the size or the nature of their memberships. Although the combination of a coherent and sincere ideology with a multifaceted organization might appear to us to have been an irresistible force, there is always the possibility that it met with an immovable object—an uninterested constituency. The next chapter examines in a comparative way the question of motivation and participation in the land-reform movement. Rescue and reconstruction of the grass roots of land reform— through company records, homestead petitions, and census reports—allow us to explore the collective identities of some of the tens of thousands of working people, in Britain and the United States, who did find the land plans compelling.

Under the Banner of Land Reform
in Britain and America

It is not now difficult . . . to understand the extraordinary appeal
which the Land Plan had for working people. Far from being an alien
imposition upon the labouring masses, it evoked a direct and striking response from them. This was what they wanted: an escape from
dependence upon wage labour, or, as in the case of the semi-
independent domestic workers, to avoid encroaching proletarianiza-
tion. The varied occupational background of the allottees is evidence of how widely diffused was the passionate desire to be liber-
ated from the grim industrial society that was closing around them.[1]

While land-reform leaders operating within the Anglo-
American tradition imagined and pursued the appeal of
the land in similar ways, those who answered this appeal in Britain
and the United States came from substantially different backgrounds. In the United States, as this chapter will show, tens of
thousands of men would respond to the call of National Reform, af-
fixing their signatures to petitions requesting either free homesteads or the exemption of the homestead from debt. From the industrializing areas of Massachusetts to the Fourierite settlements of
Wisconsin, influenced by National Reform arguments as propagated
through labor newspapers and lecturers, workingmen of varied occupations came to believe in and support the idea that land could
and should be a "safety valve" for American labor. Land reformers
were factory workers and farmers, artisans, and reformers—the
names they signed to homestead petitions provide a footprint which
we can trace, to add them to the historical record as individuals. The
average land reformer was an archetype of antebellum Northern
man—an established, married artisan, usually lacking much property, and often a proponent of other reform issues or agendas.

In contrast with the American case, about one-quarter of Chart-

ist land-company participants whose residences are known lived in
11 towns in Lancashire and Cheshire—towns which had been the
seat of much Chartist, factory-reform, and Anti–Poor Law agitation
between 1839 and 1842. Of these subscribers, a disproportionate
number were cotton-factory workers, whose trials as they adapted
to their new industrial world, and willingness to rebel violently, are
well known. About 5 percent were women; in contrast with the
American case, the British land-reform movement relied on subscription of money rather than on the ability to participate politically, and thus women were not shut out.

If the message was the same, why was the response different?
Why did land reform appeal to a wide variety of respectable artisans
in the United States, while it had a more focused appeal to less prosperous factory workers in Great Britain? As this chapter will illustrate, the answer lay in the way that the land-reform message was
disseminated more than in the message itself. In the United States,
National Reform was understood as a political intervention to save
the Republic from the scourge of monopoly. The fact that anyone
could start a National Reform auxiliary or start circulating a petition among his neighbors, and that National Reform could be
grafted onto other reform projects, increased its reach.

While the National Reform association was decentralized and
therefore seemingly democratic, the Chartist Land Company relied
on propagation by its directors. Lancashire and Cheshire cotton-
factory workers showed an interest in the land which encouraged
proponents of numerous allotment schemes to visit their region. By
conducting multiple speaking tours, the directors of the land company capitalized on the popularity that Feargus O'Connor already
enjoyed in the cotton districts on the basis of his support of the
Anti–Poor Law and factory movements. The land scheme was so
well received in Lancashire that it generated an energetic local leadership and helped maintain the continuity of Chartism.

The difference between the constituencies for land reform in
Britain and the United States was fateful as well as interesting. When
physical-force Chartism reappeared in Lancashire in 1848, supported
by the same factory poor who had subscribed in disproportionate
numbers to the land company, the government's resolve to get rid of
the land company was strengthened. Had the members of the Chartist Land Company been as respectable as the proponents of American

National Reform, the English government might not have been able to excuse its termination of the company on the grounds of protecting the savings of the uneducated working class. The British land-reform movement would estrange workers from their employers, as they sought to rescue each other through mutual assistance; the National Reform movement would attempt to smooth over the beginnings of class differences by proposing a method through which the Republic might be rescued and aristocracy averted.

By focusing on the membership and grassroots growth of the National Reform Association and the Chartist Co-Operative Land Company in turn, this chapter illustrates the way in which the message—that land reform had the potential to create independence for working people—found two audiences and two different interpretations. On the American side, petitions for free homesteads and for homestead exemption reveal not only the circumstances of particular signatories, but also their mental worlds, in which monopoly was the enemy and survival of a mythic Republic the goal. On the British side, thriving local branches of the Chartist Co-Operative Land Company show that the land plan simultaneously catered to factory workers' occupational concerns, to their land hunger, and to their political affiliations. To concentrate on the leadership of popular movements without considering the question of membership would be to ignore the diversity of the movements' reception—a diversity palpable to observers of the land-reform phenomenon in the 1840's, but hidden to the historian who fails to dig deeply into the archives.

THE SPREADING APPEAL OF NATIONAL REFORM

National Reform spread from its center among the workingmen of New York, to New England, through the infrastructure of Industrial Congresses, to upstate New York, through the Anti-Rent movement, and eventually, to the West. Using the homestead petitions which inundated Congress, this chapter will map the national geography of the movement. While attention to this national geography illustrates National Reform's breadth of appeal, analysis of National Reform in a particular state enables the historian to learn something about the background of individuals interested in National Reform. Massachusetts can be considered a microcosm of the national picture, since petitions originated in towns with artisans and machine-shop populations, in smaller manufacturing areas, and in the countryside. Examination of homestead petitions in Massachusetts reveals that although petitioners tended to be mature, settled men with families, most owned no property, and their futures were far from certain. Through its Jeffersonian politics, emphasis on the independent yeoman, and opposition to economically destabilizing monopolies, National Reform in Massachusetts united laboring people with others traditionally characterized as middle-class. All participants were united by virtue of participation in production— none hailed from the "idle classes." The very diversity of occupations and areas represented in petitions suggests that the National Reform movement had wide appeal both as a proposed method of promoting greater national prosperity and as a method of achieving greater social equality for the laborer.

New York workers turned to land reform because by 1837 they had exhausted both trade unionism and independent political activity.[2] It was a natural enough transition; behind his desk at the *Working Man's Advocate* and the *Man*, George Henry Evans had chronicled the attempt at citywide general trade unionism by projecting the struggle through a prism of Anglo-American labor theory and experience.[3] The trade-union and Working Men's Party struggles of the 1830's had been calculated to restore the primacy of labor in society and to encourage the government to assume a "policing" role in providing for the general welfare; land reform represented a change in emphasis but not in underlying values.[4] Even those political workingmen who split off to form the Loco-Foco, or Equal Rights Party in the late 1830's, who railed against monopolies and opposed the Bank of the United States, would find their views nurtured by National Reform.[5]

Continuities of personnel between trade unionism and National Reform helped establish land reform as a movement for the amelioration of working people's grievances. John Ferral, a Philadelphia handloom weaver who was elected president of the National Trade Union in 1835, and John Commerford, a member of the Chairmakers' and Gilders' Society who had edited his union's daily newspaper, the *Union*, both joined the ranks of National Reformers.[6] Other union leaders active in National Reform included K. Arthur Bailey of the Printers' Union, Benjamin Price, Andrew Day, Henry Beeny, William Rowe, Robert Blissert, Leander Thomson, and Ira B. Davis.[7]

National Reform leaders in New York labored at a wide range of skilled trades.[8] Responding to the connection between labor's elevation and land reform, entire trades' unions, like the "segar makers," declared themselves as a body in favor of land reform.[9]

National Reformers also emphasized the connection between their movement and working-class politics by forming an alliance with local politician Mike Walsh, who was already familiar to workingmen.[10] An opponent of banks and the tariff, an admirer of Calhoun and a defender of slaveholding, Walsh had founded a gang of Democrats called the Spartan Association in 1840.[11] In 1844, Walsh united his political newspaper, the *Subterranean*, with George Henry Evans's *Working Man's Advocate*, donating his services to the land-reform movement as he had to the workingmen's political cause.[12] Although the collaboration between the two newspapers ended with the December 21, 1844, issue, during that short period Walsh "helped" the National Reformers through his extreme visibility.[13]

If the leadership and membership of National Reform marked continuities from the trade-union and political movements of the 1830's, the message of land reform would not have been completely foreign either. Increasingly alienated from the city's elite, many New York workers were ambivalent about city life.[14] While, as Richard Stott notes, the work force was increasingly made up of immigrant workers with few criticisms about the actual workplace or fears about "deskilling," other components of the standard of living were less than optimal.[15] Workers shared daily exposure to a city growing out of control, its local government increasingly unable to deal with problems of housing for the poor; in 1843, 7,196 persons were living in cellars, while others lived in upper flats where daylight might enter only a single room.[16] Housing was expensive, congested, and often shoddily constructed; working people and their families were frequently injured by falling brick and timber, collapsing walls, and fires.[17] The introduction of the Croton Water supply in 1842 did not guarantee its immediate dispersal; and three-fourths of the city remained unsewered until the late 1850's. Dust and mud were endemic in the streets and that noisome preindustrial waste collection instrument, the pig, roamed freely.[18] As Edward K. Spann writes, "Manhattan had become one great, haphazardly constructed and inefficient survival machine, which converted a growing volume of the resources of the nation into the wastes of life." Visible dirt strengthened the prevailing notion that cities were naturally centers of vice.[19] In the midst of a "hidden depression," the labor force was growing at double or triple its natural rate, putting pressure on wages and rents, and exacerbating local problems of public health and crime.[20]

The National Reformers would only join a chorus in favor of westward migration for the oppressed New York mechanic. The *New York Sun* was critical of trade societies: "They are keeping thousands of men in the city . . . when they would otherwise provide for themselves well and surely by emigrating to the thinly populated cities of the West."[21] By the early 1850's, the New York Association for Improving the Condition of the Poor recommended that the labor market be evened out through emigration.[22] George Foster, perpetuating the stereotype of "Moze" and "Lize," the working-class archetypes of popular culture in the 1840's, probably surmised correctly when he imagined that urban workers looked wistfully to the countryside: "Suppose, for instance, Government should take into its head one of these days to organize an army of volunteer Agriculturalists . . . and suppose that every soldier in his grand army were . . . given in fee simple a nice little farm, sufficient for all the wants of himself and family—what a glorious chance would this be for the B'hoy!"[23]

Workers may have been receptive to the idea of migrating (or of someone else migrating, in order to alleviate pressure on the urban labor market), but they knew that migration was an expensive prospect. A worker wishing to go west needed to consider the costs of travel, livestock, fencing, and starting crops, in addition to buying land. These costs placed even the land beyond the surveyed boundaries out of the reach of poor men, and made workers—especially, as Noel Ignatiev has noted, the Irish—receptive to homestead measures.[24] National Reformers would capitalize on this receptivity, and ensured their message was ubiquitous, by tying National Reform to other issues of interest to workers, including Nativism and Thomas Dorr's quest to change the aristocratic constitution of Rhode Island.[25] As a result of this smart politics, National Reform activities were reported not only in *Young America* and Horace Greeley's *New York Tribune* but also in the *New York Weekly Sun*, which boasted a circulation of 60,000.[26]

Once they had a foothold among city workers, National Reformers made use of the Anti-Rent war in upstate New York. As Jonathan Halperin Earle has shown, the Anti-Rent agitation, already under way when the National Reform movement was inaugurated, helped the latter movement by providing a living example of the results of land monopoly in America.[27] When small farmers objected to paying extravagant rents to patroons of Dutch heritage who barred them from holding their lands outright, Thomas Devyr brought his Chartist training, natural rights beliefs, and fiercely independent attitude to their cause. Once the National Reformers saw the possibilities of Anti-Rent, Devyr was joined by other accomplished National Reform speakers. These included Lewis Ryckman, whom Evans sent by wagon and steamboat through Onandaga, Oswego, and Genessee counties, and Alvan Bovay, who conducted a lecture tour of upstate New York.[28] In 1845, Bovay alone delivered a total of 32 lectures among the Anti-Renters, sometimes before large crowds.[29] National Reformers also endeared themselves to the Anti-Renters through a propaganda campaign which helped to prevent troops being mustered from New York City to crush the Anti-Rent movement.[30]

National Reformers and Anti-Renters shared an adherence to the labor theory of value, a fear of economic monopoly (in this case embodied by the landlords), a fear of poverty, and a belief that freehold land conferred political independence; and these shared beliefs resulted in a spate of National Reform activities upstate.[31] Thus, mature, fairly prosperous, property-owning farmers and wheelwrights began to sing National Reform songs and to talk in rhetoric redolent of Paine.[32] Batavia National Reformers funded their own lecturer to proselytize in Genessee County.[33] E. M. K. Glen lectured on land reform, slavery, free trade, and direct taxation in 14 different towns in five counties, all on consecutive nights.[34] Massachusetts National Reformers and Associationist lecturers John Orvis and John Allen canvassed Utica for National Reform.[35] In Syracuse, lectures on National Reform were combined with explanations of the Working Men's Protective Union, or cooperative, movement.[36] Supported by a donation from Gerrit Smith and by passing the hat, J. K. Ingalls, editor of the land-reforming *Landmark* in Madison, New York, lectured in the area around Hamilton.[37] In Buffalo, the Free Soilers resolved "to make labor scarce and bring up its price, so that more laborers may become capitalists. ... we say, furnish inducements to become cultivators of the government lands. Let the public lands then be made free, in limited quantities, to actual settlers."[38]

Rochester developed into a particular center of interest, spurred on by the efforts of former Associationist and Clarkson Phalanx resident Jonathan Grieg.[39] Having been a center of reforming spirit since the Finneyite revivals of the 1830's, Rochester even had its own National Reform newspaper, the tabloid *National Reformer*, founded in September 1847.[40] With a handsome engraving celebrating industry on its front page, the *National Reformer* began as a National Reform newspaper but later became a general labor newspaper. National Reformers teamed with the Mechanics' Mutual Protection Organization, a consumers' cooperative movement, in the hopes that different strains of workers' activism would be mutually reinforcing.[41] When the *National Reformer* folded in 1848, the cudgels of National Reform were taken up by the *Flag of Freedom*, edited by a local doctor, Calvin Chase. In the interim between these newspapers' lifetimes, reportage of National Reform doings penetrated the mainstream press. Thus, constant visibility and easy access to information about their larger movement encouraged Rochester National Reformers to stay involved.[42]

Land reform in Rochester prospered through its connections with politics as well as with the Mechanics' Mutual Protection Organization. The *National Reformer* encouraged readers to elect land reformers to state and local office.[43] At citywide political meetings, National Reform might serve as a springboard for other issues.[44] Although at these meetings National Reform was promoted amid paeans to middle-class domesticity, Rochester National Reformers also assessed affordable dues and championed the ten-hour workday.[45] Special-interest sections flourished, including a German and a Young Men's National Reform Association.[46] "The ladies," although with no auxiliary of their own, were encouraged to convince their husbands, brothers, and sweethearts to attend National Reform meetings.[47] The interest in National Reform in New York state, nurtured in Rochester by its political connection and elsewhere by connections with Anti-Rent, culminated in a steady flow of homestead petitions into the state assembly between 1847 and 1850. This mobilization of public opinion led to the formation of several select committees on the topic. Through continual grassroots agitation, National Reformers had succeeded in putting homestead on the state's agenda.[48]

Once National Reform sentiment had thoroughly permeated New York, through newspaper exchanges and the participation of National Reform leaders at annual industrial congresses over 11 years, land-reform enthusiasm spread to other regions.[49] At the 1848 Industrial Congress, even as Europe shook with revolutions and Chartism experienced a resurgence, the National Reformers achieved their zenith of popularity. Occupying 21 of 44 congressional places, land reformers set the labor agenda that year; although resolutions in favor of Association and Protective Unions were laid on the table, free land was clearly the order of the day.[50] The executive committee nominated at this congress was directed to draw up land-reform memorials and procure signatures—these are undoubtedly the land-reform petitions which now populate the National Archives.[51] Without the regional consensus created at the industrial congresses, allowing individual reformers to take something concrete back to their hometowns, land-reform sentiment would probably not have crystallized in the localities.

Crystallize it did. The *National Reform Almanac* reported at one point that 50 National Reform auxiliaries existed in 20 states, in small towns and larger cities alike. Almost all auxiliaries were founded north of the Mason-Dixon line; many had ties with the Associationist movement, and were buttressed by newspapers which committed themselves to land reform.[52] Even in the West, where the settlement and subsequent development of open lands by free white men was a concern, National Reform caught on.[53] National Reformers in an Ohio township nominated a National Reform slate for local office.[54] John Pickering, in Cincinnati, contributed a whole book-length manifesto on National Reform to the national discourse.[55] Ranting against money rents with the moral fervor of a medieval philosopher illustrating the evils of usury, Pickering and company cultivated a view of capital-labor relations even more adversarial than that of the New Yorkers.[56]

National Reform in Wisconsin clearly owed its roots to missionary activity by New Yorkers. English emigrant Thomas Hunt of the Mukwonago settlement described the National Reform Association, noting that some of the "most advanced minds in New York" had converted those on the periphery to land reform by means of "the press, lectures, public discussions, etc. and their principles have everywhere been found to be unassailable."[57] The fruit of New York's advanced minds had been brought to Wisconsin by H. H. van Amringe for several months during the winter of 1847–48. "During his stay amongst us he completely revolutionized the minds of the more intelligent portions of the people on the subject of land reform."[58] By 1849, van Amringe was back in Wisconsin, addressing audiences in Fond du Lac, Oshkosh, Green Bay, Sheboygan, and Port Washington.[59] As Wisconsin was in the process of becoming a state just at the time homestead was being agitated, lawmakers, under pressure from a variety of petitions, contemplated incorporating homestead exemption into the new state constitution, where it was paired with the controversial proposed expansion of married women's right to property.[60] Wisconsin territory newspapers like the antislavery *Free Democrat* and the Democratic *Commercial Advertiser* helped keep the area a driving engine of land reform.[61]

Some of Chicago's most prominent citizens—most of them not manual workers—became land reformers after interest in free land caught on there around 1848.[62] The *Chicago Daily Democrat* became the local land-reform organ, and the ever present van Amringe entertained crowds with his lectures. A National Reform Association auxiliary was founded in Chicago in 1848, and by 1850 the city had proven its bona fides sufficiently to host the annual industrial congress.[63] Even California, while beyond the reach of van Amringe's evangelism, was influenced by National Reform. It was reported that "through the agency of some New York Land Reformers of the 'Young America' school (or Vote-yourself-a-farm men) the inhabitants are setting Capt. Sutter's title aside, and voting themselves any unoccupied town lots."[64]

By far the best testimony to the ubiquity of National Reform sentiment in the North and West is the volume of pro-homestead petitions sent to Congress.[65] Over the period 1845–55 alone, the legislature received at least 64,000 signatures on 533 separate petitions; the *Chicago Daily Democrat* reported more petitions for land reform were sent to Congress during the 1849 session than for any other measure save cheap postage.[66] Similar petitions were sent to state legislatures, although not all of them survive.

The petition forms on which these signatures were affixed expressed a continuum of adherence to National Reform principles.

They fell into five basic types: printed forms which called for approval of the homestead measure but were not clearly products of the National Reform Association; handwritten forms which simply called for approval of homestead; printed forms prepared by the National Reformers; handwritten preambles which expressed the philosophy behind a particular group's support of homestead; and petitions supporting homestead sent by members of the Western Farm and Village Association, which seems to have been the National Reformers in another guise.[67] Although only some of the petitions used the class- and status-conscious language of the National Reformers, all expressed adherence to the homestead measure which the National Reformers had, by constant and specific reference to the equal right of man to the soil, placed on the national agenda.[68]

Printed forms which simply called for approval of the homestead measure might have been sent in by groups for many reasons; no assumptions can really be made about their social standing or economic background. In at least one case, a group of 150 businessmen supported land reform because clients who had lost money in land speculation had failed to pay them.[69] In contrast, petition forms produced either as newspaper "extras" or separate printed sheets by the National Reformers in New York, Ohio, and Philadelphia reveal more about the motivation of the signatories.[70] The first *Young America* extra enumerated 14 reasons for the land reform.[71] Aaron Hinchman, editor of the Salem, Ohio, *Homestead Journal*, created another such form, used in 21 petitions between 1845 and 1855 in Ohio, Illinois, and New York. "We, the undersigned, legal voters of _____, being fully impressed with the evils of LAND MONOPOLY, and firmly believing that man has a natural right to a sufficiency of the SOIL from which to draw a subsistence," prayed that the Senate would pass the Homestead Act which had just passed the House of Representatives.[72]

Preprinted National Reform petitions promoted popular patriotism, and portrayed National Reform as a large and cohesive movement. One of the most prevalent forms featured the familiar unclothed, banner-wielding figure from *Young America*, flanked by land-related quotations from Leviticus and from Jefferson, from Lafayette and from Jackson.[73] One version of this form called the "system of Land Traffic" a European import.[74] The petitioners summoned up the entire future of the republican experiment, pitting it against European despotism as the Declaration of Independence had done. Their remedy proposed that the general government "shall no longer traffic, nor permit traffic, in the Public Lands yet in possession, and that they shall be laid out in Farms and Lots, for the free use of such citizens (not possessed of other land) as will occupy them."[75] A later version of this document added two additional sentences: "The expelled Aristocracy of European Despotisms are buying up our Lands for speculation, while American Republicans are *homeless*. The case admits of no delay."[76]

Another National Reform petition evoked the flag, its heading "Freedom of the Public Lands" set in a type font for which each letter was filled with stars and stripes.[77] Yet another warned of a Disraelian "Two Nations": "In view of the light and dear bought experience of the Old World—wherever the curse of land Monopoly has become fully developed, its legitimate fruit has been to create the extremes of society, the Landlord and the Landless—the Rich and the Poor—the Oppressor and the Oppressed."[78] Expressions of patriotism like these were meant to distinguish National Reformers from foreign agrarian demagogues, an important distinction since the equation of personal liberty with ownership of real property was becoming increasingly foreign to the ruling liberal political consensus.

Some land reformers, perhaps lacking access to preprinted homestead petitions, created their own. The preambles of these petitions provide insight into the political universes of ordinary people—such as Benjamin Nixon and 103 other self-professed National Reformers of Pittsford, Vermont, who painstakingly examined the Constitution in their preamble. They argued that the Congressional sale of public lands, by cutting off the natural resources of the laborer, "subjects him entirely to the mercy of the cappitalist [sic], deprives him of every right, and so far as his labor is concerned, subjects him to a system of coertion so complete and effectual, as that which coerces the labor of the chattel slave."[79] A handwritten preamble from Frederick County, Maryland, echoed the language of the Declaration of Independence:

We your Memorialists hold the following propositions to be undeniably and incontrovertibly true—That every man by the God of Nature is entitled to as much land as he can cultivate. That the right to life includes the right to a place to live and that every citizen has absolute natural rights as well as political. That the Monopoly of the Public Lands by the few to the exclusion of the many, is subversive of the absolute natural rights of man, adverse to the Genius and perpetuity of our Republican Institutions, a perversion and violation of the law of Omnipotence himself, who commanded man to cultivate the earth with much labor and to draw his subsistence from it with the sweat of his brow.[80]

Many reformers who sent personal letters or reports of town meetings to their members of Congress expressed similar fears that the Republic was doomed. Anxiety about the survival of the Republic was clear in the land-reform manifesto which William Hick, of Columbiana County, Ohio, sent to Congress; he needed a 12-page booklet, tied up with ribbon, to enumerate his arguments for the measure.[81] Time and again, land reformers in the countryside adopted a Jeffersonian stance: "Commercialism, the spirit of this Age, is but the substitute of Feudalism and is as fatal to liberty as monarchy or despotism, where the Land is or may be absorbed by the few, concentrating power and opulence unavoidably."[82] Furthermore, despite the fact that land reformers were calling for government action, they emphasized that it was only to restore the balance that monopoly had upset, and not because they wanted to expand the role of government.[83] One of the strengths of National Reform as a movement was its ability to welcome reformers who sought the legislative changes for a variety of reasons. No attempt was made to force adherents into a class-based evaluation of the problem, and as the petitions demonstrate, many Americans evaluated land monopoly in political terms.[84]

Signed in pen and in pencil, with firm strokes and flourishes or by hands unused to wielding a pen, some with the occasional "John Smith [X] his mark," testaments to the visceral appeal of homestead flooded onto the floor of the legislature. Occasionally, petitioning agents added their own editorial comments. "It is hoped your honors will take no offence at the soiling of our paper," one wrote. "We are labouring men and sign our names in the mud and out of the mud—in the house and out of the house—in the road and in the woods—by ourselves and by proxy."[85] How these signatures were actually collected is unknown. Given the relatively dispersed nature of American life, setting up shop on a street corner as Chartists and the Anti–Corn Law League did would not have borne much fruit. E. Daniels, the National Reform lecturer for Genessee County, New York, suggested interested parties devote two or three evenings or a few odd hours to visiting each family in a school district; he even encouraged ladies to circulate and sign their own petitions.[86] The names on a petition from one Massachusetts town all appear on the same two pages of the census enumeration, indicating the signers were neighbors and that someone had probably gone door to door in that instance. Petitions also may have been signed outside the workplace, and left for signature at National Reform meetings.[87]

Many petitions arrived from areas harboring Fourierite settlements. Ceresco, Wisconsin, site of the Wisconsin Phalanx, yielded two petitions.[88] Settlers at Ceresco even attempted to convert a communal village in Waukan, Wisconsin, into a "National Reform Village," by laying out 200 acres of ground in 1-acre lots for separate homes while still conducting the mills, bakeries, and washhouse on a joint system.[89] Monmouth County, New Jersey, site of the North American Phalanx, originated five petitions, three on National Reform sheets and a fourth even containing an imaginative etching of a village laid out on the National Reform plan. Although Virginia was otherwise devoid of land-reform petitioners, the town of Wheeling was home to a Fourierite phalanx and the point of origin for four petitions. Pittsford, Vermont, is another such example; besides being the location of a Fourierite group, it yielded two petitions with handwritten preambles.[90] The overlap between Fourierite settlements and homestead petitions is easy to explain. During the mid- to late 1840's, before it expired in 1849, the *Harbinger*—official newspaper of the Fourierite movement—tacitly approved the National Reform scheme. The first *Young America* petition form encouraged solidarity between the Associationists and the National Reformers, noting that free public lands would allow the Associationists the wherewithal to test their alternative organizations of society.[91] With the decline of organized Fourierism around the time homestead was beginning to emerge as a plausible plan, energies seem naturally to have drifted into National Reform.

The political overtones of many of the homestead petitions sent to Congress, and the wide appeal of National Reform, suggest that common experiences of industrialization were not crucial elements in the recruitment of land reformers. Rather, as the case of land reform in Massachusetts will illustrate, land reform was a project capable of uniting factory workers, small proprietors, and farmers.[92] Congress received a total of 22 homestead petitions from Massachusetts. In addition to some of the sites traditionally identified as labor-activist, they originated in economically diverse cities and more rural areas: Boston, Andover, Pittsfield, Northampton, and Sunderland. Massachusetts National Reformers also petitioned their state legislature, achieving legislation which exempted the homestead from distraint for debt.[93] The total number of signatures on petitions which can be positively identified as having come from Massachusetts is small when compared with New York and Ohio or with Massachusetts factory-reform petitions in the same time period.[94] Nonetheless, National Reform in Massachusetts reflects the dual crisis facing farm families and town workers, and reveals the local shadings of the movement. While farmers couched their demands in terms of protection for agriculture, the New England Labor Reform League mingled discussion of land reform with that of the ten-hour workday.[95] At a time when Americans of all backgrounds found themselves adrift in a sea of individualism, land reform seemed a particularly "republican" solution, concerned with finding and fomenting the common good.

National Reform in Massachusetts met formidable obstacles and competition. In contrast with New York, where National Reformers benefited from connections with the Democratic Party, in Massachusetts the Whigs were uniformly strong and willing to cater to working people on the issues of collective bargaining and public schools.[96] Although the Free Soil movement posed a serious challenge to the two-party system in 1848, polling 30 percent of the Massachusetts presidential vote, the Free Soilers eventually formed a shaky coalition government with the Democrats, brought a secret ballot and the ten-hour day under direct consideration in the public sphere, and actually passed a state homestead act.[97] Legislative concessions to the cause of labor may have taken the bite out of the land agitation, by showing that some reform was possible even within an unreformed system.[98]

National Reform in Massachusetts also contended with labor activists whose first loyalties lay elsewhere—especially with the ten-hour day, which had both a moral and an economic appeal. National Reform in Massachusetts also competed against antislavery.[99] The Massachusetts rank and file particularly abhorred chattel slavery; of the 925 antislavery petitioners in Edward Magdol's sample, 70 percent were born in Massachusetts.[100] Since, as I have shown, the two ideologies were sometimes incompatible, abolitionist sentiments may have deterred some otherwise likely National Reform adherents. Finally, Massachusetts National Reform competed with the Working Men's Protective Union Movement, a series of consumers' cooperatives. Although contemporaries indicated that weekly business meetings of the 56 Protective Unions, reaching 8,000 members, would have provided the perfect structure for dissemination of information on land reform, and some discussion of National Reform did go on there, the movement as a whole resisted introducing such politics into its framework.[101]

As examination of particular localities illustrates, those reformers who did feel strongly about land reform were clustered predominantly in factory work and artisanal production, with a few in farming. Very few were professionals or men of property, although some seem to have achieved their "competency." Although there were exceptions in a few places, the majority were native-born, in their twenties or thirties, married and with children, living with only their families and perhaps a few boarders, but not in communal boardinghouses. Throughout Massachusetts, the friends of National Reform were generally neither rabble-rousing agrarians nor young revolutionaries; rather, they were mostly settled, mature family men, most of them native to Massachusetts or at least to New England. In contrast with the men of industrial Lancashire who sought land, these were men who had something to lose rather than men who had already lost almost everything; they were the very constituency implied by the rhetoric of equal rights.[102]

In industrializing Worcester, National Reform was guided by Appleton Fay, a 44-year-old married patternmaker with two children, who had lived in New York in the late 1830's and perhaps had become acquainted with land-reforming ideas there.[103] Fay took advantage of possible National Reform assistance from farmers by calling a Massachusetts-wide organizational meeting for National Reformers on the day of the Worcester cattle show.[104] The meeting was a success, and a National Reform convention was then scheduled to take place in the second week in October.[105] So organized, Worcester's National Reformers nominated a slate of Worcester County senators, representatives to the state legislature (including, coincidentally, one Appleton Fay), and Congress.[106] A personal visit by George Henry Evans in 1846 and support from the local newspaper helped to sustain the momentum.[107] Fay also attended the 1847

Industrial Congress and in that year called a Massachusetts National Reform state convention in Worcester to nominate gubernatorial candidates pledged to freedom of the public lands, the ten-hour workday, and downgrading the salaries of all public officials.[108] By the time he became National Reform corresponding secretary for the entirety of Massachusetts, Fay had achieved a certain regional popularity. His interest in land reform continued at least into the mid-1850's, when Worcester became the center of another westward movement, Eli Thayer's plan to settle Kansas for free labor through the New England Emigrant Aid Society.[109]

Although one signatory to the Worcester National Reform petition was arrested in 1850 for blowing up the mayor's office with a six-inch grenade (for reasons unknown), the other signatories appear a remarkably settled and "respectable" group.[110] They were in the prime of their lives, with a median age of 33 in 1851. Of those whose names could be found in the census and/or the city directory, almost all were married and had children, and the minority with assets listed owned from $350 to $6,000 worth of property. Some of the signatories were politically active in other reform movements or occupational organizations; 7 could be identified among signers of a Worcester temperance petition, 5 had signed petitions in favor of a ten-hour day, and 35 were among the members of the Worcester Mechanics' Association in either 1854 or 1861.[111] The occupational breakdown of the 104 signatories whose occupations could be identified reveals that, although the occupations represented were diverse, participation was strongest among skilled workmen and in the metal trades.

The National Reform pattern seen in Worcester would be replicated in Lowell, with a few variations.[112] Already a site of ideological contention over the meanings of industrialization in a free and democratic country, and the impact of factories on workers, Lowell was the American city which most resembled industrial England.[113] Correspondence indicates many of the workplace-environment and fatigue problems of which English workers complained were common to Lowell; contemporary observers were sure that operatives fantasized about leaving the mills and going off to the country.[114] Some New England factory workers did look westward; William Mann, working in a mill in Slatersville, Rhode Island, suggested to a friend that eight or ten families might club together, and with

$1,000 form a neighborhood on the best soil in Wisconsin.[115] After 14 years in the United States, one Mr. Kellett, a foreman in the Middlesex Factory in Lowell, wrote to a friend rejoicing to see that members of the middle classes were moving westward: "I tell you, Sir, I am happy to see the growing disposition in men generally to be the possessors of a little 'Free Soil,' where they can sit under their own vine and fig-tree, none daring to make them afraid."[116]

Lowell residents interested in land reform could find pertinent information in the Lowell Courier, Tri-Weekly American, and Vox Populi, and especially the Voice of Industry, with incarnations in Fitchburg, Lowell, and Boston.[117] This avowedly pro-labor newspaper had various editors, all clearly National Reformers. Even its banner incorporated the National Reformers' motto, "For Me, for Thee, for All," as well as iconography joining industry and agriculture.[118] Former farmer and harness maker William Field Young, who edited the Voice of Industry, believed nine out of ten workingmen reformers were in favor of land reform even if this interest was not reflected at regional conventions.[119] Again, support for land reform was linked to fears for the political health of the union: "The people are beginning to realize that the nation's independence and property are based upon the landed interest of the country. We must have a landed Democracy or a ragged Democracy." In addition to touting the clear benefits of free homesteads for city workers, Young felt speculation in the soil to be the greatest evil affecting the agricultural interest, and stressed the importance of preserving the family homestead from mortgage or execution.[120] Like George Henry Evans, Young followed the progress of the British land-reform movement during his tenure as editor, and even defended the reputation of "Fergus O'Conner" against the disparagement of other newspapers.[121] The editors who followed Young were also land reformers: John Allen, D. H. Jacques, and John Orvis.[122]

Lowell labor reformers integrated National Reform into a wider framework which included a Female Labor Reform Association, an Industrial Reform Association, the Middlesex Mechanic Association, and a Laborers' Union Association.[123] It is likely the issue of public lands was initially discussed by "friends of Labor Reform" who met weekly at 76 Central Street.[124] Land reform was also bolstered by Lowell's own 61-member Union of Associationists.[125] By the early 1850's, Lowell had sprouted its own National Reform organization.[126] Yet despite the presence of influential land-reform agitators in Lowell, coverage of the homestead issue in the press, and the operations of speakers and local organizations, the Massachusetts state legislature received just two National Reform petitions from Lowell, one with 123 names and the other with 15; and Congress received none.[127] Lowell signatories to National Reform petitions represented 70 percent of the occupational categories listed in the census, illustrating the wide appeal of the homestead measure.[128] Although the sample of names the petitions provides is too small to draw any firm conclusions, clearly, compared with the census, metalworkers were disproportionately numerous in the movement. Joel Hatch, who worked in the Lowell Machine Shop and ardently supported National Reform at a workingmen's convention, may have been the main evangelist among metalworkers.[129]

Although Associationists and skilled workers were prominent among Lowell's National Reformers, factory workers and operatives did participate in the National Reform movement. West Chelmsford, near Lowell, submitted a simple petition calling for passage of the Homestead Act. The shakiness of the signatures to this document suggests that, in contrast with the Lowell petition, many of the signatories had had marginal educations, and may have been either factory workers (who notoriously had little time for schooling) or other unskilled laborers. Similarly, a petition from Amesbury and Salisbury was annotated "chiefly from workers in the factories."[130] But lest we be tempted to equate these workers with their Lancashire counterparts, it must be noted that the Americans were much more prosperous—a fact which links them to the Lowell signatories.[131] Upon closer examination, the petition from Amesbury revealed four carders, a dyer, three fullers, three finishers, nine self-described laborers, five machinists, two "manufacturers," 19 spinners, and five weavers, all probably working in the mills; but they also had the support of one blacksmith, three carpenters, a clergyman, two clerks, and a clothier, a dentist, a farmer, a postmaster, a printer, a ship's carpenter, two shoemakers, a tailor, and three traders. Interestingly enough, those of the signatories recorded in the census as being from England, Ireland, or Scotland were only employed in the mill trades. The average signatory had a median age of 39.5, and two children; almost all past their mid-twenties were married. Although only 27 of the signatories had any property, the aver-

age amount they owned was $1,515—not a particularly impover-
ished lot. Furthermore, even those signatories who owned no property, if they were married and heads of household, tended to live in a
separately enumerated domicile, suggesting at least some room of
their own. A petition like this one, with both factory and nonfactory
workers participating, suggests that a sense of identity and common
purpose united artisans and wage earners in pursuit of National Reform. It also suggests that just as George Henry Evans argued, National Reformers were not propertyless agrarians, but rather men of
some substance who embraced a Jeffersonian ideology.

To find National Reform among millworkers and metal forgers is
well enough, but to argue that National Reform attracted Massachusetts workers, it would be almost necessary to find evidence of
support for free public lands among the shoemakers. The manufacture of boots and shoes was the leading industry in Massachusetts
between 1837 and 1855, accounting for a third of all the industrially
employed at the beginning of that period, and 31.7 percent at the
end.[132] Working in groups in their individual "ten-footers," far from
the prying eyes of the capitalists who supplied them with leather
and thread, male shoemakers in this period were notoriously jealous
of their social standing and their supposed rights as citizens. While
factory workers may have shared shoemakers' concerns about wages
and hours, and possibly temperance and moral reform, they lacked
the shoemakers' autonomy and opportunity for serious discussion;
and thus shoemakers have come down to us as some of the most
"radical" of all antebellum workers.[133] This radicalism and willingness to protest grew toward the 1850's and 1860's, as the introduction of outwork, then factory methods and sewing machines,
threatened to diminish the importance of their skills.[134] That National Reform was popular among the shoemakers of Lynn, therefore, testifies to its ability to appeal to the self-proclaimed independent artisan without personal experience of the factory.

Lynn cordwainers not only contributed a land-reform petition to
the Massachusetts state legislature; they also formed and docu-
mented their own National Reform auxiliary. By some unknown
means, they had been exposed to land-reforming and Associationist
ideas even before December 1844, when fellow shoemaker and then
Brook Farm resident L. W. Ryckman gave three lectures at the Lynn
town hall.[135] By October 1844 the editors of the shoemakers' official

organ, the *Lynn Awl*, were calling George Henry Evans "friend Evans," subscribing to *Young America*, and printing advertisements for National Reform meetings and accounts of land-related speeches and New York developments.[136] In the midst of this enthusiasm, all workingmen and their sympathizers, regardless of "color, sect or party," were invited to join the Lynn National Reformers.[137]

Reformism was generally rampant in Lynn. In addition to land reform, the *Awl* dabbled in Fourierism and Owenism, and promoted producers' cooperatives.[138] Workingmen with strong feelings about slavery could vent their spleen at weekly discussions hosted by the Lynn Mechanics' and Laboring Mens' Institute.[139] Members of the Cordwainers' Society also expressed some interest in temperance, leading meetings of the Samaritan Temperance Society and the Young Men's Washingtonian Association. A true proponent of reform could have attended some type of meeting six days of every seven.[140]

Although Lynn cordwainers are best known as labor reformers, jealously clinging to their rights through their patriotism-charged rhetoric, opposing "distinctions, anti-republican in their character, which assimilate very nearly to those that exist between the aristocracy and the laboring classes of Europe," land reform was not alien to their quest.[141] "Equal rights"—the shoe workers' constant refrain—implicated the whole community, women shoe binders as well as male heads of household. "Equal rights" also suggested that ownership of property was central to independence, yet until the 1850's fewer than half of Lynn voters owned any real property.[142] Land reform, with its promises of more widespread property ownership, was especially interesting to shoemakers.

Boasting the highest circulation of any local newspaper in 1844–45, the *Awl* was the main source for information on the National Reform movement.[143] Lest the idea of freeing the soil for actual settlers seem remote to shoemakers who had no intention of laying down the last and taking up the spade, correspondents to the *Awl* presented access to the soil as a natural right, and a component of the "equal rights" worldview—a matter of principle.[144] The *Bay State* also reprinted material supporting homestead exemption, and printed the Massachusetts senate's rather long 1851 homestead-exemption report in its entirety.[145] Its flame fanned by these newspapers, National Reform in Lynn touched off discussion of other grievances. At any National Reform meeting, one member might speak against slavery, another of political action to free the public lands, another in favor of free public education, another in favor of the idea that "the laboring classes should be their own orators and make their own laws."[146] In Lynn the name National Reform was nebulous enough to attract reformers of all stripes. One Johnson noted he was "induced to come here on account of the name given to these meetings. It sounded noble to him. He had faith in every reform that came from the working classes."[147]

Although the freedom of the public lands clearly was insinuated into the larger body of shoemakers' demands, only some of the men who were listed in the *Awl* in connection with National Reform signed the Lynn petition, and the absence of only one of the missing men can be explained.[148] Of the 56 men who did sign the Lynn homestead petition, 19 could not be located in city directories or in the census; among the rest, all were cordwainers with the exception of two carpenters, a mason, two traders, and a laborer. Most of the signatories were married and native-born, with several children, and the capital they individually owned, where it was listed, ranged from $200 to $2,000. They ranged in age from 20 to 76, with a median age of 35. Some but not all of the signatories had a visible history of activism, leading meetings of various types or serving as regional delegates.[149] In Lynn, as elsewhere, those National Reformers who can be identified were largely settled, respectable workingmen who, while they had a trade, perceived that they had a harder time than their forefathers did achieving a competency. While they might not have moved out West themselves, it was natural that they might consider opposition to land monopoly, and recognition of a natural right to a portion of the soil, as parts of a general program to improve the position of labor. The shoemakers' program for equal rights, developed in the unique political hothouse of the ten-footer, included a bid for large-scale property ownership, without which true political autonomy was impossible.

While land reform appealed to urban working people, petitions for land reform also originated in rural towns, illustrating that the market revolution was beginning to transform social relations there as well, and to cause social strains.[150] While it would be inappropriate to call them manifestations of "class," status distinctions, even in the countryside, caused working people to feel threatened.[151]

Thus, 16 men from Greenfield did sign a homestead petition, its preamble written out by the local shoemaker. One might rightfully conclude that the rhetoric of "equal rights" had seeped into the consciousness of these rural artisans, who included two other carpenters and a cabinetmaker, a chairmaker, a machinist, a laborer, and three printers.[152] Together, they comprised almost a stereotype of the proud if slipping worker during this period: almost all were from Massachusetts originally; almost all were married (some with children, as their median age of 31.5 would suggest); only two owned any property.[153]

In the countryside as in the city, printers were central to the dissemination of National Reform ideas. The junior editor of the *Northampton Democrat* decried the "impropriety as well as the absolute injustice of allowing speculators, many of them with borrowed capital, to buy up these lands for the purpose of raising their prices and preying upon the hardy yeomanry who wish to settle and cultivate them."[154] With a wistful reference to white slavery, he urged his readers to look to the West, where "we believe that when the Millenium shall come, they shall sit, *every* man under *his* vine and under his fig-tree, and that it is the duty of all to do their part to produce such a state of things as is expected to exist in the Millenium, and one of the things which ought to be done is to put it in the power of every man to labor for himself—to enjoy the entire fruits of his industry and have a home of his own."[155] Despite his enthusiasm for land reform, the editor may have been fighting an uphill battle. The land-reform petition from Northampton, although submitted on a form printed by the National Reform Association, bore only five signatures.[156] It was not atypical in this respect.[157]

Like Northampton, the central Massachusetts town of Chester, also primarily a farming town, produced a petition.[158] Of 36 signers to that petition, a full third could not be identified through the census. Of the remaining 24, 15 were listed in the census as farmers, ranging in age from 24 to 71, most of them married and with some capital—in one case as much as $7,000. The remainder of the signatories included four laborers in their early twenties, a mechanic, a shoemaker, a tailor, a carpenter, and a Methodist minister who, born in England, was the only signer not native to the northeastern seaboard. All the signers appear to have signed their own names, with the exception of the petition's lone woman, Sarah Kingman, who marked an X. Of the Chester petition signers who could be traced, almost all were located on the same two pages of the 1850 census, which suggests they were near neighbors.[159]

Eleven residents of Wendell, a farming town of 920 inhabitants in 1851, signed a petition which argued for a law exempting a homestead of between $300 and $500 in value. They claimed this would obstruct the tendency "of Real Estate being eventually swallow'd absorb'd and passing into the hands of large monied landholders; that the tendency would be to elevate the Farmer in Society to that position which his occupation justly entitles him—That it would hasten the time when he is to be looked upon as a 'being equal to the Lawyer, Physician or Divine' and no longer consider'd as a mere clodhopper, a digger of bogs, ditches and dung heaps, and only fit to wallow in the 'free soil' he cultivates." The signatories to this document fit the pattern of relative maturity noted elsewhere among Massachusetts land-reform supporters, with a median age of 35. Four could be identified as farmers, one a lumberman, one a shoemaker, one a miller, and one a clerk, while two had no occupation listed in the census. Nine were married, and eight had at least one child; eight owned between $400 and $2,600 in assets.[160]

Why would farmers and rural dwellers, like those in Northampton, Greenfield, Wendell, and Chester, have been interested in National Reform? Massachusetts farmers faced with the difficulty of eking out a living there may have looked west and dreamed of other farms. Clearly, National Reform also promised to raise the status of agriculture, restoring the small farmer to his place in the center of the American political cosmos.[161] Like the workmen of Lynn, the farmers of the Massachusetts countryside jockeyed for the rights of the independent, republican individual against the forces of federalism, monopoly, and hard cash. Nor did National Reform require any activity that seemed subversive—rather, petitioning was considered to be one of Americans' natural political rights.

As examination of both the scope and the breadth of National Reform has shown, land reform was an issue which, invested with the labor theory of value and the importance of land in maintaining independence, could unite the farmer, the artisan, and the factory worker. Although its rhetoric was driven from a New York center, National Reform took on the local shadings and enthusiasms of its participants, becoming a political caucus in Rochester, a meeting of reforming minds in Lynn and Lowell, a natural extension of the Anti-Rent agitation elsewhere in upstate New York, and a way to recoup the privileged ideological position of the farmer in western Massachusetts. If the doctrines of National Reform would eventually attract some of its adherents on the basis of "Manifest Destiny" or even the need to settle the West for free white labor, as seems to have been the case by the mid-1850's, they still carried their original connotations—that the producer was the center of American society and that every worker had a right to a living on the soil.

One student of National Reform, Sean Wilentz, has called for historians to broaden their examination of working people's concerns and to reject a model of class formation supposedly gleaned from the German or English experience. This model asks why America did not follow a pattern while at the same time neglecting to weigh the significance of what did happen. At the same time, however, like Norman Ware before him, Wilentz sympathizes in his romantic narrative with traditional, institutional labor protest, and especially the General Trades Unionists, the journeymen seeking shorter hours and better working conditions and going on strike. Despite his admission that National Reform capitalized on popular appreciation of the importance of land redistribution which dated back to at least 1829, and that National Reform leaders sought free land *for the workers*, sometimes in confrontational tones which bespoke "class" as much as any antebellum American rhetoric, Wilentz on the basis of the occupations of such leaders appears to consider it only "the semblance of a radical labor milieu" rather than a true expression of working people's hopes.[162]

I would suggest that the significance of National Reform has been obscured by the historical tendency to wall off "working-class" from "middle-class" protest. As analysis of the grassroots composition of National Reform outside New York suggests, small employers and employees, factory hands, and farmers collaborated in a political movement to change a social situation. To call National Reform "the city's first truly petit bourgeois radical movement" obscures the diversity inherent in the national movement, of which, by the late 1840's, New York was only a small part. Nor does referring to it as a "populist" movement accommodate the heavy overtones of political economy inherent in National Reform, or the extent to which National Reform was tied up with other traditional labor concerns like the ten-hour day and free public education. In Massachusetts as in New York and probably elsewhere, National Reform for the rank and file was a particularly flexible and inclusive movement, but its overarching goal was to eliminate monopoly and elevate the "producers," however defined.

THE CHARTIST LAND COMPANY IN
THE LOCALITIES

Determining the composition of the Chartist movement at the grassroots level has been an intractable problem for historians; it is not surprising, then, that the subject of membership in the Chartist Land Company has received little attention until recently.[163] We know that the land company's membership hailed from all parts of Great Britain, and even France and Belgium.[164] We also know that the company's members pursued a wide variety of occupations, from farming to factory work and even the professions. Yet in spite of this diversity, examination of land-company legal documents also shows two important trends not noticed earlier. The industrial North of England was a particular stronghold of land-plan activity: 11 Lancashire and Cheshire cotton-producing towns of varying sizes supplied about one-fourth of the subscribers to the land plan.[165] They were some of O'Connor's strongest supporters, springing to O'Connor's defense when the first allegations against the plan were made and continuing to support the plan after it had been attacked in the House of Commons.[166] In each of the 11 towns studied, cotton-factory workers not only comprised a plurality of land-plan subscribers, but also were substantially overrepresented compared with their proportion in the larger population.

Cotton-factory workers, followed in number by manual laborers, were both pushed and pulled to the dream of land-based autonomy and economic competence which O'Connor's land scheme promised. The towns in which they lived were suffering from a combination of increasing population and inadequate infrastructure; middle-class contemporaries flocked to the crowding, bad smells, nonexistent sewers, and scarce drinking-water supplies of Lancashire to make notes and thereby condemn the ills of industrialization. Within this already undesirable environment, cotton-factory workers were personally imposed upon by industry in a number of ways.

Their entry into industry as workers regulated their movements, regulated the structure of their families and the distribution of their neighborhoods, and perhaps most crucially, deprived them of the economic security and predictability which they believed their fathers and grandfathers had enjoyed. Every day as the factory bell rang, individuals whose cyclical poverty gave them reason to be discontented were brought together and exposed to fellow workers for the greater part of their waking hours—and from this routine a spirit of common purpose and opportunities for discussion and the formation of values and ideologies emerged.

Land-company Chartism flourished in cotton towns in part because the experience of cotton-factory workers opened their minds to the revealed truth that a life on the land was to be preferred to an urban subsistence. It also prospered because the towns had historically been strongholds of Chartist activity, strike protest, and the cooperative movement. Prior radicalism in the cotton towns had trained local leaders. It had created relationships of opposition or attempts at paternalism and co-option by local authorities and other reforming groups (especially the Anti–Corn Law League). Most important, it had created ties of loyalty between large groups of workers and men who represented themselves as labor's tribunes: Joseph Rayner Stephens and later, Feargus O'Connor. Taking advantage of the opportunity to make a strong showing for his land company early, O'Connor made Manchester and its environs a center of land-reforming proselytization, crossing and recrossing the cotton district with his message. Not only was he wildly successful in the short run, as factory workers and laborers lined up to sign the register of land-company members; but the development of local land-company organizations in the cotton towns helped political Chartism to reemerge quickly in 1848, by keeping leaders and followers in touch with each other.[167] This section illustrates the way in which the land's push and pull, combined with O'Connor's cultivation, worked itself out in 11 Lancashire towns, and examines the effect of land company organization on the resurgence of Chartism in Lancashire in 1848.

A case study of Lancashire has repercussions for the history of Chartism there as well as for the history of land reform—making it necessary to reverse some earlier assumptions about the nature of radicalism there. As Donald Read noted, the predominantly cotton-producing towns of southeastern Lancashire had been stalwart bastions of support for Chartism in 1839 and 1842, culminating in the violent "general strike" of that year. After 1842, Read claimed, bad trade conditions which had impelled thousands to seek a solution in Chartism improved, and workers' energies were funneled into the more clearly economic ten-hours and Anti–Poor Law agitations.[168] While Read's conclusions were based on the assumption that the land plan was a movement distinct from authentic Chartism, closer examination of the issue reveals that such a distinction is faulty. The upturn in trade conditions which Read identified did not alienate Chartists from the land plan, but rather gave them more leisure to ponder their positions in society and feelings about industrialization, and more cash to afford the price of shares. As Feargus O'Connor himself pointed out, the land plan had a wide appeal in good times: "The great advantage of the land movement is this—that it supplies food for sensible agitation in good times and bad times. Good times have always been destructive of Chartism but now assist it, because it is then that the working classes have the best opportunity of subscribing to the land plan."[169] The extent of southern Lancashire's involvement in the land plan demonstrates no significant desertion of Chartism; workers remained interested in substantial social reform, including agrarian reform, until 1848–49, when this option collapsed under pressure from the government and internal mismanagement. Far from fleeing the ranks of the Chartists, workers in Greater Manchester reshaped Chartism to correspond with a new vision of themselves as independent property holders and land tillers, and sought to realize this vision through mutual assistance and the aid of an apparently benevolent and charismatic leader.

ENGLAND'S GRIM UNPLEASANT LAND?

By the 1840's, the towns of the industrial Northwest were bound together by the experience of working in cotton. A preponderating 40 percent of adult males in the textile-producing ring around Manchester worked in textiles; only 5 percent of residents were officially classified as professional and white-collar.[170] Forty percent does not express appropriately the totalizing hold that cotton had over these lives. Many male and female adults working outside mills or in the home at the time of the census had worked as mill hands at some point in the life cycle.[171] Local merchants, accountants, and agents all depended on the health of the cotton trade for their own prosperity. The predominance of Lancashire and Cheshire cotton workers in the Chartist Land Company becomes understandable when one contrasts the standard of living which workers experienced in Manchester towns with their memories and expectations.

Given the pervasiveness of factory organization, the structure of life in the factory towns, down to the movements of their residents, was determined by the needs of the cotton industry. Workers and nonworkers moved through the streets in waves, responding to the demands of the factory.[172] Even the elderly and children, who brought food for the workers or delivered babies to be nursed, were at the beck and call of the factory bell.[173] Throughout the 1840's, factories were still running from 5:30 in the morning until 6 or 7 P.M. or later at night in a schedule which varied with the seasons and the amount of available light.[174] Fines for late arrival were a serious grievance alienating workpeople from their employers.[175] The needs of the operatives for rest and leisure were subjugated in favor of the needs of the machinery and the pressure of filling orders.

Middle-class observers who wrote horrified tracts recounting the living conditions of working people also noticed the contrast between the lush and rolling hills of the English countryside and the sooty dankness of the cotton towns.[176] Over each town the mill chimneys presided, arrogant monuments to industry. Around each mill, row upon row of close brick houses followed the contours of the landscape.[177] Workers in the cotton towns lived in neighborhoods segregated by class and notable for the absence of sanitation, ventilation, and running water.[178] Lyon Playfair's study of sanitary conditions throughout Lancashire condemned all the towns with charges of ambient pollution and insufficient water supplies.[179] Given that it was nearly impossible to drag enough water up to one's rooms to take a decent bath, it was no wonder that middle-class observers described factory operatives as faceless masses who had imbibed the dinginess of their surroundings.[180]

Economic historians have claimed that rational nineteenth-century working people were happy to trade poor surroundings, dirt, and crowding for the prospect of higher wages than might be earned in the countryside. To state such a case is to ignore that workers lacked perfect economic information by which to make such rational decisions. For example, even though in the wake of the general strike the fortunes of the cotton district improved, workers widely believed that the industry had created a long-term decline in the standard of living for the workers, especially weavers.[181] Furthermore, even when factory wages were good, there was no guarantee of their permanence. Every jump and dip in the fortunes of the industry—such as the slump which occurred in 1847—had wide repercussions:[182]

Cotton workers were often forced to accept wage reductions or endure periods of layoffs or working "short time." Their experiences clashed with the popular mythology that at some point in the past, workers had experienced a golden age of short hours and high wages.[183] The poet and handloom weaver William Thom, whose literary work raised him from the edge of literal starvation in the 1840's, remembered that a weaver in 1770 earned 40 shillings for four days' work. The wage was enough to enable him to wear lawn frills, a gilt-buttoned coat, and hair powder, and carry a cane.[184] Prestonians spoke of handloom weavers in the good old days who earned good wages even after playing two or three days a week. In their leisure time, they swaggered about in top boots, baiting badgers, cockfighting, poaching, and drinking.[185] According to local myth, however, as machinery expanded into new sectors of production, formerly proud workers like these would lose jobs. Although the cost of final goods would decline, these workers would not benefit.

The wages-for-environment tradeoff was complicated by the structure of wage payments in the industry. The wages for given tasks were determined on the basis not of effort or skill required, but rather of whether a given task was traditionally male or female.[186] Rare male jobs were defined as skilled jobs; women and children were hired, whenever practicable, at wages kept low on the grounds that they were not the principal breadwinners. Almost no cotton industry worker, male or female, earned a wage which would tide a family over in periods of working short time, illness, or high prices. Only one in seven of all working-class families was permanently free from "primary poverty," and relative poverty was exacerbated by one's stage in the life cycle or by economic depression.[187] Low wages and economic uncertainty were exacerbated by occasional survivals of labor practices of an earlier time, including the company store or "truck system."[188]

The problems which all working residents of textile towns experienced—pollution, lack of drainage, water, and public services, insecure incomes—were redoubled, for those who actually worked in cotton factories, by the physical and mental strains of their accommodation to the machinery. Cotton workers and those who had once worked in cotton understood the meaning of, and were bound together by, endless, repetitive, unchanging toil.[189] For ten hours or more, operatives were deafened by the rhythmic clacking of the shuttle in the loom, suffocated by heat, humidity, and smells, fatigued by endless bouts of standing, walking, staring. No matter what the task at hand, the long hours between breaks would have been rendered less bearable by the repetitiousness of the toil. Opportunities for serious injury, occupational disease, or at the very least fatigue and crushing boredom abounded from the first step of production to the last.[190] While occupational illness was largely ignored in nineteenth-century Britain, spectacular workplace accidents were harder to pretend not to see.[191]

The removal of the work process from the home, and the end of worker control over the time in which the work was done, had spelled the end of variety and autonomy.[192] Demeaning sets of prohibitions also sharply delineated factory labor from the supposedly "independent" labor of the fields.[193] Ashton weavers, led by Chartist Richard Pilling, publicly protested being fined for petty offenses.[194] It is easy to understand how the drawbacks of the factory might overcome the benefits, even in a rational economic calculus.

For Lancashire and Cheshire factory workers, the nearness of the countryside was particularly poignant; and, according to contemporary observers, workers found themselves drawn to nature. Samuel Bamford described the Lancashire cotton towns as dotted with villages, houses, and factories, "presenting an appearance somewhat like that of a vast city scattered amongst meads and pastures, and belts of woodland; over which, at times, volumes of black furnace smoke go trailing their long wreaths on the wind."[195] Surrounded by reminders of the countryside before its corruption, working people may have tried to beat back the stereotypical city by cultivating plants indoors, as among the weaving families at Shaw: "They generally had flowers and green shrubs in the windows, and before the doors were small gardens with flowers and a few pot herbs."[196] Reporter Angus Bethune Reach noted that a great many Manchester operatives were interested in botany: "Every holiday sees hundreds of peaceful wanderers in the woods and fields around, busily engaged in cutting specimens of grasses and flowers."[197]

The most telling evidence of cotton workers' interest in the land in general is the widespread support, throughout Lancashire, for home-grown allotment schemes of various types. One Salford Christian Socialist proposed a Christian Co-operative Joint-Stock Community, "to locate its members on the land, with the view of ensuring to them constant and regular employment, a competent supply of food and raiment, comfortable homes, support in old age, and a certain prospect of provision for their children." He and others planned to lease a plot of land, bring it into cultivation, and use any profits to buy a freehold.[198] Oldham spinners developed their own land scheme, renting a ten-acre field and installing their unemployed workers upon it for 2s 6d a day wages each. Like the Chartist allotments, the little Oldham experiment became a tourist attraction.[199]

Examination of the physical geography and the work experience of residents of the cotton towns illustrates that living and working conditions left much to be desired. In communities noted for their social homogeneity, families often dependent on the cotton industry struggled with the boom-and-bust cycle of poverty and prosperity, and dealt with debt and credit, pollution, crowding, and unreliable water supplies. Those who worked in the cotton industry spent the majority of their waking hours sharing mental and physical strains and the attempted regulation of, and incursions upon, their bodies by the factory system. The few opportunities for entertainment and personal betterment available to operatives in the cotton towns may well have been outweighed by the overcrowding, resentment of working conditions, loss of autonomy and variety, low and unpredictable wages, and aesthetic monotony which middle-class observers described. Furthermore, the serenity of the country was close by, both physically and in terms of the myth of the independent farmer-weaver, the world which cotton operatives felt they had lost. But experience, while powerful, was not the only factor which would push these workers out of the cities. Their experience was mediated by past histories of radicalism—and especially of Chartism—in each of the towns.

Greater Manchester was the site of some of the most sustained and impressive Chartist participation in all of England; and it was participation with standard-of-living concerns, just the kind to make the land plan seem a great opportunity.[200] The factory and Anti–Poor Law campaigns had been hugely popular in the cotton areas—especially Ashton and Stalybridge, which were star speaker Reverend Joseph Rayner Stephens's home localities.[201] O'Connor savvily built upon these campaigns, making his *Northern Star* a central source of information about them before the Charter became a rallying point. The Chartism which grew up in the towns never lost this tinge; the suffrage was commonly spoken of in Lancashire as a means to the end of social and economic betterment rather than as an end in itself.

The character of participation in the land company in each town studied was complicated by other political factors.[202] Some Lancashire towns, like Bolton and Bury, were particular bastions of the Anti–Corn Law League, which could make visibility or access to meeting rooms difficult.[203] Although members of Bolton's middle classes initially supported the Chartists, their support quickly faded in favor of interest in Free Trade. The alienation between Bolton Chartists and middle-class Free Traders was exacerbated by the Chartist strategy of interrupting Anti–Corn Law League meetings, and by Chartist Anti–Free Trade screeds in the local newspapers.[204] Similarly, Bury's grand demonstrations and displays of unity were those of the Anti–Corn Law League rather than the Chartists. Thousands of working people from the local mills and artisans in every trade paraded to celebrate the triumph of Free Trade in 1846—more, in fact, participated than watched.[205] In Rochdale, devotion to Free Trade was similarly fierce.[206] It is reasonable to conclude that the extent of enthusiasm for Free Trade in these towns made the land plan more difficult to pursue.

In other towns, conciliatory labor relations might provide working people with hope that they could be accommodated within the factory system, without making the jarring transition to a life on the land. Thus, while Preston had a strong Chartist presence, it was the town in the district most famed for attempts at reconciliation with factory owners.[207] Gardner's mill became an object lesson in economy for all of Lancashire; its proprietor unilaterally reduced mill hours to see whether dire warnings about the inability of short-hours mills to compete in a global marketplace would prove true. When they proved false, a thousand people celebrated the reduction of hours as a newfound reconciliation between master and man.[208] When visiting Preston to promote the land plan, O'Connor had to combat this trend, telling audiences that such reconciliation was illusory.[209] Thus, the land company prospered in Preston, but may have been held back from its full potential by the spirit of paternalism.

The land company faced a similar obstacle in Rochdale, home of the fledgling consumers' cooperative movement; but the possibility of ameliorating working people's suffering through cooperation was not the only reason why. In Rochdale, as in the Manchester suburb of Salford, municipal politics was professedly democratic. Members of the working class were called upon to ratify many locally made decisions at town meetings, and had their own representatives on local governing boards. Ironically, the most influential of the local working-class representatives was an O'Connorite Chartist, Thomas Livsey. Although Livsey was respectable enough to be elected police and improvement commissioner and, in 1852, chief constable, he was also a shareholder in the National Land Company and reaped local disapproval for encouraging the Rochdale Oddfellows to send £100 to O'Connor's National Land and Labour Bank.[210]

The political background of Lancashire and Cheshire towns could aid as well as hinder the development of the land company. Ashton-under-Lyne and Stalybridge had been flash points of the O'Connorite phase of Chartism, and of the factory and Anti–Poor Law agitation, and this interest naturally extended to the land plan.[211] In Ashton and Stalybridge, the legacy of Joseph Rayner Stephens, local favorite son and advocate of a more equitable distribution of the produce of the land, was appropriated by O'Connor.[212] At one point Stephens had proposed self-sufficient home colonies, supported by spade husbandry, but also with schools, public buildings, churches, libraries, and reading rooms, museums, laboratories, studios, and lecture rooms. Although Stephens might be seen as a rival to O'Connor since he had intended his collective plan as a corrective to small farms, Stephens also fomented general worker interest in the land through his newspaper, the *Ashton Chronicle and Lancashire Advertiser.*[213]

Ashton and Stalybridge had also come to be strongly associated with Feargus O'Connor and physical-force Chartism through their central role in the 1842 general strike.[214] Like the rhetoric of the land scheme, local appeals produced during the turbulent strike period expressed in melodramatic language earnest appeals to a Christian moral economy concerned with material wealth and the juxtaposition of poverty and plenty.[215] In response to this concern with acquiring one's daily bread, the idea "that property belonged in common to all, and all had a right to an equal share" percolated through Ashton meetings in 1842.[216] As a result of their history of political and social action and organization, Ashton factory hands were particularly aware of the disadvantages of a factory life. One Ashton emigrant to America noted that if there was one thing he had come to America to avoid, it was having his sons brought up between a pair of power-looms: "As Hard as my work is or irregular the weather I would not exchange it for a factory Dresser's life."[217] Buoyed by such sentiments, Stalybridge and Ashton remained dynamic centers of Chartism throughout the 1840's, providing their land company meetings with the kind of numbers and enthusiasm which *Northern Star* reporters so enjoyed.[218]

In a small town, the interest which one activist took in the land company might revive the fortunes of Chartism itself. The number of active Chartists in Bacup had declined from 100 around the time of the 1842 General Strike, to 15 by late 1843, as the Anti–Corn Law League's attractiveness grew.[219] A local leader, weaver William Linn Tagg, used his interest in the land company, and the town's strategic situation near a large commons, to resuscitate Bacup Chartism.[220] By June 1845 Bacup had its own branch of the land company, attracting regional leaders who lectured on the land.[221] The Bacup local also held weekly meetings and participated in making land-company policy.[222] In 1848, the branch even resolved to establish a branch bank in connection with the larger Land and Labour Bank.[223] The relationship between the land company and the 1848 revival of Chartism seems particularly clear in Bacup, where William Tagg took the chair at both land-company and more threatening meetings, which coincided with reports of unemployed Bacup men arming and drilling under cover of darkness.[224]

Land-company leaders attempted to overcome the political differences among the towns of the Lancashire and Cheshire cotton district by intensively cultivating the region with national and local lecturers and by playing upon the particular concerns of cotton operatives. Because the Chartist Co-operative Land Company appeared on the scene at a time when many operatives were employed but retained recent memory of severe economic depression, company rhetoric directed at them wisely focused on the relationship between work, wages, and independence on the factory and farm. Other prospective shareholders were no doubt attracted by the energy O'Connor invested in building and promoting strong and (relatively) spacious cottages for the allottees—to the "better sort" of thrifty operatives, the land company could have been viewed as a building society.[225] In any case, for financially strapped workers like Benjamin Wilson's friends, who "although trade was bad . . . cheerfully made great sacrifices to raise the money," the land scheme must have seemed a viable alternative for them to have parted with any of their incomes.[226] Their concentration on Lancashire as a lecturing venue early in the land company's formation encouraged experienced local leaders to reinvigorate an already extant Chartist infrastructure.

Because the main body of the working classes was alienated from mechanics' institutions, meetings addressing working-class concerns—including, in the 1830's and 1840's, Chartist and land-company meetings—were not generally held under the watchful eye of middle-class patrons.[227] Although larger public meetings might be held at town halls or temperance halls depending on the disposition of the local authorities, smaller indoor meetings were held in rented rooms at public houses, which over time would become identified as the "Chartist Rooms" or the "Land Company's Rooms."[228] Such rooms might also be rented or let free to other sympathetic groups, thus defining a space for working-class political activity within an already working-class pale of settlement.[229] Outdoor meetings ranged from "camp meetings" of several thousand people, usually held on some locally famous bit of waste ground, to smaller meetings held on a town dweller's property.

Speaking in these largely class-segregated spaces, lecturers in Lancashire simply did not allow excitement about the land cheme to die down.[230] O'Connor, who had begun to cultivate Lancashire as early as 1841, moved through Lancashire on several propaganda blitzkriegs, visiting a different town each day.[231] Working from set agendas, O'Connor gave long speeches, wearing down his audiences' objections. He addressed a Bolton audience for nearly two hours, giving them an inkling of the capabilities of the land.[232] His blessing for some sort of land project catalyzed Oldham's local organizers into action before a national plan was even contemplated.[233] Rarer than visits by O'Connor were addresses by Ernest Jones, but he made at least one visit to the area in early April 1847.[234]

Regional delegates maintained the excitement which O'Connor had sparked.[235] William Dixon began promoting land reform in Lancashire in 1843, in lectures and addresses expressing the sentiment "the land, the land, the land, is the only hope of our salvation." The following year, he was sent on an intensive mission to enroll Chartists in the National Charter Association, with good results.[236] After representing Lancashire at the 1846 annual convention, Dixon was still circulating through the cotton district in 1847, lecturing to a "crowded and raptly attentive rooms" in Wigan, Manchester, and Bacup. For his unrelenting application to the cause, he was appointed a director of the land company in that year.[237] Similar fortune smiled upon George Candelet, of Hyde, who spoke on the land company in Stalybridge. His tract enticing friendly societies to contribute to the Land and Labour Bank was distributed to the tune of 15,000 copies.[238] For those whose tastes inclined more to the morally reforming, Peter Murray McDouall, the attractive young Chartist doctor from Ramsbottom, near Bury, promoted the land plan in 1847–48.[239] Appealing to local temperance sentiment, he told his audiences that "when employed on the land they would have time to improve their minds, and the body would not be fatigued so as to require artificial stimulants to support it, which was one cause of the intemperance which prevailed."[240]

O'Connor's associates Thomas Clark, Philip McGrath, and Christopher Doyle toured southern Lancashire together, dividing their oratorical labor.[241] McGrath invoked the Charter, telling the assembled how refreshing it was to rcpresent a truly working-class agitation, throwing rhetorical barbs at the Anti–Corn Law League and emigration. "Paddy" Clark, as always playing up his Irishness, followed, enumerating the principles of the land plan, painting it as a just reward for the wealth the working classes had created. He appealed to the historical memory of his audience by describing a supposed conversation with an aged handloom weaver (the apotheosis of workingman displaced by machinery) who was said to have spoken of a time when there was little social distance between men and their masters, when weavers could address masters by their Christian names and look them in the eye. Clark invoked the custom of the weavers to have small allotments of land around their cottages, so that if the price of cuts threatened to get too low, the weaver could take himself out of the market, and cultivate his land until the price rose again. Having whetted the appetites of his hearers, Clark descanted on the capabilities of the soil, estimating a return for labor of £2 a week, which after five months could match the income of a handloom weaver for the entire year.[242]

At these meetings, the land issue was often conflated with the factory question—a phenomenon that may go a long way toward explaining the great rush of cotton-factory workers into the ranks of land-plan subscribers. The plan of William Peel, missionary of the National Association of United Trades, "appeared to be much the same as the land scheme propounded by the chartists," and he dwelt "at some length at the great benefits to be derived by placing those now idle on the land, and thus draining the surplus hands out of the labour market."[243] Preston trades unionist Hartley Holdgate at a union meeting "referred to the anticipated advantages, in elevating the condition of the labouring classes, of the Chartist land scheme—the land being, he considered, the inalienable birthright of the people."[244] The senior and junior Isaac Holts of Bolton, both land-company subscribers, spoke eloquently at an 1845 land-reform meeting in favor of curtailing the "long-hour system." John Dutton, another land-company subscriber, railed against workingmen creeping through the streets, more like shadows than realities. "Was it because they worked too little, were confined too little? No, but quite the reverse. If a child born into the world had a right to live in the world, it ought not to be slowly murdered by the system of long hours. It was said they were too ignorant, let those who said so give

them time, and they would put an extinguisher at once to much of
their ignorance."[245] The support that outspoken men like these gave
the land company was doubtless potent.

Land reform was tied up with union activism among another
group of powerful Lancashire workers—the miners. Like the factory
hands, colliers in the 1840's experienced a large gap between real
wages and working conditions and expectations based on institutional memory. Unlike the factory hands', the colliers' complaints
were compounded by the constant specter of violent death in the
mines.[246] The mid-1840's marked a high point of union activism for
Lancashire miners. The land company came to their attention at
this time because William Prowting Roberts, the "Miners' Attorney
General," served as both legal counsel to the miners' union and
treasurer to the Chartist Co-Operative Land Company.[247] Roberts
spoke of obtaining the land as well as on the benefits of a National
Consolidated Trades Union.[248] He was joined in this by Chartist William Dixon, who spoke on behalf of both the miners' cause and the
land company, and Martin Jude, a union activist who was treasurer
of the Newcastle branch of the land company.[249] Feargus O'Connor
even managed to insinuate a letter on small farms into the normally
apolitical *Miners' Advocate*.[250]

While action by land-company directors played a key role in
piquing interest in the land company in Lancashire and Cheshire,
they were aided by promoters of other land-based schemes who also
operated in the cotton district. David Ross, a Manchester teacher of
rhetoric and elocution, gave penny lectures urging the discontented
not to emigrate, but rather to "stop in their own native country as
every man [h]as a right to have a piece of Land of his own to cultivate so that he could live in peace and quietness and from beneath
the Iron hand of the oppressor."[251] On the ideological Right, Buis-
field Ferrand promoted the enclosure of wastelands and the employment thereon of surplus labor. When he promised every man
happiness, the audience was reported to have erupted in loud
cheers.[252] On the ideological Left, Bronterre O'Brien spent two days
in Rochdale, promoting land nationalization and expressing his disapproval of O'Connor.[253] In the center, former Ashton preacher Joseph Barker, now the republican middle-class editor of the *People*,
spoke at various places in the cotton district.[254] He attacked a property qualification for the vote, censuring primogeniture and entail

in particular.[255] Favoring a single tax on land, Barker was also an energetic and well-informed proponent of emigration to the United States.[256] Furthermore, no matter who in Lancashire was speaking on the land on any particular night, audiences might use post-lecture discussion periods to discuss the benefits of the Chartist Co-Operative Land Company.[257]

The cultivation of pro–land reform sentiment in Lancashire quickly paid off. Once the rules of the Chartist Co-Operative Land Company had been published, local leaders encouraged the formation of branches, intended to enroll members, collect money, and entertain regional lecturers.[258] In Bacup and Salford, local branches of the land company held weekly meetings; in Preston, they were held monthly.[259] In Oldham, a group educational effort on the subject of land reform was molded into a branch of the land company.[260] In Ashton, the excitement was such when the branch first opened that 41 people took out shares in 24 hours.[261] Organization was contagious—discussion of the land plan spread from local branches to union and ten-hours meetings.[262]

Once these branches were set up, local energies flowed in a number of different directions. The localities funded land-plan lecturers, subsidized struggling allottees, collected honoraria for Chartist political widows, made suggestions which appeared in the *Northern Star*, or submitted addresses. The Bolton branch printed 1,500 copies of O'Connor's address on the capabilities of a three-acre farm, and met to discuss some allegations against the land plan which had been printed in the *Manchester Examiner*.[263] The Ashton branch issued a peroration against government oppression and industrial uncertainty, tinged with millenarian yearnings. While workingmen were presently hedging against depression by saving their money in banks which, by buying securities, in turn helped finance government oppression, "hundreds, nay thousands, may be snatched from overcrowded cities, and an overcrowded labour market, to enjoy the free air of heaven, and labour for himself on a free soil where, in the language of scripture, every man may 'Sit under his own vine and fig tree none daring to make him afraid.'"[264] Excitement over the land plan flourished especially through the allotment lotteries, and ran rampant whenever a local resident was chosen as an allottee, providing an excuse for a grand political tea party with speeches and dancing.[265] The excitement continued long after the band stopped playing, as representatives from the cotton district became ambassadors to the new Chartist spaces, the allotments themselves.[266]

The strength of local branches was intimately connected to the degree of involvement local leaders chose.[267] Weaver William Pickvance, secretary of the Bolton branch of the land company, was one of the more active leaders.[268] For Pickvance, involvement with the land company was ideal, since he believed that a positive environment and self-help were both crucial for creating moral individuals.[269] Pickvance illustrates the ingenuity which a single leader could bring to bear. He used local newspapers to spread the good news about the land company, titling one letter to the *Bolton Free Press* "THE LAND! THE LAND!!" after O'Connor's letters in the *Northern Star*. He appealed to Bolton Poor Law Guardians' self-interest, urging them to consider the possible savings should able-bodied paupers be employed on a town farm.[270] Pickvance also sent the *Bolton Times and Lancashire Advertiser* an advertisement for the Land and Labour Bank clothed as an informational article on the land company. It detailed the company's successes and its objects: "to pioneer the way in the glorious work of social emancipation. . . . Its particular aim is the benefit of its members . . . to point out the means of rendering permanently prosperous the condition of the industrious millions."[271] The land company in Bolton in turn spurred interest in Chartism.[272] Bolton Chartists met in their association room to petition the House of Commons for the release of Frost, Williams, and Jones, and passed another petition, with 7,000 signatures, to Ainsworth, their local MP.[273] The popular Pickvance was elected representative to the 1848 Chartist convention by over 3,000 Chartists.[274]

Contrasting with Bolton was Preston, where a feud between local leaders over the land question accelerated a split among the town's Chartists.[275] Richard Marsden, a Chartist stalwart and secretary of the powerloom weavers' union in Preston, supported land nationalization but not O'Connor's plan.[276] Despite Marsden's stellar reputation, the post of secretary of the Preston Chartist association was reserved for powerloom weaver James Brown, an active supporter of the land plan.[277] Marsden's refusal to support O'Connor's land company until 1847 compromised his standing in the regional

Chartist leadership, but he was able to repair the damage once he changed his stance and publicly favored the land company.[278]

The decision to direct one's energies toward support of the land company was complicated. Although the land company was in theory nonpolitical, in practice it was seen as an outgrowth of political Chartism. Thus, local newspapers often opposed the land plan, warning of difficulties between prospective shareholders and employers or other authority figures. "O Worchin Man," a Rochdale pundit, warned in Lancashire dialect:

Oi tel yo heauw aw thynk it is we Fergus—e olis loiks fur to be differunt to uther foke, un wen other hagitaturs takken op we thoose things us ur loikly fur to benefit ther felley kraturs, e starts oppo summut differunt, other is lond scheyme [i.e. his land scheme] ur elze Fraust, Williums un Jones. . . . Waw, Furgus's long scheyme us o moonshoine, so ol hadvyse yo to tak kare o yor brass.[279]

The editor of the same newspaper would later call for a Parliamentary investigation of the land scheme.[280] The *Preston Chronicle* pronounced the land plan "visionary and impracticable" after the first Preston lecture on the subject, and poked fun at its anti-technology bias.[281] The *Preston Guardian* was just as damning, commenting that "the allottees are taught to gamble for their chances, to gamble for their locations, and to gamble for the crops, just as Mr. O'Connor has been gambling against law and parliament for the chance of a lucky throw which would relieve him from the penalties he has incurred, and give him the opportunity of keeping his word to the ear of the poor men whose money he has wasted."[282]

In contrast, worker-friendly politicians like John Fielden supported home colonization. "I like to see the people contented in their native land," said Fielden at his triumphal entry into Oldham in 1847, witnessed by 18,000 people. "I ask you to stay at home, and cultivate your own soil and produce as far as you can, all you want for your comfort and support. . . . We have the means to provide for our own people at home, without passing laws for their transportation, as recommended by the new-fangled political economists."[283] The political economists to whom Fielden alluded would soon catch on to the depth of feeling in favor of the land in Lancashire.

Before the land company fell prey to politically motivated repression, the most serious threat to its success in Lancashire came from rival schemes, including one developed by the Anti–Corn Law League. As Richard Cobden explained when he introduced his scheme in Oldham in 1845, the only way to ensure the dominance of Free Trade principles was to increase the number of really active Free Trade members in Parliament. He proposed that adherents of Free Trade purchase freeholds in order to create new voters who would then favor Free Trade. Cobden knew it was nearly impossible for an operative to save the total amount necessary for such a purchase, but suggested that any operative who could manage to save £15 or £20 could be trusted with a loan for the rest. Although Cobden warned that it would be unjust to influence the votes of these newly made freeholders, since there was no secret ballot, and given the possibility of blacklisting by employers, influence in such a system would have been unavoidable.[284] In contrast with the Chartist land scheme, in the freehold land scheme the vote was the main consideration. The freehold investment might house a cottage, if its purchaser were a small tradesman, or the landowner might sublet the property; but the freeholds were not intended for agricultural use.

Lancashire workers who could afford them snapped up shares in political and nonpolitical land societies alike.[285] By 1846 a Freeholders' Building Society with district branches had been formed in Greater Manchester; more than 2,500 persons, the majority of them operative artisans, mechanics, millwrights, powerloom weavers, and craftsmen, purchased a total of 6,000 shares.[286] Between 1850 and 1855, the Oldham Freehold Land Society purchased 52 acres of land, laid it out in 363 small plots, and built 109 houses there.[287] In Bolton, the Anti–Corn Law League Building Society moved 1,015 shares between January and July 1849; by November, the number of shares taken up had jumped to 12,500.[288]

The intense cultivation of Lancashire by various land societies benefited the Potters' Joint-Stock Emigration Society as well as the Chartist Co-Operative Land Company. By 1849, the Potters' Emigration Society, in need of cash, had opened its membership to non-potting trades, and its directors targeted Lancashire for development. Thomas Twigg, the Emigration Society's estate manager in America, in late 1849 and early 1850 visited six cotton towns, emphasizing the relationship between worker independence and a life on the land.[289] *Potters' Examiner* editor William Evans also spoke in

Ashton, where he benefited from an attention-attracting disagreement with Joseph Barker.[290] Emigration quickly caught on in South Lancashire; local branches of Evans's society were formed and provided the funds which were its lifeblood. Of the £349 7s 7d received between September 11 and December 8, 1849, the cotton districts contributed £82 15s 9d, or about 23 percent of the total. Money flowed in from the "Land of the Free" and "Spinners' Home" branches in Preston, the "New Paradise" branch of Ashton, the Hyde "Poor Man's Refuge" branch, and the "Poor Man's Hope" branch in Dukinfield. Bury had its own branch, the "Hope of Freedom," and Wigan had its "Workman's Refuge" branch. Bolton's "Vulcan" branch contributed, as did Oldham's two branches, the "United Labour," and the "Labour's Refuge" branch, which had already yielded four successful emigrants.[291]

As had the branches of the Chartist Co-Operative Land Company, cotton-district branches of the Potters' Joint-Stock Emigration Society made the land scheme their own, peppering their leaders with influential suggestions.[292] A regional gathering representing Lancashire made statements of policy and studied and rebutted local opposing public opinion.[293] Great rejoicing reigned when families received news of their Lancashire emigrants.[294] William Scholes, an emigrant Oldham cotton worker, wrote from America to deny reports that the colonists had nothing to eat and that their land was bad. John Goulding, another emigrant from Oldham, informed his wife back in England that he never intended to return to the old country. "A person should not come here without consideration," he reflected. "We have no towns, no fairs, no places of amusement,—a person must give up all these when he comes here." But he also warned that "factory life in America is little better than factory life in England. The American farmer is the most independent man in the world, and to emigrate from the factory in England to the factory in America, is not worth while." William Evans set these two emigrants' letters in pamphlet form for circulation in the cotton district, and boasted he had sold 500 at a halfpenny apiece because the men in question were so well known in Oldham.[295]

The popularity of the Potters' Emigration Society and of other building and freehold land societies testifies to the power of land in the public imagination in Lancashire. Yet for the Chartist Land Plan members, the connection between the Charter and the land was still central.[296] In Lancashire, the role of the land plan as a continuation of O'Connorite Chartism is clear, especially if one considers the symbolism of the two movements rather than looking for continuity of leadership alone. "The Charter and the Land" were often bandied about together, although which was to bring about which was never clear. Land-plan activity in the cotton district was kept at a high pitch by the activities of acknowledged Chartist luminaries, and those who were repulsed by Chartist principles could not have been expected to support a Chartist organization with their hard-earned wages. While for some subscribers the connection with Chartism may have been tenuous, and the land company viewed it as an inexpensive and possibly lucrative investment, it was an investment which presupposed some political commitment. As investigation of the Lancashire lecture circuit has illustrated, the Chartist Land Company was not the only possible land-investment choice for working people—but it was the most controversial choice.

The most powerful evidence which supports the assertion that the land company was a phase of the Chartist movement is the ease with which Chartists were able to return to their petitioning activities in 1848. The resurgence of older forms of Chartist activity—memorializing, demonstrating, petitioning—was facilitated by the organizational structures for radicalism which the land company had maintained in place.[297] Active participants in the land company were mainstays of the physical-force Chartism which swept through Lancashire in 1848.[298] As Manchester swore in special constables, thousands of Chartists listened to inflammatory speeches. The numbers of Chartists meeting during this time swelled from a few hundred to many thousands, and meetings were presided over by local Chartist chieftains who had been land-plan organizers or promoters months before—Richard Pilling, Richard Marsden, and, of course, O'Connor.[299]

Reports of insurgency in Lancashire and Cheshire reached to the government. Home Office informants reported that a national guard of several thousand was meeting in Ashton-under-Lyne.[300] In Oldham, Chartists seeking to found a national guard openly advertised their intention, and their recruiting poster found its way to the Home Office. The mayor of Wigan begged Lord Grey not to move the military from his town, and Bolton police sergeant Martin Finnegan reported that Chartists there were marching in military file.[301]

Even in Bacup, it was reported that 2,000 unemployed operatives were meeting at night and drilling.[302] Subscribers to the land company were involved in this new and more violent agitation.[303] Finally, after many months of fears about arming, minor scuffles, and the shooting of a constable during a riot in Ashton, the government arrested 46 Chartist leaders, Ernest Jones among them.[304]

Physical-force Chartism owed its resurgence to an infrastructure which the land company had kept alive. Just as the land company had earlier benefited from the loyalties to O'Connor held by the physical-force Chartists of 1839 and 1842, so Chartism could rise again because the names of land-company leaders, and the connection between the Charter and the land, had been continually bandied about in the cotton district. Thus, as they had been some of the first to sign on for the land company, so Lancashire operatives were some of the last to desert the idea, cemented to it as they were by admiration for O'Connor.[305] Especially where localities' Chartist leaders were not split over the questions of conciliation with the middle-class reformers or with the Anti–Corn Law League, workers made connections between the factory and Anti–Poor Law movements and the land plan's promises to address economic instability and inequity.

In the towns of the cotton district, O'Connor and his cronies saw and responded to operatives' fears of long hours, overcrowding, environmental degradation, and the failure of most municipal governments to represent their interests. The Chartist Co-Operative Land Company, presented in Lancashire again and again by numerous speakers, condemned the factory, appealed to a desire for independence and for a living wage, and rested on a Christian moral economy which contradicted the harshness of a burgeoning science of political economy. Although speakers never pretended successful implementation would mean the end of industry, they played upon the perceptible nostalgia for a time when the handloom weaver, ancestor of these industrializing workers, had supposedly worked a plot of land to make ends meet. The Chartists—with the help of many other social schemers who looked to the land—were successful in creating and nurturing a land hunger in Lancashire which was able to sustain several types of land movement, not all of which were political. Yet even where local political contexts were unfriendly to the continuation of Chartism in the mid-1840's, in almost every town several hundred workers, even in the midst of what must have been a weekly financial shortfall, dedicated some of their earnings to the purchase of a share in the Chartist Co-Operative Land Company. Especially for workers in cotton—whose everyday lives conformed with the nightmare of factory production which could elicit transatlantic fears—the land plan could not have seemed more tailored to their needs.

Examination of the composition of the British and American land-reform movements reveals a central difference between their memberships which is invisible when only discourse and leadership are the objects of study. In the cotton districts of Lancashire and Cheshire, promoters of the Chartist Co-Operative Land Company appealed to a constituency already attracted to the idea of allotments of land. Exerting constant pressure through lecture tours, these promoters promised direct economic amelioration, reaching out to a great number of less well-off workers who lived in crowded and unhealthy conditions in clearly industrial areas. The response they received was overwhelming—not only did hundreds of operatives in each town respond, but the land company helped to revitalize the organizational equipment of Chartism in the localities, making possible a renewed mass movement in 1848.

In contrast, National Reform leaders encouraged petitioning for economic amelioration, thus mixing new industrial and older radical metaphors of protest. The republican message resonated, not only among the workingmen of New York City, but also among the Fourierite Associationists of Wisconsin and western Virginia, the factory workers of Lowell, the metal forgers of Worcester, the shoemakers of Lynn, and the farmers of rural Massachusetts. The British government looked at the membership of the Chartist Land Company and saw uprisings, general strikes and the hungry eyes and the bent backs of a thousand cotton operatives. At the same time, observers of National Reform saw a constituency so respectable, and so seemingly representative of America, that its requests to save the Republic through land reform could hardly be denied. As the chapter which follows will illustrate, these differences in the movements' social compositions, and the way in which they were perceived, would have repercussions for their disposition, as each encountered authority in a way which would determine its success or failure.

7

The Land Plans, Politics, and the Press

Were the name of Chartism altered to some other ism, still preserving however the principles whole and entire, how many thousands
of persons would exclaim, "Ah, this is indeed a glorious system! I
shall give my instantaneous adhesion to it." . . . Those who have
been taught by influential friends, by habit, by the press, and by constant outpourings of aristocratic and middle class virulence to look
upon Chartism as a monstrosity and its adherents as brigands, would
rush to array themselves under the standard of the same doctrine
with another name.
                                              —*Reynolds' Political Instructor*[1]

Resolved, That the land monopoly is at the foundation of the state
of things, and that it is the duty of the State, which is but another
name for the people, to adopt the policy of land limitation . . .
                                              —1851 Industrial Congress[2]

In the case of American and British land reform, as I have
tried to demonstrate, the ideologies developed were similar
on both sides of the Atlantic, having come from a common store-
house of ideas; and organizational structures mirrored each other,
having evolved through a process of transatlantic communication.
Thus it is (at least in part) to the state and other institutional structures that the historian must look for an answer to the question of
why in the end the paths of American and British working-class
land reform diverged.[3] This chapter discusses the way in which political contexts, and oppositional public opinion managed by the
middle-class press, influenced the course of radicalism. In Britain,
an increasingly centralized and autonomous state was able to justify
direct intervention into the working-class land-reform movement
through a Select Committee investigation. Because working people
were not considered to be free agents, the government had to protect

their interests. In the United States, a weaker federal government acknowledged workers as citizens rather than subjects (at least when it came to politics, if not the law). Land reformers, by forming voluntary associations to influence public and political opinion, were simply following a venerable American tradition. Furthermore, while British authorities perceived the land company as a threat because of the checkered history of Chartism and O'Connor's recent political rabble-rousing, leaders of the American land-reform movement dispelled possible threatening aspects by distancing themselves from "agrarianism" and forging links with middle-class legislators and publicists who would carry their cause to the highest levels of government.

In their reception of and reaction to the land-reform movements, the press and government in Britain and the United States were reacting in part to the popular composition of the movements. In the United States, overwhelmingly "respectable" workers—whose inclusion in the political process was vital to the myth of democracy—approached the question of land reform through what were seen to be the proper channels. The very praise of the sanctity of "contract" and the doctrine of the assumption of risk which made the industrial workplace so dangerous in the 1840's invested workers with the notion that they were free agents and independent political actors.[4] Empowered by the right to vote, their position in law, and the theory that the government should respond to the exercise of their collective will, they promoted their own vision of the state, as a machine which might be driven by the people to secure citizens' pursuit of happiness as well as their personal freedom. In contrast with the British case, for the Americans, the public sector was the logical place to pursue social happiness—not only because the government did own public lands which could be opened up to the workers, but also because producers saw the "freedom" of the public lands as something which they could reasonably demand.[5]

Although their view of government's potential to effect economic and social change clashed with both the reigning vision of government's responsibility and the real distribution of power, the "respectable" American proponents of land reform were able to find legislative friends to advocate their cause—the battle over the responsibilities of government had not yet been lost to the "liberals." As one-issue politicians, the National Reformers anticipated the post-1850 breakdown of the second-party system, and provided a bridge to a new political system. Their program to populate the West with free laboring men cohered well with the ideology of the fledgling Republican Party; conflating free land with Free Soil suggested a practical way to combat the Slave Power. Furthermore, the land reformers' sense of urgency about using land reform to save the Republic cohered with the political alarmism of the time.[6]

In contrast with the participatory, federal, United States, England was undergoing a staggering centralization of governmental administration, and it was this government, in a tremendous position of power vis-à-vis the unrepresented Chartists, which brought all its force to bear upon the land plan.[7] Impelled by the press, a legislature bolstered by the triumph of Free Trade worked to create the same stability domestically which Free Trade aimed to create in the world system. In contrast, the Chartist Land Company represented an "irrational" leap sideways toward a society of peasant smallholdings, achieved through a significant exercise of workers' combined power: Thomas Martin Wheeler captured the weightiness of the issues involved when he called the company "the grand palladium which was to ensure the future prosperity of England, combated by the whole press of the empire, defying the government." And yet, hinging on O'Connor's personal sway as it did, the land company was a symbol of power out of control, of the irrational demagoguery of an earlier age.[8] While O'Connor in Parliament in 1848 made treasonous suggestions about the union with Ireland, France convulsed in revolution, and the Chartists mustered signatures for their third petition and secretly drilled in Lancashire. These events lay outside the purview of the state, but the Chartist Land Company, which had raised so many working people's hopes, did not. And so, rather than allow the company to die a lingering death by financial mismanagement, a Select Committee intervened against the company, in such a way as to destroy it and leave no doubt about the need for paternalistic protection of the British working people.

LAND REFORM AND THE MAINSTREAM PRESS

In both Britain and the United States, the land-reform movements encountered powerful allies and enemies in the mainstream press. Newspapers in the early nineteenth century could build up a movement or bring it down by controversy. Within each state or city, the press might choose to dignify land reformers with a mention—and even a critical mention could stir interest—or ignore them entirely. George Henry Evans understood this when he asked, "How happens it that, while [the newspapers] tell us all about Victoria and her brats, they tell us nothing about the landless Chartists, who, within the last year or two, have raised a fund of £70,000, and are now collecting from five to ten dollars a week, to buy back bits of the soil of which they have been robbed in order that they may get votes to recover the remainder?"[9]

The Chartist Land Plan came under heavy, and in the long run harmful, press fire because it faced off against the Anti–Corn Law League, a lobbying contingent of considerable organization and financing. The stage had been set for enmity between the two groups since the early 1840's, when the Chartists began to interrupt league meetings to pass Chartist resolutions. The press crusade against the land company was carried out by the Free Trade journalist Alexander Somerville, also known as "One Who Has Whistled at the Plough." While he was far enough removed from the leadership of the Anti–Corn Law League to prevent rumormongering and scandal, his political proclivities were known. Since 1842, Somerville had traveled to agricultural areas, reporting on the penalties the Corn Laws exacted from laborers. He traveled wholly among the poorest, "feeling by anticipation how the narrative of what they said was to move readers, perhaps to tears."[10]

Alexander Somerville alleged in a tract written in the 1850's that the leaders of the Anti–Corn Law League had funded press attacks on Chartist Co-Operative Land Company. Because this tract is in part a polemic against Anti–Corn Law League leader Richard Cobden, it cannot be considered a completely reliable source; Somerville's anger may have led him generally to exaggerate Cobden's faults.[11] Yet Somerville had no conceivable reason to blame Cobden and co-leader John Bright for the demise of the land company had they not in fact had a part in it. By making such an accusation, Somerville was, after all, identifying Cobden as the whistle-blower on a scheme which was, by 1850, thoroughly unpopular; having killed the land company was more likely to endear Cobden to the general public than alienate him from it. Somerville claimed that Cobden was embarrassed to hear that O'Connor had praised him in the *Northern Star*—any hint of a connection between himself and the Irish demagogue made him furious. He "urged me to proceed in my exposure of O'Connor's scheme. It was then that expenses were spoken of, when several persons present said they would take care to stand between me and loss as to expenses. In private, Mr. Cobden spoke more virulently against Mr. O'Connor than any man whom I have ever heard utter his name."[12] In an 1849 letter to fellow Free Trader John Bright, Cobden suggested that a history of Chartism, "with a temperate but truthful narrative of the doings of its leaders," might help to counteract any attempted revival of the Chartist movement. "A series of letters or articles in the *Examiner*, to be afterwards printed in a volume . . . would be certain to elicit a howl from the knaves who were subjected to the ordeal of the pillory and this would be useful in attracting attention to the book."[13]

On the basis of this evidence, one may fairly conclude that Somerville was in the pay of the Anti–Corn Law League when he began his journalistic exposé of the land company. He made several visits to O'Connorville in 1846, visited the Land Office in London, and perused the land company's documents on file at the Joint-Stock Company registration office. His almost unprecedented investigative journalism culminated in a series of damning articles in the *Manchester Examiner*, and then the collation of a digest of the letters which Somerville sent to members of Parliament, newspapers, trade societies, and branches of the land company. Somerville incurred £10 of debt, and was later imprisoned, for his pains.[14]

Published in the *Manchester Examiner* in December 1846, Somerville's criticisms of the land company were craftily integrated into the newspaper's regular offerings and made to seem more innocent than they really were.[15] Although pretending to be letters from a disinterested reader, Somerville's interventions were prominently titled and situated above the fold of the page, and the columns of text were spaced wider apart than were surrounding articles, to render his the most eye-catching item on two facing pages. His early letters drew in the simply curious by inviting the reader along on a purely descriptive visit to an aesthetically pleasing Chartist colony at Herringsgate. He described an imposing school building and a series of three-room cottages, noting that "it is hardly possible to conceive anything more pretty than these houses, seen in perspective from the school on the gentle height overlooking them, unless it be the view upward, with the school buildings in the high distance. But apart from the prettiness of the perspective, each erection is in itself tasteful."[16]

Having laid his trap for the naive, in each succeeding letter, Somerville portrayed himself as progressively disillusioned with the Chartist experiment. He found a young man who volunteered to accompany him around the Herringsgate estate, and soon Somerville was seeing potential problems everywhere. The young man told him the cottages' window sashes had been made from wood cut on the estate, which made him think it must be green and unfit for use. He saw some carpenters and plasterers, who were being paid with land-plan money, idling in the schoolhouse because the rest of their compatriots were down at the pub. Somerville visited one house occupied by a handloom weaver, who refused to be drawn into conversation because he was weaving—clearly not the right occupation when a whole farm lay beyond the threshold to be tilled. The weaver's wife was very lonely, and sold him a handkerchief for 10d—signifying that the supposed economic independence of the farming lifestyle did not prevent her from having to pawn her possessions. The weaver's wife also wished other people would move in, as it was very dark and isolated and they feared setting forth from their plot in the dark. Somerville noticed that the wells that had been sunk on the estate yielded little water, and worried about the expenses of irrigation. The evolution of Somerville's perspective from optimist to pessimist based on firsthand knowledge and observation established his bona fides and allowed him to broach the subject of the legal problems of the land scheme with greater credibility.[17]

Having taken the position that the land plan was a pyramid scheme to bilk the working classes, Somerville worked like a man possessed to discredit it. He described an unannounced visit to the offices of the company; when he demanded to see its publications, he was told that only the rules and one balance sheet were available for perusal. The signed balance sheet he was shown falsely claimed that the company was under the protection of the Joint-Stock Companies Act (the company was still only provisionally registered). Like a Chadwick investigating the Poor Laws, Somerville gathered together every relevant paper he could find, sat down and read them all, and came to his own conclusion—that the company was unsound as a business speculation.[18]

In article after article, Somerville exploited the fears for their savings of people unacquainted with the law. He claimed that every shareholder of the company was liable to be prosecuted not only for the penalties incurred by the directors and agents, but also for the company's debts. He likened the company to other friendly societies which had recently been brought up before magistrates for fraud. His scathing prose mocked O'Connor's promises:

A pretty prospect for O'Connorville, in the county of Hertford. It is quite enough that the genius of 'Feargus O'Connor. Esq., barrister-at-law,' is to provide each family of prizeholders at O'Connorville out of the sum of *fifteen pounds*, from February first to harvest first, with a 'Happy home,' bread, meat, butter, cheese, sugar, tea and trimmings; spades, rakes, hoes, forks, dibbles, lines, baskets, plants, seed wheat, seed of every kind, barn, cowhouse, pigstye, yard, fowlhouse, cesspool, cistern, four young cows, six pigs, fowls and *water*; quite enough that this marvellous barrister-at-law has all this to do without having to provide for all those pains and penalties which he has brought upon his dupes.[19]

Somerville occasionally descended to ad hominem assassination. Judging the merits of O'Connor's *Small Farms*, he wrote, "I am amazed that, with a pen to write and as much mechanical sense as enables him to handle it, there should be a blockhead that could have conceived and written the incoherent nonsense that is in this book, and that there should be any men so intellectually blind as to believe and follow it and him with their money."[20] But the substance of his criticism was philosophical. A subscriber to liberal political economy, Somerville believed in the inviolability of private property, the right of every man to work where, when, and for whom he chose to work, and the right of every employer to employ what men he chose; these were all corollaries of Free Trade. The land company's precept of mutual aid and its heavy overtones of paternalism did conflict with this liberal vision, and Somerville fastened on this conflict.

Somerville's criticisms of the land scheme continued into the autumn of 1847, when O'Connor finally challenged him to defend his views in public debate.[21] While Somerville evaded the challenge, Joshua Hobson, former editor of O'Connor's *Northern Star*, now also publishing negative letters about the land scheme in the *Examiner*, challenged O'Connor to "a fair fight."[22] Hobson, who had his own pedigree as a long-standing friend of the people, feared that workers were letting themselves down by bowing to the dictation of one man rather than exercising independent judgment.[23]

The charges made against the land plan in the mainstream press prompted O'Connor to respond in a public forum, making use of his charisma and oratorical power. The crowds at the Hall of Science in Manchester on October 23, 1847, were such that the reporter for the *Examiner* had to be hauled into the hall through an upstairs window, while Peter McDouall stuck his head out another window to lecture to several thousand people who had been crowded out. In a four-hour speech, O'Connor fulminated against the press and against the editors of the *Examiner*, Ballantyne and Ireland, for having hired Somerville. He was, however, careful to distance himself from Richard Cobden, about whom he said—perhaps desperately trying to make peace—that he would never say another unkind word.[24]

While the speech must have satiated O'Connor's devotees, the combination of Somerville's sustained criticism with O'Connor's indirect defense was beginning to have some impact on the company's cash flow. Friendly societies which had seen the Land and Labour Bank as a good investment now withdrew their funds.[25] Land-company director Philip McGrath bravely claimed that negative articles in the *Manchester Examiner* and some London journals had done nothing but evoke a vote of confidence in O'Connor.[26] Working people knew that the mainstream press was never on their side, and the stir Somerville created might have died down, or percolated only among the mill owners and Manchester middle classes, had not O'Connor exacerbated the situation by printing extracts from Somerville's attacks in the *Northern Star* in order to refute them.[27] Although Somerville's muckraking letters had ceased, Hobson's continued, and the *Examiner* was also inundated with letters from readers who castigated O'Connor and railed at the foolishness of the land plan.

Alexander Somerville was not the only investigative journalist who visited the Chartist allotments and threw doubt on the future of the land scheme; other newspapers objected to the scheme for its Irish associations. The *Gloucester Journal* warned of the introduction of "Hibernian" ways of life into the formerly pristine countryside. Its editor claimed that O'Connor's cottages, shoddily built, would not last 20 years. Their floors, level with or below the outside soil, would be damp in winter; their slated roofs would suffocate in summer. The plots of land which accompanied them would prove too small to keep cows properly, much less families. "If as appears not improbable, in a few years the occupants should fall behind in their rent, and 'the company' should resort to dispossession and the location of new tenants on a large scale, we are afraid the wild vengeance of Chartist Englishmen would not be more scrupulous than that of Whiteboy Irishmen." A correspondent in the same issue extended the metaphor, calling Lowbands a "model Tipperary" for its small one-story cottages and spade husbandry. The *Journal* concluded that the land scheme was a social retrogression rather than a social advance.[28] Local newspapers added fuel to the fire, preventing reconciliation between middle-class and working reformers with claims that the success of Free Trade had hammered a nail into the coffin of the Chartist land scheme.[29]

Just as damaging as the clearly antagonistic attacks of the mainstream press were attacks on O'Connor's plan from other Chartists who, while sympathetic to the idea of social amelioration, found flaws in the machinery of the land plan. Bronterre O'Brien not only detailed his opposition to the land plan in his own *National Reformer*, but also called readers' attention to Somerville's attacks.[30] The *Poor Man's Guardian and Repealer's Friend* borrowed O'Connor's principles but mocked his methods:

As for the working classes buying the land with accumulated pence, or club-money, it is too ridiculous a project to occur to anybody not a rogue or a fool. The purchasing of a few acres in that way for the purpose of experiment might be practicable enough. . . . But supposing such a thing possible on a large scale, or as to leading the working classes to expect a termination of their sufferings through a process of that sort, we most sincerely pity the unfortunate dupes who can put faith in such delusions; and we as cordially detest the heartless knaves who, knowing better can cold-bloodedly trifle with honest men's feelings and resources, for such a purpose.

The editor of the *Poor Man's Guardian* suggested running up a million pounds of national debt in order to secure wasteland for working people to cultivate—not necessarily a more practical plan than O'Connor's scheme, but potentially a more popular one.[31]

Lloyd's Weekly London News was scathing, printing "The Last Word on Land Societies" on its front page. Its editors noted that if any of the paper's readers wished to avail himself of a chance to win an allotment, he would be provided with an illustrated ticket, "on which he may see rural felicity delineated; and, if he never obtain a

cottage for his money, he may make sure of the picture of one . . .
there stand at the door Hodge and Mary, in hose and doublet of lin-
sey-woolsey, mockingly seeming to say, 'Don't you wish you may
get it?'" The newspaper portrayed both O'Brien and O'Connor as de-
luded Irishmen, presumptuous for thinking they could address the
problems of the English, and belittled the idea that the land plan accomplished anything toward the emancipation of the working
classes.[32] "In what way can the 'social emancipation' of the people
be promoted? In drawing lots for £30 cottages, and hiring them at
rack-rents, *for ever*, from grinding capitalists?"[33]

Although the critics of the land plan seemed to outnumber—if
not outtalk—its proponents, O'Connor's side of the slate was not
completely blank.[34] Besides the positive press attention granted the
land company by the American National Reformers, O'Connor's
group attracted the attention of Friedrich Engels. In an article which
was translated and reprinted in the *Northern Star*, Engels attributed
the attacks on the land company to bourgeois nervousness, precipitated by the fact that O'Connor's scheme threatened to make the
workers more independent than they had ever been. Engels sympa-
thized with O'Connor's battle against the slanderous middle-class
press: "Imperturbable amidst all these attacks, the indefatigable patriot continues his work, and the unanimous confidence of the English people is the best proof of his courage, his energy and his incor-
ruptibility." Although this was high praise indeed, it was short-
lived; within three years Marx and Engels were calling the land
company a distraction from the real working-class land-reform
measure—nationalization and rental of land, as proposed by
Bronterre O'Brien.[35]

Some newspapers also supported the land scheme. *Jerrold's
Weekly Newspaper*, aimed at a mainstream market, expressed opinions on the land broadly similar to O'Connor's.[36] The *Spirit of the
Age*, a newspaper promoting communal societies, at first denied
that O'Connor carried any financial blame for the land company's
problems, and accused middle-class newspapers of using the land
plan as a vehicle for gross personal attacks.[37] Over time, however,
even its editors became more critical, on the grounds that the
scheme was "a most lamentable running to seed of individualism
and isolation, with no advantage but wholesome air; and that even
has the drawback of creating an appetite, where the means of sup-

plying it are exceedingly limited."[38] A member of the land company who had not drawn an allotment in the lottery wrote to *Reynolds' Political Instructor*, denying that O'Connor had made extravagant claims: "If I remember rightly, Mr. O'Connor's letters were not particularly poetical, but rather prosaic and filled with statistic about peas, potatoes, manure and cattle."[39]

The newspaper of the Oddfellows—another notable vehicle for working-class mutual assistance—also supported land-company principles.[40] Its editor, swayed by favorable demonstrations of spade husbandry, suggested a farm of 500 acres should be divided into allotments from 2 to 8 acres each, and each allotment provided with a clean cottage, according to the size of each family. Home colonies might be financed by groups of workers, by building societies, joint-stock companies, benevolent societies, or even a single capitalist.[41] Like Feargus O'Connor's plan, the Oddfellows' proposed experiment rejected any community of property: "That theory has been tried, and it has failed. . . . it was only an utter ignorance of one of the first principles of the human mind, that should have prompted any man to make the experiment."[42]

From its zenith in 1847 to its demise from 1848 onward, the Chartist Co-Operative/National Land Company was at the center of a great whirl of discussion by the press, little of which was favorable. Funded by middle-class Free Traders, Alexander Somerville helped to draw public attention to the shortcomings of the land company, and impelled other editors to investigate the popular scheme. O'Connor's method of rebutting the charges helped to sow doubt among people who may not have had access to the *Manchester Examiner*. In contrast, the supporters of the land company made their arguments from the pages of the working-class press. Thus, O'Connor's enemies in government, who were spoiling for a way to get to him, saw only the attack, not the defense.

It was the Chartists, and O'Connor in particular, rather than the idea of providing a safety valve to the land for workers, who were so distasteful to the middle classes. The negative impact of the press on the Chartist Co-Operative/National Land Company is clear when contrasted with the experiences of the Potters' Joint-Stock Emigration Society. Although the *Manchester Examiner and Times* did discuss the potters' society, printing letters from both satisfied and dissatisfied Wisconsin colonists, the scheme was spared a press onslaught.[43] The communitarian *Spirit of the Times* criticized the potters' scheme for failure to hew to cooperative principles, but also for its poor odds, estimating that the chances of procuring passage and a farm in Wisconsin lay 50 to 1 against the drawer in any lottery.[44] Yorkshire radical Joseph Barker also attacked the scheme.

When letters of complaint about the potters' scheme did surface, William Evans was almost as bombastically indignant as O'Connor. He poked fun at the emigrants, claiming that they, who had been the aristocrats of labor, simply felt "disgusted at the rough log cabins, and the days of hard, persevering toil to make those cabins into independent landed homes. They ... rush back to some large city, full of the most dreadful tales of Indian lands, log pigsties, and big rough men that want shaving!"[45] Nonetheless, because press attention to the potters' scheme was very limited, and perhaps because Feargus O'Connor was the potters' main opponent, the potters' scheme did not elicit government opposition. As Evans triumphantly pointed out later, while his scheme achieved less notoriety than the Chartist Land Company, the potters had been able to snap up a great deal of land and support a printing establishment, all for under £6,000, and to do it legally besides.[46]

The National Reformers fared better than either the land-plan Chartists or the Potters' Society in their relationship to the press, and this in turn was a key factor in maintaining a good relationship with state and federal legislatures. Horace Greeley's conversion to the cause of land reform was particularly significant. Although George Henry Evans, Thomas Devyr, and other workingmen prepared the ground for National Reform, Horace Greeley, politician and editor of the *New York Tribune*, received much of the credit for popularizing the homestead idea. He adopted a reform which in its original incarnation was aimed at wage workers, removed some of the more controversial aspects, and recast it as part of a destined westward movement.[47] Coming to National Reform through an interested in Fourierite Associationism, Greeley evolved to a position of sympathy with labor.[48] He saw in the West a healthier sphere for the city operatives whose plight he chronicled weekly in his newspaper.[49] At first Greeley was not prepared to give wholesale support to the plan, since it threatened to shortchange the older states by giving away any title they might claim to proceeds from the public lands, but by November 1845 he characterized the plan as "deserving of the most candid and earnest consideration."[50]

Between 1845 and 1848, Greeley was an avowed friend of land reform—at least in public—writing and speaking on the issue at venues which transcended class boundaries, and even introducing a homestead bill into Congress (where it was promptly tabled).[51] "National Reform is the broad and sure basis whereon all other Reforms may be safely erected," he wrote in George Lippard's journal *Nineteenth Century.* "A single law of Congress, proffering to each landless citizen a patch of the Public Domain—small but sufficient, when faithfully cultivated, for the sustenance of his family, and forbidding further sales of the Public lands except in limited quantities, would promote immensely the independence, enlightenment, morality, industry and comfort of our entire laboring population evermore."[52] Greeley thought the homestead idea progressive, inasmuch as it promised to elevate the masses, both morally and economically.

Working-class land reformers gladly accepted Greeley's support until it ebbed in the early 1850's in favor of other reforms.[53] Yet this support was double-edged: influential because Greeley was unmistakably middle-class, but also interested, because Greeley was foremost a Whig politician, whose private views toward the working class were less charitable than those he presented in public.[54] Greeley may not even have voted for the land-reform candidate in 1848.[55] Nonetheless, although the contradictions in Greeley's personality and career were evident to National Reformers at the time, most of them were happy to accept his assistance.[56]

The National Reformers also benefited from having few enemies. Rather than revile the National Reformers, as mainstream British newspapers would revile the Chartists, mainstream American newspapers at first ignored Evans and his colleagues. Ever the optimist, Evans was cheered: "The present silence of the Commercial Press and of those above it in the social hierarchy only proves that the idea is yet novel. . . . within twenty years of agitating the subject, three fourths of the States composing this Union will have secured the home of every family against legal confiscation for debts of its owner."[57] A few newspapers publicly switched sides. After Thomas Devyr lost editorial control of the *Albany Freeholder* in 1845 and began editing a rival newspaper, the editor of the *Free-*

holder at first cast the National Reform movement as a foreign import, advocated by frustrated Chartists.[58] After a few attempts at an exposé of National Reform, including the claim that the National Reformers numbered fewer than a thousand members, and that those were limited to New York, the editor of the *Freeholder* finally gave his qualified support to National Reform measures. He would be in good company; National Reform measures were rapidly taken up by a number of far-flung newspapers.[59] Even in the West, where clogged labor markets were as yet unknown, editors supported National Reform. Thus, O. F. Macmillan, editor and publisher of the Illinois *Chester Reveille*, supported homestead exemption in his newspaper, used National Reform's man-atop-the-world icon, and made National Reform tracts available for circulation throughout the West, even though Chester at this time was particularly hungry for able workmen.[60]

In both Britain and the United States, the attitude that the mainstream press took toward each land-reforming group helped influence the government. In the United States, relative freedom from press criticism, combined with the adoption of their cause by a wide variety of labor and reforming sheets, insulated National Reformers from charges of being a geographically limited, ideologically extreme, or disreputable, foreign-influenced group. National Reformers were clearly no Jacobins, such as the American government might have suppressed in the 1790's, but rather were a voluntary association among a plethora of other associations seeking the betterment of American society. On the British side, however, the relationship between disapproval of working-class efforts and government intervention was clear. In the case of the Potters' Joint-Stock Emigration Society, press comment was limited, and raised no alarm bells in Whitehall. In contrast, unfortunately for O'Connor's group, sustained criticism in the mainstream press, compounded by the Chartists' history of controversial radicalism, had made the Chartist Land Company much more visible—visible enough to fall into the tentacles of an increasingly activist government.

LAND REFORM AND THE BRITISH GOVERNMENT

Land-reforming Chartists knew in advance that they could expect little sympathy from their government. In 1847 Thomas Frost predicted, "In vain shall we look to Parliament to take up the Land

Plan, until that Parliament is composed of the people's representatives, fairly and truly chosen by the people. . . . The working classes must achieve their own salvation, rely only upon themselves, and success will attend their noble endeavors."[61] Although O'Connor had at first considered his land company to be an experiment which the government might fruitfully take up and fund, in practice it relied on working-class cooperation and mutuality and tried to give the state a wide berth.[62] Nonetheless, there were certain legal formalities which had to be observed. At first, the company attempted legal registration of the company as a friendly society. When the Registrar of Friendly Societies, Tidd Pratt, ruled that it could never be accommodated within the rules of friendly societies, the directors attempted to register it as a joint-stock company. Registration as a joint-stock company was much more expensive and complicated, because of the need for collection of signatures from and information about tens of thousands of shareholders, and the procurement of costly stamps for every page of the company deed.

Eileen Yeo has noted that the rules and regulations surrounding joint-stock company registration constructed legal barriers to any large, democratic organization seeking to make use of working-class funds; but as the example of the Potters' Joint-Stock Emigration Society illustrates, the government did not always choose to enforce these legal barriers.[63] I would argue that the government enforced them in the case of the Chartist Co-Operative Land Company because Feargus O'Connor, then sitting in Parliament, was a high-profile troublemaker. O'Connor looked upon Parliament as a gentleman's game; and while he thought he knew the rules, he constantly exceeded the bounds of tolerance. Most egregiously, in addition to transacting his Chartist business, O'Connor (who had, after all, first entered Parliament on the coattails of Daniel O'Connell) used his Parliamentary seat to announce his unpopular opinions on the union with Ireland.

O'Connor's attack on the union was sustained and, at times, flouted Parliamentary proprieties. On December 7, 1847, he moved that a committee be appointed to inquire into the means by which the Anglo-Irish union had been effected, and into its results: it was defeated by 255 votes to 23.[64] In July 1848, in the House of Commons, O'Connor viciously and publicly attacked Lord John Russell on his Irish policy: "The noble Lord had resorted to an invariable

Whig practice—coersion first, and conciliation afterwards; but he
warned the noble Lord that this measure, like all his previous ones
of coersion, would fail, and only hasten the rupture that was ap-
proaching." Although O'Connor said that he did not support a repeal of the union, he did advocate total separation of England and
Ireland. Russell pushed the oath of allegiance over the table in
O'Connor's direction, as if to remind him that he had taken an oath
to support the present form of government, which included union
with Ireland. Sir Robert Peel warned O'Connor was treading on dangerous ground: "The allegiance promised [in the oath] was allegiance on the part of Ireland as fully and completely as on the part of
England; and does the Hon. Gentleman mean that he took the oath
with a secret reservation that he would be a faithful and loyal subject in this part of the united kingdom, but that he reserved a perfect
latitude for treason in Ireland?"[65]

On another occasion in Parliament, O'Connor responded to an
account of occurrences in Ireland by alleging that the legislature
was always on the side of the landlords, and warned that boatloads
of starving Irish would soon be knocking at England's door: "You
express sympathy for Poland, but the condition of Ireland is worse
than that of Poland. The air of Poland is redolent with the fresh
smelling blood of the martyrs slain in battle in defence of their
country's liberty, while the putrid atmosphere of Ireland stinks from
the effluvia of the wasted bodies of famished slaves." O'Connor's
vehemence—and surely his language—horrified MP's; Sir Harry
Verney hoped aloud that "it would never be his fate to hear such another speech in that house, as that delivered by the honourable
member for Nottingham, which was unfounded in fact, and violent
in the extreme."[66]

Members of Parliament found O'Connor's behavior unaccepta-
ble on many occasions, including moments in which he acted as the
Chartists' Parliamentary representative. On April 10, 1848, O'Connor submitted the third Chartist petition in favor of universal suffrage. Upon examination, the petition was found to have only
1,975,496 signatures instead of close to six million, as O'Connor had
claimed. Various consecutive sheets were in the same handwriting,
and there were false names—"No Cheese," "Pug-Nose," and "Flat-
nose"—and some obscenities. Furious at O'Connor for mocking the

House of Commons, the Conservative member for Cirencester, William Cripps, politely called O'Connor a liar. When O'Connor responded by stalking out of Parliament, his colleagues in the Commons, worried that he might seek violent revenge, sent the sergeant-at-arms of the House of Commons to the *Northern Star* office to bring him back. Cripps apologized (rather ungraciously), but more important, the House extracted O'Connor's promise that he did not plan to avenge his honor.[67]

O'Connor's colleagues in Parliament had no way of knowing that his Parliamentary behavior in 1847 and 1848 had a physical and mental underpinning—that he was slowly going mad. Rather, their minds were full of memories: of O'Connor's bombast at the torchlit Chartist meetings of the late 1830's; of the fanatical crowds which had cheered his release from York Castle in 1841; of his suspected connection with the industrial unrest of 1842. All these historical specters must have sprung to the forefront whenever O'Connor stood up to speak. With a huge, personal, working-class following, he embodied inversion of the theory that working people should submit to be ruled by their social betters.

O'Connor's efforts in early 1848 to secure legislative legalization of the land company must be seen against this backdrop of Parliamentary unease. O'Connor had unwisely procrastinated about registering the company as a joint-stock company, in hopes that the laws governing friendly societies would be amended to include the land company. On March 16, 1848, O'Connor and radical coroner Thomas Wakley were allowed to bring before the House of Commons a bill which proposed to amend Acts 9 and 10 Victoria, the laws relating to friendly societies.[68] The bill was phrased in such a way as expressly to legalize the National Land Company:

Whereas, by an act passed in the tenth year of the reign of her present majesty, intitled 'An Act to amend the laws relating to friendly societies', certain purposes for which societies might be established under the provisions of the said laws relating to friendly societies were enumerated and defined . . . be it therefore enacted . . . that societies already at the time of the passing of this act established . . . for the purposes hereafter mentioned . . . be within the said laws relating to friendly societies . . . for the purpose of purchasing land in the United Kingdom of Great Britain and Ireland, and of erecting on such land dwellings to be allotted to the members of the society, together which certain portions of such land for agricultural purposes.[69]

Members of Parliament knew that O'Connor's bill was specifically aimed at legalizing the land company because, to prepare the House for the introduction of his legislation, O'Connor had arranged for it to receive a series of petitions from "outdoors." These petitions requested either that the Friendly Societies Act and its benefits be applied to the land company, or that joint-stock-company-style legal protection be advanced to the company and the prohibitive stamp duty on the deed reduced.

A petition seeking these objects (although it was submitted in 1849) reveals the style of such pleas. The memorialists described the destitution and unemployment wracking their region, and expressed their determination to earn their livings by the sweat of their brow. They urged Sir George Grey to convince the queen to register the land company, on the grounds that huge amounts of money had already been expended on the project of registration. The petitioners politely urged the government to help them protect themselves against the ignominy of the workhouse; but they also hinted at possible violence: "We declare ourselves friends to Peace, Law, Order, but our social condition must be improved."[70] Written by Thomas Cooper's old crony James Sweet, the petition was signed by 104 residents of Nottinghamshire, including two women. A cross-section of the community, the petitioners displayed various degrees of handwriting ability, ranging from the confident penmanship of a bookseller to the somewhat shaky writing of lacemakers and framework knitters to the hardly legible scrawl of a laborer's hand unused to holding a pen.[71]

Petitions like that from Nottingham, which subtly invoked the threat of violence, could not have endeared O'Connor to the rest of the House of Commons. O'Connor exacerbated the situation by constantly upbraiding his fellow MP's for their failure properly to provide for the poor, and warned them that through the neglect of the middle classes, the workers might turn to vice.[72] To add insult to injury, when O'Connor introduced his and Wakley's bill, he subjected his Parliamentary audience to a very long speech, eloquent on the finer points of the land plan but with scant attention to the bill he actually promoted. Although his eloquence probably sustained his popularity among his readers when the speech was reprinted, it fell upon deaf ears in Parliament.

The Friendly Societies Amendment, first read in Parliament on

May 12, was an obvious target for O'Connor's political enemies to attack. Sir Benjamin Hall, a Whig member for Marylebone, thus raised the question of why the land company remained only provisionally registered.[73] Flustered, O'Connor was forced to admit that since complete registration was so expensive, he did not plan to move in that direction until his amendment bill was disposed of.[74] Hall came forward again on May 30 with specific charges against the land company, and called for a rigid and searching inquiry into its operation. O'Connor, in his naiveté and assurance that the land company was based on impeccable principles, said that an inquiry would not only absolve him of any hint of blame, but also give him the opportunity to promote his scheme at the highest level.[75] By the time the second reading of his friendly-societies bill was brought up (and deferred) on June 10, the land plan was already under scrutiny by a Select Committee; and the only member on the committee who cared about the survival of the land company was O'Connor himself.[76] The Free Trade forces which had raised official hackles about the land scheme through the press now began to work against O'Connor in politics; Select Committee member George Hayter pumped muckraker Alexander Somerville for anti–land company information. Somerville received £25 from Hayter for a (presumably biased) summary of the land scheme and accompanying land bank.[77]

The early phases of the Select Committee investigation examined the questions of the legality and possible financial mismanagement of the land company, as the interlocutors traced the path of funds and their possible diversion to finance the *Northern Star*. Was the land company an illegal lottery? Was it a mass swindle perpetrated on an unsuspecting populace? Brought to the witness stand, O'Connor portrayed himself as no devious leader, but rather an innocent man who had been mercilessly importuned by his working-class constituency: "When I first established [the company], I had no more notion of receiving £5,000 than I had of flying in the air. The people became, however, so fascinated with [the company], that the receipts went on at a speed which I had had no reason to contemplate."[78]

When John Revans, an assistant Poor Law commissioner and professed expert on allotments, was summoned before the committee, he shifted the hearings' focus from the legality of the land scheme to its practicality—and there, to O'Connor's detriment, it would stay. Revans vehemently opposed the scheme, and not only because his visit to the allotments had revealed town laborers unaccustomed to farm work and cold weather. Revans believed the whole system of small farming was inefficient, and plumped for larger, consolidated efforts: "It does appear to me that the plan of buying large farms, and dividing them into three- and four-acre allotments, to be cultivated by spade by artisans and weavers from the manufacturing towns, is about as hopeful as would be a scheme for buying large power-loom factories, pulling down the steam machinery and appropriating each of the looms to be worked by a farm-labourer."[79] Revans warned that the allotments could become a machine for providing successive waves of laborers with a settlement in the allotment parishes (thus allowing them to collect poor relief if they needed it), and then pauperizing them. The chairman of the Select Committee seemed to agree with Revans, at one point asking him, "Then your views do not much differ from mine, as to the result of those locations; that they will tend to pauperize the districts in one way or the other?"[80] Revans's testimony construed the land company as a possible economic threat to the parishes in which the allotments were located.

In the face of this evidence, Feargus O'Connor inappropriately attempted to employ the same tactics he had used to promote the land company. He brought John Sillett to the stand to report on the amazing crop yields he had achieved on a two-acre farm.[81] O'Connor was good at self-promotion, but he struggled against the testimony of John Finlaison, who claimed that O'Connor's "reproductive principle"—that settled lands could be mortgaged and the funds used to buy more allotments—was spurious, given the particular tenants involved in the National Land Company. Overall, the questioning over the course of the hearings presupposed wrongdoing or impracticality in the land scheme. Although evidence of (for example) embezzlement was not uncovered, it was impossible, given this weeks-long onslaught of negativity, that the committee could recommend anything less than the winding-up of the company.

The committee did recommend that the company fold, although the language used in the Sixth Report was diplomatic. It was announced that, while the National Land Company was an illegal scheme, and would not fulfill the expectations held out by the directors to the shareholders, "it should be left entirely open to the parties concerned to propose to Parliament any new measure for the purpose of carrying out the expectations and objects of the promoters of the Company." The committee also proposed that those involved might be exonerated of the penalties they had incurred by transacting business before the company was completely registered, as long as they agreed to wind up the scheme.[82] The committee painted its actions against the company as a move to protect the small savings of the working classes. This is significant, especially when this is viewed in the contemporary milieu of laissez-faire attitude toward business practice. The hypocrisy did not go unnoticed by the *Spectator*, which commented, "The working classes have a right to make experiments for the purpose of bettering their own condition, or indeed for any other purpose not in itself bad; they have as much right to pursue even their hobbies as any other class."[83] That the directors and founders of the company were largely working-class, and that many shareholders had very little to spare, legitimated direct intervention into the company. Similarly paternalistic action in "protection" of working-class interests had, after all, been taken by Select Committees on other occasions, mostly having to do with the regulation of work practices. Because most workers were still excluded from the political process, it was easy for Parliamentarians to cast doubt on their abilities to think and to invest for themselves—much easier than it would have been in the United States.[84]

O'Connor quickly moved to put as positive a spin on the situation as possible.[85] Implausible as it seems, neither O'Connor nor others connected with land reform thought the Select Committee's final report tolled the death knell for the land company. Even John Stuart Mill, later an agitator for reform of land distribution himself, thought as late as 1849 that O'Connor had successfully cleared a major obstacle, noting that O'Connor had "successfully repelled (before a tribunal by no means prepossessed in his favour, a Committee of the House of Commons) the imputations which were lavished upon the project, and upon his mode of executing it."[86] In most cases, however, newspapers published the results of the Select Committee and editorialized that the Chartist Land Company was dead, although the principle of peasant proprietorship was not completely vanquished: "it does remain without dispute, that a man having only a small family, and being possessed of two acres in his own right, well situated near to a town, may by his own industry keep his head above water."[87]

Governmental refusal to sanction the land company was compounded by the arrest and detention of the Chartist movement's leaders in 1848. Ernest Jones, arrested for sedition after a speech in London during which he avowed himself a physical-force Chartist, was sentenced to two years' solitary confinement, removing him from his position as publicist for the land plan at a crucial moment.[88] Nor was Jones the only prominent arrestee; the convergence of the Chartist petitioning and the Irish union repeal movements in early 1848 meant that, once the Irish leaders were arrested, much Chartist energy was diverted toward memorializing for their release. In the absence of its leaders, and with much of its funding cut off as prospective shareholders lapsed into doubt, the land company foundered.

The sky over O'Connorville darkened further, as those allottees who had been given farms turned against their benefactor. On March 1, 1850, the ubiquitous Sir Benjamin Hall produced in the House two petitions against the land company, one from Snigs End and one from O'Connorville. As the land scheme became pressed for cash, O'Connor had begun trying to collect back rents. Although his tenants had ostensibly known deferred rents were piling up, they had never yet been called upon to pay. Their meager crops were insufficient to make payment possible, and O'Connor made matters worse by blaming the weakness of the company on the allottees' failure to pay. Harassed from both sides, O'Connor requested a bill to wind up the land scheme, but in the meantime became embroiled in a libel suit. The attorney for the defendant used the courtroom as a platform to cast aspersions on O'Connor's motives, continuing the paternalistic discourse which had been such a feature of Select Committee testimony:

In order . . . to induce the people to join his society, he went to the manufacturing towns, where vast populations were employed for many hours during the day in labour, and who, by reason of their ignorance of the country, were most likely to be worked upon, and he told them that scenes of rural bliss and an actual paradise, awaited them if they would enroll themselves members of the society. He described in glowing terms the beauties of the country, the tranquil homesteads, the lowing of cattle, the slumbering pigs, the glorious harvest prospects, and other scenes of contentment and plenty, and used other expressions which were likely to make an impression on the minds of a population long accustomed to a factory atmosphere.[89]

Although the land scheme itself was not under examination in the libel case, the judge overreached himself to declare the scheme illegal, and O'Connor immoral.[90]

Ultimately, the act which wound up the land company encompassed some of the main charges against the land scheme. Its language, while completely vindicating the investors of any charges, did construct them as helpless dupes. The Winding-Up Act also mentioned that the land company may have contravened the Act for the Suppression of Societies Established for Seditious and Treasonable Purposes. The Winding-Up Act proposed that the assets of the company be seized, the costs paid, and the rest of the funds divided up. O'Connor and any other trustees and directors would be legally protected from any liability for the remaining monies owed, but subscribers were free to pursue monetary claims. Subscribers did eventually try to recoup their claims, under the supervision of a Master in Chancery, who appointed an outside manager for the company. The manager, Goodchap, ran the company for a few years, and had just as much trouble squeezing rent out of the allottees as O'Connor had had.[91] Anyone who was able to pay his back rent would be assigned a title in fee simple; but few allottees were well enough off to take advantage of this offer.[92]

The drawn-out failure of the land scheme, and the disillusionment and disappointment it occasioned, engendered scathing rhetoric; even former believers in the scheme began to adopt the presentation of land-company investors as understandably gullible people misled by a cunning and evil demagogue. The *Gloucester Journal* likened O'Connor to the great railway fraud George Hudson, and accused him of despoiling the environment and bilking innocent working people. The *Journal*'s editor accused O'Connor of wasting the people's money in order to bring carloads of people in from all over the country to laud him as the king of the Chartists. Now, mournfully enough, easily led working people were going to lose their homes.[93]

The government's suppression of the Chartist Land Plan, impelled as it was by pressure from the mainstream press, illustrates how a discourse of paternalism might be used to disguise the exercise of power against a weaker group—here, working people. Although all kinds of business investment flourished unregulated in Britain in the mid-nineteenth century, the Chartist Co-Operative/National Land Company was regulated on the grounds that workers' investments needed to be protected. Ironically, the same workers who could not be trusted to safeguard their savings were, under law, thought the most fit to risk lives and limbs by analyzing the danger level of their own workplaces.[94]

But the demise of the Chartist Land Company was more than just an interesting episode in the exercise of unequal power; I would argue that the forceful end put to the Chartist Land Company led many to lose interest in Chartism. Gareth Stedman Jones has claimed that Chartism ebbed because social amelioration had been achieved under an unreformed system. Yet the 1847 Factory Act on which Stedman Jones's argument is largely based encompassed only a small part of Chartists' demands. The Chartist Co-Operative/National Land Company, which reached its pinnacle in 1847–48, envisaged a much more substantial reorganization of society than any factory act could encompass. More important to the decline of Chartism is that all of its forms of organization had failed.[95] Petitioning had not worked, armed rebellion was not the answer, and even a private company proved within the reach of government's regulatory energies. By 1848, a short-lived trade boom and a loss of experienced leadership had sapped some of the motivation and guidance from the movement, and the land issue been co-opted by the Liberals.[96] Furthermore, while not all Chartists may have felt betrayed by O'Connor, the myth of the end of the land company which lived on, and which was resurrected during the smallholdings debate of the 1870's, emphasized O'Connor's mismanagement and even, perhaps, deceitfulness.[97] Although his bad judgment in the House of Commons was undeniable and the finances of the scheme were probably unworkable, the myth failed to remember O'Connor's good intentions. Yes, he had acted as paternalistic as the Select Committee proved to be, viewing the allottees as grateful and loyal subjects to him rather than as independent actors—but he seems to have intended the best for them until they withdrew their loyalty. The eventual rent revolt which cast him in the role of rack-renting Irish landlord was too much for him to bear. He died emaciated, penniless, and insane, after a stay at Dr. Tuke's asylum—where he recognized no one, and absently sang the Chartist hymn "The Lion of Freedom," unaware now that he had been its inspiration.

If the Chartist Land Company fell to pieces with a resounding crash, the Potters' Joint-Stock Emigration society died with a whimper—evidence, again, that it was not the economics of land reform which precipitated government intervention. The Potters' Joint-Stock Emigration Society had been allowed to register under the Friendly Societies Act even though certain factors might have set off alarm bells. The Emigration Society's operative principles mirrored those of the land company; "Joint-Stock" blazoned forth from its very title; and available tracts of American land were parceled out by a possibly illegal lottery, very similar to the lottery adopted by the Chartists.[98] Yet the Potters' Joint-Stock Emigration Society suffocated for want of cash, by 1851 dying the peaceful death that the land company might have had, had the government not intervened.

The contrast between the fates of the Emigration Society and O'Connor's land company supports the contention that political factors bulked large in the destruction of the land scheme. Given the exclusion of working people from political participation, it was easy for members of the House of Commons to move against O'Connor—and the bigger target of Chartism which O'Connor represented—on the grounds that the working classes needed their aid.[99] The financial mismanagement of the land company, and the fact that O'Connor flouted the joint-stock registration laws, simply gave them an opportunity to intervene. In contrast, in the United States, homestead reformers took advantage of the myths of political inclusion and classlessness to force their reform onto the political agenda—and after long years of lobbying, to achieve their goals.

FROM NATIONAL REFORM TO
THE HOMESTEAD ACT

In contrast with the government hostility shown to the Chartist Land Plan, the planks of the National Reform platform were both popular in many state legislatures and eventually adopted by Congress.[100] Helene Zahler accurately described the National Reformers as being ineffectual in politics but as having influenced, surprisingly, a number of "respectable" politicians in high places.[101] National Reform discourse proclaimed many concepts which were not controversial in mainstream American politics: the intrinsic worth of the actual settler, the importance of a family home, and the desirability of furthering republicanism with a widespread distribution of land. In contrast with Britain, American legislators were dissuaded by political necessity, and perhaps by real belief, from classifying American workers as unfree agents who needed paternalistic protection, or from marginalizing their concerns entirely.[102] The myth of the small farmer as the most virtuous unit of American society made National Reform doctrine extremely attractive; and this became more true in the 1850's, as the new Republican Party, seeking to combat the "Slave Power," made free soil, free labor, and free men the cornerstone of its platform. Furthermore, even as land reform entered the choppy sea of mainstream politics in the 1850's, leaders kept a broad base of supporters by maintaining voluntary and fraternal organizations and petition drives dedicated to land reform.

As Michael Holt has pointed out, the Democratic and Whig national parties converged and seemed to lose effectiveness between 1848 and 1853, and state parties searched for anything which might excite the electorate and clarify the parties' differences.[103] In this atmosphere, individual issues like temperance, nativism, or homestead might benefit. For the developing Republican Party, with its allegiance to an idiosyncratically defined "free labor," homestead exemption was a perfect issue, a method for potentially providing social mobility.[104] Thus, homestead exemption bills began to pass, shepherded by state legislators who in turn were influenced by the National Reformers.[105] Frederick Robinson of Massachusetts explained in 1851 that he began to champion homestead exemption when "a movement in favor of the homestead exemption law was made in New York, and a paper was devoted to this subject, which for several years demonstrated, by unanswerable arguments and facts, the justice, the importance, and the necessity of such a law."[106] Robinson's cause was also advanced by the fact that Connecticut, Vermont, Maine, and Rhode Island had all recently enacted homestead exemption laws.[107]

In New York, petitions to the state assembly helped ensure the appointment of almost annual select committees on homestead exemption and land limitation, over which the National Reformers exercised ideological sway, sometimes through direct participation. This first New York Select Committee espoused all three National Reform measures: homestead exemption, land limitation, and freedom of the public lands. The 1847 Select Committee report, avowedly in response to National Reform memorials, adopted the safety-valve theory of the public lands, used natural-rights language, and borrowed the exact words of the National Reformers' memorial to Congress: "Poorhouses and prisons, dark alleys and noisome, pestilential cellars and hovels in our crowded cities, would soon become tenantless, and that promised day spoken of in scripture would arrive, when 'they shall sit, every man under his vine and his fig tree, and none shall make them afraid.'"[108] The 1848 Select Committee quoted Horace Greeley's speech before the New York Young Men's National Reform Association.[109] The influence of the National Reformers on the Select Committees, through borrowed language and through the participation of avowed land reformers as members, continued until the end of the decade.[110] The presence of pro-land-reform representatives in the state legislature, and the participation of Horace Greeley as land reform's lobbyist, underlined the intrinsic respectability of homestead exemption.[111]

Yet the exemption of a family homestead from distraint for debt was uncontroversial compared with a legislated limitation on the amount of land any man might own, or free grants of the public domain to the poor. While espousal of land limitation or free homesteads would have represented opposition to some of the basic doctrines of market economics, politicians might portray homestead exemption as an apolitical and humanitarian attempt to preserve for the debtor a few basic necessities, and to protect women and children who were not free agents under the law. Still, homestead exemption debates might serve as a springboard for larger discussions about entitlements; New York's 1851 Select Committee Report proclaimed that "the land belongs to man as an inalienable heritage. It is not only necessary to his support, but necessary to his independence, and . . . a limited quantity sufficient for the maintenance of himself and offspring, should be granted to him as a right, the same as his undisputed title to the air and sunlight."[112]

New York was not the only state in which legislators consciously adopted National Reform reasoning; in the West, state leg-

islators interested in the compact settlement of their communities
by free white farmers, rather than the acquisition of land by speculators, took note of the measures.[113] In Wisconsin, National Reformers
quizzed candidates for state offices on land reform and claimed to
have influenced the 1848 election. A homestead exemption proposal
debated at the Wisconsin constitutional convention became a stick-
ing point between two groups of delegates, both claiming to be the
poor man's friend.[114] Members of the first group worried that the
measure would subsidize imprudent behavior.[115] A second group,
spearheaded by Fourierite Warren Chase (founder of the Ceresco co-
operative community), used the language of the National Reformers; if a man had a right to life, he argued, surely he had a right to
somewhere to live.[116] Another proponent, Horace Patch, delivered a
prose poem on home, with sentiments that epitomized the contemporary view of home as a gendered oasis of calm in the midst of a
capitalist storm:

I would give [the debtor] a home, the permanency of which is fixed and
immutable, that amid the changing vicissitudes which characterize the
business transactions of life and amid calamities that beset his path a man
can rise above the ruin that surrounds him and exclaim with a heart filled
with gratitude and countenance beaming with joy—"My home is left!"
Sir, home is an endearing word; it has associations accompanying it that
touch the tenderest fibers that vibrate the human mind.[117]

When the Wisconsin legislature omitted land limitation from the
state constitution, local National Reformers lobbied until a land
limitation bill was introduced in 1851. A report submitted in favor
of the bill's passage invoked man's natural right to the soil but also
wielded a general populism against threats of commercial monopoly: "Those who have some property, and who live by manufactures
and commerce, are exposed to the ruinous operations of specula-
tions and competition by overgrown capitalists."[118] The debate over
land reform led naturally to larger questions of private property,
monopoly, and freedom in a democracy.[119] Although land limitation
was always too controversial a measure to make much progress, by
1854, sentiment in favor of the homestead bill was entrenched in
the Wisconsin state legislature.[120]

Although their showing was not as impressive at the federal
level as it was in the states, National Reform measures received
some Congressional support.[121] At first the petitions and draft legislation which National Reformers sent were summarily dismissed,

in spite of many eloquent speeches made on the issue by Western representatives.[122] But National Reform coincided with a cultural moment in which the "West of the imagination" flourished, and, given the pressure to settle the free or slave status of Western lands, the momentum was hard to ignore. "It is to the West, the agricultural West, her community of independent farmers, who eat the bread of their own industry, that the eye of the statesman must turn with prophetic hope for the patriotic race who are destined to preserve the principles of democratic liberty," one Congressman enthused.[123] Although National Reformers produced little Manifest Destiny rhetoric themselves, they surely benefited from these effusions.

This is not to imply that National Reform measures were uncontroversial at the national level. Often tarred with the designation "agrarianism," signifying equal division of property, land reform elicited heated emotions. During an 1845 debate on a land-price graduation bill, Thomasson of Kentucky reported that he had seen a copy of *Young America* and decried its doctrines: "I solemnly declare that I entertain for the doctrine they promulgate the most ineffable detestation and abhorrence. It is ultra-agrarianism."[124] When Congressman Herrick presented a memorial from the National Reformers in March 1846, a majority of sixteen voted not to print, much less to discuss it.[125] When homestead bills did come before the attention of Congress, they were often not taken seriously:

Mr. Mc Connell—"Mr. Speaker, I rise to a privileged question. I gave notice some time ago, of my intention to introduce a bill to give a homestead to every head of a family." [Laughter]
A dozen voices in various parts of the hall—"Read the bill, read the bill." ... The Clerk proceeded to read the bill, and after he had finished the first two or three lines, some of the members appeared to be satisfied, and cried out, "That's enough," and others, "Oh, no" "Go on," "Let's hear it all," followed by peals of laughter.[126]

National Reform in this period was still new and associated almost exclusively with a band of New York activists whose other claim to fame had been their brief infatuation with Skidmorism in 1829. All this was soon to change.

As Helene Zahler noted, 1850 marked a turning point in Congressional reception of the homestead idea. A major intellectual shift had taken place, related to an increased sense of urgency about settling the frontier with free white labor, but also to the espousal of

National Reform ideas in temperate language by some influential legislators and to the reception of petitions from a wider area than just New York City. From then on, rhetoric evocative of National Reform was rampant.[127] On August 13, 1850, Senator Walker introduced a bill proposing that the public lands be ceded to the several states, which would then parcel them out free in limited quantities for actual settlers. His argument rested partly on a claim that a right to life means a right to subsistence, a key contention of the National Reformers. He also used the statistics of their Cincinnati Industrial Congress, and, as the National Reformers were wont to do, alluded to the dark example of Great Britain.[128] More and more, advocates of homestead were able to tie National Reform measures to the greater destiny of the nation.[129]

When homestead came under discussion in Congress in 1851, Senator George Julian advocated a homestead act on the grounds of natural right, and was able to give the topic a fairly conservative shading. "I am no believer in the doctrines of agrarianism, or socialism, as these terms are generally understood," he explained. "The friends of land reform claim no right to interfere with the laws of property of the several States. . . . They simply demand, that in laying the foundations of empire in the yet unpeopled regions of the great West, Congress shall give its sanction to the natural right of the landless citizen of the country to a home upon its soil." As Jefferson had, Julian identified a rural life as the one most conducive to virtue; by siphoning surplus workers onto the public lands, the government would increase productivity, decrease the number of the idle, and increase public morality.[130]

Another great debate on homestead followed in 1852, as a homestead bill actually managed to pass in the House of Representatives—only to be killed by the Senate, which refused to be swayed by a large influx of petitions.[131] Despite constant explanation in the labor press of the term "agrarian," and distancing of the National Reformers from agrarianism—as evil and un-American in the 1840's as communism was in the 1950's—enemies occasionally pointed an accusing finger at the way in which workers had banded together to ask for the measure.[132] "Who asks for it?" J. Sutherland of New York asked of land reform. "Certain associations, called 'Industrial Congresses'—offsprings of the German school of socialism, and of the

American school of 'higher law' transcendentalism—partly political, partly agrarian. . . . They ask for it as a gift, as a charity to better their condition and to enable them to live without working."[133] In some quarters, the specter of demagoguery and demands made by workers from the industrial cities was too frightening to permit a concession.[134] "If this agrarian precedent is established by Congress in the middle of the nineteenth century . . . on petitions emanating from our large commercial cities or other sectional locations, what may be the demands from the same quarter before the close of the century?" the members of a Delaware Agricultural Society fretted.[135]

Such aristocratic objections to proposals from the masses were few; most legislators who opposed homestead rather claimed philosophical, economic, or nativist reasons. Representative Timothy Jenkins of New York thought relief of the poor should also be a state rather than a federal concern, but denied that it was a concern at all "so long as forty acres of good land can be purchased for fifty dollars, and eighty acres for one hundred dollars, a farm is within the reach of every one who is not disabled by sickness or old age."[136] To give free land was to reward those who lacked the industry or frugality to save. In June 1853, John Welch of Ohio argued against homestead on the grounds that many farmers had already bought land, and freeing the public lands would depress the prices of their holdings. S. H. Rogers thought the homestead bill would depopulate the older states, and played on nativist sentiment when he argued that it would bring to the United States people from all over the globe who had no sympathy for American political institutions but who wanted a free meal ticket.[137]

To these legislators, homestead advocates responded with rhetoric which sang the praises of free labor. Albert Brown of Mississippi asserted that those who would benefit from homestead were those without land and home: "Hardy sons of toil, slighted by the world for the crime of being poor, and elevated to the dignity of freemen only on election days. In the new States, under the operations of this bill, they will become freeholders and householders, and will be at all times, and in every season, equal to the proudest nabobs in Christendom."[138] Gerrit Smith powerfully argued that the logical end of land monopoly was the degradation of the American worker to the condition of the Irish peasant.[139] Or, perhaps, the unsaid argument would have been, the American slave. The political party which adopted the homestead issue could claim to be the friend of workingmen as well as the opponent of the extension of slavery.

While the debates continued, as did the annual process of introducing homestead bills which were then rejected, land reformers in the United States reached out to those who were already cynical about achieving change through political means. They thus pursued their ends through a new, voluntarist, fraternal organization, the Brotherhood of the Union, as well as through petitions and political activism.[140] Like the National Reform Association in the 1840's, the Brotherhood of the Union served as a school and social outlet for workingmen interested in land reform. The Brotherhood was the invention of an eccentric young Philadelphian, George Lippard, who since 1848 had edited the pro-land-reform newspaper *Quaker City*.[141] Besides being a familiar name to workingmen who read story papers, he was a romantic and charismatic figure.[142] Handsome, young, and highly literate, Lippard trained as a lawyer and then turned his hand to fiction, writing a novel, *The Quaker City*, while still in his teens. Lippard's personal life was shot through with suffering; he survived both his wife and two children, and had to cope with heavy debt before his premature death. By becoming the tribune of the working classes, people with even less power than he, he could keep his mind off an unfulfilling personal life, benefit from a certain amount of adulation, and to a certain extent remake the immediate world in his own image.

Frustrated with do-nothing industrial congresses, Lippard planned to right the world through a Mason-style secret society formed to battle workingmen's oppressors, including bankers, land monopolists, and "all Monied Oppressors who use their money, to make the rich richer and the poor poorer."[143] Founded on September 1, 1849, Lippard's Brotherhood recruited members, held rituals whose words and gestures Lippard had designed, circulated land-reform petitions, and inculcated a religion of workingmen's patriotism. By 1850 it had "planted its white banner" in 20 states.

The Brotherhood of the Union combined producerism and the natural-rights arguments common to most land reformers with popular evangelical Christianity, as in its motto: "The Continent of America is the Palestine of Redeemed Labor."[144] Eschewing party politics, members of the Brotherhood sought to render labor and capital harmonious, and more concretely, to secure every worker a homestead. According to Brotherhood propaganda, its secret rites "trace the history of labor through every age and point to the Future, when the acceptable year of the Lord shall come to the sons of men, blessing every man with a place to work, with the fruit of his work (not wages nor alms) and with a bit of land that he may call by the sacred title of home."[145] The Brotherhood also officially approved cooperation, and Lippard originally planned a series of Brotherhood cooperatives, although the national records do not indicate whether any were formed.[146]

Members were instructed to do all that was in their power to achieve passage of a free homestead act, and land limitation was vital to secure to every producer the full products of his toil, "the most of which under the present system of Land Monopoly finds its way into the pockets of the Land Lords and the capitalist, in the form of Rent and Interest." The adoption of these measures would nerve Americans against every internal and foreign foe, because the government secured to him "the shelter of his own 'vine and fig tree, with none to make him afraid.'"[147] Although members of the Brotherhood of the Union shared a consciousness of oppression which they couched in terms of class, they were committed to healing the breach between labor and capital by the power of positive thinking and mutual spiritual regeneration—the New Agers of the railroad era.[148] The Brotherhood's Christian component promoted quietism, patience, and martyrdom, rather than revolution. In 1852, when the Senate rejected the homestead bill, the Brotherhood called upon "every true man to retreat from politics and seek land reform through the Brotherhood with a martyr spirit."[149]

Although the Brotherhood of the Union attempted to undertake some of the same methods of ideological dissemination that the National Reformers had tried, it was hampered by lack of funds. Lippard proposed a national journal to be called the *White Banner*, with essays, stories, and biographies, "illustrative of the Right of Labor, of Homestead Exemption, Land Reform—of all Cognate Reforms—and of the word Brotherhood, in its largest and holiest sense." When insufficient money was raised from the Brotherhood's members, the *White Banner* was produced as a handbook, to be supplemented by tracts and pamphlets.[150] Another of the group's national initiatives was to translate certain documents of the organization into German, so that a German-language circle could be formed.[151]

As the National Reformers had done in the 1840's, the Brotherhood catered to workingmen's desire to be entertained and amazed even as they were educated. When the Brotherhood proselytized, it used a multimedia program complete with magic-lantern slides illustrating the degrees of the order, and an Indian costume, ostensibly for the presenter to wear.[152] Each of the circles had a set of officers whose titles were chosen from the luminaries of history. These included a Grand Chief Jefferson, a Grand Chief Franklin, a Grand Chief Wayne, "named after Anthony Wayne, the Knight of the Revolution," a Grand Chief Fulton, named after Robert Fulton, "who by his life illustrated that the Labor of a mechanic is more glorious than the battle-field of Kings," and a Grand Chief Girard, named after Stephen Girard, "who atoned for his immense wealth by dedicating it to the education of Orphanage and the elevation of Labor."[153] The highest office of all was Supreme Washington, to which Lippard was continually elected. Induction ceremonies, featuring stirring set speeches, were undertaken in costume; local circles could buy from the central office the merino collars and cambric robes, urns, torches, and rules of membership which lent an air of mystery to the whole.

The correlation between land reform and the Brotherhood was strong even at the top levels of leadership. It is probable that George Evans joined the organization; a letter sent to Congress from the "Ouvrier Circle" of the Brotherhood of the Union is in his distinctive handwriting.[154] Writings by Lippard and Evans indicate that both men knew each other, and each extended to the other a grudging respect.[155] Among those who certainly joined were Albert Brisbane, John Commerford (elected District Supreme Washington in the late 1850's), and Gilbert Vale, Jr.; Ira B. Davis, a tailor active as an agrarian in the 1840's and a cooperationist in the 1850's, Rochester land reformer John Grieg, and Samuel Champion, a delegate to the 1848 Industrial Congress; and J. K. Ingalls, president of the National Land Reform Association, and Benjamin Franklin Price, a land reformer who later became a leader in the Carpenters' Protective Association and Amalgamated Trades' convention in 1853.[156] By the height of its influence in the 1860's, almost 150 circles of the

Brotherhood had been founded in 24 states. Thirty-seven of these were in Ohio, six in Illinois, and others in Wisconsin, Indiana, Iowa, Minnesota, and Texas, the Brotherhood's centers of strength coinciding with areas of greatest petitioning for land reform in the 1850's.[157]

Although Lippard's Brotherhood of the Union was the premier nonpolitical land-reform organization of the 1850's, having siphoned off many of the top activists, it was not the only spiritual or voluntarist land-reform association in those years. Fannie Lee Townsend's Philadelphia pro-land-reform Jubilee grouping held religious mass meetings, listened to sermons, and even enjoyed occasional cultural events in the early 1850's.[158] National Reformers properly so-called also continued to agitate politically in New York, their cause taken up by other newspapers with the demise of *Young America* and kept alive by the convention of a New York City Industrial Congress in June 1850 at which more than fifty organizations were represented.[159] K. Arthur Bailey, a member of the Church of Humanity, president of the Industrial Congress and of Typographical Union no. 6, and a prominent land reformer, delivered the main address at a major meeting in City Hall Park in August—a meeting also attended by John Commerford and Lewis Ryckman. Riding this wave of energy, four wards, the ninth, tenth, sixteenth, and seventeenth, ran insurgent labor-land-reform tickets.[160] In February 1854, more than four thousand people came out for a mass rally, organized by land reformers, to protest the Kansas-Nebraska Act.[161] In Philadelphia, the National Reform Association continued to meet and draft memorials for Congress.[162] Finally, although homestead is traditionally associated with the Republican Party at least one attempt was made to graft land reform onto the Democratic Party. The National Reformers and Free Democracy held a mass meeting at Tammany Hall on June 2, 1851, under the motto "Free Homes for All in '52," at which I. P. Walker of Wisconsin was nominated as the Land Reform presidential candidate, and influential Democratic proponents of land reform were publicly thanked.[163]

The industrial congresses, staffed by an almost entirely different set of activists than during the 1840's, continued to meet and primarily to address homestead legislation (although they also reflected the increasingly slavery-oriented concerns of the day). Some reformers evidently stayed away from the 1852 congress, fearing that the Philadelphia delegation might try to slip a "colored" delegate past the doorman (a threat which failed to materialize). Despite this evidence of racism, the 1854 congress railed at the Slave Power and lauded the efforts of emigration societies to settle Kansas and Nebraska, hoping that these might successfully serve as the first states granted free to actual settlers.[164] Serious resolution-passing continued even as attendance dropped off, but by 1856 only eight long-bearded enthusiasts were present, and the congress petered out after the first day.[165]

The Free Soil movement also adopted and perpetuated National Reform measures. At the Free Soil convention at Pittsburgh held on August 12, 1852, the majority report of the Committee on Platform demanded the land free in limited quantities for actual settlers. The prospect was still controversial; when Booth of Michigan offered a resolution declaring that all men had a natural right to a portion of the soil, "living and dying—at their birth and their death; that those who opposed this doctrine would bottle up God's sunshine for speculation," several delegates responded with "humbuggery and nonsense." Sheldon of Pennsylvania looked on the subject as the entering wedge to the destruction of slavery. Smith of Indiana said no man could sell the soil, only the improvements, and insisted government had no right even to protect those who were presently on the soil. Bright of Massachusetts hoped the resolution would pass, and Gerrit Smith, now a thoroughgoing land reformer, said he saw it as completing the platform. It was adopted almost unanimously.[166]

Some workers moved away from politically connected movements and joined building societies.[167] National Reformer Parke Godwin suggested this tactic in 1848, and by 1852, Edward Spann notes, there were more than seventy such in operation.[168] In New York, individual land reformers led projects like the "Western Farm and Village Association," the object of which was to take up a whole township of public land and divide it among, and actually settle it with, its members. The village of Minnesota in Minnesota had been colonized by the first cohort of Western Farm members. By 1852, a second cohort, called the Western Homestead Association, was organized, intended to provide implements, provisions, and dwellings as well as land. John Commerford served as president of another society, Industrial Home Association no. 3. Commerford's company collected $1,500 to purchase 500 acres along the Harlem Railroad.

Each claimant would enter for an acre, a half, or a quarter, and then lots would be drawn; it was a copy of the Chartist Land Company on a smaller scale.[169]

By the late 1850's and early 1860's, responsibility for the petitioning process had fallen to a handful of New York groups, especially the National Land Reform Association, composed of National Reform veterans, and the New York circle of the Brotherhood of the Union.[170] John Commerford and Thomas Devyr still personally lobbied Democratic legislators for approval of the measure. Besides sending a circular on the measure to every member of Congress, Commerford courted longtime homestead advocate Andrew Johnson, warning Johnson that the labor-capital issue rather than slavery was the real wedge dividing Americans.[171] Thomas Devyr, also a lifelong Democrat, felt the land-reform issue was bound up with the survival of that party. As he wrote to Andrew Johnson in 1859, if the Democrats, even now in the eleventh hour, could just get behind the issue of land reform, they would pick up all the disaffected Northerners who had been forced to turn to the Republican Party. "For they will not have the sense, even now, to proclaim a free home to every 'enterprising citizen,' and the comparative bagatelle of whether a slave will work on the hither or thither side of a line will continue to swallow up public attention, and lose to your Presidential candidate such states as New York," he exclaimed in despair.[172] Devyr also continued to further the cause of transatlantic reform in the late 1850's, traveling to England and while there, staying with cooperative pioneer George Jacob Holyoake, to whom he had been introduced by Horace Greeley.[173]

Despite Commerford's and Devyr's attempts to graft land reform to the Democratic Party, where it had had its roots, by the 1860's the political landscape had changed. The diffusion of land-reforming energies into political, religious, and economic spheres contributed to the general acceptance of the homestead idea by broadening its reach while emphasizing its respectability. At the same time, in the political free-for-all of the 1850's, the Republican Party had appropriated free land as part of free soil. The culmination of almost twenty years of National Reform lobbying, of Brotherhood of the Union ritual, and of industrial-congress resolution passing was a bit of an anticlimax. In 1862, in the midst of the Civil War, the Homestead Act was signed into law. The view that it was a sop to retain the loyalty of white workingmen is probably not misplaced. This political context, combined with the long delay from the start of the land-reform agitation to its end, makes it seem less of a "victory" than it might otherwise. The real victory had in fact come by the early 1850's, when under the relentless pressure of their logic and persistence, and in a Northern atmosphere increasingly concerned with the Western movement of free labor, the tide in Congress had begun to turn in their favor. The land reformers, unlike the Chartists, set forth a movement with the potential for real inclusiveness, and—unlike O'Connor and the Chartist Land Company—showed themselves too innocuous to be feared and too ubiquitous to be crushed. The emphasis they had placed on opposition to land monopoly had evolved into a canny, positive quest for "homes for all"—and by playing down "leveling" in favor of "raising," gained them many more adherents. Instead of charity, free homesteads now stood for opportunity.

Most of the energy had dissipated from National Reform by the passage of the Homestead Act; there was almost no one left to greet the measure with rejoicing. John Commerford was busy running unsuccessfully for Congress and advising Napoleon to invade Mexico and to distribute the lands of Mexico to the landless.[174] J. K. Ingalls continued to preside over a "National Land Reform Association" in New York, possibly into the 1870's. This group continued to take some of its inspiration from a new generation of English land reformers, including John Stuart Mill.[175] Thomas Devyr continued to publicize land redistribution with the self-publication of his autobiography in 1882, and agitated for the cause of Irish independence through his journalism. Significantly, however, there was no great movement of poor urban workers to the West. The safety-valve effect failed to materialize; perhaps its moment had passed.

The real tribune of National Reform was long gone. George Henry Evans had died—penniless—of a cold in 1856.[176] The remaining members of the National Land Reform Association celebrated George Henry Evans's birthday annually, as radicals had once fêted Tom Paine. Having raised some money, they visited Shaker elder Frederick Evans and shared with him their plan to have a bust of his brother put up in Central Park.[177] Although no bust was ever erected, these friends did finance a tombstone in a New Jersey cemetery, which bore the proud inscription, "G. H. E. the Radical. The great object of his life was to secure homes for all by abolishing the traffic in land and limiting the individual possession of it. As editor of the *Man*, the *Radical*, the *People's Rights*, and *Young America*, he triumphantly vindicated the right of every human being to a share of the soil, as essential to the welfare and permanence of the Republic." Despite the similarities between Henry George's suggestions and George Henry's (which caused a temporary elevation in the stock of the latter), labor's business was increasingly transacted through unions, and the land reformers whose struggle had assumed a different form were forgotten.[178] Somewhat fittingly, weeds grew over the tombstone of George Henry Evans, and it lay lost for almost a hundred and fifty years.[179]

Epilogue

The Chartist Land Plan and the Potters' Joint-Stock Emigration Society were short-lived, killed off by power politics and financial mismanagement. National Reform slogged on for almost twenty years before culminating an anticlimactic partial victory—partial because, while homestead was achieved, the original fears of the National Reformers about America's antidemocratic tendencies were never addressed. Yet nothing can erase this: for one bright moment in the 1840's workers on both sides of the Atlantic saw in land reform a shining future. As they sought to accommodate to, variously, the inception of a market economy and the increasing demands of industrialization, the question of the disposition of natural resources and its relationship to the quality of their lives bulked large. In both Britain and the United States, the quest for free farms was in part a reaction to dissatisfaction with urban overcrowding and the paucity of good housing—yet there were larger philosophical questions being contested.

Although cotton factories already dotted the hills of Lancashire, even there the distribution of land was far from being a settled question. Having little to be enthusiastic about in their daily routines and in the unpredictability of their yearly survival, captivated by Feargus O'Connor, who had been their public voice since the late 1830's, workers envisioned an alternative but still possible mix of industry and agriculture which would raise wages for both city and country workers. In contrast, while removed by relative prosperity from the direct effects of industry, Massachusetts farmers, factory laborers, and skilled workers incorporated land redistribution into a series of demands which, when satisfied, would elevate the status of labor to its proper position in a democracy, by ensuring equal rights. American workers in particular strove to amalgamate the ideal of

the yeoman farmer advanced by Jefferson with a producerist ideology rooted in their own experiences.

While the experiences of the factory and some of the economic
dislocations attendant upon industrialization helped convince the
masses to sign on to land reform, the ideologies of the British and
American movements owed their similarities to communication
and a common intellectual heritage. Drawing on a fairly ancient and
closely reasoned body of works on the land, and crafting their own
solutions in the land-reforming hothouse atmosphere of the 1830's
and early 1840's, American and British land-reform leaders created a
language of land reform which, while it may not have grown directly out of the experience of the mass of workers, was able to appeal to them on many levels, ranging from the promise of more and
better food to that of more and deeper respect. Land reform on both
sides of the Atlantic was a reaction to fears that factory production
threatened artisanal independence. It was fashioned by its leaders to
connote not only higher wages for workers but also increased independence and autonomy on the job. Economic autonomy and political autonomy were linked, given the specter of chattel slavery lurk-
ing in the background. The discourse of land reform was gendered—
reformers conjured up a vision of the family roles which they would
like to see "restored," or perhaps invented. Their vision was based
on a family wage and women's presence in the home rather than in
the labor market. In contrast with the increasing premium put on
individual responsibility in both Britain and the United States, all
these goals were to be achieved through the concert of working-
class efforts, and in the United States, through the exercise of government responsibility for the well-being of the people. Even as
workers distinguished themselves from some of their intellectual
forebears, and partly accommodated themselves to industrial capitalism by insisting on the sanctity of individual private property,
they tried to buffer some of capitalism's less humane aspects and re-
capture something of village society by espousing life on the land.

If the transatlantic working-class land-reform movements illustrate the interaction of language and ideology with experience, do
they illustrate the action of class? In both Britain and the United
States, the quest to secure man his natural right to the land grew out
of a perceived opposition between the interests of the producer and
the nonproducer. While the leaders of the movements which sought

land for workers were not uniformly workers themselves, their concepts evolved through tension and competition with the overwhelmingly "middle-class" Anti–Corn Law League and abolitionist
movement, both of which promoted the classic liberal position that
individual freedom—freedom to trade, freedom of the person—
should be the highest social value. The call for land reform, in both
countries, was a natural outgrowth of the ideological position that
there should be some standard below which the laborer should not
be allowed to fall; it was part of a platform of reforms containing
such measures as the ten-hour day, universal suffrage, and universal
education. These goals reinforced each other, creating so coherent a
vision of labor's interests that the Seventh Annual Industrial Congress of the United States called for a third party, a Labor Party.

But to call the land-reform movements "class movements" is to
oversimplify. The stated intention of these movements was, after
all, to elevate the status of production and restore harmony between
status groups—eventually to erase the lines of social difference
which divided employers from employees. This casts doubt on
whether these activists perceived class to be permanent. The rhetoric that demanded redistribution of the land—like the rhetoric of
many other movements—was contradictory: at times as full of gree-
dy capitalists and exploited laborers as the most thoroughgoing
Marxist could wish, and at other times quietist, evoking the feudal
world of the happy peasant. It is impossible to say with conviction
that one construction was for public and one for private consumption.[1]

Examination of the land-reform movements in a transatlantic
context has illustrated that even with its much-vaunted frontier,
the United States was not perceived to be a haven for the land-
hungry workingman in the antebellum period. Although the conflict which the American land reformers engendered encompassed
artisans, factory workers, shop owners, and other producers, the
language which they used was confrontational in its own way. So
close was it to the language used in the British land-reform movement, and so sympathetic were the personnel of each movement
toward the other, that the movements were thought to be entwined
in pursuit of a common goal. In the end, American working people
achieved their goal because the myth of the republican state stood
or fell on the basis of their political participation. British working

people's independent activity was subtly repressed by a centralized, hierarchical government supported by a sympathetic middle class. British workers were not free agents and needed to be controlled; American white workers were free agents, and it was one of their only consolations.

While the place of working people within the social institutions of each state determined the outcome of each land-reform movement, perhaps the most impressive achievement of the land-reform movements is not what any of the three groups accomplished, but rather the worker-based culture they made in the process. In both Britain and America, land-reform movements overcame the constraints of geography and time to develop similar organizational strategies—lectures, print, leadership, the creation of specific spaces for land-reforming activities. Thousands of people, representing a wide range of occupations and experiences, after exposure to this transatlantic movement, considered themselves land reformers. They were bound by the common notions that the right to life entailed the right to the wherewithal to live, that society bore a responsibility for the physical welfare and social happiness of its citizens, and that the independence inherent in farming created the most responsible citizens and the most acceptable and ample definition of freedom. While their particular movements met ends which were disastrous at worst and indifferent at best, the vitalization of this ideology, together with an abiding mystique in, and nostalgia for, the land, would be the land reformers' greatest legacy to the future.[2]

Reference Matter

Notes

INTRODUCTION

1. "My Wants," by P.S.A., *The Field, the Force and the Factory* (Ashton-under-Lyne), vol. 2, no. 19, Oct. 20, 1849.

2. The simultaneous land-reform movements have been mentioned in Kirk, *Labour and Society*, vol. 1; Zahler, *Eastern Workingmen*; Boston, *British Chartists in America*; Schlueter, *Lincoln, Labor and Slavery*; and Wilentz, *Chants Democratic*.

3. David Montgomery points out that the search for rural land was linked to rising urban rents and a housing shortage in American cities, and writes, "among working people, struggles over land, rent and housing—the physical domain of the reproduction of daily life—provided, as Powderly said, a keynote that did 'reach the human heart' every bit as powerfully as the more famous battles that arose directly out of working for wages." *Citizen Worker*, p. 114.

4. The land-reform movements illustrate the way in which ideologies helped workers interpret different experiences in similar ways. On the role of language in the interpretation of experience, see Gray, *Factory Question*; Zonderman, *Aspirations and Anxieties*; Stedman Jones, "Rethinking Chartism"; Kirk, "In Defense of Class." But see also Scott, "On Language, Gender and Working Class History"; Epstein, "Constitutional Idiom."

5. On the extent of producerism in Britain and America, see Hattam, *Labor Visions*, pp. 93–111. On the value of comparative studies of producerism, see Fredrickson, "From Exceptionalism to Variability."

6. See Sellers, *The Market Revolution*; for an excellent corrective to some of the romanticism inherent in Sellers's narrative, see Stokes and Conway, eds., *Market Revolution in America*. A full bibliography of recent works on the emergence of capitalism in the United States appears in Gilje, "Rise of Capitalism in the Early Republic."

7. Claeys, "Example of America a Warning to England?"

8. For harsh judgments of the British land-reform movements as impractical distractions from unionism, see Burchill and Ross, *History of the Potters' Union*, p. 84. Burchill and Ross followed the judgments of two earlier writers on the emigration society; see Warburton, *History of Trade Union Organization*, and Owen, *Staffordshire Potter*. Malcolm Chase has discussed the generally negative representation of the Chartist Land Company

in "We Wish Only to Work for Ourselves." For equally harsh judgments on
the American side, see N. Ware, *Industrial Worker*, p. xvii; Roediger and
Foner, *Our Own Time*, p. 63.

9. I agree with Edward Pessen, who argued that a movement should be
considered to have been a workers' movement as long as it sought workers
at least as supporters and sought to promote the causes and the welfare of
workers. See Pessen, *Most Uncommon Jacksonians*, p. 28.

10. On the right to property in labor, see Wilentz, *Chants Democratic*;
Faler, *Mechanics and Manufacturers*; Dawley, *Class and Community*. On
the rent issue, see Blackmar, *Manhattan for Rent*.

11. Murphy, *Ten Hours' Labor*; Lazerow, "Religion and Labor Reform"
and "Religion and the New England Mill Girl."

12. Bridges, *City in the Republic*, p. 80.

13. Goodman, "Emergence of Homestead Exemption."

14. John Saville, "Introduction," p. 59.

15. Chase, *People's Farm*, p. 188; Flett, "To Make That Future Now";
Guarneri, *Utopian Alternative*, p. 5.

16. Gronowicz, "Revising the Concept of Jacksonian Democracy," p.
117.

17. A wealth of basic information about the Chartist Land Plan can be
found in Hadfield, *Chartist Land Company*; Koga, "Chartist Land Scheme";
D. Jones, *Chartism and the Chartists*, pp. 128–37; D. Thompson, *Chartists*,
pp. 299–307; Armytage, "Chartist Land Colonies." The main source for the
Potters' Joint-Stock Emigration Society is Foreman, "Settlement of English
Potters in Wisconsin," although see also the brief discussion in J. F. C. Harrison, *Robert Owen and the Owenites*, pp. 228–29. Although there are several scholars currently working on the topic, the definitive monograph on
National Reform remains Zahler, *Eastern Workingmen*; the subject is also
treated in Wilentz, *Chants Democratic*, pp. 335–43.

18. G. Howell, "Ernest Jones, the Chartist."

19. For other case studies which use the Board of Trade lists of Chartist
subscribers to the land company, see Ashton, "Chartism in Gloucestershire"; Chase, "Chartism, 1838–58" and "Chartist Land Plan and the Local
Historian"; Little, "Liverpool Chartists" and "Chartism and Liberalism";
D. Jones, *Chartism and the Chartists*, pp. 133–37; D. Thompson, *Chartists*,
pp. 178, 342–68. For a case study of National Reform participation in upstate New York, see Huston, "Land and Freedom," pp. 471–86.

20. Malcolm Chase claims that the land plan did in fact cause such a re-
surgence of Chartist violence. See "Chartism, 1838–1858," p. 164. Thomas
Frost argued that such a land-impelled revival had occurred in his native
Croydon. See Frost, *Forty Year's Recollections*, p. 96.

21. Lause, "Progress Impoverished" and "Voting Yourself a Farm."

CHAPTER 1: THREE MOVEMENTS, ONE GOAL

1. *Voice of Industry*, vol. 1, no. 21, Nov. 21, 1845.

2. *Northern Star*, vol. 6, no. 304, Sept. 9, 1843.

3. Read and Glasgow, *Feargus O'Connor*, p. 111.

4. This short summary is assembled from Armytage, "Chartist Land Colonies," and Hadfield's heavily dramatized *Chartist Land Company*, which takes most of its information from the 1848 Select Committee on the National Land Company. See also MacAskill, "Chartist Land Plan"; Tiller, "Charterville and the Chartist Land Company"; Jebb, *Smallholdings*, chapter 3.

5. Stevens, *Memoir of Thomas Martin Wheeler*, p. 30.

6. The financially complicated, but comfortingly authentic-sounding, rules and objects of the land company are reprinted in D. Jones, *Chartism and the Chartists*, p. 201.

7. For an example of top-down communication, see *Northern Star*, vol. 10, no. 478, Dec. 19, 1846.

8. According to one estimate, 19,000 subscribers paid their shares in full, and 50,669 paid in part, the average payment being 2s 2d each. *Northern Star*, vol. 11, no. 565, Aug. 19, 1848.

9. *Northern Star*, vol. 9, no. 422, Dec. 13, 1845.

10. D. Jones, *Chartism and the Chartists*, p. 133.

11. *Northern Star*, vol. 10, no. 521, Oct. 16, 1847. George Whitmore Chinery, managing clerk for the treasurer of the National Land Company, 7,566 shareholders, representing £33,000 of the £130,000 subscribed, had signed the final deed, but it could not be handed in because it was later found that the list had to be in alphabetical order. Parliamentary Papers, *Reports from Committees*, vol. 19 (1847–48), First Report from the Select Committee on the National Land Company, Together with the Minutes of Evidence and Appendix, p. 14.

12. *Cheltenham Free Press*, no. 730, July 7, 1849.

13. This lack of knowledge would become legendary. See Parliamentary Papers, *Reports from Commissioners*, Royal Commission on Agriculture, 1882 (1), vol. 14, p. 251.

14. *Northern Star*, vol. 12, no. 628, Nov. 3, 1849.

15. *Northern Star*, vol. 13, no. 633, Dec. 8, 1849.

16. *Northern Star*, vol. 14, no. 702, Apr. 19, 1851.

17. Armytage, "Chartist Land Colonies," p. 95.

18. Margot Finn mentions O'Connor's "syphilitic decline" in *After Chartism*, p. 82.

19. *Northern Star*, vol. 13, no. 672, Sept. 7, 1850.

20. *National Union*, no. 3, July 1858; no. 6, Oct. 1858.

21. Personal observation of O'Connorville, Apr. 1994. The best description of the contemporary appearance of the Chartist allotments is Dennis Hardy, *Alternative Communities*, pp. 89–105.

22. The others present included Thomas Devyr, James Pyne, James Maxwell, and Lewis Masquerier. According to Boston, *British Chartists in America*, Pyne, a picture-frame maker, hailed, like Devyr, from Newcastle. Boston refers to Pyne as "possibly a Chartist" in his appendix (p. 94), and as a "former Chartist" twice in his text (pp. 26, 54); the source of these refer-

ences is unclear. Jonathan Halperin Earle has emphasized in his recent dissertation that Devyr, with his recent experience in the Anti-Rent movement of upstate New York, was a motive force behind the organization of the National Reform movement. Earle, "Undaunted Democracy," p. 82.

23. *Working Man's Advocate*, vol. 1, no. 2, Mar. 30, 1844.

24. Ibid.

25. *Northern Star*, vol. 7, no. 342, June 1, 1844.

26. *Northern Star*, vol. 7, no. 343, June 8, 1844.

27. *Working Man's Advocate*, vol. 1, no. 30, Oct. 19, 1844.

28. *New York Daily Tribune*, vol. 5, no. 48, June 4, 1845.

29. Goodman, "Emergence of Homestead Exemption."

30. On the Emigration Society, see Owen, *Staffordshire Potter*; Boston, "William Evans and the Potters' Emigration Society"; Foreman, "Settlement of English Potters in Wisconsin"; Warburton, *History of Trade Union Organization*. On the character of radical politics in Hanley and Stoke-on-Trent in this period, see R. A. Lowe, "Mutual Improvement in the Potteries."

31. To operate the jolly, the potter picks up one of a series of open molds, which resemble flowerpots, whose insides are contoured to the shape of the desired item. The molds have been filled with clay beforehand by the operative's helper, often a child. The entire mold is then spun at a high rate of speed while a contoured tool, resembling a small meat-hook on a flexible arm, is brought down from above into the filled mold, distributing the clay all around the inside of the mold—throwing the pot from the inside out. The mold is then left to dry, the entire mechanical process having taken only a few seconds. A similar machine, the "jigger," was invented to do the same for plates. Display, May 1994, Gladstone Pottery Museum, Longton, Stoke-on-Trent.

32. W. Evans, *Art and History of the Potting Business*, p. x.

33. Burchill and Ross, *History of the Potters' Union*, p. 83.

34. *Potters' Examiner and Workman's Advocate*, vol. 1, no. 8, Jan. 20, 1844.

35. *Potters' Examiner and Workman's Advocate*, vol. 6, no. 24, Dec. 12, 1846.

36. Seeing themselves as working-class diplomats, Hamlet Copeland, John Sawyer, and James Hammond detoured to Washington in an abortive attempt to present a hand-thrown handled vase to General Land Commissioner Thomas Blake, who had helped negotiate the land purchase. Although Blake was not in the Land Office at the time of their arrival, they did manage to present the urn, along with a rhetorical flourish, to one of Blake's brothers, who worked in the same building. The entire gift consisted of a Doric vase and "beautiful lizard candlesticks" on a pedestal, grounded in morone and inscribed in gold, "A tribute of respect; presented by the Potters' Joint-Stock Emigration Society and Savings Fund to the Hon. T. H. Blake, General Land Commissioner of the United States of North America,

Anno Domini 1846." Copeland and Sawyer also managed to meet the president. See *Potters' Examiner and Workman's Advocate*, vol. 5, no. 8, Jan. 17, 1846, and vol. 5, no. 26, May 23, 1846.

37. *Potters' Examiner and Workman's Advocate*, vol. 7, no. 17, Apr. 24, 1847.

38. On the idea of a "moral economy," see E. P. Thompson, "Moral Economy of the English Crowd."

39. *Potters' Examiner and Workman's Advocate*, vol. 7, no. 25, June 19, 1847.

40. For the original handwritten, and printed revised, rules of the society, originally called the Potters' Emigration Society and Savings Fund, see Public Record Office, Kew, FS 1 657/607. For the registration of the company under the Friendly Societies Act, see FS 2/4. *Potters' Examiner and Emigrant's Advocate*, vol. 9, no. 88, p. 699. I thank Jodie Minor for locating the Friendly Society records.

41. The existence of at least one branch was recorded in Airdrie, Ashton-under-Lyne, Ayrshire, Bedford, Belshill, Bingley, Birmingham, Bolton, Broseley, Burslem, Bury, Clitheroe, Cornwall, Crewe, Dalehall, Dukinfield, Dundee, Enfield, Farnworth, Glasgow, Greenock, Halifax, Hanley, Huddersfield, Hull, Hyde, Lanark, Leeds, Lees, Lenoxtown, Liverpool, London (seven branches), Kilburnie, Kirkady, Macclesfield, Manchester, Newcastle, Oldham, Paisley, Poynton, Rochdale, Sheffield, Stoke, Stratford, Swindon, Tunstall, Whitburn, Wigan, and Wishawtown. Grant Foreman counted a total of 39 branch societies. See Foreman, "Settlement of English Potters in Wisconsin," p. 382.

42. *Potters' Examiner and Emigrant's Advocate*, vol. 9, no. 65, p. 522; vol. 9, no. 72, p. 570; vol. 9, no. 77, p. 608; vol. 9, no. 78, pp. 620–22; vol. 10, no. 12, p. 93. The newspaper under its new title no longer contains the date of each issue.

43. *Potters' Examiner and Emigrant's Advocate*, vol. 9, no. 68, p. 540; vol. 9, no. 73, p. 579.

44. *Potters' Examiner and Emigrant's Advocate*, vol. 10, no. 14, p. 159.

45. Boston, "William Evans and the Potters' Emigration Society," pp. 36–37.

46. *Northern Star*, vol. 13, no. 669, Aug. 17, 1850.

47. Boston, "William Evans and the Potters' Emigration Society," p. 42.

48. Public Record Office, Kew, FS 1 657/607. There may once have been a letter in the envelope, but if so, it is no longer in the file.

CHAPTER 2: THE INTELLECTUAL
HERITAGE OF REFORM

1. O'Connor, *The Land and Its Capabilities*. John Saville noted that this wide-ranging discussion of land as a viable option for alleviating social distress had included interventions from conservative Tories, moderate middle-class men, and fringe radicals alike. Saville, "Introduction," p. 51.

2. Parliamentary Papers, *Reports from Committees*, Select Committee to Inquire into Allotment System, and Propriety of Setting Apart Portion of Waste Land for Labouring Poor, 1843 (402), vol. 7.

3. Harrington, *Commonwealth of Oceana*. Harrington, himself the scion of an aristocratic family, spent time at Oxford and in Europe before writing his tract. Despite the fact that he was not personally involved in the Civil War, when the Restoration came, he was arrested on suspicion of wanting a change of government. Upon his release from prison, he drank himself into oblivion and was never quite the same until his death in 1677. Leslie Stephen, ed., *Dictionary of National Biography*, vol. 24 (New York: Macmillan, 1890), pp. 434–36.

4. On Paine's background and influence, see E. Foner, *Tom Paine*.

5. Thomas Paine, *Agrarian Justice*, p. 183. Gregory Claeys argues that Paine turned to a "progress"-based argument because his religious views made it uncomfortable for him to made a deity-based argument. Claeys, "Paine's *Agrarian Justice*."

6. On Paine's *Agrarian Justice*, see also Claeys, *Thomas Paine*, pp. 196–208.

7. This distinction was not lost on Paine's contemporaries. See T. Spence, "Rights of Infants," in Gallop, ed., *Pigs' Meat*, p. 124.

8. On the impact of Harringtonian and agrarian thought generally during the early years of the United States' existence, see Conkin, *Prophets of Prosperity*. On land as a recurring trope in American thought, and on Jefferson's view of farming in particular, see L. Marx, *Machine in the Garden*; and Bender, *Toward an Urban Vision*.

9. Jefferson, *Notes on the State of Virginia*, pp. 164–65.

10. Ibid.

11. Ogilvie (1736–1819) was born into a landowning family and attended King's College, Aberdeen, and Edinburgh University before taking up a chair at King's College, Aberdeen, where he was a noted classical scholar and numismatist. Also interested in agriculture, he sold his estate in 1772 to buy some poor land in the hopes of cultivating it to full flower; he made a profit of £2,500 on the deal. Ogilvie was known in America during his lifetime; he received an honorary degree from Columbia University, and George Washington owned a copy of his *Essay on the Right of Property in Land*. Sidney Lee, ed., *Dictionary of National Biography*, vol. 42 (New York: Macmillan, 1895), pp. 21–22. For more on Ogilvie as an English agrarian, see Eayrs, "Political Ideas of the English Agrarians." Max Beer grouped Ogilvie with Spence and Paine in his *Pioneers of Land Reform*.

12. Ogilvie, *Essay on the Right of Property in Land*, p. 154.

13. Ibid., p. 11.

14. Ibid., p. 193.

15. Hall (1745–1825) became a medical student at Leiden in 1765, and then took the degree of M.D. He published the *Medical Family Instructor, with an Appendix on Canine Madness* in 1785, and his *Effects of Civilization* twenty years later. At the time of the publication of the latter, he was

bankrupted by a lawsuit and soon after had to move to the Fleet Prison, where he died at age 80 in 1825. See Leslie Stephen, ed., *Dictionary of National Biography*, vol. 24 (New York: Macmillan, 1890), pp. 60–61. Hall also corresponded with Thomas Spence, which correspondence was preserved by Francis Place and is in the British Library, BM Add. MS 27,808.

16. C. Hall, *Effects of Civilization*, pp. 70–88.

17. Ibid., p. 210.

18. Much later, American novelist Edward Bellamy would devise a similar plan for producing manufactures for the public good, and minimizing the cost of such work to the laborer. See *Looking Backward*. Bellamy's work, which also draws heavily on the Associationist theories of Charles Fourier, demonstrates that Hall's ideas were not necessarily "backward-looking" but rather might be compatible with an industrial society.

19. C. Hall, *Effects of Civilization*, p. 213.

20. Ibid., p. 205.

21. Ibid., p. 175.

22. Hodgskin, *Natural and Artificial Rights*.

23. Epstein, *Radical Expression*, pp. 22–23.

24. Chase, *People's Farm*, p. 18; for the later history of the Spenceans, see McCalman, *Radical Underworld*.

25. Notes for a Biography of Thomas Spence, Francis Place Collection, BM Add. MS 27,808, p. 154.

26. Ibid., p. 153.

27. Ibid., p. 152.

28. Gallop, ed., *Pigs' Meat*, p. 16; Chase, *People's Farm*, p. 33.

29. T. Spence, *Constitution of Spensonia*, in Waters, ed., *Trial of Thomas Spence*, p. 95.

30. In this way, Spence's proposal was a forerunner of that of Henry George. P. M. Kemp-Ashraf claims that Spence was a proto-Marxist, and that his version of "the land" encompassed all natural resources, including man-made improvements and permanent structures: "The intention is to make the sources of wealth, as well as of primary subsistence, common property." See Kemp-Ashraf, "Introduction," p. 271.

31. Gallop, ed., *Pigs' Meat*, p. 105.

32. T. Spence, *Description of Spensonia* (London: Hive of Liberty, 1795); reprinted in Waters, ed., *Trial of Thomas Spence in 1801*, p. 91.

33. Ibid., pp. 89–101.

34. Gallop, ed., *Pigs' Meat*, p. 31.

35. Wood, *Radical Satire*, pp. 64–90.

36. George Henry Evans was an admirer of Spence but felt Spence's prescriptions more appropriate to a thickly settled country than to the United States. *Radical*, no. 7, July 1841, p. 97. Evans reprinted Spence's "Meridian Sun of Liberty" in his newspaper.

37. *Working Man's Advocate*, vol. 1, no. 1, Mar. 16, 1844.

38. *Working Man's Advocate*, vol. 1, no. 11, June 8, 1844.

39. Based on an examination of the contents of the British Library catalog.

40. *Northern Star*, vol. 1, no. 35, July 14, 1838.

41. *Gloucester Journal*, vol. 125, no. 6503, Aug. 21, 1847.

42. *Gloucester Journal*, vol. 126, no. 6538, Apr. 17, 1848.

43. Campbell, *Theory of Equality*, p. 46. See also Public Record Office (hereafter PRO) HO 45/249C, no. 215, poster.

44. For the Owenite backgrounds of land reformers Lewis Masquerier and George Henry Evans, see Claeys, "Lewis Masquerier."

45. J. Wiener, *Radicalism and Freethought*, p. 105. Carlile was not, however, an adherent of Spence.

46. For Wedderburn's writings, see McCalman, ed., *Horrors of Slavery*.

47. For the link between Spence and violence, see T. Spence, *End of Oppression*, p. 7. On Davenport: only a thousand copies of his 1836 *Life, Writings and Principles of Thomas Spence* were ever printed. See Davenport, *Life and Literary Pursuits*, p. 68.

48. Ibid., p. 42.

49. Ibid., p. 58.

50. Davenport, *Life, Writings and Principles*, p. 5.

51. Compare an editorial in the *Northern Star*, vol. 9, no. 472, Nov. 7, 1846: "all the armed forces at the disposal of European monarchs dare not invade a people entrenched in their own cottages, bivouacked upon their own inheritance, and ready as one man to fly to the cry of 'my cottage is in danger.'"

52. Davenport, *Life, Writings and Principles*, pp. 14–24.

53. *Reasoner and Herald of Progress*, no. 10, Aug. 6, 1846, p. 158.

54. *Northern Star*, vol. 1, no. 31, June 16, 1838. Malcolm Chase convincingly posits Spenceanism and the Chartist Land Plan as common opponents of centralized government, in contrast with land nationalization schemes like that of O'Brien. See Chase, "The Land and the Working Classes," p. 233. A direct influence of Spence on O'Connor is, however, very hard to prove. Harney's mention of Spence was one of only two I was able to locate in the entire 13-year run of the *Northern Star*.

55. *Northern Star*, vol. 8, no. 407, Aug. 30, 1845, contains a review of Allen Davenport's biography of Spence. See also Chase, *People's Farm*, p. 1; Claeys, *Citizens and Saints*, pp. 239–40. For another *Northern Star* reference to the "people's farm," see Allen Davenport's poem "The Land, the People's Farm," reprinted in Chase, ed., *Life and Literary Pursuits of Allen Davenport*, p. 120.

56. Kemp-Ashraf, "A Selection from the Works of Thomas Spence," p. 289 n. 12. Among the tracts on land reform in Harney's library was Allen Davenport's autobiography; see Hambrick, *Chartist's Library*, p. 83.

57. *London Democrat*, no. 3, Apr. 27, 1839, p. 20. This definition of social equality echoed the words of Joseph Rayner Stephens, a social democrat who was *not* a political democrat. See *infra*, Chaps. 3 and 6. The only article by Allen Davenport which appears in the existing issues of the *London Democrat* ran on June 8, 1839, in the ninth number, and focused on universal suffrage rather than the land.

58. *Democratic Review*, Feb. 1850, p. 352.

59. Norman Ware supposed both National Reformer George Henry Evans and his father had been Spenceans in England, and fled to America in the 1810's to avoid being jailed for their political opinions. Ware seems to have based this conclusion on a coincidence of names: both George Henry Evans's uncle and his grandfather were named Thomas Evans, and a senior and junior Thomas Evans published Spencean works. As Newman Jeffrey has shown, however, this purported relationship, however tantalizing, could not exist; both Spencean Thomas Evanses were in an English prison in March 1818, six months after the Thomas Evans who was George Henry Evans's relative had come to New York. N. Ware, *Industrial Worker*, p. 181; Jeffrey, "Social Origins of George Henry Evans," p. 151.

60. On the equation of land with political power in America, in contrast with its economic usefulness in England, see Griswold, *Farming and Democracy.*

61. Gilbert, "Sketch of the Life of Thomas Skidmore," in *Free Enquirer*, vol. 1, no. 24, Apr. 6, 1834. See also Pessen, *Most Uncommon Jacksonians*, pp. 59–65.

62. Skidmore, *Rights of Man to Property!*

63. Ibid., p. 99.

64. Ibid., p. 59.

65. Cf. Malthus, quoted in Himmelfarb, *Idea of Poverty*, p. 122: "A man who is born into a world already possessed, if he cannot get subsistence from his parents on whom he has a just demand, and if the society do not want his labour, has no claim of *right* to the smallest portion of food, and in fact, has no business to be where he is. At nature's mighty feast there is no vacant cover for him. . . . If these guests get up and make room for him, other intruders immediately appear demanding the same favour . . . the order and harmony of the feast is disturbed, the plenty that before reigned is changed into scarcity and the happiness of the guests is destroyed by the spectacle of misery and dependence in every part of the hall."

66. Skidmore, *Rights of Man to Property*, pp. 137–44.

67. Ibid., p. 390.

68. Even Thomas Spence had trouble romancing his radical audiences from the idea of private property. In his scathingly satirical recantation of his ideas, he mentions "the dread of not being able to buy land, according to my system . . . it is a sin to lessen even the ideal comforts of the poor by destroying their hopes of distant greatness: I leave them therefore to the enjoyment of their golden dreams, and give up that system which I *foolishly* conceived for their happiness, that they may yet have a right to buy land! Yes, that pennyless beggars may yet have a right to buy land!" *Spence's Recantation of the End of Oppression*, p. 6. Edward Pessen thinks it possible that Jacksonian labor leaders questioned private property, but his evidence for this is questionable. See Pessen, *Most Uncommon Jacksonians*, p. 148.

69. *Working Man's Advocate*, vol. 1, no. 4, Apr. 20, 1844.

70. This episode, and the impact of British radicalism upon it, are discussed in detail in Wilentz, *Chants Democratic*, pp. 172–216.

71. On Skidmore's position vis-à-vis a movement of "workers," see Dorfman, "Jackson Wage-Earner Thesis." On the type of political economy to which Skidmore may have been reacting, see Hamilton, *Progress of Society*.

72. Savetsky, "New York Working Men's Party," p. 23.

73. Hugins, *Jacksonian Democracy and the Working Class*, p. 149.

74. Savetsky, "New York Working Men's Party," p. 13. John Jentz, taking a sample of 515 members of the Working Men's Party in 1829–30, discovered 69.7 percent of them were artisans, in marked overrepresentation to their numbers in the population. Only 3.3 percent were laborers, 17 percent shopkeepers, 3.1 percent merchants, and 6 percent professionals. Jentz, "Artisans, Evangelicals, and the City," pp. 139–45.

75. Emphasizing that Skidmore's ideas did have complete sway over the Working Men for a short time is Edward Pessen, in "Thomas Skidmore: Agrarian Reformer."

76. *Working Man's Advocate*, vol. 1, no. 12, Jan. 16, 1830.

77. *Working Man's Advocate*, vol. 1, no. 22, Mar. 27, 1830.

78. *Working Man's Advocate*, vol. 1, no. 23, Apr. 3, 1830.

79. *Working Man's Advocate*, vol. 1, no. 47, July 28, 1830; Pessen, *Most Uncommon Jacksonians*, p. 63.

80. Ibid.; Commons, *History of Labor in the United States*, p. 245.

81. Quoted in *Working Man's Advocate*, vol. 1, no. 6, Dec. 5, 1829.

82. Skidmore, *Rights of Man to Property!*, pp. 137–44.

83. *Radical*, vol. 1, no. 4, Apr. 1841, p. 52.

84. Another American writer on political economy, Langton Byllesby, expressed views similar to those of Skidmore in his *Observations on the Sources and Effects of Unequal Wealth*. In 1852, Langton Byllesby was one of about eighteen hundred signers to a pro-homestead petition sent to Congress from Philadelphia. See petition from Philadelphia, Apr. 26, 1852, Sen 32A H2o, National Archives.

85. See, for example, Gaskell, *Artisans and Machinery*, p. 49.

86. Cobbett remained a folk hero even among Chartists. W. E. Adams remembered how, as a small boy, his mother had made sure he knew the difference between Cobbett and Free Trader Richard Cobden. "The old lady . . . was careful to explain to me that Cobbett and Cobden were two different persons—that Cobbett was the hero, and that Cobden was just a middle class advocate." Adams, *Memoirs of a Social Atom*, p. 163.

87. O'Connor, *Practical Work on the Management of Small Farms*, p. 5.

88. For Cobbett's role as popular politician, see Dyck, *William Cobbett and Rural Popular Culture*.

89. Cobbett, *Cottage Economy*, p. 5.

90. William Evans, editor of the emigrationist *Potters' Examiner*, thought Cobbett would have been horrified at O'Connor's suggestion that the main item of cultivation on the Chartist farms, as well as a staple of the

diet, was to be Cobbett's "damnable root," the potato. Cobbett was a bread-and-beer man, and for him and other Olde Englishmen the potato brought to mind the unsavory conditions of the Irish peasant. See *Potters' Examiner and Workman's Advocate*, vol. 4, no. 6, July 5, 1845; and Cobbett, *Cottage Economy*, p. 49.

91. Blacker, *Essay on the Improvement*, pp. 28–32.

92. Ibid., p. 59.

93. Allen, *Colonies at Home*, p. 21.

94. Although between 1795 and 1835, 184 pamphlets were printed suggesting allotments for the poor (a third of these between 1830 and 1833), there were some lingering fears that allotments might be taken to justify a global right to the soil. See Barnett, "Allotments and the Problem of Rural Poverty, 1780–1840," pp. 175–77. For the vindication of the idea of peasant proprietorship based on contemporary examples in other countries, see Thornton, *Plea for Peasant Proprietors*, p. 220. Arguing that proprietorship impelled peasants to undertake long-term improvements, Thornton suggested a scheme for granting wasteland in Ireland to the landless. On Thornton's relationship to later nineteenth-century land reformers, including J. S. Mill, see Dewey, "Rehabilitation of the Peasant Proprietor."

95. The writings of the society influenced social commentator Peter Gaskell, who advanced the idea that the land was unique in combining economic amelioration with moral encouragement for the poor. Gaskell, *Artisans and Machinery*, p. 56.

96. *Labourer's Friend*, vol. 1, no. 1 (1833). On the question of allotments for the poor, see also Young, *Inquiry into the Propriety of Applying Wastes*, p. 32: "What evil would be felt, what scarcity would be thought of while a system was maturing and gradually coming into effect which was to place every man under the shade of his own vine, his wife milking her cow, and his children weeding the potatoes?"

97. See also Gaskell, *Artisans and Machinery*, pp. 51–53.

98. J. Burn, *Familiar Letters*, pp. 6, 51; *Labourer's Friend*, n.s., no. 87, June 1838, p. 76.

99. This was not an idea completely foreign to Chartists, either. See "Factory System," p. 8.

100. *Labourer's Friend*, vol. 1 (1833), pp. 60–61.

101. *Labourer's Friend*, vol. 2 (1834), p. 69.

102. *Labourer's Friend*, vol. 2 (1834), p. 99.

103. *Labourer's Friend*, vol. 1 (1833), p. 327.

104. "Useful Hints for the Labourer," *Labourer's Friend Tracts*, no. 102 (Nov. 1840), p. 41.

105. For example, he advised his O'Connorville allottees not to patronize the beer shop adjoining the land, not to become poachers, not to discuss religion in the schoolhouse, not to grumble, and not to neglect their families' educations. *Northern Star*, vol. 10, no. 498, May 8, 1847.

106. *Labourer's Friend*, vol. 1 (1833), p. 51.

107. *Labourer's Friend*, vol. 1 (1833), p. 285. Cf. Charles Hall: "If every

man had an allotment of land, had his patrimony, his inheritance, every man would fight bravely, expose himself to the greatest danger, to maintain his stake." C. Hall, *Effects of Civilization*, pp. 126–29. For similar views, see *Cheltenham Free Press*, no. 703, Dec. 30, 1848.

108. *Northern Star*, vol. 2, no. 55, Dec. 1, 1838; vol. 5, no. 213, Dec. 11, 1841; vol. 4, no. 202, Sept. 25, 1841.

109. *Labourer's Friend*, n.s., no. 48 (Mar. 1835), p. 57; C. Hall, *Effects of Civilization*, pp. 229–32.

110. As Malcolm Chase has pointed out, a belief in the efficiency of spade husbandry was one of the only factors which united William Cobbett, Robert Owen, and O'Connor. See Chase, "We Wish Only to Work for Ourselves," p. 142.

111. O'Connor, *A Practical Work on the Management of Small Farms*, p. 46; Parliamentary Papers, *Reports from Committees*, Select Committee on the National Land Company (1848) 1, vol. 19, Third Report, pp. 26–29; Letter from Archibald Scott, *Labourer's Friend*, vol. 2 (1834), p. 113.

112. *Northern Star*, vol. 5, no. 241, June 25, 1842, p. 6. An editorial said of such allotment systems: "The small allotment system is but an ekeing out of the slender means of the under-paid operative . . . it does not place the man or the family in an independent position! He is not as the Englishman ought to be. . . . The position we should wish man to occupy on the land, is one of independence! To be there his own master! To have sufficient of surface in his occupation to occupy his labour hours, and return him an adequate LIVING." *Northern Star*, vol. 6, no. 270, Jan. 14, 1843.

113. The *Manchester Guardian* suggested dissemination of the report would do great good, and agreed that the desire to obtain allotments was universal among mechanics and laborers. See, no. 1514, July 12, 1843.

114. Parliamentary Papers, *Reports from Committees*, Select Committee to Inquire into Allotment System, and Propriety of Setting Apart Portion of Waste Land for Labouring Poor, 1843 (402), vol. 7, p. iii. Members of the Select Committee were Cowper, John Stuart Wortley, Stanton, Estcourt, Escott, Lord Worsley, Lord Ashley, Lord Robert Grosvenor, Wyse, Lord John Manners, Ferrand, Stansfield, Childers, Sir Edward Knatchbull, and Viscount Barrington.

115. Ibid., p. 82.

116. Ibid., pp. 26, 52, 78.

117. Select Committee to Inquire into Allotment System, and Propriety of Setting Apart Portion of Waste Land for Labouring Poor, 1843 (402), vol. 7, pp. 80–85.

118. Ibid., p. 108.

119. Ibid., pp. iv–vii.

CHAPTER 3: LAND-REFORM RHETORIC

1. Quoted in *Albany Freeholder*, vol. 5, no. 5, May 2, 1849.

2. Shannon, "Homestead Act and the Labor Surplus." For a recent review of the question, see Deverell, "To Loosen the Safety Valve."

3. On a visit to the United States in 1834, French social commentator Michael Chevalier was already propagating a myth of a "safety-valve" connection between the West and a relatively quiet—because powerful— American work force. See Chevalier, *Society, Manners and Politics*, p. 144.

4. Such language seems to have appealed even to those who had no first-hand knowledge of the factory. See Chapter 6 *infra* for rural American land-reform petitions.

5. Campbell, *Theory of Equality*, p. 44. Campbell, who described him-self as a former member of one of O'Connor's executive committees, was in contact with the National Reform movement by July 1845. *National Reformer*, vol. 1, no. 2, Oct. 10, 1846.

6. Pessen, *Most Uncommon Jacksonians*, p. 128.

7. Address of the workingmen of Charlestown, Mass., 1840, quoted in *Boston Quarterly Review*, vol. 1, Jan. 1841, p. 121.

8. Ibid., p. 123. For a similar view of the possible encroachments of ma-chinery, see *Young America*, Gerrit Smith Collection pamphlets, no. 217.

9. *Northern Star*, vol. 5, no. 255, Oct. 1, 1842.

10. *Northern Star*, vol. 6, no. 281, Apr. 1, 1843; vol. 6, no. 282, Apr. 8, 1843.

11. W. E. Adams noted the similarities between O'Connor's rhetoric and Stephens's in his 1903 *Memoirs of a Social Atom*, p. 178.

12. For use of this trope by National Reformers, see van Amringe's arti-cle on machinery in *Harbinger*, vol. 2, no. 24, May 23, 1846.

13. Stephens, *Political Pulpit*, p. 48.

14. For female roles in contributing to the family income during the pe-riod of protoindustrialization, see Berg, *Age of Manufactures*.

15. *Working Man's Advocate*, vol. 2, no. 46, Feb. 7, 1846.

16. Malcolm Chase discusses this and other rhetorical aspects of the Chartist Land Plan in "The Land and the Working Classes," pp. 217–33.

17. Faucher, *Manchester in 1844*, p. 118.

18. *Labourer*, vol. 1 (1847), p. 48.

19. *Jubilee Harbinger*, vol. 3 (1854), p. 105. See also *English Chartist Circular*, vol. 2, no. 138, p. 341: "We rejoice to see that the concoctors of the new plan or organization for the Chartist body have embodied in that plan certain ends which, if energetically worked out, may enable thousands to bid a glad farewell to their present filthy town courts and alley habitations, and become the cheerful denizens of comfortable country homesteads, erected by and for themselves."

20. *Ashton Chronicle*, no. 62, Aug. 18, 1848.

21. *Voice of Industry*, vol. 1, no. 24, Nov. 28, 1845; Adams, *Memoirs of a Social Atom*, p. 33; *Blue Hen's Chicken*, vol. 3, no. 5, Sept. 17, 1847.

22. According to Richard Carwardine, the culture of revivalism in the Great Awakening in Britain and America lent popular politics organiza-tional as well as rhetorical modes; political songs were set to hymns, speak-ers rotated as in camp meetings, and political campaigners, like religious

ones, drew a world divided between good and evil. See "Evangelicals, Politics, and the Coming of the American Civil War."

23. On the association of virtue with natural surroundings, see *Working Man's Advocate*, vol. 1, no. 40, Dec. 28, 1844. Avner Offer has asserted that English middle class was drawn to the land and to nature by a combination of religious arousal, sexualized vigorous activity, and aesthetic pleasure, and asserts that working people may not have responded to this appeal with quite the same fervor. *Property and Politics*, pp. 328–49.

24. *Massachusetts Ploughman*, Dec. 1842, quoted in *American Laborer* (1843), p. 259. See also *The People* (Wortley), vol. 2, no. 75, p. 179.

25. *Potters' Examiner and Workman's Advocate*, vol. 1, no. 14, Mar. 2, 1844.

26. *Potters' Examiner and Workman's Advocate*, vol. 1, no. 23, May 4, 1844.

27. Campbell, *Theory of Equality*, p. 105.

28. July 2, 1852, Sen 32A H20, National Archives.

29. Crèvecoeur, *Letters from an American Farmer*, pp. 51–65.

30. The Cincinnati National Reformers were a rare exception, claiming that the difficulty of subduing the frontier was a central reason why pioneers should not have to pay for these lands. *National Reformer*, vol. 1, no. 26, Mar. 27, 1847.

31. On New Jersey's role in this time as market gardener to New York City, see Spann, *New Metropolis*, p. 123. For a contrasting view on Evans's presentation of farm life, see Conkin, *Prophets of Prosperity*, p. 247.

32. *Potters' Examiner and Workman's Advocate*, vol. 2, no. 3, June 15, 1844.

33. Parry, *Letter to Feargus O'Connor, Esq.*

34. *Northern Star*, vol. 8, no. 411, Sept. 27, 1845. Perhaps compromised by his excited descriptions of life on the land, O'Connor was forced publicly to refute the assertion that he wanted all the laborers to go on the land: "if there were three millions of labourers in the labour market, and two millions could supply the demand, he did not wish the whole three millions to go upon the Land; nor the two millions; but the one million: those who were a 'surplus population' for the employers to fall back upon." *Northern Star*, vol. 6, no. 296, July 15, 1843. But compare vol. 8, no. 384, Mar. 22, 1845: "one and all can return from an artificial to a natural state, and can become cultivators of the soil. "

35. O'Connor, *Practical Work on the Management of Small Farms*, p. 156. O'Connor may have been drawing on the work of Charles Hall, who had similarly speculated on the output of an imaginary family tilling 3.5 acres of land: "By this method, I presume, five persons may be supported comfortably on three acres and a half of land," Hall had calculated—almost exactly O'Connor's estimate. See C. Hall, *Effects of Civilization*, pp. 236–39. For similar American appeals to plenty proceeding from a couple of acres, see *Working Man's Advocate*, vol. 1, no. 12, June 15, 1844. For a com-

parison of the arithmetical discourse of plenty in Paine, Spence, and O'Connor, see Chase, "Paine, Spence and the 'Real Rights of Man.'"

36. *Northern Star*, vol. 8, no. 399, July 5, 1845.

37. Erickson, *Invisible Immigrants*, pp. 27–28.

38. Joseph Hollingworth to William Rawcliff, Nov. 8, 1830, in Kulik, Parks, and Penn, eds., *New England Mill Village*, pp. 382–83.

39. Erickson, *Invisible Immigrants*, p. 164.

40. Ibid., p. 168.

41. For a demonstration of this fear, see "A Steam Cotton Mill," in *Awl*, vol. 1, no. 45, May 24, 1845. For the importance of the English example on the American consciousness, see Pessen, *Most Uncommon Jacksonians*, p. 157.

42. Gregory Claeys has identified belief in the perfectibility of man as a key characteristic of Owenite socialists in the 1840's, and it was completely shared by land-plan Chartists and American National Reformers. Belief that men's characters were made for them by their environments, and that poverty led to dissipation and not the other way around, helps to explain the lack of overlap between land reform and, for example, the temperance movement. Claeys, *Citizens and Saints*, p. 73.

43. Some of the land reformers seem to have deployed the language tactically; see Campbell, *Theory of Equality*, p. 94: "Although the opinions of [authorities] cannot make that which is true in fact, to be false in theory, or vice versa, yet their opinions carry a certain weight with the mass of mankind. The republican will admire the doctrines of a Jefferson and a Jackson, and the practical Christian will yield a ready assent to the law of the New Testament."

44. See, for example, *Monthly Jubilee* (May 1852), p. 79, which contains a land-reform sermon by Rev. J. L. Fairly, entitled "The Jubilee," delivered on Mar. 14, 1852 at the Third Presbyterian Church in Philadelphia.

45. Leviticus 25, quoted in Gallop, ed., *Pigs' Meat*, pp. 87–88.

46. In his periodical *Pigs' Meat*, Thomas Spence reprinted Leviticus 25: 8–28, with the editorial comment "Thus you see God Almighty himself is a very notorious leveller." See ibid., p. 69.

47. Ibid., p. 42. This verse can be sung nicely to the tune of "God Save the King," as Professor Peter Linebaugh demonstrated at the E. P. Thompson memorial conference, Conway Hall, London, July 1994.

48. J. F. C. Harrison categorizes the use of religious—or any familiar—discourse by reformers as habitual rather than intentional: *Robert Owen and the Owenites*, p. 91.

49. Robert Wedderburn came to land reform through Methodism, illustrating that the two movements could be complementary. McCalman, *Radical Underworld*, p. 66. On Spence's religious background, and its importance for his thought, see Knox, "Thomas Spence."

50. *Potters' Examiner and Workman's Advocate*, vol. 2, no. 8, July 20, 1844.

51. *Monthly Jubilee*, vol. 3, no. 7 (May 1853), p. 309.

52. For a Chartist land-reforming gloss on Psalm 33, see *Labourer*, vol. 3 (1848), p. 23. See also N. Ware, *Industrial Worker*, p. 18.

53. See, e.g., Bronterre O'Brien's *National Reformer*, vol. 1, no. 12, Dec. 19, 1846.

54. *National Reform Almanac for 1848*, p. 30.

55. See, e.g., Robert Lowery's 1839 *Address on the System of Exclusive Dealing*, reprinted in B. Harrison and Hollis, eds., *Robert Lowery*, p. 202; *Northern Star*, vol. 10, no. 502, June 5, 1847; vol. 12, no. 612, July 7, 1849; land-plan advertisement quoted in the *Manchester Examiner*, vol. 2, no. 53, Jan. 9, 1847; Parliamentary Papers, Reports of Commissioners, Royal Commission on Agriculture, 1882 (1), vol. 14, p. 250. For other contemporary usages, see *American Labourer*, May 1842, p. 49. Horace Greeley, later a National Reform supporter, served on a committee considering the effect of Free Trade on American labor. "We disclaim all aggressive protection. . . . We demand simply that the toiling masses of our own goodly land may be enabled to sit in peace beneath their own vine and fig tree secure in their several employments, and finding a just reward and stimulus for their industry in ministering to each other's wants and enjoyments to mutual advantage."

56. *Gloucester Journal*, no. 6655, Sept. 7, 1850.

57. *The People*, vol. 1, no. 38, p. 307.

58. *Northern Star*, vol. 2, no. 79, May 18, 1839. See also *Northern Star*, vol. 1, no. 50, Oct. 27, 1838.

59. This fact did not escape contemporary comment. As John Jackson commented to O'Connor, "he had now discovered the truth of what the Reverend J. R. STEPHENS said 3 years before, namely that 'The charter, of itself, was not worth two straws, without something else, and that something was the LAND.'" Jackson, *Demagogue Done Up*, p. 47. Cf. Stephens, *Northern Star*, vol. 2, no. 57, Dec. 15, 1838: "I would not give two straws either for Household Suffrage or Universal Suffrage, unless Universal Suffrage brought peace and plenty to the cottage, and light work and heavy wages."

60. See "Our National Defenses," *Labourer*, vol. 3 (1848), p. 44.

61. *Northern Star*, vol. 10, no. 458, Aug. 22, 1846.

62. *Monthly Jubilee* (May 1852), p. 61.

63. *Young America*, Gerrit Smith Collections, pamphlet no. 217.

64. On the evangelical climate in America in this period, see Wilentz, *Kingdom of Matthias*; P. Johnson, *Shopkeeper's Millennium*; Brooke, *Refiner's Fire*; C. Johnson, *Redeeming America*.

65. *Potters' Examiner and Workman's Advocate*, vol. 26, no. 5, Dec. 26, 1846. The importance of a religious/moral element in the construction of the identity of working people is recognized in Murphy, *Ten Hours' Labor*; and Lazerow, "Religion and Labor Reform."

66. *Young America*, vol. 2, no. 7, May 10, 1845.

67. Devyr, *Our Natural Rights*, p. 56.

68. *National Reformer* (Rochester), vol. 1, no. 35, May 25, 1848; *Jubilee; Radical*, vol. 1, no. 1, Jan. 1841.

69. Jentz, "Artisans, Evangelicals, and the City," pp. 119–20.

70. *Young America*, vol. 2, no. 50, Mar. 7, 1846. As noted in Chapter 5 *infra*, Vale met Holyoake, cementing an interest in American land reform which extended into the 1870's, J. K. Ingalls, a National Reformer working for cooperative colonies, also met George J. Holyoake when he was on a visit to America. Ingalls, *Reminiscences*, p. 62.

71. Petition from Boston, May 20, 1852, Sen 32A H20, National Archives.

72. *Voice of Industry*, vol. 3, no. 16, Oct. 29, 1847. For accounts of the various printers' freethought activities, see Post, *Popular Freethought*, pp. 34–74.

73. Apart from Spence, see Hodgskin, *Natural and Artificial Rights*, p. 55; Eayrs, "Political Ideas of the English Agrarians."

74. *Potters' Examiner and Workman's Advocate*, vol. 2, no. 7, July 13, 1844.

75. *Evening Star*, no. 56, Sept. 27, 1842. For other references to man's natural right to the soil, see *Northern Star*, vol. 8, no. 392, May 17, 1845; vol. 10, no. 481, Jan. 9, 1847; see also Noakes, *Right of the Aristocracy*.

76. Faler, *Mechanics and Manufacturers*, pp. 164–88; Dawley, *Class and Community*, pp. 73–96; Wilentz, *Chants Democratic*, pp. 107–42; Laurie, *Artisans into Workers*, pp. 38–46.

77. *Quaker City*, vol. 2, no. 24, Dec. 29, 1849.

78. *National Reform Almanac for 1848*, p. 44.

79. *People's Rights*, vol. 1, no. 19, July 27, 1844. For more on the Dorr War, see *Working Man's Advocate*, vol. 1, no. 19, Aug. 3, 1844; no. 20, Aug. 10, 1844.

80. Devyr, *Odd Book*, American Section, p. 49. For more revolutionary rhetoric, see *Voice of Industry*, vol. 3, no. 5, Aug. 14, 1847.

81. *Harbinger*, vol. 2, no. 7, Jan. 24, 1846.

82. Huxhorn, "United We Stand," p. 31.

83. This pamphlet, which Paul Conkin describes as a sloganeering attempt to disguise National Reform ethics, shares a remarkable rhythm with a passage from the March 2, 1844, issue of the *Potters' Examiner*: "Do you wish for health and longevity, go upon the land; do you wish for pure air, pure food, and wholesome exercise, go upon the land; do you wish to see your children, hardy in body, energetic in mind, and a prop to your declining years, go upon the land." See Conkin, *Prophets of Prosperity*, p. 256.

84. *True Workingman*, Jan. 24, 1846, reprinted in Commons, *Documentary History of American Industrial Society*, vol. 7, p. 307.

85. On the republican discourse, which has been described as "outdated" but one of the only discursive options at this time, see Berthoff, "Independence and Attachment"; Baker, "From Belief into Culture"; Appleby, "Republicanism and Ideology"; Rodgers, "Republicanism."

86. Campbell, *Theory of Equality*, p. 21.

87. Ibid., p. 25. Jefferson also used a natural-rights argument for return-ing the unemployed to the soil. See Jefferson, *Writings*, Monticello ed., vol. 19, p. 18: "Whenever there are in any country uncultivated lands and un-employed poor, it is clear that the laws of property have been so far ex-tended as to violate natural right. The earth is given as a common stock for man to labor and live on. If for the encouragement of industry we allow it to be appropriated, we must take care that other employment be provided to those excluded from the appropriation." Quoted in Hibbard, *History of the Public Land Policies*, p. 143.

88. Campbell, *Theory of Equality*, pp. 40–44.

89. Ibid., p. 80. Fourier made a similar division of society.

90. Ibid., pp. 44–45.

91. Finn, *After Chartism*, pp. 106–88.

92. T. Spence, *Meridian Sun of Liberty* (1796), reprinted in Gallop, ed., *Pigs' Meat*.

93. O'Connor, *Employer and the Employed*, p. 56.

94. O'Connor, *A Practical Work on the Management of Small Farms*, pp. 14–15.

95. *Northern Star*, vol. 10, no. 442, May 2, 1846.

96. *Jubilee Harbinger* (1854), p. 311.

97. Colley, *Britons*, illustrates the potential of working people for popu-lar patriotism; Joyce, *Visions of the People*, makes a case for paternalism having prevented the emergence of class solidarities in many cases until the end of the century.

98. Maps of Chartist allotments at Public Record Office, M.R. 105, M.R. 641, M.R. 104; *Northern Star*, vol. 10, no. 458, Aug. 22, 1846; vol. 9, no. 473, Nov. 15, 1846; and personal examination of the O'Connorville estate at Rickmansworth. This section is also based on descriptions of the Chartist allotments in Hadfield, *Chartist Land Company*, p. 90, and in Armytage, "Chartist Land Colonies."

99. Parliamentary Papers, *Reports from Committees*, Select Committee on the National Land Company (1848), vol. 19 Fourth Report, p. 23.

100. M. Anderson, *Family Structure*, p. 104.

101. Warnes, "Early Separation of Homes."

102. *Labourer*, vol. 1 (1847), p. 48.

103. Letter from Henry Smith, President, Monmouth County National Reform Association, May 22, 1852, Sen 32A H20, National Archives. The letter is in George Henry Evans's handwriting.

104. "Principles and Objects of the National Reform Association," *Pot-ters' Examiner and Workman's Advocate*, vol. 6, no. 25, Dec. 19, 1846. On the U.S. Rectangular Survey System, see H. Johnson, *Order upon the Land*.

105. Evans and his fellow planners would not have known that although de facto Western settlements lacked these planned public spaces, a sense of community was often heightened as settlers worked together to supply miss-ing roads and church buildings. See Faragher, "Open-Country Community."

106. Dennis Hardy's book illustrates that many "alternative communities" conceived in this period, including the Chartist Land Plan, sprang full-blown from the brain of single individuals. See *Alternative Communities*.

107. Masquerier, *Scientific Division*. This tract, which paid homage to the National Reformers and recommended they colonize Nebraska (which Masquerier renamed "Nebrashevil") was on sale at the Young America office. Masquerier himself was a native of Paris, Kentucky, scion of an English father who had traveled to Java and Calcutta before settling down in the wilds of the American frontier. Raised in Boonslick, Masquerier studied law and (ironically) speculated on land to support himself. In 1830, he was struck with an idea for a phonetic alphabet, and went to New York in search of type to propagate his new system. Once there, he began to deliver lectures on social subjects and soon fell in with the reforming crowd. Masquerier, *Sociology*, p. 135.

108. Claeys, "Lewis Masquerier."

109. Masquerier, *Sociology*, pp. 15–21.

110. *Potters' Examiner and Workman's Advocate*, vol. 7, no. 5, Jan. 30, 1847.

111. Erickson, *Invisible Immigrants*, p. 54. See also *Boston Chronotype*, vol. 2, no. 18, Sept. 23, 1847.

112. Christine Stansell describes New York workers' habits of sociability, and the extension of the "domestic sphere" into streets and yards and onto front stoops, in *City of Women*, p. 41.

113. On the uses of gender within factory reformers' rhetoric, see Gray, *Factory Question*, pp. 23–27.

114. Michael D. Pierson argues that patriarchy was a cornerstone of the antebellum Democratic Party, but underestimates its importance among reformers, including Free Soilers, in "Guard the Foundation Well."

115. In this way, the male-centered vision of "class" which Joan Scott describes as prevalent among historians reflects the aspirations of men— and many women—in the period of industrialization. See "On Language, Gender and Working Class History," pp. 53–67.

116. A. Clark, "Rhetoric of Chartist Domesticity"; Schwartzkopf, *Women in the Chartist Movement*, pp. 220–46, 264–82; Belchem, "Beyond Chartist Studies." Compare Joseph Rayner Stephens: "I argue from the word of God that man is to be the bread provider, and woman the bread distributor. . . .The woman's factory is on the hearthstone and over the kitchen fire; there is the woman's world. Her desire is to be at her husband's hearth and at her husband's bed." *Northern Star*, vol. 2, no. 53, Nov. 17, 1838.

117. *English Chartist Circular*, vol. 2, no. 70, p. 69.

118. O'Connor, *Practical Work on the Management of Small Farms*, p. 41; *Northern Star*, vol. 3, no. 131, May 16, 1840; vol. 10, no. 498, May 8, 1847.

119. *Voice of Industry*, vol. 1, no. 23, Nov. 21, 1845. While Evans cared enough to write the women an encouraging letter, none of the core National Reformers could be spared to address an audience of women at Lowell. See *infra*, Chapter 6.

120. *Albany Freeholder*, vol. 4, no. 43, Jan. 24, 1849. In Wisconsin, where lawmakers contemplated writing protection of the homestead into the new state's constitution, the issue was considered in tandem with women's property rights. On this aspect of homestead exemption, see Goodman, "Emergence of Homestead Exemption," p. 488.

121. *Voice of Industry*, vol. 2, no. 43, May 7, 1847. See also John Commerford's comment quoted in the *Northern Star*, vol. 7, no. 347, July 6, 1844: "Adopt this measure of freeing the land, and you would not see poor girls compelled to walk miles every morning, in all seasons and through all weather, to earn, by a long day's toil, the means of supporting their widowed mothers in some miserable garret or cellar up town. If the men of New York have a spark of manhood left, they will combine to break up a system that may subject their sisters, wives, and daughters to this misery and degradation."

122. *Voice of Industry*, vol. 1, no. 21, Nov. 7, 1845.

123. June 8, 1852, Sen 32A H20, National Archives.

124. *National Reformer* (Rochester), vol. 1, no. 11, Dec. 11, 1847. The most complete statement of the vision of National Reform leaders on the position of women in their movement can be found in the address "To the Working Women of New York," in *Working Man's Advocate*, vol. 1, no. 51, Mar. 15, 1845.

125. *Working Man's Advocate*, vol. 2, no. 43, Jan. 17, 1846.

126. The role of women was similar within the Anti-Rent movement of upstate New York. See Huston, "Land and Freedom," p. 342. For rhetoric about women at meetings, see *Working Man's Advocate*, vol. 1, no. 20, Aug. 10, 1844, and Lewis Ryckman's comments at George Henry Evans's commemorative ball, Feb. 25, 1847, reported in *Northern Star*, vol. 10, no. 493, Apr. 3, 1847.

127. *Voice of Industry*, vol. 1, no. 19, Sept. 25, 1845.

128. *Harbinger*, vol. 1, no. 1, June 14, 1845; *Working Man's Advocate*, vol. 2, no. 12, June 14, 1845.

129. Zboray and Zboray, "Political News and Female Readership."

130. David Zonderman has pointed out one reason why the National Reformers might expect a lack of interest in homestead from working women: "Men may have derived some ultimate satisfaction from working the land if they owned their farms and believed in the ideal of the independent yeoman. But women's farm labour was often done in an environment that offered little in the way of ownership or independence." *Aspirations and Anxieties*, p. 266.

131. This is not to claim that there are no signatures of women on the petitions. See, e.g., petition received from unknown location, Jan. 22, 1847, Sen 29A G19.1, National Archives. On the female operatives, see *Voice of Industry*, vol. 1, no. 28, Dec. 19, 1845; Roediger and Foner, *Our Own Time*, p. 60. For more on Cluer, see Murphy, *Ten Hours' Labor*; N. Ware, *Industrial Worker*, pp. 140–42; Magdol, *Antislavery Rank and File*, pp. 70–71.

132. Stone invited the National Reformers to come to Lowell on Octo-

ber 29, to share with the working people there the great principles behind National Reform: "Come and make known the fair prospects and bright hopes which open up to your far sighted visions—to our more obtuse and dull perceptions of the beautiful and true in National Reform." *New York Tribune,* vol. 5, no. 164, Oct. 18, 1845. See also her praise of National Reform in *Voice of Industry,* vol. 1, no. 31, Jan. 30, 1846.

133. *Young America,* vol. 2, no. 39, Dec. 20, 1845.

134. *Young America,* vol. 5, no. 27, Sept. 23, 1848.

135. The epitaph on the grave of George Henry Evans's wife, Laura, suggests that she impelled the movement by her stoic suffering: "she bore, without murmuring, all the privation necessary for the cause her husband had espoused, and now while we mourn the vacant chair, she sleeps calmly, with the branches above waving a requiem over her grave." Nothing more is known about her contribution. Masquerier, *Sociology,* pp. 102–3.

136. *Voice of Industry,* vol. 2, no. 50, June 25, 1847.

137. Ibid.

138. Ibid.

139. *National Reformer* (Rochester), vol. 1, no. 52, Sept. 14, 1848.

140. *Monthly Jubilee,* vol. 5, no. 9, Sept. 1855, pp. 111–16. Contemporary newspapers disagreed whether she had divorced her first husband or whether his death left her free to marry. General Jones, who ran a carpet-weaving mill capitalized to the amount of $400,000, with 300 handlooms and powerlooms, was a controversial figure himself, having been indecisively court-martialed for raising militia troops for his own company without official permission. *Monthly Jubilee,* vol. 3, no. 7, May 1853, p. 297; vol. 5, no. 9, Sept. 1855, p. 130.

141. *Monthly Jubilee,* vol. 4, no. 3, Mar. 1854, pp. 102–5.

142. *Monthly Jubilee,* vol. 5, no. 9, Sept. 1855, p. 125.

143. *Voice of Industry,* vol. 2, no. 51, July 2, 1847.

144. *Jubilee Harbinger* (1854), p. 342.

145. The one late Chartist female leader who appeared on the platform, Mrs. Theobald, was a proponent of temperance and Irish repeal and does not seem to have mentioned the land plan, although she did show some nostalgia for the land. *Preston Guardian,* no. 277, May 26, 1849; *Manchester Guardian,* no. 2045, Aug. 12, 1848.

146. *Northern Star,* vol. 10, no. 503, June 12, 1847; vol. 11, no. 543, Mar. 18, 1848; *Preston Guardian,* no. 214, Mar. 11, 1848.

147. *Northern Star,* vol. 10, no. 513, Aug. 21, 1847.

148. *Working Man's Advocate,* vol. 1, no. 7, May 11, 1844.

149. On the importance of spade husbandry for Chartist, Owenite, and Tory land-reform prescriptions alike, see Plummer, "Spade Husbandry."

150. *The People,* vol. 1, no. 5, p. 33. For a view which classifies land reform as primarily nostalgic, see Martin, "Land Reform."

151. For natural-rights rhetoric among the radical shoemakers of Lynn, see *Awl,* vol. 1, no. 19, Nov. 23, 1844.

CHAPTER 4: THE COMPETITION FOR
REFORMING ATTENTIONS

1. Frothingham, *Gerrit Smith*, p. 111.

2. E. Foner, *Free Soil*, p. 4.

3. Bestor, "Patent-Office Models of the Good Society." The situation was little different on the other side of the Atlantic, as the millennial prose of John Francis Bray suggests: *Labour's Wrongs*, p. 216.

4. For the relationship between antislavery and factory reform, see Gray, *Factory Question*, pp. 37–47; Drescher, "Cart Whip and Billy Roller." On the discourse of slavery in the Anglo-American context, see Cunliffe, *Chattel Slavery*.

5. *English Chartist Circular*, vol. 2, no. 119, p. 265.

6. Ignatiev, *How the Irish Became White*, p. 69.

7. T. Spence, *Restorer of Society to Its Natural State* (1803), in Gallop, ed., *Pigs' Meat*, p. 131.

8. For a contrasting view on the significance of land reformers' rhetoric on slavery, see Goodman, "Emergence of Homestead Exemption," p. 483.

9. Frederick Robinson, "Homestead Exemption Report," in Massachusetts Acts—1851, Chap 340, Act to Exempt from Levy on Execution the Homestead of a Householder Having a Family, Approved May 24, 1851. Massachusetts Archive, Columbia Point, Boston.

10. Schlueter, *Lincoln, Labor and Slavery*, pp. 54–55.

11. The Fourierite movement also viewed abolition as a major rival, and for the same reasons. See Guarneri, *Utopian Alternative*, pp. 252–58; Wennersten, "Parke Godwin."

12. Jentz, "Artisans, Evangelicals and the City," p. 55. For a statistical treatment of national antislavery petitions, see Magdol, *Antislavery Rank and File*; Fladeland, *Abolitionists and Working Class Problems*.

13. *Pleasure Boat*, quoted in the *Voice of Industry*, vol. 2, no. 33, Feb. 26, 1847.

14. See Earle, "Undaunted Democracy."

15. Ignatiev quotes Evans out of context, suggesting that he would have opposed the abolition of slavery even after land-reform measures had been gained. Evans's writings, when looked at in their entirety, do not support such an interpretation. See Ignatiev, *How the Irish Became White*, p. 80.

16. *Northern Star*, vol. 10, no. 440, Apr. 18, 1846; *Voice of Industry*, vol. 2, no. 50, June 18, 1847. Timms had been one among forty-odd New Yorkers who petitioned for the establishment of an Owenite branch there, and was also the Social Reformers' representative at the National Reform convention held at Croton Hall on May 10, 1845. See Claeys, "Lewis Masquerier."

17. Devyr to Johnson, Dec. 9, 1859, Andrew Johnson Papers, Library of Congress. See also Devyr's letter to the *Tribune*, reprinted in the *Albany Freeholder*, vol. 6, no. 9, Feb. 27, 1850.

18. Schlueter, *Lincoln, Labor and Slavery*, p. 73. See also J. Pickering, *Working Man's Political Economy*, p. 69.

19. Boston, *British Chartists in America*, pp. 57–64. For one demonization of labor reformers, see Rayback, "Industrial Workman." Racism did permeate the land-reform rank and file; see C. Plant's hapless parody of *Uncle Tom's Cabin* in *Monthly Jubilee*, vol. 3, no. 7, May 1853, p. 298.

20. John Campbell (1810–74) was an Irish weaver, elected to the executive of the National Charter Association in 1840. He was arrested and tried with O'Connor in 1843, and appeared in Philadelphia later that year. In 1844 he became the first secretary of the Social Reform Society and served as Horace Greeley's labor stringer for Philadelphia. Dorfman, *Economic Mind in American Civilization*, pp. 689–92.

21. Campbell, *Negro-Mania*, pp. 437–59.

22. Of course, land-reform prophet Thomas Jefferson did share similar views on black inferiority. See *Notes on the State of Virginia*, pp. 130–43.

23. T. Spence, *An Interesting Conversation*, reprinted in Gallop, ed., *Pigs' Meat*, p. 69. Cf. Fitzhugh, *Cannibals All!*

24. "Principles and Objects of the National Reform Association," reprinted in *Potters' Examiner and Workman's Advocate*, vol. 6, no. 25, Dec. 19, 1846.

25. Jonathan Glickstein tempers this view, asserting that abolitionists felt poverty built character and encouraged industry, and was therefore necessary; on the other hand, they wanted poverty to be escapable through hard work. See Glickstein, "Poverty Is Not Slavery."

26. See also E. Foner, "Abolitionism and the Labor Movement."

27. E. Foner, *Short History of Reconstruction*, pp. 35–54.

28. *Voice of Industry*, vol. 3, no. 5, Aug. 13, 1847.

29. *Working Man's Advocate*, vol. 1, no. 15, July 6, 1844; no. 17, July 20, 1844.

30. "Gerrit Smith," *Dictionary of American Biography*, vol. 27, ed. Dumas Malone (London: Oxford University Press, 1935), pp. 270–71 notes the following: born in 1797, Smith eventually succeeded to the entire control of his father's property, which was valued at $400,000. and was able to increase its extent and value. He therefore became a philanthropist. Besides giving away land, he was a reformer in the cause of the Sunday school and Sunday observance, was an anti-Mason, a vegetarian, a teetotaler, and an opponent of smoking, a dress reformer, and a believer in women's suffrage, prison reform, and the abolition of capital punishment. He was also probably an accessory before the fact to John Brown's raid on Harper's Ferry but was never punished; he died in 1874.

31. *People's Rights*, vol. 1, no. 18, July 24, 1844. This newspaper, also printed by Windt and Evans, came out several times a week but was eventually subsumed in the weekly paper.

32. The correspondence continued in *Working Man's Advocate*, vol. 1, no. 20, Aug. 10, 1844, and no. 21, Aug. 17, 1844, and Smith's wife sent the National Reformers ten dollars. By May 1845, at the New York National Reform convention, Smith was nominated as a possible friend of the agitation. See *Young America*, no. 7, May 10, 1845. By 1848, the National Re-

formers were selling his four-page tract "Letter on Land Monopoly" for 40 cents a hundred. See *Young America*, Apr. 29, 1848. Smith was finally nominated as the presidential candidate by the 1848 Free Soil convention; *Working Man's Advocate*, vol. 5, no. 27, Sept. 23, 1848.

33. Smith to Ingalls, Aug. 15, 1848 (n.p., 1848), State Library of New York, Albany. Another of Smith's letters, sent to one Brother Ritchie, was also reprinted as a tract. In it, Smith appealed to peace advocates by predicting that if there were no land monopoly, war would starve itself to death for "lack of food for powder." *National Reform Almanac for 1848*, p. 44.

34. Ibid.

35. This may not have been completely altruistic. Like the Free Traders' freehold land program in Britain in 1849–51, such a scheme could be expected to produce loyal (here, abolitionist) voters.

36. Frothingham, *Gerrit Smith*, pp. 102–3.

37. Ibid., p. 107. Between 1849 and 1852, the parcels Smith had supposedly given away were sold to pay his taxes, forcing the men cultivating these lands to buy them from the new owners at short notice. In 1852, one "poor coloured man" of Kingston, who had received 40 acres from Smith, was "very illy able to defray the expenses of a search" into his title, and a friend asked the Essex County clerk to perform this service gratis. B. M. Hasbrouck to Clerk of Essex County, Mar. 19, 1852, State Library of New York, Albany, MS 17710. It is not known how many of Smith's recipients were able to hold on to their plots after this incident.

38. News of Smith's philanthropy reached English working people through *The People* (Wortley), vol. 2, no. 61, p. 72.

39. "Circular," May 1, 1849, Gerrit Smith Papers, Syracuse University Archive, Syracuse, N.Y.

40. Frothingham, *Gerrit Smith*, p. 109. This episode was also reported under the heading "An American Nobleman," in Joseph Barker's *The People*, vol. 2, no. 61, p. 72.

41. Smith to John Cochran, Isaac T. Hopper, Daniel C. Eaton, George H. Evans, and William Kemeys, Jan. 4, 1850, Gerrit Smith Papers, Syracuse University Archive, N.Y.; *Albany Freeholder*, vol. 6, no. 15, Apr. 10, 1850.

42. Frothingham, *Gerrit Smith*, p. 111. In the long run, Smith's experiment in free black farming failed. Although the land was admittedly intractable and the climate harsh, Frothingham blamed the blacks for not having the gumption to become farmers, commenting sourly, "The disabling infirmities and vices of the black people Mr. Smith had the courage to admit. He had little hope of them as they were; on the best land they would have done nothing." *Gerrit Smith*, p. 112.

43. Garrison, ed., *Gerrit Smith on Land Monopoly*.

44. Devyr to Smith, Dec. 18, 1856, Gerrit Smith Papers, Syracuse University Archive, N.Y.

45. Despite his forays into land philanthropy, Smith's beneficence did not extend to Evans and *Young America*. Thomas Devyr later denounced Smith for refusing to donate thirty or forty dollars a month to support Evans

in publishing his land-reform newspaper, forcing an ignoble end to the affair: "Evans was literally starved back to his mortgaged spot of ground in New Jersey. Greeley held a mortgage on it for $200—had imperative need and must get the money he lent—but would take no interest. . . . Instead of cultivating the stony public mind George went to cultivate melons." Devyr, *Odd Book*, American Section, p. 115.

46. *Northern Star*, vol. 7, no. 347, July 6, 1844. The editors also argued, more controversially, that freed slaves were entitled to the vote, and arms with which to protect themselves.

47. Lovett, *Life and Struggles*, p. 237. *Northern Star*, vol. 4, no. 183, May 15, 1841.

48. This was not the first time the subject of the land and its relationship to workers had been brought before the *Star's* readership—a series of articles by John Finch on Ralahine, the abortive Irish utopian community, ran from April 21 to May 19, 1838.

49. The Anti–Corn Law League, headquartered in Manchester, was an extremely well-funded lobbying organization composed of manufacturers and liberals. Using speeches, newspapers, and Parliamentary representatives, it sought to have repealed a series of laws which protected the English agricultural interest by taxing incoming grain. The act repealing the Corn Laws was passed in the wake of the Irish famine in 1846. Two books detailing the work of the league are McCord, *Anti–Corn Law League*, and Longmate, *Breadstealers*.

50. *Bolton Free Press*, vol. 5, no. 218, Jan. 18, 1840.

51. On the nature of this antagonism, see Brown, "Chartists and the Anti–Corn-Law League." As Paul Pickering has shown, some operatives in the Manchester area opposed the Corn Laws, but were soon won over to proposing Chartism as a primary measure: *Chartism and the Chartists*, p. 103.

52. *Bolton Chronicle*, vol. 16, no. 759, Feb. 15, 1839; *Bolton Free Press*, vol. 4, no. 169, Feb. 16, 1839; PRO HO 45/249C, no. 51, letter from Shaw dated July 18, 1842. *Manchester Guardian*, no. 1372, Mar. 5, 1842; no. 1448, Nov. 23, 1842.

53. Helene Zahler describes National Reformers infiltrating union meetings; but the sense of antagonism which characterizes the relationship between the Chartists and the Anti–Corn Law League was absent. *Eastern Workingmen*, p. 64.

54. *Manchester Examiner*, no. 42, Oct. 24, 1846. See Chartist petitions to Joshua Lancashire, Chief Constable of Rochdale, Apr. 13, 1840, Rochdale Local Studies Library, R.L. 604, Political Ephemera coll., no. 42. The petitions are signed by Chartist householders.

55. *Manchester Guardian*, no. 1614, June 26, 1844.

56. See also *Northern Star*, vol. 4, no. 203, Oct. 2, 1841. The connection between opposition to Free Trade and championship of the land plan is clearest in the career of Scottish Chartist and popular public speaker Samuel Kydd. S. Roberts, *Radical Politicians and Poets*, pp. 107–27.

57. Campbell, *Examination of the Corn and Provision Laws*, reprinted in *Chartist and Anti-Chartist Pamphlets*, pp. 27–28.

58. Ibid., p. 52.

59. See the positively Oastlerian speech "Altar, Throne and Cottage," which O'Connor gave at O'Connorville in August 1847, reprinted in Hadfield, *Chartist Land Company*, p. 102. For a provocative, if not completely satisfying, revision of the concept of Tory radicalism, see Driver, "Tory Radicalism?"

60. The two concepts of liberty are Isaiah Berlin's; for the importance of positive liberty in the context of Victorian radicalism, see Finn, *After Chartism*, p. 104. Berlin's original "Two Concepts of Liberty" can be found in his *Four Essays on Liberty*, pp. 118–72.

61. O'Connor on Apr. 1, 1848, quoted in Armytage, "Chartist Land Colonies," p. 93.

62. *English Chartist Circular*, vol. 2, no. 67, p. 57. O'Connor also pointed out that a four-acre allotment could confer the franchise. *Northern Star*, vol. 7, no. 364, Nov. 9, 1844.

63. *Labourer*, vol. 1 (1847), p. 45.

64. *Northern Star*, vol. 5, no. 211, Nov. 27, 1841.

65. *Leeds Mercury*, quoted in *Manchester Examiner*, vol. 1, no. 50, Apr. 24, 1849. As Harold Perkin demonstrated, the middle-class land-reforming efforts of the later nineteenth century self-consciously traced their roots back to the Anti–Corn Law League's early discussion of free trade in land rather than to the Chartist Land Plan or even to Paine and Spence. In contrast with the Chartist effort, which was based upon a desire for self-improvement, Perkin claims Cobden and Bright's land reform was intended both as a logical extension of Free Trade to the land and as an unsubtle challenge to the landed social order. One reason this failed was that formerly middle-class industrialists, having achieved a certain level of income, sought to join rather than reject the landed elite. See Perkin, "Land Reform and Class Conflict in Victorian Britain," esp. p. 196.

66. *Preston Chronicle*, no. 1944, Dec. 1, 1849.

67. *Preston Guardian*, no. 313, Feb. 2, 1850.

68. *Reynolds' Political Instructor*, vol. 1, no. 9, Jan. 5, 1850. See also an editorial on the freehold land societies in *Gloucester Journal*, no. 6507, Sept. 25, 1847.

69. In 1842, William Galpin, a former Owenite, proposed a home colonization company to settle people on the land and provide them with housing and education privately, because the government expressed unwillingness to do so: Home Colonization Company, *Prospectus*. In 1845, James Hill founded the National Land and Building Association, a land-savings bank enrolled under the Friendly Societies Act. Hill promoted his scheme as extending to the working classes all the benefits of landed proprietorship, and allowing all members who wished for healthy habitations to gain them. See *Commonweal*, Hill's propaganda organ.

O'Connor not only created working-class interest in acquiring the land, but also created a template which other, smaller groups could use to organize their own settlements. An Independent Cooperative Land Association in Kidderminster located between 25 and 30 families on Hooborough Estate. Samuel Bowly of Gloucester volunteered to form a company of middle-class investors to put up the money for a working-class allotment community. *Gloucester Journal*, no. 6504, Aug. 28, 1847.

In 1849, 18 Gateshead workingmen subscribed nearly £400 to buy an estate, then divided it into portions on a regular plan, ranging from a half-acre to an area large enough to build a cottage on. *Manchester Examiner*, vol. 1, no. 42, Mar. 27, 1849.

70. "Association" throughout refers specifically to the system of communal living propounded by Fourier and popularized in the United States by Albert Brisbane.

71. *Harbinger*, vol. 1, no. 26, Dec. 6, 1845. By far the most complete study of Fourierism is Guarneri, *Utopian Alternative*.

72. *Harbinger*, vol. 2, no. 7, Jan. 24, 1846.

73. *Harbinger*, vol. 1, no. 11, Aug. 23, 1845. For a more negative assessment of National Reform, see the article from the *Phalanx* excerpted in the *Working Man's Advocate*, vol. 1, no. 23, Aug. 31, 1844. It claimed that while in England "bloated monopoly has indeed most effectually shut out the laborer from the soil, and there the cry of the English Chartists, who are of the same class as the men here who are advocating the agrarian doctrine, is rightly enough, *to the Land! to the Land!* The cry is not applicable here."

74. *Working Man's Advocate*, vol. 2, no. 29, Oct. 11, 1845.

75. *Harbinger*, vol. 3, no. 18, Oct. 10, 1846.

76. *Harbinger*, vol. 4, no. 17, Apr. 3, 1847. Guarneri also describes this transition in *Utopian Alternative*, chap. 11.

77. Brisbane, *Social Destiny of Man*, p. 394. Guarneri has shown, however, that the more egregiously impractical elements of the system were toned down in practice, and that artisans were numerous among phalanx dwellers. *Utopian Alternative*, p. 170.

78. Guarneri, "Reconstructing the Antebellum Communitarian Movement."

79. As Paul Conkin writes: "On close inspection, proprietary and cooperative ideals rarely reflected contrasting social ideals, but rather the outer extremes of carefully nuanced differences of emphasis, as illustrated by the appeal of both to American transcendentalists. Proprietary advocates assumed specialization and interdependence plus a wide range of cooperation and sociability. Collectivists argued that true communalism did not mean centralized control but the fullest and most authentic individualism." Conkin, *Prophets of Prosperity*, p. 224. For a discussion of the nexus between land reform and Association from the Fourierite perspective, see Guarneri, *Utopian Alternative*, p. 308.

80. National Reformer Charles Sears worked together with Horace Greeley to arrange Associationist schools. See Charles Sears to Horace Greeley, Nov. 17 and 24, 1852, Box 1, Horace Greeley Papers, New York

Public Library. Sears served as the secretary of one of the industrial congresses. On Godwin, see Wennersten, "Reformer's Odyssey."

81. On Brook Farmers' appreciation of agriculture on moral grounds, see Rose, *Transcendentalism as a Social Movement*, p. 138. For Ryckman's early republican principles, see his tract *Largest Liberty Defined*.

82. *Harbinger*, vol. 1, no. 1, June 14, 1845.

83. Guarneri, *Utopian Alternative*, p. 71; van Amringe, *Association and Christianity*. See also *Harbinger*, vol. 1, no. 11, Aug. 23, 1845; vol. 4, no. 15, Mar. 20, 1847; vol. 4, no. 13, Mar. 6, 1847; vol. 4, no. 12, Feb. 27, 1847.

84. *Boston Chronotype*, vol. 2, no. 5, June 24, 1847. In 1849, van Amringe was lecturing in Fond du Lac, Wisconsin, and then was to go off to Oshkosh, Green Bay, Sheboygan, and Port Washington: *Young America*, vol. 6, no. 8, May 12, 1849. English émigré Thomas Hunt reported van Amringe spent a winter in Spring Lake, Wisconsin, and "completely revolutionized the minds of the more intelligent portion of the people on the subject of Land Reform." *Spirit of the Age*, no. 16, Nov. 11, 1848.

85. *Harbinger*, vol. 2, no. 24, May 23, 1846.

86. On the career of Albert Brisbane, see Pettit, "Albert Brisbane."

87. On Brisbane's life, see Bestor, "Albert Brisbane"; Fellman, *Unbounded Frame*.

88. Brisbane, *Social Destiny of Man*, p. 102.

89. Brisbane, *Concise Exposition*, p. 2.

90. Brisbane, *Social Destiny of Man*, p. 380.

91. Brisbane, *Concise Exposition*, p. 9.

92. As Guarneri points out, the opportunity to blame "the system" rather than the individual for failure to achieve economically may have endeared Fourierism to the workingman; I would allege the same to have been true of National Reform. See *Utopian Alternative*, p. 67.

93. Brisbane, *Concise Exposition*, p. 11.

94. *Working Man's Advocate*, vol. 2, no. 7, May 10, 1845.

95. Ibid. For some of Brisbane's other speeches, see vol. 1, no. 46, Feb. 8, 1845.

96. *Young America*, vol. 2, no. 47, Feb. 14, 1846.

97. *Working Man's Advocate*, vol. 2, no. 38, Dec. 13, 1845.

98. *Northern Star*, vol. 10, no. 481, Jan. 9, 1847.

99. Claeys, *Citizens and Saints*, pp. 261–62; this chapter contains a comparison of the rhetoric, beliefs, and interactions of Chartists and socialists in the mid-1840's. See also Armytage, "Manea Fen."

100. *Northern Star*, vol. 8, no. 404, Aug. 9, 1845; *Potters' Examiner and Workman's Advocate*, vol. 4, no. 11, Aug. 9, 1845.

101. Morgan, *Christian Commonwealth*.

102. Green, *Claims of the Redemption Society Considered*. The Leeds Redemption Society was formed in October 1845 under the Friendly Societies Act, to collect money to endow a cooperative community. Officers

were appointed and lectures held, and tracts explaining the society were published. The collectors went house to house, taking the tracts with them, making converts and pocketing funds. By June 1848, the society had an estate burdened with a £1,200 mortgage, but only four members were on the farm.

103. Although see Wellwood, *Letter to Feargus O'Connor, Esq.*, a thinly disguised Associationist screed.

104. On the importance of one's environment, see Bray, *Labour's Wrongs and Labour's Remedy*, pp. 25–29.

105. Bray, *Labour's Wrongs and Labour's Remedy*, p. 213. Bray was well known to the Chartists; two public lectures given in 1842 were entitled "The Nation's Wrong and the Nation's Remedy," a takeoff on Bray's title. The speaker, a Manchester packer, "contended that the land was not in the hands of its rightful owners but that the people must take it and cultivate it themselves." PRO HO 45/249, nos. 347, 349.

106. *Spirit of the Age*, no. 4, Aug. 19, 1848, p. 56; J. F. C. Harrison, *Robert Owen and the Owenites*, p. 58.

107. Claeys, *Citizens and Saints*, pp. 270, 324. On the conceptual content of Owenism and other early socialist alternatives, see Claeys, *Machinery, Money and the Millennium*.

108. *Northern Star*, vol. 6, no. 283, Apr. 15, 1843.

109. For O'Brien's contribution to British thought on land reform, see Plummer, *Bronterre*, pp. 179–88. *Working Man's Advocate*, vol. 1, no. 1, Mar. 16, 1844, contains a column headed "The People's Right to the Soil," with aphorisms from men who influenced National Reform. These included Bronterre O'Brien, Spence, Paine, Byrdsall, Mike Walsh, Thomas Devyr, John Hunt, John A. Collins, James Napier Bailey, John Francis Bray, Samuel Bower, Feargus O'Connor, Richard Carlile, J. K. Fisher, L. W. Ryckman, E. G. Buffum, and Thomas Skidmore. For views similar to O'Brien's, see also *The Land of England Belongs to the People of England*, available in the Goldsmith's Library, University of London.

110. *Northern Star*, vol. 1, no. 29, June 2, 1838; vol. 1, no. 32, June 23, 1838.

111. *National Reformer*, no. 15, Jan. 9, 1847. *Manchester Guardian* agreed, seeing reason in this to wish O'Connor godspeed: no. 1837, Aug. 15, 1846.

112. O'Brien, *Bronterre's Letters*, vol. 2, no. 93, letter 7, Mar. 26, 1836, British Library 8139.eee.39. Former Chartist Thomas Cooper proposed a similar measure: "Let the state buy up at once all the land of the country, and all the public funds of the nation, and pay them by instalments without interest, the amounts of instalment to be reckoned in fair proportion to the wants of each family and the amount of individual riches. That being done, labour could be organized immediately in every agricultural and individual parish, where all interest would centre in one common stock." T. Cooper, *Land for the Labourers*, p. 9.

113. *National Reformer*, vol. 1, no. 3, Oct. 17, 1846.

114. O'Brien to Allsop, Apr. 4, 1847; O'Brien to Allsop, Sept. 27, 1847. Allsop Collection, British Library of Political and Economic Science, London School of Economics.

115. O'Brien to Allsop, Aug. 4, 1840. Allsop Collection, British Library of Political and Economic Science, London School of Economics.

116. *National Reformer*, vol. 1, no. 27, Apr. 3, 1847.

117. Although O'Brien had visited the United States in 1845, his newspaper's name was not borrowed from the American land-reform movement, but rather was a carryover from *Bronterre's National Reformer*, his own 1837 publication. The 1846 newspaper, in addition to promoting his own scheme, was also the official organ for Johannes Etzler's Tropical Emigration Society, and an advertiser of Dr. Bowkett's freehold societies, showing O'Brien's wide-ranging interest in land-based solutions. For the adventures of the Tropical Emigration Society, which sought to shunt off surplus labor to Venezuela, see Claeys, "John Adolphus Etzler." The Bowkett Provident Freehold Societies were groups of at least a hundred people contributing slightly more than £2 per year, which combined sum would be awarded once annually to a member chosen by lot. It was to be used to buy freehold property. *National Reformer*, vol. 1, no. 23, Mar. 6, 1846.

118. *National Reformer*, vol. 1, no. 1, Oct. 3, 1846.

119. *National Reformer*, vol. 1, no. 3, Oct. 17, 1846.

120. *National Reformer*, vol. 1, no. 2, Oct. 10, 1846.

121. *National Reformer*, vol. 1, no. 7, Nov. 14, 1846; vol. 1, no. 9, Nov. 28, 1846; vol. 1, no. 10, Dec. 5, 1846.

122. *National Reformer*, vol. 1, no. 2, Oct. 10, 1846. O'Brien here underestimated American perceptions of the boundlessness of their own frontier. National Reformers confronted the issue of potentially running out of space by stating that, if necessary, the original 160-acre allotments could some day be divided into 80- or 40-acre plots.

123. *National Reformer*, vol. 1, no. 6, Nov. 7, 1846; vol. 1, no. 12, Dec. 19, 1846.

124. *National Reformer*, vol. 1, no. 29, Apr. 17, 1846. O'Brien was not wrong about the salutary effects of land-scheme reportage on the *Northern Star*, as Chapter 5 *infra* illustrates.

125. *National Reformer*, vol. 1, no. 15, Jan. 9, 1847.

126. A compromise between the O'Connorite and the O'Brienite positions was proposed by pamphleteer Ebeneezer Jones, who called a board of national-land managers, to whom laborers could appeal for a portion of the land if they were feeling insufficiently remunerated: "This plan would not only secure for such Home Colonizers their share in exchange for the labour of producing it, but it would also produce and maintain an equally just arrangement for all other labourers left in the labour market. For it is evident, that for the labour market to retain any labourers, it would be obliged to raise the remuneration of their labour, and their general treatment also, until they would be as well situated as if they were to avail themselves of their

right to location on the land." Ebeneezer Jones, *Land Monopoly*, p. 9. On Ebeneezer Jones, see Lindsay, "Ebeneezer Jones." William Linton wrote in a similar vein in *The People's Land*.

CHAPTER 5: MAKING WORKING-CLASS ACTIVISM

1. *Northern Star*, vol. 2, no. 86, July 6, 1839.

2. *Northern Star*, vol. 10, no. 493, Apr. 3, 1847.

3. At the 1852 Industrial Congress, land-reform poet A. H. Duganne proposed the most radical formulation of this internationalism: "That if the American People as individuals, choose to assist another people *struggling for Liberty*, by sympathy, by money or by men, then let the Government of the United States declare the broad doctrine of non-interference with its own people." This was amended to read "that no Government has a right to intervene to obstruct the success of revolution or other means adopted by any other people or nations to ameliorate their conditions and institutions." *Proceedings of the Seventh Annual Industrial Congress*, p. 8.

4. Although this was the culture of a movement, it was largely an alternative received culture rather than the type of "movement culture" Lawrence Goodwyn defines. See *Populist Moment*, p. xix.

5. Emerson, for example, was disturbed by Association's systematic attention to each detail of an all-encompassing order. See Pettit, "Albert Brisbane," p. 178.

6. As Jean Baker has suggested, we need not confine our definition of "political" to partisan behavior; the political expressions of individuals in the early nineteenth century often occupied other forms, including participation in reform movements. See Baker, "Politics, Paradigms and Public Culture."

7. O'Connor was the soul of the land movement, and as he wrote himself in 1847, "it is my boast, that neither the living denouncer, nor the unborn historian can ever write of Chartism, leaving out the name of Feargus O'Connor." *Labourer* (1847), p. 175. O'Connor also used any forum he could to promote the land scheme. See, e.g., his introduction to *Trial of Feargus O'Connor, Esq.*

8. In an autobiographical fragment, O'Connor described his childhood, in a house with a father who was loveless and domineering until his old age. "Life and Adventures of Feargus O'Connor, Esq., MP," *National Instructor* supplement (1850–51), p. 26.

9. The mid-1840's controversy over O'Connor's leadership style is chronicled in O'Connor, *Letter from Feargus O'Connor*; W. Hill, *Scabbard for Mr. O'Connor's Sword*; W. Thomason, *O'Connorism and Democracy Inconsistent*; Jackson, *Demagogue Done Up*. Although Hill quarreled with O'Connor, both supported home colonization. See J. Hill, *Life Boat*.

10. Holyoake, *Sixty Years of an Agitator's Life*, pp. 106–7.

11. Harrison and Hollis, eds., *Robert Lowery*, p. 125. On the importance of physique among working-class leaders, see Stott, *Workers*, p. 255.

12. William Henry Chadwick, famed as the last living Manchester

Chartist, wore one such pendant around his neck all his life. Newbould, *Pages from a Life of Strife*, p. 32.

13. *Labourer*, vol. 2 (1847), frontispiece.

14. *Preston Chronicle*, no. 1854, Mar. 11, 1848. See also Chase, "We Wish Only to Work for Ourselves," pp. 136–37.

15. Adams, *Memoirs of a Social Atom*, p. 157.

16. O'Connor's biographers claim his interest in land can be traced to his Irishness and to the writings of his uncle, Arthur O'Connor, on small-holdings. Read and Glasgow, *Feargus O'Connor, Irishman and Chartist*, p. 108; D. Jones, *Chartism and the Chartists*, pp. 128–30.

17. As he wrote breathlessly to Robert Burrell, "Robert, I think of the land by day, and I dream of it by night. My mind is set upon it. My every thought is occupied with it, because through its just application I see the enfranchisement of man—the freedom of man—and the independence of man." O'Connor to R. Burrell, Aug. 1845, quoted in D. Jones, *Chartism and the Chartists*, p. 128.

18. *Northern Star*, vol. 11, no. 534, Jan. 15, 1848.

19. *Northern Star*, vol. 10, no. 524, Nov. 6, 1847.

20. *Cheltenham Free Press*, no. 615, enlarged series, no. 390, Feb. 6, 1847.

21. There is no proper biography of Ernest Jones. Saville's *Ernest Jones, Chartist* has some biographical information, but is more a useful compendium of Jones's political writings. There is also a short sketch of Jones in G. D. H. Cole's *Chartist Portraits*, pp. 337–35; and see Crossley, *Ernest Jones: Who Is He? What Has He Done?* George Howell intended to write a biography of Jones, and the complete handwritten manuscript of this effort is available for consultation in the Howell Collection at the Bishopsgate Institute Library in London. Some of this mammoth effort was distilled into "Ernest Jones, the Chartist," a scrapbook of articles originally printed in the *Newcastle Weekly Chronicle* in 1898, also at the Bishopsgate Institute.

On Jones's coeditorship of the *Labourer*: when Jones was jailed in 1848, and his wife Jane approached O'Connor for payment for some of Jones's articles in the *Labourer*, O'Connor denied Jones had written them, claiming O'Connor had just used his name. Jane Atherley Jones to Ernest Jones, Sept. 2, 1848, Ernest Jones Papers, MUN 1 0 10 (6), Chetham's Library, Manchester.

22. Ernest Jones to the Earl of Aberdeen, Mar. 14, 1842, BM Add MS 43239.

23. Jones was evidently quite shaken by his brush with debt. As he wrote in his diary on Feb. 18, 1845, the day the auctioneers took possession of his house, "Here I am after the storm, hiding from my creditors. We have saved our clothes and a few pet books and boxes etc. A great deal of china, glass, plate and books has been claimed—the whole hangs at issue. My position is critical in the extreme." Ernest Jones Diary, n.p.

24. Jones was also a member of the Committee for Poland's Regeneration and the Fraternal Democrats. See Jones's diary for May 25, May 26,

June 2, July 14, July 18, 1846. No matter which meeting he attended, Jones was soon called to the chair.

25. Jones may have used his family connections to aid in the registration of the land plan. See "Carl" to "Tuttie" (these were their pet names for each other), undated letters, Ernest Jones Papers, Seligman/Jones Collection, Columbia University.

26. Ernest Jones Diary, Oct. 8, 1846.

27. "Blackstone Edge," reprinted in G. Howell, "Ernest Jones, the Chartist," n.p.

28. Ernest Jones Diary, Aug. 10, 1846.

29. Jones to Jane Atherley Jones, Aug. 7, 1845, Ernest Jones Papers, Seligman/Jones Collection, Columbia University.

30. Ernest Jones Diary, Jan. 14–15, 1847.

31. C. Bubb to Ernest Jones, Dec. 19, 1846, Ernest Jones Papers, Seligman/Jones Collection, Columbia University. Bubb later became an editor of Jones's *People's Paper*. See no. 35, Jan. 1, 1853.

32. *Manchester Guardian*, no. 2036, July 12, 1848. An undated, unaddressed letter-draft, probably intended for O'Connor, detailed Jones's suffering in prison (letter 10). In response to such pleas for aid, O'Connor offered to adopt and educate the Jones's new baby, but they declined the offer (letter 12). MUN 1 0 10, Ernest Jones Papers, Chetham's Library, Manchester.

33. Jane Atherley Jones to Ernest Jones, July 23, 1848, Ernest Jones Papers, Seligman/Jones Collection, Columbia University.

34. Ernest Jones to Jane Atherley Jones, Dec. 10, 1851, Ernest Jones Papers, Seligman/Jones Collection, Columbia University.

35. Zahler, *Eastern Workingmen*, p. 38.

36. Evans Family Bible, Shaker Museum, Old Chatham, New York. Evans filed a Declaration of Intention of Becoming a Citizen in 1823, but failed to complete his papers for citizenship until 1829 on the day of the Working Men's Party election. Jeffrey, "Social Origins of George Henry Evans," p. 270.

37. Ibid., pp. 10, 207. Jeffrey's thesis is to date the only lengthy biography of Evans (and covers his life only up to 1829). Interestingly enough, it also contains a photocopy of the only known photograph of Evans, which was discovered in a barn near Pontiac, Michigan, in 1937, in a trunk belonging to the English Chartist and American radical John Francis Bray. See ibid., p. iv. On Evans's thought specifically pertaining to the Working Men, the bank crisis, and land reform, see Helton, "George Henry Evans."

38. Jeffrey, "George Henry Evans," p. 71.

39. Ibid., p. 265.

40. On the Working Men, see Pessen, *Most Uncommon Jacksonians*, pp. 9–33. George's younger brother Frederick started out with him in New York as an agent for the *Working Man's Advocate* (see vol. 1, no. 47, July 28, 1830) but soon after went upstate to join the Shakers. Although their births are not recorded in the Evans Family Bible, two sisters of George's evidently also joined the Shakers. George remained a steadfast freethinker, and prob-

ably refused to have any connection with his brother not only for his religious enthusiasm but also because the Shakers refused to vote, much less vote themselves farms. See Horace Greeley to F. W. Evans, Apr. 6, 1852, Shaker Museum, Old Chatham, N.Y. Nonetheless, being above all a compassionate man, George Henry Evans did reconcile with Frederick toward the end of his life. See MSS 10347B, Logbook of the Shaker Settlement, p. 195, Wed., Jan. 10, 1851; 10347A, Logbook, pp. 57–58, Wed., June 11, 1851, Shaker Museum, Old Chatham, N.Y.

41. Bradshaw, "George Henry Evans," p. 185. See also McFarland and Thistlethwaite, "20 Years of a Successful Labor Paper." The authors refer to the *Working Man's Advocate* as the leading labor paper of its time. Although the political confrontation carried on through its pages probably achieved only small gains, the *Advocate* kept many social issues alive and helped to maintain solidarity, just as the *Northern Star* did for the Chartist movement.

42. *Working Man's Advocate*, vol. 1, no. 3, Nov. 14, 1829.

43. *Working Man's Advocate*, vol. 4, no. 29, Mar. 2, 1833. The land question was raised at a convention of the National Trades Union in 1834. *Man*, Aug. 30, 1834, quoted in Commons, "Horace Greeley," p. 479.

44. *Radical*, vol. 1, no. 1, Jan. 1841, p. 15. For Evans's debts, see vol. 1, no. 3, Mar. 1841.

45. *Radical*, vol. 1, no. 4, Apr. 1841, p. 52.

46. Bray was born in 1809 in Washington, D.C., to English parents, emigrated back to England, became a Chartist, and wrote *Labour's Wrongs and Labour's Remedy*, a work of equalitarian political economy influential in both countries. He moved to Boston in 1842, then, perhaps motivated by Evans or Owen, went west and took up farming in Pontiac, Michigan. He worked as a printer and trade unionist in Detroit until his death in 1897. Boston, *British Chartists in America*, pp. 65–69.

47. Masquerier, *Sociology*, p. 99.

48. Ibid., p. 69.

49. Ibid., p. 93.

50. And he was absolutely right about that. *Young America*, vol. 6, no. 8, May 12, 1849.

51. Byrdsall, *History of the Loco-Foco or Equal Rights Party*, pp. 14–15.

52. For more on Devyr's life and ideology, see Huston, "Land and Freedom," pp. 408–15; Swajkowski, "Chartist Contributions," pp. 137–232.

53. Devyr's *Odd Book* is not the only place his story is told; he liked to recount it to establish his reformist pedigree. See also Devyr to Andrew Johnson, Jan. 23, 1875, Andrew Johnson Papers, Library of Congress; Devyr to Gerrit Smith, Dec. 18, 1856, Gerrit Smith Papers, Syracuse University.

54. As a small boy, gathering potatoes in an Irish field, he set fiercely upon another little potato-harvesting boy who dared to call him "upstart." *Odd Book*, p. 38.

55. Ibid., p. 108.

56. Ibid., p. 19.

57. Ibid., p. 111.

58. Ibid., p. 140.

59. *Northern Liberator*, vol. 1, no. 58, Nov. 17, 1838.

60. *Northern Liberator*, vol. 1, no. 38, July 7, 1838.

61. *Northern Liberator*, vol. 2, no. 82, May 11, 1839.

62. *Northern Liberator*, vol. 2, no. 84, May 25, 1839; vol. 2, no. 91, July 13, 1839.

63. The first volume appeared on October 21, 1837, predating the *Northern Star* by several months. It was not an inexpensive paper, but rather cost the same as the *Star* would—4.5d—for half as many pages. It did, however, contain original reporting of the movements in the Newcastle area which the *Star* would cover in less detail.

64. Devyr, *Odd Book*, p. 161. Devyr's land-reforming influence was not completely invisible at the newspaper. In July 1839, under the title "Blessings of Aristocratic Rule in Ireland," one paragraph was published which Devyr might well have written: "Immense tracts of soil is [sic] lying barren in Ireland and immense numbers of men willing to labour are going about unemployed. The blasphemous aristocracy will not let the people reclaim the soil, except upon the condition that all its enhanced value shall go to the accursed rent roll, leaving the people still at the old level of rags and famine." *Northern Liberator*, vol. 2, no. 93, July 27, 1839.

65. *Northern Star*, vol. 3, no. 121, Mar. 7, 1840. His views remained behind. In November, the *Liberator* received numbers of a circular entitled "The Land of England Belongs to the People of England," which claimed the land was the immediate gift of God, like air or water. It suggested the elected commissioners acting for the state hold the land for the benefit of all, and dedicate its rents to education, infrastructure, defense, justice, recreation, and free emigration. *Northern Liberator*, vol. 2, no. 96, Aug. 17, 1839; vol. 3, no. 110, Nov. 23, 1839.

66. Devyr, *Odd Book*, American Section, p. 26.

67. Ibid., pp. 33–38.

68. For more on Anti-Rent, see Huston, "Land and Freedom"; and Christman, *Tin Horns and Calico*, pp. 57–58. See also Boston, *British Chartists in America*, pp. 49–56.

69. Devyr, *Odd Book*, p. 39.

70. Ibid., p. 41; *Albany Anti-Renter*, June 6, 1846.

71. Devyr to Gerrit Smith, Dec. 18, 1856, Gerrit Smith Papers, Syracuse University.

72. Christman, *Tin Horns and Calico*, p. 163

73. Devyr to Gerrit Smith, Dec. 18, 1856, Gerrit Smith Papers, Syracuse University.

74. W. Evans, *Art and History of the Potting Business*; on Evans's background, see J. F. C. Harrison, *Robert Owen and the Owenites*, pp. 228–29.

75. Burchill and Ross, *History of the Potters' Union*, p. 83.

76. *Potters' Examiner and Workman's Advocate*, vol. 1, no. 6, Jan. 6, 1844.

77. W. Evans, *Art and History of the Potting Business*. He wrote this painstakingly descriptive work to banish the mystery which shrouded potterymaking. Evans felt workers had less bargaining power when only their employers, and not they, understood every step of the potting process. On the question of Christianity and the Corn Laws, see *Potters' Examiner and Workman's Advocate*, vol. 5, no. 20, Apr. 11, 1846.

78. J. F. C. Harrison, *Robert Owen and the Owenites*, pp. 228–29; Boston, "William Evans and the Potters' Emigration Society," pp. 5–19. Although Boston claims Evans wrote letters to the *Star in the East*, none I looked at for 1838–39 could be identified as his.

79. *Potters' Examiner and Workman's Advocate*, vol. 6, no. 16, Oct. 17, 1846.

80. *Potters' Examiner and Workman's Advocate*, vol. 4, no. 3, June 14, 1845.

81. *Potters' Examiner and Workman's Advocate*, vol. 6, no. 22, Nov. 28, 1846. In a handbill reprinted in this issue, the land-company members referred to Evans's scheme as "transportation," accused him of being a paid agent (he never denied being paid), and blamed him for being divisive, noting that "your name has never been mentioned, nor your Society either, by any Land Meeting that has been held at Hanley, from first to last, among the Chartists; we are not *one-half* Potters, therefore your affairs do not interest us." O'Connor himself was no kinder, heading an article on the Emigration Society "Emigration Humbugs of the Potteries Unmasked." See *Potters' Examiner and Workman's Advocate*, vol. 6, no. 24, Dec. 12, 1846.

82. *Potters' Examiner and Workman's Advocate*, vol. 6, no. 24, Dec. 12, 1846. Evans strenuously denied being anti-Chartist: "Feargus O'Connor is not the Charter! Home colonization, with its small farms, is not the Charter! The little local party in this neighborhood, who at a sacrifice of all truth, libel us and the society to which we belong, are not the Charter!" *Potters' Examiner and Workman's Advocate*, vol. 5, no. 20, Apr. 11, 1846.

83. *Potters' Examiner and Workman's Advocate*, vol. 4, no. 6, July 5, 1845.

84. *Potters' Examiner and Workman's Advocate*, vol. 4, no. 9, July 26, 1845.

85. For an engaging discussion of the self-presentation of workingmen's leaders in this period, see Vernon, *Politics and the People*, pp. 252–91. Vernon argues that much followership during this period was based on personalities, and that working-class audiences had a say in the roles their leaders adopted. The trope of the gentleman leader is also discussed in Joyce, *Democratic Subjects*, pp. 213–23.

86. Vernon, *Politics and the People*, pp. 105–60.

87. Stott, *Workers*, p. 51.

88. Saxton, "Problems of Class and Race in the Origins of the Mass Circulation Press."

89. Zboray, "Technology and the Character of Community Life."

90. On the idea of "imagined community," including the importance of a shared language and of print culture, see B. Anderson, *Imagined Communities*. Although Anderson was concerned with the construction of nationalisms, the concept can be generalized.

91. *Northern Star*, vol. 8, no. 396, June 14, 1845.

92. *Working Man's Advocate*, vol. 1, no. 5, Apr. 27, 1844.

93. Adams noted that, like Adams's mother, Larry the shoemaker was a follower of Cobbett, holding two volumes of Cobbett's works among his most cherished possessions. Adams, *Memoirs of a Social Atom*, p. 165.

94. Brierley, *Home Memories*, p. 23.

95. *Northern Star*, vol. 13, no. 636, Dec. 29, 1849.

96. *Potters' Examiner and Workman's Advocate*, vol. 6, no. 26, Dec. 26, 1846.

97. *Northern Star*, vol. 6, no. 301, Aug. 19, 1843.

98. G. Howell, "Ernest Jones, the Chartist," chap. 24.

99. Tracts and land-company rules were also distributed at meetings for other types of reform—the Irish coercion bill, for example. *Preston Chronicle*, no. 1756, Apr. 2, 1846.

100. O'Connor, *Remedy for National Poverty*, p. 22. O'Connor proposed the government buy wastelands from landlords at a cost of £20,000,000. This would be consolidated into a national debt.

101. O'Connor, *The Land and Its Capabilities*.

102. Parry, *Letter to Feargus O'Connor, Esq.*; O'Connor, *Letter from Feargus O'Connor to John Humphreys Parry*; White, *Answer to John Humphreys Parry*.

103. Sillett, *Practical System of Fork and Spade Husbandry*, pp. i–vi.

104. O'Connor, *What May Be Done with Three Acres of Land*.

105. *Manchester Examiner*, vol. 2, no. 53, Jan. 9, 1847. See also Tiller, "Charterville and the Chartist Land Company."

106. Quoted ibid., p. 256.

107. *Potters' Examiner and Workman's Advocate*, vol. 1, no. 8, Jan. 20, 1844.

108. *Potters' Examiner and Workman's Advocate*, vol. 1, no. 9, Jan. 27, 1844.

109. *Potters' Examiner and Workman's Advocate*, vol. 1, no. 10, Feb. 3, 1844.

110. Foreman, "Settlement of English Potters in Wisconsin," p. 382.

111. McFarland and Thistlethwaite, "20 Years of a Successful Labor Paper."

112. Bradshaw, "George Henry Evans."

113. Jeffrey, "Social Origins of George Henry Evans," p. x. Perhaps not coincidentally, Kansas was also the site of an 1870 attempt by British O'Brienites to form a joint-stock emigration company on the same principles as the Potters' Emigration Sociey, and for the same reasons that their predecessors in the 1840's had done so. Among its catalysts was John Days, an

English emigrant–cum–California state senator who had visited London promoting land reform. See Whitehead, "*New World* and the O'Brienite Colony in Kansas," pp. 40–43.

114. Ingalls, *Reminiscences*, p. 25.

115. Sometime between September 1848 and May 1849, the banner picture changed, and the formerly naked man, possibly bowing to Victorian moralism, acquired a suit of clothes. *Young America*, vol. 6, no. 8, May 12, 1849. This single copy of the newspaper is at the American Antiquarian Society in Worcester, Massachusetts. According to Eric Hobsbawm, the naked individual represented the ideal type in eighteenth-century aesthetic theory, but the use of a naked man rather than a partly clad woman in labor or populist iconography at this early date is rare. See "Man and Woman: Images on the Left."

116. *National Reform Almanac for 1848*; see also *Homestead*.

117. *Young America*, vol. 6, no. 8, May 12, 1849.

118. *Young America*, vol. 1, no. 50, Mar. 7, 1846.

119. *Jubilee*; Gerritt Smith Pamphlet Collection, no. 216; *Young America*, Smith Collection, no. 217; *Vote Yourself a Farm!* Smith Collection, no. 218, Syracuse University.

120. James Vernon has argued that radicals' decisions to meet in new public spaces—on commons, or in their own purpose-built halls—were often symbolic and purposeful, part of a larger struggle to define inclusion in the public sphere. See Vernon, *Politics and the People*, p. 229.

121. *Manchester Examiner*, vol. 1, no. 13, Apr. 18, 1846.

122. *Manchester Examiner*, vol. 3, no. 177, June 13, 1848.

123. *Jerrold's Weekly Newspaper*, no. 59, Aug. 28, 1847, p. 1071.

124. Gammage, *History of the Chartist Movement*, p. 95.

125. *Northern Star*, vol. 9, no. 420, Nov. 29, 1845.

126. *Northern Star*, vol. 9, no. 421, Dec. 6, 1845.

127. Ibid.

128. *Northern Star*, vol. 10, no. 501, May 29, 1847.

129. For the importance of banners, bands, and other symbolic communication in the Chartist movement, see P. Pickering, *Chartism and the Chartists*, chap. 9.

130. Hadfield, *Chartist Land Company*, p. 107.

131. *Northern Star*, vol. 10, no. 458, Aug. 22, 1846; Armytage, "Chartist Land Colonies," p. 92.

132. Ernest Jones, *Chartist Songs and Fugitive Pieces* (n.p.). Allen Davenport also wrote an O'Connorville poem shortly before his death, which reads, in part, "Bold was the genius that first planned / That scheme of restoration. / There is no road but through the Land / to man's regeneration! / The Jubilee has come at last, / the day of restoration. / The Rubicon has now been passed / by the grand Demonstration." See *Northern Star*, vol. 10, no. 459, Aug. 29, 1846. The "genius" to whom Davenport refers is probably Spence, not O'Connor.

133. *Northern Star*, vol. 10, no. 460, Sept. 5, 1846; vol. 10, no. 503, June

12, 1847. Today, a hand-colored copy of this engraving hangs in the little pub directly across from the Heronsgate Estate.

134. *Northern Star*, vol. 10, no. 501, May 29, 1847.

135. *Gloucester Journal*, vol. 125, no. 6503, Aug. 21, 1847.

136. *Northern Star*, vol. 10, no. 512, Aug. 14, 1847; vol. 10, no. 513, Aug. 21, 1847.

137. *Northern Star*, vol. 12, no. 602, May 5, 1849.

138. *Northern Star*, vol. 10, no. 512, Aug. 14, 1847.

139. *Albany Freeholder*, vol. 1, no. 7, May 21, 1845.

140. A list of the locations and hosts of ward meetings appears in *Working Man's Advocate*, vol. 2, no. 20, Aug. 9, 1845.

141. *Northern Star*, vol. 7, no. 344, June 15, 1844. As Vernon illustrates, nineteenth-century radical oratory often made use of visual symbols, and was often much more theatrical than speeches as we know them today. Vernon, *Politics and the People*, pp. 117–31.

142. *Voice of Industry*, vol. 2, no. 39, Apr. 9, 1847. According to Marianne Dwight, future wife of Brook Farmer and land reformer John Orvis, Brisbane was in the habit of speaking of man's right to the soil during his lectures on Association: "The whole soil of England is owned by about a hundred families. Twelve or fifteen millions of her people have no other way of subsistence ... than to cultivate the soil, so they are wholly in the power of the first landed proprietors; they must starve or cultivate it on the owner's terms! What a state of things!" Marianne Dwight to Anne W. T. Parsons, Dec. 23, 1844, in Reed, ed., *Letters from Brook Farm*, pp. 54–55.

143. *Northern Star*, vol. 7, no. 336, Apr. 20, 1844.

144. *People's Rights*, vol. 1, no. 22, Aug. 10, 1844.

145. *Northern Star*, vol. 7, no. 349, July 20, 1844.

146. *Northern Star*, vol. 10, no. 444, May 16, 1846. Reports of a meeting of the German National Reform Association can be found in *Young America*, vol. 2, no. 33, Nov. 8, 1845.

147. *Working Man's Advocate*, vol. 1, no. 17, July 20, 1844.

148. Ingalls, *Reminiscences*, p. 28.

149. *People's Rights*, vol. 1, no. 22, Aug. 10, 1844.

150. Zahler, *Eastern Workingmen*, p. 47. Similarly, the Chartist land reformers occasionally used Irish coercion or Frost, Williams, and Jones as methods of entering into discussion of the land. *Preston Guardian*, no. 122, June 6, 1846.

151. *Working Man's Advocate*, vol. 1, no. 42, Jan. 11, 1845.

152. Ingalls described how, at the Canastota Free Church convention, the land reformers held a reception at Gerrit Smith's house, where Ingalls regaled the company with a rendition of J. H. Duganne's "Acres and Hands," set to the tune of "The Carrier Dove," an old English folk song. See Ingalls, *Reminiscences*, p. 34. See also Masquerier, *Sociology*, which includes songs written to the tune of "Battle Cry of Freedom" and "Star-Spangled Banner."

153. The song is printed in full in J. Pickering, *Working Man's Political*

Economy, p. 195. Other songs of the National Reform movement are reprinted, with accompanying discussion, in P. Foner, ed., *American Labor Songs*, pp. 47–51.

154. "Dan Tucker," like "Oh, Susanna," was originally a minstrel song, the melody of which was appropriated many times in the cause of working-class politics. On this issue, see Lott, *Love and Theft*, chaps. 3, 7.

155. J. Pickering, *Working Man's Political Economy*, p. 203.

156. Gammage, *History of the Chartist Movement*, p. 203.

157. *Voice of Industry*, vol. 3, no. 26, Dec. 31, 1847. On the reader requests, see vol. 3, no. 29, Jan. 28, 1848. William Lovett called Feargus O'Connor "the great 'I AM'" of Chartism, in ironic allusion to the biblical reference. Lovett, *Life and Struggles*, pp. 294–97.

158. *Voice of Industry*, vol. 1, no. 30, Jan. 9, 1846. Unfortunately, Young wrote, it would have cost him $25 to attend, which money would be better spent printing another issue of his own newspaper.

159. *Voice of Industry*, vol. 2, no. 29, Jan. 15, 1847; the event was also reported in the *Northern Star*, vol. 10, no. 491, Mar. 20, 1847.

160. *Northern Star*, vol. 10, no. 493, Apr. 3, 1847. It is unclear whether the "single exception" refers to a particular word or a particular woman in the audience.

161. *Boston Chronotype*, vol. 3, no. 1, May 27, 1848.

162. *National Reformer* (Rochester), vol. 1, no. 41, July 6, 1848; vol. 1, no. 42, July 13, 1848.

163. Baker, *Affairs of Party*.

164. *Working Man's Advocate*, vol. 1, no. 24, Sept. 7, 1844. On Moore, who had been president of New York's General Trades Union in the 1830's, see Hugins, "Ely Moore." On Parke Godwin, Brook Farmer and Fourierite attorney, see Wennersten, "Parke Godwin."

165. *Working Man's Advocate*, vol. 1, no. 48, Feb. 22, 1845.

166. *Young America*, vol. 2, no. 33, Nov. 8, 1845.

167. R. Taylor, *Autobiography of Robert Taylor*, Feb. 5–Aug. 1, 1846–47, p. 18, Manuscript Division, New York Public Library.

168. *Harbinger*, vol. 4, no. 19, Apr. 14, 1847; *Voice of Industry*, Apr. 23, 1847, vol. 2, no. 41.

169. Ingalls, *Reminiscences*, p. 26.

170. *Potters' Examiner and Workman's Advocate*, vol. 7, no. 12, Mar. 20, 1847.

171. *Working Man's Advocate*, vol. 1, no. 9, May 25, 1844; on their insistence that land reform originated in America, see vol. 1, no. 24, Sept. 7, 1844. For contemporary association of radicalism with English emigration, see Ernst, *Immigrant Life*, p. 19; but compare N. Ware, *Industrial Worker*, p. 171, who notes that "alien ideas" do not take root unless the soil is primed for them.

172. *Working Man's Advocate*, vol. 2, no. 17, July 19, 1845.

173. *Working Man's Advocate*, vol. 1, no. 52, Mar. 22, 1845. See also

Evans's response to a letter from O'Connor, *Working Man's Advocate*, vol. 2, no. 15, July 5, 1845.

174. *Northern Star*, vol. 8, no. 398, June 28, 1845.

175. An exception to this general rule is the excellent treatment of transatlantic political radicalism in Thistlethwaite, *America and the Atlantic Community*, pp. 39–75. Thistlethwaite focuses on the contributions of John Cluer, John Campbell, and Thomas Devyr, but also considers George Henry Evans culturally an Englishman.

176. See Zahler, *Eastern Workingmen*, p. 78. The continuities between the movements are listed on pp. 78–79. Hermann Schlueter may have been the first historian to take note of the correspondence between American and British land reform in *Lincoln, Labor and Slavery*. See also Lillibridge, *Beacon of Freedom*, p. 68.

177. Hardy, *Alternative Communities*, p. 244.

178. For a model of a comparative and transatlantic examination of ideologies, see J. F. C. Harrison, *Robert Owen and the Owenites*.

179. Devyr told New York audiences that the arguments of the National Reformers had been read by two million English readers; *Northern Star*, vol. 7, no. 348, July 13, 1844. The *Star* was also receiving Devyr's *Williamsburg* (Long Island) *Democrat*.

180. *Northern Star*, vol. 8, no. 392, May 17, 1845.

181. *Working Man's Advocate*, vol. 1, no. 10, June 1, 1844.

182. *Northern Star*, vol. 7, no. 336, Apr. 20, 1844.

183. *Northern Star*, vol. 7, no. 337, Apr. 27, 1844.

184. *Northern Star*, vol. 7, no. 345, June 22, 1844.

185. *Northern Star*, vol. 7, no. 338, May 4, 1844; see also vol. 9, nos. 473, 474, Nov. 21 and 28, 1846.

186. *Northern Star*, reprinted in *Working Man's Advocate*, vol. 2, no. 17, July 19, 1845.

187. Brook, "Lawrence Pitkeithly," pp. 79–84.

188. *Working Man's Advocate*, vol. 1, no. 37, Dec. 7, 1844.

189. *Spirit of the Age*, no. 24, Jan. 6, 1849; see address from the workingmen of Salford to the workingmen of America, *Northern Star*, vol. 10, no. 432, Feb. 21, 1846.

190. *Spirit of the Age*, no. 25, Jan. 13, 1849.

191. According to the *Northern Star*, there were not half a dozen Chartists in the American movement; not being citizens yet, Chartists could not sign the agrarian pledge. *Northern Star*, vol. 7, no. 363, Nov. 2, 1844.

192. *Northern Star*, vol. 10, no. 500, May 22, 1847; vol. 10, no. 480, Jan. 2, 1847. It was, in fact, through the *Star*'s coverage that *Young America* became apprised of the Wisconsin reformers' activities.

193. *National Reformer* (Rochester), vol. 1, no. 39, June 22, 1848.

194. The Chinese Museum, where this meeting was held—the largest public space in Philadelphia—had also been the site of a series of Sunday lectures on National Reform in 1848. See *National Reformer* (Rochester), vol. 1, no. 39, June 22, 1848.

195. *Monthly Jubilee*, vol. 3, no. 7, May 1853, p. 309.

196. *Young America*, Apr. 29, 1848.

197. Ray Boston has speculated that "it is . . . probable, but no more, that [William Evans] was related to Frederick William Evans, the Shaker leader, and his labour leader brother, George Henry Evans." The American Evanses and William Evans both had cousins who were printers in the Worcester area; this, and radical politics on both sides, are the only evidence for such a link. See Boston, "William Evans and the Potters' Emigration Society," p. 5.

198. *Potter's Examiner and Workman's Advocate*, vol. 6, no. 25, Dec. 17, 1846.

199. This first connection made a second wave of international communication possible in the early 1870's. The remnant of the National Reformers, now the Land Reform Association, led by old unionist Henry Beeny, corresponded with J. S. Mill's Land Tenure Reform Association; and J. K. Ingalls, then secretary of the Cooperative Colony Aid Association, met G. J. Holyoake, who was visiting the United States. See Ingalls, *Reminiscences*, p. 67.

200. Letter dated July 30, *New York Tribune*, vol. 4, no. 117, Aug. 22, 1844.

201. *Young America*, vol. 2, no. 50, Mar. 7, 1846.

202. G. J. Holyoake, Engagement Diary, Oct. 2, Oct. 9, Nov. 28, 1847, Bishopsgate Institute, item no. 293.

203. *Reformer* (London), May 26, 1849, quoted in Shepperson, *Emigration and Disenchantment*, p. 75.

204. Boston, *British Chartists in America*, pp. 47–48.

205. *Boston Chronotype*, vol. 2, no. 50, May 6, 1848. *Working Man's Advocate*, vol. 1, no. 22, Aug. 24, 1844; vol. 1, no. 36, Nov. 30, 1844; vol. 1, no. 37, Dec. 7, 1844. *Voice of Industry*, vol. 3, no. 16, Oct. 29, 1847. Murphy, *Ten Hours' Labor*.

206. *Voice of Industry*, vol. 1, no. 31, Jan. 30, 1846.

207. *Working Man's Advocate*, vol. 1, no. 35, Nov. 23, 1844.

208. Bussey appears in New York in 1844 at a celebration of Thomas Paine's birthday, indicating that his interest in radical causes—as well as his trade of tavernkeeping—followed him across the Atlantic. See Jentz, "Artisans, Evangelicals, and the City," pp. 38–42.

209. *Northern Star*, vol. 10, no. 504, June 19, 1847. John Campbell reported later that year that a crowded meeting at the Filbert Street Hall had, on September 7, celebrated O'Connor's election to Parliament for Nottingham. *Northern Star*, vol. 10, no. 519, Oct. 2, 1847.

210. "Land Question in America." *The People*, vol. 2, no. 83, p. 242; vol. 3, no. 117.

211. Wittke, *Utopian Communist*, pp. 99–123; Ernst, *Immigrant Life*, pp. 112–14. Kriege and Weitling, like the Chartist leaders, disagreed over whether land should be held as private property.

212. Schlueter, *Lincoln, Labor and Slavery*, p. 76. Although the German labor movement was more "radical" in the traditional sense than its Amer-

ican counterpart, its stress on land reform, among a whole platform of issues, was constant. Nadel, "From the Barricades of Paris," pp. 47–75.

213. Ernst, *Immigrant Life*, p. 113.

214. *Northern Star*, vol. 10, no. 442, May 2, 1846; *Young America*, vol. 2,
no. 42, Jan. 10, 1846.

215. Ibid.

216. Hunt was a prominent London Owenite who, dissatisfied with the
way British communities were run, left for America. He arrived at Milwaukee in July 1843 with 21 people, purchased 263 acres of land, and tried to
farm it. Despite a second injection of English colonists, the settlement petered out by 1846. See J. F. C. Harrison, *Robert Owen and the Owenites*, p.
175.

217. *Notes to the People*, vol. 1, p. 337; *Northern Star*, vol. 13, no. 677,
Oct. 12, 1850; *Star of Freedom*, vol. 15, no. 755, May 1, 1852; *Red Republican*, vol. 1, no. 4, July 13, 1850; *National Instructor*, no. 9, July 20, 1850.

CHAPTER 6: UNDER THE BANNER
OF LAND REFORM

1. Saville, "Introduction," in Gammage, *History of the Chartist Movement*, p. 6.

2. See Wilentz, *Chants Democratic*, for the best work on this transformation.

3. *Northern Star*, vol. 10, no. 474, Nov. 21, 1846; See also *Man*, Aug. 30,
1834, quoted in Commons, "Horace Greeley," p. 479; Bridges, *City in the
Republic*, p. 113.

4. As Christopher Tomlins has explained, the view that government had
a role to "police" or ensure prosperity for all its citizens was a residual republican viewpoint coming under severe attack by mid-nineteenth-century
liberalism; but working people remained some of its strongest proponents.
See his *Law, Labor and Ideology*, pp. 33–59.

5. Hammond, *History of the Political Parties of the State of New York*,
vol. 2, pp. 491–95. For George Henry Evans's own pedigree as an antimo-
nopolist, see Helton, "George Henry Evans."

6. Pessen, *Most Uncommon Jacksonians*, pp. 97–99; *Working Man's
Advocate*, vol. 2, no. 24, Sept. 6, 1845.

7. On the other hand, National Reformer J. K. Ingalls noted that they
"were never able to enlist any considerable number of the union men to listen to the discussion of the land question." Ingalls, *Reminiscences*, p. 47.
See also Commons, *History of Labor in the United States*, vol. 1, p. 532.

8. *Voice of Industry*, vol. 1, no. 8, July 17, 1845. One list of National Reformers included a carpenter, a printer, a teacher, a saddler, a cigar maker,
an editor, a shoemaker, a clockmaker, a cabinet maker, a tailor, a chairmaker, a bookbinder, a cooper, a physician, a blacksmith, a granite cutter, a
locksmith, a silversmith, an iron-rail maker, a pianoforte maker, a brick-
layer, a painter, a scene painter, and a machinist. Few National Reformers
whose occupations were mentioned in newspapers were among the 39.2

percent of New Yorkers who fell into the lowest category—laborers and domestic servants, drovers, and policemen. For the breakdown of the occupations of New Yorkers in this period see Bridges, *City in the Republic*, p. 46.

9. *Albany Freeholder*, vol. 1, no. 12, June 25, 1845; *Working Man's Advocate*, vol. 2, no. 13, June 21, 1845.

10. For an address to the "Sons of Vulcan" (blacksmiths), see *Working Man's Advocate*, vol. 1, no. 9, May 25, 1844.

11. Bridges, *City in the Republic*, p. 112.

12. *Working Man's Advocate*, vol. 1, no. 29, Oct. 12, 1844.

13. In addition to proposing a land-reform resolution at the Boston Working Men's convention, he was fined twice, and sentenced to 60 days in jail, for libels in the *Subterranean*. See Ernst, "One and Only Mike Walsh," pp. 43–65; *Northern Star*, vol. 8, no. 372, Dec. 28, 1844; *Working Man's Advocate*, vol. 1, no. 39, Dec. 21, 1844.

14. The development of class-based cultures in New York is the subject of Buckley, "To the Opera House."

15. Stott, *Workers*, p. 66

16. Reform leaders, beginning with a more pessimistic view than most, made great capital out of what problems did exist. See Pessen, "Workingmen's Movement," pp. 428–43. On the question of sanitation, see the New York Public Library exhibition *Trash!* Dec. 23, 1994.

17. By the late 1840's, land reformers like John Commerford and Irish nationalists like Michael T. O'Connor would create a Tenants' League to address these problems directly, and even espoused urban homesteading on city common lands. See especially the *Homestead*, which has a long section on rents and overcrowding; and Blackmar, *Manhattan for Rent*, pp. 246–47; Dayton, *Last Days of Knickerbocker* Life, pp. 131–32; Ernst, *Immigrant Life*, pp. 49–51.

18. Ernst, *Immigrant Life*, p. 22. One of the most engaging descriptions of working-class life in antebellum New York City appears in Stansell, *City of Women*, pp. 3–10.

19. Spann, *New Metropolis*, pp. 130, 156.

20. Fogel, *Without Consent or Contract*, p. 356.

21. *New York Sun*, 13th year, no. 619, Oct. 14, 1848, p. 2.

22. New York Association for Improving the Condition of the Poor, *Annual Report*, p. 17; Degler, "West as a Solution." Thomas Devyr suggested social-welfare agencies could participate in the exodus to the West by appropriating part of their budgets to relocate the poor through loans. *Working Man's Advocate*, vol. 1, no. 4, Apr. 20, 1844.

23. George Foster, *New York in Slices*, p. 45.

24. Ignatiev, *How the Irish Became White*, p. 87.

25. John Commerford was censured for injecting National Reform principles into one Nativist meeting, and of bringing a group of dissidents, including Evans, to disrupt it. The attempt to capture the Nativists for National Reform was far from absurd—both groups had faith in the theory of

surplus labor, although the Nativist scapegoat was alien low-wage labor rather than land monopoly. *Champion of American Labor,* vol. 1, no. 1, Apr. 3, 1847. For some Nativists, the land did have an appeal. See the sentiments of journeyman hatter and Bativist James Flagler of Poughkeepsie, in *Champion of American Labor,* vol. 1, no. 5, May 1, 1847.

26. *New York Sun,* 12th yr., no. 573, Nov. 27, 1847; 12th yr., no. 592, Apr. 8, 1848; 14th yr., no. 697, Apr. 13, 1850.

27. Earle, "Undaunted Democracy," p. 116.

28. The best treatment of the connection between National Reform and the Anti-Rent movement is Huston, "Land and Freedom." See also *Working Man's Advocate,* vol. 2, no. 46, Feb. 7, 1846.

29. Many of these areas forwarded homestead petitions to Congress. For Bovay's report, see *Voice of Industry,* vol. 1, no. 19, Sept. 25, 1845.

30. Thomas Devyr, *Odd Book,* American Section, p. 41; *Working Man's Advocate,* vol. 2, no. 24, Sept. 6, 1845.

31. Huston, "Land and Freedom," pp. 325–32.

32. *Working Man's Advocate,* vol. 1, no. 16, July 13, 1844; Huston, "Land and Freedom," p. 482.

33. *National Reformer* (Rochester), vol. 1, no. 39, June 22, 1848.

34. *National Reformer* (Rochester), vol. 2, no. 4, Sept. 28, 1848.

35. Their tour is also described—and interpreted as a mainly Fourierist effort—in Guarneri, *Utopian Alternative,* pp. 239–41.

36. *Harbinger,* vol. 5, no. 15, Sept. 18, 1847.

37. I have been unable to locate a copy of the *Landmark* anywhere, but a short excerpt, giving an indication of the flowery and sentimental nature of its prose, can be found in *National Reformer* (Rochester), vol. 1, no. 39, June 22, 1848. Ingalls went on to a career in individualist anarchy, and wrote articles for the anarchist journal *Liberty.* To the end of his life, he remained a land reformer. See Brooks, ed., *Individualist Anarchists,* pp. 149–63.

38. *Albany Freeholder,* vol. 5, no. 3, Apr. 18, 1849. The National Reformers began using the term "Free Soil" to refer to their own agenda as early as 1846. See *Northern Star,* vol. 10 [sic], no. 444, May 16, 1846.

39. For Grieg's Fourierism, see Guarneri, *Utopian Alternative,* p. 277.

40. A fairly comprehensive catalog of reformism in Rochester is McElroy, "Social Reform in the Burned-Over District." For the Fourierite and socialist agitation in Rochester which immediately preceded National Reform, see esp. pp. 191–97.

41. The banner featured an eagle sitting atop an oval frame, within which a blacksmith worked at his anvil. On either side were men and women working in the field, and an industrial scene, with a train passing over an elevated bridge, a boat going along a canal, and masts of ships and corners of buildings in the background. *National Reformer,* vol. 2, no. 6, Oct. 26, 1848.

42. *National Reformer,* vol. 1, no. 38, June 15, 1848; the *National Reformer* also printed Auburn National Reform news. *Rochester Daily Democrat,* Mar. 12, 1849, printed a report of a committee of the National Reform-

ers and also explained that the National Reformers' own newspaper had been discontinued. See also *Rochester Republican*, vol. 31, no. 42, Oct. 19, 1847.

43. *National Reformer*, vol. 1, no. 2, Oct. 5, 1847; *Rochester Daily Advertiser*, vol. 22, Feb. 17, 1848.

44. *National Reformer*, vol. 1, no. 35, May 25, 1848.

45. See J. C. Chumasero's speech, in *National Reformer*, vol. 1, no. 4, Oct. 11, 1847; also vol. 1, no. 11, Dec. 11, 1847; vol. 2, no. 1, Sept. 21, 1848.

46. *Rochester Daily Advertiser*, vol. 22, Aug. 15, 1848; John Grieg, a tailor, ran an advertisement in the *National Reformer* announcing he was working at Smith and Waterman's clothing store, and describing himself as a private in the ranks of the foot artillery of the great army of National Reformers. *National Reformer*, vol. 1, no. 36, June 1, 1848; *National Reformer*, vol. 1, no. 7, Nov. 9, 1847.

47. *National Reformer*, vol. 1, no. 11, Dec. 11, 1847.

48. *Journal of the Assembly of the State of New York* (1850) notes the petitions for homestead exemption, most of which were referred to a Select Committee. Some of the petitions also prayed for land limitation, a mechanics' lien law, and/or an end to further traffic in the public lands. For 1847: Westchester County, Jan. 16; sundry citizens, Jan. 18; Tioga Co., Jan. 21; sundry citizens of New York, Jan. 26; Albany Co., Mar. 22; Rensselaer Co., Mar. 25: pp. 100, 105, 126, 173, 576, 605. No petitions were noted for 1848. For 1849: three petitions from Monroe and Orleans Co., Jan. 18; Delaware Co., Jan. 23; Alabama, Gennessee Co., and six petitions from Steuben and Wyoming Co., Jan. 24; Brookfield, Madison Co., Jan. 25; Covington, Wyoming Co., Jan. 27; 58 inhabitants of Mentz, Cayuga Co.; Feb. 3; Watertown, Jefferson Co., Feb. 5; sundry inhabitants of New York, Feb. 6; Cattaraugus Co., Feb. 10; Oswego Co., Feb. 12; sundry N.Y.C. citizens, Feb. 17; Wyoming Co., Feb. 19; Cohoes, Feb. 26; Madison Co., Mar. 5: *Journal* (1849), pp. 159, 205, 212, 225, 311, 324, 342, 402, 418, 491, 509, 579, 663. For 1850: Oneida Co., Jan. 10; Buffalo, Jan. 12; Chenango Co., Jan. 21; Erie Co., Jan. 24; Rochester, Jan. 30; Delaware Co., Feb. 6; sundry citizens of Lockport, Feb. 15; Niagara Co., Feb. 18; Oswego Co., Feb. 19; Herkimer Co., Feb. 26; Westchester Co., Feb. 27; Niagara Co., Mar. 6: *Journal* (1850), pp. 82, 105, 160, 196–97, 236, 291, 382, 390, 396, 460, 482, 594.

49. For the proceedings of the first Industrial Congress, see *New York Tribune*, vol. 5, nos. 161–64, Oct. 15–18, 1845. While National Reform policy was formulated at the industrial congresses, to maintain their pride of place, land reformers deferred to other issues—the ten-hour day, a variety of cooperative retailing schemes, and women's rights. *Voice of Industry*, vol. 2, no. 1, June 19, 1846. See also N. Ware, *Industrial Worker*, p. 226. At the 1847 Industrial Congress in Philadelphia, reformers settled upon a series of "prospective measures" meant to follow freedom of the soil: prohibition of government debts, repeal of debt-collection laws, direct taxation, free trade, elimination of any standing army or navy, the consideration of various plans of cooperation and association, and township education, to be paid by

a tax raised within the township. *Nineteenth Century*, vol. 2, Jan. 1848, p. 183.

50. *National Reformer*, vol. 1, no. 40, June 29, 1848.

51. *National Reformer*, vol. 1, no. 39, June 22, 1848.

52. *National Reform Almanac for 1848*; see also *Voice of Industry*, vol. 3, no. 21, Dec. 3, 1847. For a full list of these newspapers, see Bronstein, "Under Their Own Vine and Fig Tree," app. 2.

53. Norris, "Land Reform Movement," pp. 73–82.

54. *Working Man's Advocate*, vol. 2, no. 4, Apr. 19, 1845; vol. 2, no. 5, Apr. 26, 1845. Even in Ohio, New York newspapers kept emigrants informed about the Chartist movement. See letter marked Glens Run, Ohio, Nov. 26, 1838, in Erickson, *Invisible Immigrants*, p. 305.

55. J. Pickering, *Working Man's Political Economy*. Almost nothing is known about Pickering's background, although it is alleged that he spent some time in an experimental community run by Josiah Warren. Dorfman, *Economic Mind in American Civilization*, vol. 2, p. 685.

56. J. Pickering, *Working Man's Political Economy*, p. 100.

57. *Power of the Pence*, vol. 1, no. 1, Nov. 11, 1848.

58. Ibid. The same letter was also printed in the *Spirit of the Age*, no. 16, Nov. 11, 1848. Wisconsin land reformers had been in touch with the land-plan Chartists since 1846, when Mineral Point reformers wrote to the *Northern Star*, "At no time have our hopes of the speedy triumph of your principles assumed so substantial a character as since the publication of your 'Jubilee' on the 17th of August last. Now we know that you have attacked the monster 'Monopoly' in the right quarter. Get the land—and all turmoil of faction, all the brutality of a bloated aristocracy, all the cunning of a grasping, monopolising, shopo-mill-ocracy will be unable to subvert your cause." *Young America*, vol. 3, no. 50, Mar. 6, 1847.

59. *Young America*, vol. 6, no. 8, May 12, 1849.

60. Between October 21 and December 3, 1846, 16 pro-homestead petitions were sent in from Wisconsin Territory, Dane Co., G. W. Green and 85 others (no county listed), Iowa Co., Racine Co., Dodge Co., Milwaukee Co., Washington Co., and Rock Co. See Quaife, "Convention of 1846," pp. 210, 402, 444, 452, 470, 524, 626. Between December 23, 1847, and January 26, 1848, 17 pro-homestead petitions were received from Ceresco, Dane Co., Fond du Lac Co., Milwaukee Co., Iowa Co., Dodge Co., Racine Co., Waukesha Co., Marquetta Co., and Rock Co. See Quaife, "Attainment of Statehood," pp. 240, 300, 348, 469, 492, 586, 593, 616, 793.

61. J. Gregory, "Land Limitation Movement," p. 95.

62. Among the land reformers Joe Norris lists are the editor of the *Illinois Staats-Zeitung*, a lawyer, a physician, a member of Congress who was also the editor of the *Chicago Daily Democrat* (John Wentworth), a contributor to the *Chicago Daily Democrat*, a printer, an entrepreneur, three real-estate operators, a dry-goods merchant, a publisher, and the pastor of the local Episcopal church. Norris, "Land Reform Movement," pp. 78–79 n. 14.

63. Ibid., pp. 73–82.

64. *Quaker City*, vol. 2, no. 12, Sept. 22, 1849.

65. A list of the newspapers reported to have endorsed National Reform appears in Bronstein, "Under Their Own Vine and Fig Tree," pp. 387–88.

66. The petitions are available at the National Archives, Tabled Petitions and Committee on the Public Lands records for both houses of Congress, under the following classification numbers: HR 29A G17, HR 30A H1.3, HR 31A G18.4, HR 32A H1.9, HR 33A G20.2, HR 30A G19.2, HR 32A H1.6, LC HR (Library of Congress House of Representatives Collection in the National Archives) Box 227, LC HR Box 232, LC HR Box 237, LC HR Box 243, LC HR Box 246, LC Territorial Papers (1 box), Sen 28A G17.2, Sen 29A G19, Sen 29A H7, Sen 30A H17.2, Sen 31A H19.1, Sen 31A H19.5, Sen 31A J4, Sen 32A H20, Sen 32A H20.2, Sen 32A H20.4, Sen 32A J2. The number of petitions is exact, but because of the sheer volume of material, the number of signatures was estimated rather than counted on the longer petitions (numbers on shorter petitions were counted exactly). Having settled on 60 signatures per page as a rough average for a sheet with two columns of names, and 30 per page for one column of names, I multiplied that figure by the number of pages per petition. More details of this project are described in Bronstein, "Under Their Own Vine and Fig Tree," p. 279. On the *Chicago Daily Democrat*, see Norris, "Land Reform Movement," p. 80.

67. According to this petition form, the members of the "Western Farm and Village Association of the City of New York" were "temperate and industrious Mechanics and Farmers from different sections of our country, and organized for the purpose of settling in close proximity, on a small portion of the public domain, with a view of obtaining a free grant thereof from Congress." They called for a quarter-section each, specifying that it lie between Lake Michigan and the Rocky Mountains. Andover, Mass., to Congress, May 25, 1852, Sen 32A H20, National Archives.

68. The Congressional discussion of the land-reform measure, in Chapter 7 *infra*, illustrates that homestead continued to be associated in the national mind with the National Reformers, urban workers, and the dangerous concept of "agrarianism" until at least the early 1850's. Those who petitioned for homestead were therefore doing so even in the face of its controversial origins.

69. John Commerford to Andrew Johnson, New York, Feb. 9, 1858, Sen 35A J1, National Archives.

70. In the absence of a printed blank, petitioners might copy the wording from a *Young America* form. See Duaresburgh, Schenectady Co., N.Y., Mar. 22, 1852, Sen 32A H20, National Archives.

71. Kalamazoo, Mich., Feb. 9, 1846, Sen 29A H7, National Archives.

72. Washington Co., Ohio, July 12, 1852, Sen 32A H20. For a second *Homestead Journal* extra, which goes into considerably more detail, see Ohio, Jan. 24, 1855, HR 33A G20.2, National Archives.

73. A petition featuring this icon and these quotations was also printed up specifically for residents of Ohio. See James Townsend and others, Ohio,

Feb. 13, 1847, HR 29A H1.5. Another petition, without these icons, was produced for New York signers. See New York City, Jan. 17, 1851, Sen 31A J4, National Archives.

74. D. Lamb and others, Mar. 21, 1848, Sen 30A H17.2, National Archives.

75. Ibid.

76. Dunleavy, Ohio, Jan. 19, 1852, Sen 32A H20.4, National Archives.

77. New York, July 12, 1852, Sen 32A H20, National Archives.

78. Pope Leo, Ill., July 6, 1852, Sen 32A H20, National Archives.

79. Benjamin Nixon and 103 others, Pittsford, Vt., Mar. 18, 1850, Sen 31A H19.5, National Archives.

80. Frederick Co., Md., May 20, 1852, Sen 32A H20, National Archives.

81. William J. Young to Congress, June 4, 1852, received June 8, 1852, Sen 32A H20. William Hick to the Congress of the United States, Columbiana Co., Ohio, HR 31A G18.4. For public-meeting reports sent to Congress, see Philadelphia, May 15, 1854, Sen 33A J2; Cincinnati, Jan. 15, 1851, Sen 31A H19.6, National Archives.

82. William J. Young to U.S. Senate, New York, May 25, 1852, Sen 32A H20; see also David Bryan to Congress of the United States, Philadelphia, Pa., Aug. 10, 1848, LC HR Box 232; K. Bailey to Congress of the United States, May 25, 1852, HR 32A H1.6, National Archives.

83. North Newburgh, Me., July 6, 1852, Sen 32A H20, National Archives.

84. The resolution is in Thomas Devyr's handwriting. J. K. Ingalls to U.S. Senate, Williamsburgh N.Y., June 3, 1852, Sen 32A H20. Land reformers John Commerford and Benjamin Price were members of Mechanics' Mutual Protection no. 41 of New York City. See Mechanics' Mutual Protection to the Congress of the United States, New York, N.Y., July 29, 1850, Sen 31A H19.6, National Archives.

85. North Newburgh, Me., July 6, 1852, Sen 32A H20, National Archives.

86. *National Reformer* (Rochester), vol. 1, no. 49, Aug. 31, 1848.

87. New York, N.Y., Jan. 23, 1851, Sen 31A J4, National Archives. This petition, sent by the Ouvrier Circle of the Brotherhood, was signed by Benjamin Price, later president of the National Land Reform Association, and William Rowe, later president of the New Jersey National Reformers.

88. The Wisconsin Phalanx, consisting of 170 persons, had 1,700 acres of land, more than 700 of these cultivated, and was entirely debt-free in 1847. *Harbinger*, vol. 5, no. 10, Aug. 15, 1847. National Reformer and associationist Lucius Alonzo Hine visited Ceresco in that year. *Harbinger*, vol. 5, no. 11. For Hine as a land reformer, see Zahler, *Eastern Workingmen*, p. 47.

89. *Weekly Tribune* (London), vol. 2, no. 52 (enlarged series, no. 1), Feb. 16, 1850.

90. Pittsford, Vt.: May 25, 1852, HR 32A H1.6; Mar. 18, 1850, Sen 31A H19.5. Wheeling, Va.: May 27, 1852, Sen 32A H20; June 3, 1852, Sen 32A H20; June 21, 1852, Sen 32A H20. Monmouth Co., N.J. June 3, June 7, June

8, 1852, Sen 32A H20; Jan. 28, 1850, Aug. 8, 1852, HR 31A G18.4. Ceresco, Wisc.: June 7, June 14, 1852, Sen 32A H20, National Archives.

91. Kalamazoo, Mich., Feb. 9, 1846, Sen 29A H7, National Archives.

92. The economic diversity of Massachusetts in the 1840's allows it to stand as a microcosm of the developed North. Although Lowell and incipient factory textile production almost monopolized the imagination of European visitors, bootmaking and shoemaking, neither factory-centered nor highly mechanized before the Civil War, employed 77,287 Massachusetts residents, as compared with 34,787 in textiles. Furthermore, much of Massachusetts was still agricultural, although this sector was in decline. Farm families increasingly either made an expensive and uncertain move west, or went into domestic production, factory industry, or the trades. They therefore had a vested interest in finding an outlet for their labor— including new farms. See Field, "Sectoral Shift in Antebellum Massachusetts," p. 165.

93. Information about the homestead-petition signatories from those Massachusetts towns not featured in this discussion can be found in Bronstein, "Under Their Own Vine and Fig Tree," chap. 7.

94. Approximately 24 petitions in the National Archives bear no distinguishing clue to their geographic origin. Petitions from Massachusetts are: Amesbury/Salisbury, n.d., Sen 32A H20; Andover, May 25, 1852, HR 32A H1.6; Andover, June 3, 1852, Sen 32A H20; Ashburnham, June 3, 1852, Sen 32A H20; Boston, June 3, 1852, Sen 32A H20; Boston, May 14, 1852, Sen 32A H20; Boston, May 20, 1852, Sen 32A H20; Cambridge, Mar. 14, 1852, Sen 32A H20; Chicopee, May 17, 1852, HR 32A H1.9; Franklin Co., July 13, 1852, Sen 32A H20; Holyoke, Jan. 17, 1851, Sen 31A J4; Northampton, n.d., Box 245 LC Territorial Papers; Pittsfield, Feb. 4, 1847, HR 29A G17; Pittsfield, June 3, 1852, Sen 32A H20; Roxbury, May 25, 1852, Sen 32A H20; Sunderland, May 20, 1852, Sen 32A H20; Sunderland, May 25, 1852, Sen 32A H20; Three Rivers, June 3, 1852, Sen 32A H20; West Chelmsford, June 3, 1852, Sen 32A H20; Winchendon, Mar. 30, 1852, HR 32A H1.6. I am grateful to Dr. Mark Lause for providing me with two further citations: Newton Upper Falls, May 20, 1852, Sen 32A H20; Pittsfield, n.d., HR 30A G19.2.

95. At a New England Workingmen's convention which began September 11, 1845, most of the proponents of a ten-hour day hailed from Fall River, one area where land-reform sentiment seems to have been weak. No state petition for homestead from Fall River has been found. *Harbinger*, vol. 1, no. 16, Sept. 27, 1845. See also Zahler, *Eastern Workingmen*, p. 181.

96. Goodman, "Politics of Industrialism," p. 177.

97. Goodman, "Politics of Industrialism." See also Sweeney, "Rum, Romanism, and Reform."

98. Gareth Stedman Jones makes an analogous claim for the decline of Chartism in "Language of Chartism."

99. *Voice of Industry*, vol. 3, no. 17, Nov. 5, 1847.

100. Magdol, *Antislavery Rank and File*, p. 62. There are interesting

parallels between Magdol's findings and those of this study. He also had difficulty finding occupational information for about half his sample, and imputed this to the mobility of the antebellum population. Of the people who signed who could be located, a plurality were between 19 and 29 years of age, with the 29- to-39-year-olds being the next-largest group. Most either owned no property or were skilled laborers with small amounts of property credited to them in the census.

101. A similar situation developed with regard to the cooperative movement in Rochdale. *Voice of Industry*, vol. 2, no. 50, June 18, 1847; *New Era of Industry*, vol. 1, no. 6, July 13, 1848. Albert Brisbane did try to link the various reforms in a speech in Boston, reported in the *Voice of Industry*, vol. 2, no. 1, June 19, 1846. Protective unions and National Reform were also linked in a resolution passed at a New England Labor Reform League meeting: *Voice of Industry*, vol. 1, no. 31, Feb. 12, 1847. On the protective unions, see Rozwenc, *Cooperatives Come to America*.

102. As John Brooke has noted, the political insurgencies which wracked central Massachusetts in the nineteenth century were predicated on a Harringtonian worldview—something that cohered very nicely with National Reform. See *Heart of the Commonwealth*.

103. U.S. Census, Massachusetts, Worcester Co., Worcester, p. 165.

104. *Voice of Industry*, vol. 2, no. 14, Sept. 18, 1846.

105. *Voice of Industry*, vol. 2, no. 15, Sept. 23, 1846.

106. *Voice of Industry*, vol. 2, no. 21, Nov. 6, 1846.

107. Zahler, *Eastern Workingmen*, p. 39; *Bay State Farmer and Mechanic's Ledger*, vol. 1, no. 23, June 10, 1846.

108. *Voice of Industry*, vol. 2, no. 50, June 18, 1847; vol. 3, no. 11, Sept. 23, 1847. The involvement of Massachusetts reformers in National Reform may have helped centrally codify the ten-hour day as part of the National Reform pledge by 1849. See *Young America*, vol. 6, no. 8, May 12, 1849.

109. *Boston Weekly Chronotype*, vol. 4, no. 36, Oct. 17, 1850; *Voice of Industry*, vol. 3, no. 12, Oct. 1, 1847; S. Johnson, "Genesis of the New England Emigrant Aid Company."

110. *Lowell Tri-Weekly American*, vol. 1, no. 148, May 15, 1850; vol. 1, no. 145, May 8, 1850.

111. Information for this section was compiled from the *Worcester Almanac*; a temperance petition reprinted in the *Massachusetts Cataract and Temperance Standard*; petition from Worcester, Massachusetts House, Unpassed Legislation (1845), box 252, no. 1587, Massachusetts Archive, Columbia Point, Boston; U.S. Census, 1850; *Historical Sketch of the Worcester County Mechanics Association*; and a list of politically active Worcester residents kindly provided to me by Professor John L. Brooke of Tufts University.

112. For conditions in Lowell and activism there, see N. Ware, *Industrial Worker*, pp. 87–134; for the cultural struggle over the meaning of industrialization, see Bender, *Toward an Urban Vision*; Zonderman, *Aspirations and Anxieties*.

113. Dix, *Local Loiterings*, pp. 44–50; Aiken, *Labor and Wages, at Home and Abroad*; see also Miles, *Lowell as It Is and as It Was*. Two contemporary views of Lowell are reprinted in Beaudry, "Lowell Boott Mills Complex." As Beaudry points out, archaeologists rooting around in Lowell trash pits found many flowerpot shards, eloquent testimony to the attempts of boardinghouse residents to sweeten their surroundings. Other important secondary sources addressing the experiences of Lowell operatives include Josephson, *Golden Threads*; P. Foner, ed., *Factory Girls*; and Dublin, *Women at Work*.

114. Charles Metcalf to his parents, Apr. 27, 1844; Charles A. Metcalf to Mrs. Joseph Metcalf, June 8, 1844, box 3 folder 1, Metcalf-Adams Papers, Museum of American Textile History; Zonderman, *Aspirations and Anxieties*, pp. 24, 66–70; Dix, *Local Loiterings*, pp. 78–80.

115. William Mann to Chloe Metcalf, Jan. 20, 1849, box 3 folder 16, Metcalf-Adams Papers, Museum of American Textile History.

116. Enhancing the international connection, this letter was seen and reprinted by British land reformer Joseph Barker on an emigration-scouting visit to America. See *People* (Wortley), vol. 2, no. 69, p. 135. Kellett was interested in a Seneca Falls–based emigration society which bought tracts in the far West from which shareholders then selected allotments.

117. *Lowell Tri-Weekly American*, vol. 1, no. 1, May 28, 1849; vol. 2, no. 102, May 25, 1850; vol. 2, no. 187, Aug. 16, 1850. *Lowell Courier*, vol. 13, no. 2157, Feb. 20, 1847; vol. 13, no. 2216, May 1, 1847. *Vox Populi*, vol. 5, no. 20, Apr. 11, 1845.The *Voice of Industry* supported National Reform in almost every issue throughout that newspapers three-year run.

118. The new banner showed Justice with rays emanating from her head, sitting on the world like *Young America*'s nude man, with the motto scrolling under her body. Next to Justice sat a muse with a lyre and a book, and beyond the muse lay the sea, where ships blew about at full sail. Flanking Justice on the other side stood Industry, bedraggled but smiling, his sleeves rolled up and his right hand on a spade, his left holding a scroll. Behind Industry a man plowed with an ox, and then farther in the background were a railroad and some mills and buildings. "The Voice of Industry" appeared on a curling ribbon in the immediate foreground, interwoven with ferns, flowers, and the produce of a bounteous earth. *Voice of Industry*, vol. 1, no. 31, Feb. 12, 1847. The possible cultural meanings of this banner are dissected in Zonderman, *Aspirations and Anxieties*, p. 95. On the *Voice*, which Norman Ware considered to be the longest-lived labor paper of this period, see his *Industrial Worker*, p. 213.

119. *Voice of Industry*, vol. 1, no. 20, Oct. 2, 1845.

120. *Lowell Tri-Weekly American*, vol. 2, no. 205, Sept. 27, 1850. For a biographical account of Young, which emphasizes his religious beliefs but perhaps exaggerates his shrinking from direct action, see Lazerow, "Religion and Labor Reform." Young was also one of the two principal leaders of the protective-union movement. See Rozwenc, *Cooperatives Come to America*, p. 96.

121. *Voice of Industry*, vol. 1, no. 41, Mar. 27, 1846.

122. For Jacques's support of National Reform and admiration for Fear-gus O'Connor, see *Voice of Industry*, vol. 3, no. 31, Feb. 11, 1848.

123. *Voice of Industry*, vol. 1, no. 28, Dec. 19, 1845. Six signatories to the Lowell National Reform petition could be found in the membership list of the Middlesex Mechanic Association. See *Catalogue of the Library of the Middlesex Mechanic Association*, pp. 19–21.

124. *Voice of Industry*, vol. 3, no. 18, Nov. 12, 1847.

125. *Harbinger*, vol. 3, no. 12, Aug. 29, 1846; N. Ware, *Industrial Worker*, p. 213. Pierce's bona fides as a land reformer became evident with the 1848 petition he submitted to the Massachusetts legislature on behalf of the Lynn Labor Reform League. *Voice of Industry*, vol. 2, no. 37, Mar. 26, 1847. Petition from the Lynn Labor Reform League, Massachusetts House, Unpassed Legislation (1848), box 275, no. 2919, Massachusetts Archive, Columbia Point, Boston.

126. *New York Daily Tribune*, vol. 12, no. 3474, June 5, 1852.

127. National Reform petitions from Lowell are in a completely differ-ent league from the ten-hours factory-reform petitions which originated there. According to one report, 2,139 signatures were submitted in favor of ten-hours legislation—a large proportion of them by women. Massachusetts House, Unpassed Legislation (1845), box 252, no. 1587, Massachusetts Ar-chive, Columbia Point, Boston.

128. Of the signatories to these petitions, 50 could not be located either in the 1850 U.S. Census or in the 1851 Lowell City Directory, or else had no occupation listed. Massachusetts Senate, Unpassed Legislation (1847), box 297, no. 12103, Massachusetts Archive, Columbia Point, Boston.

129. *Voice of Industry*, vol. 1, no. 43, Apr. 10, 1846.

130. Amesbury and Salisbury to U.S. Senate, n.d., Sen 32A H20, Na-tional Archives. Amesbury and Salisbury shared between them the Salis-bury Manufacturing Company, a water-powered wool-weaving complex with 840 employees spread among six mills, dye houses, drying houses, and machine shops and a sorting house. It is likely that the petition, with 99 signatures, emanated from this workplace. DeWitt, ed., *Statistical Informa-tion*, pp. 162–63.

131. Ironically, what they did share with their Lancashire counterparts was lack of job security. These same workers would be dismissed en masse during an 1853 strike over the question of a customary 15-minute break. Despite the fact that the town was on the workers' side, the company was too powerful and refused to rehire the workers—in the wake of which deba-cle many families pulled up and went west. C. Ware, *Early New England Cotton Manufacture*, p. 294.

132. Goodman, "Politics of Industrialism," p. 168.

133. For an excellent discussion of this cross-cultural phenomenon, see Hobsbawm and Scott, "Political Shoemakers."

134. On the shoemakers, see the classic D. Johnson, *Sketches of Lynn*; Blewett, *Men, Women and Work*; Dawley, *Class and Community*; Faler, *Mechanics and Manufacturers*.

135. *Awl*, vol. 1, no. 21, Dec. 7, 1844.

136. *Awl*, vol. 2, no. 13, Oct. 11, 1845.

137. *Awl*, vol. 1, no. 26, Jan. 11, 1845. The first advertisement for the NRA featured a drawing of a ship and the caption "The National Reform's final destination is not exactly known; but she will sail from *Grinder's Row*, through the gulf of oppression, and touch at the island of aristocracy; and capture a few *land-sharks*, and then sail for the freedom of public lands; and on her return passage she will touch at association islands for provisions," etc.

138. Members of the society were addressed by "Mr. Allen of Boston, editor of the *Social Reformer*." *Awl*, vol. 1, no. 21, Dec. 7, 1844.

139. *Bay State*, vol. 1, no. 1, Oct. 11, 1849.

140. Among the leaders of the cordwainer's society, William A. Fraser and Walter Sherrod were also officers of the Samaritan Temperance Association, whose meetings were reported in the *Awl*, vol. 1, no. 24, Dec. 28, 1844. Of 1,514 men employed in the manufacture of women's shoes in 1844, 583 were reported to belong to the cordwainers' society. *Awl*, vol. 1, no. 7, Aug. 28, 1844.

141. *Mechanic* (Fall River), vol. 1, no. 14, July 27, 1844.

142. See the appeals to women in the *Awl*, vol. 1, no. 23, Dec. 21, 1844; vol. 1, no. 25, Jan. 4, 1845. Women acted as organizers of cordwainers' social events. See *Awl*, vol. 1, no. 23, Dec. 21, 1844; Dawley, *Class and Community*, p. 81.

143. *Awl*, vol. 1, no. 12, Oct. 2, 1844; vol. 1, no. 20, Nov. 30, 1844; vol. 1, no. 2, July 24, 1844; vol. 2, no. 5, Aug. 18, 1845.

144. See the letter from "A Poor Man" in *Awl*, vol. 1, no. 30, Feb. 8, 1845. As David Johnson points out, many Lynn shoemakers would have been intimately acquainted with the benefits of the soil, since it was customary until at least the depression of 1837 for a shoemaker to keep a garden and a pig. See his *Sketches of Lynn*, p. 157.

145. *Bay State*, vol. 1, no. 52, Oct. 3, 1850.

146. *Awl*, vol. 1, no. 30, Feb. 8, 1845; vol. 1, no. 34, Mar. 8, 1845.

147. *Awl*, vol. 1, no. 30, Feb. 8, 1845.

148. *Working Man's Advocate*, vol. 1, no. 47, Feb. 15, 1845; petition of Richard A. Fleming and 57 others for land limitation and homestead exemption, Massachusetts Senate, Unpassed Legislation (1848), box 309, no. 12388, Massachusetts Archive, Columbia Point, Boston; *Awl*, vol. 1, no. 31, Feb. 22, 1845; vol. 1, no. 34, Mar. 8, 1845; vol. 2, no. 12, Oct. 4, 1845; vol. 2, no. 13, Oct. 11, 1845. Walter Sherrod, active in both the cordwainer's association and National Reform, was said to have seduced and ruined a young girl and then skipped town in 1845. *Awl*, vol. 2, no. 6, Aug. 23, 1845.

149. *Awl*, vol. 1, no. 4, Aug. 7, 1844.

150. This process is well illustrated in regard to both Millerites and Associationists in Barkun, *Crucible of the Millennium*; the specifics of the transformation are set out in C. Clark, *Roots of Rural Capitalism*.

151. Greenfield did have two industries employing substantial numbers

of people in 1855: a woolen mill employed 120, and the mechanics' tools industry another 80. DeWitt, ed., *Statistical Information*, pp. 185–86. On manifestations of status anxiety, see Edward S. Carpenter Diary (1844–55), July 17, Sept. 4, Sept. 14, 1844, American Antiquarian Society.

152. On republicanism in rural Massachusetts, see Prude, "Town-Factory Conflicts in Rural Massachusetts," p. 86.

153. Franklin Co., Mass., July 15, 1852, Sen 32A H20, National Archives.

154. *Northampton Democrat*, reprinted in *Voice of Industry*, vol. 2, no. 23, Nov. 20, 1846.

155. *Northampton Democrat*, reprinted in *Voice of Industry*, vol. 2, no. 36, Mar. 21, 1847.

156. Northampton, Mass., to Congress, Feb. 16, 1847, Library of Congress, Territorial Papers, box 257 (new numbering box 78), National Archives.

157. See also Franklin Co., Mass., July 15, 1852, Sen 32A H20, National Archives.

158. DeWitt, ed., *Statistical Information*, pp. 213–14.

159. Massachusetts State Legislature, Acts—1851, Chap 340, Act to Exempt from Levy on Execution the Homestead of a Householder Having a Family, Approved May 24, 1851 (with bundle of supporting information), Massachusetts State Archive, Columbia Point, Boston.

160. Petition of Jabez Sawyer and others, Feb. 4, 1850, Massachusetts House, Unpassed Legislation (1850), box 290, no. 2910, Massachusetts Archive, Columbia Point, Boston.

161. One homestead-petition signatory claimed elsewhere that the government of the United States increasingly ignored the yeomanry of the country; "those by whose toil [the country's] solid wealth is dug out of the ground." Massachusetts Senate, Unpassed Legislation (1847), box 296, no. 12051, petition of Henry M. Clapp and others, Massachusetts Archive, Columbia Point, Boston.

162. Wilentz, *Chants Democratic*, p. 342. Norman Ware had a very circumscribed definition of an "authentic" labor movement, and considered George Henry Evans inauthentic and the "reformist" movement a distraction from the workers' real causes, which had to reflect their economic interests directly (and the more they prefigured later unionism, the better). N. Ware, *Industrial Worker*, pp. xvii, 181. Edward Pessen—rightly, I think—broadened the definition of "authenticity" to include movements which explicitly sought workers as members or supported programs designed to promote the causes and the welfare of workers. Pessen, *Most Uncommon Jacksonians*, p. 28. While Wilentz has acknowledged the latter view, his treatment of Jacksonian workers' activism suggests he sympathizes with the former.

163. But see Saville, "Introduction," p. 61.

164. D. Thompson, *Chartists*, pp. 341–68, contains a listing of land-company branches by town.

165. My conclusions are based on a study of Chartist Co-Operative Land Company subscribership for eleven towns in southeastern Lancashire: Ashton-under-Lyne, Bacup, Bolton, Bury, Colne, Preston, Oldham, Rochdale, Salford, Stalybridge, and Wigan. Subscribership was abstracted from Board of Trade Papers 41/474–76, Registration of the National Land Company, Public Record Office, London. Each town's subscribership was entered into a data base and separated into occupational groupings in line with those suggested by the 1851 census, Parliamentary Papers, *Accounts and Papers* (Census Abstracts), vols. 85–88 1852–53 (1631–32, 1691-I and 1691-II) and vol. 43 1851 (1399). The 1851 census for males over 20 years old was grouped using the same rules, to find out the percentages represented by each occupational group. This process resulted in two sets of percentages, which can fairly be compared—the percentage of any occupational group within the land plan, and the percentage the same group represented within the whole town. The results of this exercise, arranged collectively and by town, appear in the appendix of my dissertation, "Under Their Own Vine and Fig Tree."

166. *Northern Star*, vol. 10, no. 449, June 20, 1846; vol. 8, no. 411, Sept. 27, 1845; vol. 13, no. 646, Mar. 9, 1850.

167. As Joy MacAskill pointed out, the ring around Manchester provided some of the earliest and strongest support for the land company. See MacAskill, "Chartist Land Plan."

168. Read, "Chartism in Manchester."

169. Feargus O'Connor, quoted in Chase, "Land and the Working Classes," p. 216.

170. Michael Anderson arrived at a figure of 17 percent of men aged 20 and over in Lancashire in cotton manufacture, along with some 15 percent of the county's adult women. Nearly 38 percent of those in employment were in cotton (the discrepancy is reconciled by the 40 percent of cotton employees between 1841 and 1851 who were under 20 years of age). Anderson also points out that working in a cotton mill was a lifestyle stage, affecting many people who had experienced such work in their adolescence. When men moved out of cotton because of loss of eyesight and dexterity as they aged, few opportunities were available for them at the same status level. M. Anderson, *Family Structure*, pp. 22, 29; Fleischman, *Conditions of Life*, p. 235.

171. Gadian, "Comparative Study," pp. 88–92.

172. Kohl, *Ireland, Scotland, and England*, quoted in Dennis, *English Industrial Cities*, p. 78; Waugh, *Sketches of Lancashire Life*, p. 185; Warnes, "Early Separation of Homes," p. 126.

173. Dodd, *Factory System Illustrated*, p. 129.

174. *Jerrold's Weekly Newspaper*, no. 20, Dec. 12, 1846, p. 470.

175. Bowman, *England in Ashton-under-Lyne*, p. 444.

176. Reach, *Manchester and the Textile Districts in 1849*, p. 1. Richard Dennis reminds us, however, that Reach, dramatizing unfamiliar scenes for his audience, had an interest in simplification, and perhaps, if he expected

government intervention, an interest in globalizing problems. Dennis, *English Industrial Cities*, p. 24.

177. Kohl, *Ireland, Scotland, and England*, p. 133.

178. See the letter from "Working Man," in *Bolton Chronicle*, vol. 21, no. 1033, Aug. 16, 1845; Gadian, "Comparative Study," p. 15; Reach, *Manchester and the Textile Districts in 1849*, p. 3. For similar sentiments from another quarter, see *Public Health Act . . . Pendleton*; Hardwick, *History of the Borough of Preston*, p. 427. For a contrasting view, see *Public Health Act . . . Preston*.

179. Health of Towns Commission, *Report on the Sanitary Condition of Large Towns in Lancashire*. But for a reassessment of the conditions of working-class life in Preston, see Hunt, *History of Preston*, pp. 161–64.

180. Reach, *Manchester and the Textile Districts in 1849*, p. 2.

181. George F. Foster, *Ashton under Lyne*, p. 30. W. Cooke Taylor thought cotton operatives blamed their struggles, in times of depression, on the instability of the industry rather than on capitalists; because this was a factor no man could control, it was an even more potent argument for leaving the industry altogether. W. Cooke Taylor, *Notes of a Tour*, p. 46.

182. *Manchester Examiner*, vol. 2, no. 70, May 8, 1847.

183. Preston workers' wages were reduced in 1842 and 1847–48. See Hardwick, *History of the Borough of Preston*, p. 418.

184. Thom, *Rhymes and Recollections*, p. 9. See also *McDouall's Chartist Journal and Trades Advocate*, Apr. 1, 1841.

185. Hewitson, *History of Preston*, p. 170. For a similar description of the good old days, see Butterworth, *Historical Sketches of Oldham*, p. 105.

186. *Jerrold's Weekly Newspaper*, no. 19, Nov. 21, 1846, p. 443. Compare Fleischman, *Conditions of Life*, p. 166, which illustrates variation in wage levels between 1820 and 1840; and R. Hall, "Work, Class and Politics," table 11, p. 276. Neville Kirk's table of percentage changes in the average weekly earnings of various classes of cotton operatives in Lancashire and Cheshire between 1839 and 1874 shows that over 1839–50, the earnings for eight out of fifteen grades of workers fell, and three remained even; only four advanced. Piecers, spinners, and tenters saw the biggest losses; warpers, weavers, blowing and cardroom women, and little piecers saw the gains. In other words, this period featured an advance in the wages of women and children while the wages of traditional "male" tasks decreased. Although the family wage may have stayed steady, the continuing reversal of roles was likely to have repercussions. Kirk, *Growth of Working-Class Reformism*, pp. 95–96.

187. M. Anderson, *Family Structure*, pp. 24, 32.

188. George F. Foster, *Ashton under Lyne*, p. 37; Bamford, *Walks in South Lancashire*, p. 10.

189. Reach, *Manchester and the Textile Districts in 1849*, pp. 15–17.

190. On the cotton-production process, and on early nineteenth-century mill architecture, see Williams and Farnie, *Cotton Mills in Greater Manchester*; Dodd, *Narrative of the Experience and Sufferings of William Dodd*;

Hall, "Work, Class and Politics"; museum displays at Styal Mill, Styal, Cheshire, visited Mar. 1994; and at Boott Mills, Lowell, Massachusetts, visited Aug. 1994.

191. *Manchester Examiner*, vol. 1, no. 43, Oct. 31, 1846; *Jerrold's Weekly Newspaper*, no. 19, Nov. 21, 1846, p. 443; *Manchester Guardian*, no. 1934, July 21, 1847.

192. E. P. Thompson, "Time, Work-Discipline and Industrial Capitalism," pp. 56–97.

193. "Rules to Be Observed by the Hands." Of course, it would be hasty to assume such rules were ever read—as James Archer, a weaver dismissed from Gardner's Mill in Preston testified in court, where he was seeking back wages, "There were rules printed in large type hung up on the walls, but they were never read up. . . . I can just read the alphabet, that's all." *Preston Guardian*, no. 136, Sept. 5, 1846.

194. *Manchester Guardian*, no. 1698, Apr. 16, 1845. Pilling was a powerful figure of continuity in Ashton throughout this period. Born in 1799, he had led a hard life and looked like a man of 60. He had been a handloom weaver from the age of 10, but when wages declined below the subsistence level, he entered a Stockport factory. He became a public figure in Chartist circles when he was tried for participation in the 1842 general strike. He emigrated to the United States in 1848. *Trial of Feargus O'Connor, Esq*, p. 254; Reid, "Richard Pilling," pp. 216–23.

195. Bamford, *Walks in South Lancashire*, p. 10. One contemporary lithograph, titled "View of Rochdale from Broadfield," shows cows grazing in the foreground, rolling hills and church spires in the far background, and 12 smoking mill chimneys—somehow not jarring to the eye—in the middle. The lithograph can be found in the Political Ephemera Collection, Rochdale Local Studies Library, Rochdale local history scrapbook 2A, no. 14.

196. Bamford, *Walks in South Lancashire*, p. 33.

197. Reach, *Manchester and the Textile Districts in 1849*, p. 20. Malcolm Chase and Alan Little described the appeal of the land to the factory worker in terms of familiarity with the land right outside the city boundaries, as well as the perception of increased autonomy in rural labor. See Chase, *The People's Farm*, p. 9; Little, "Chartism and Liberalism," p. 157, and especially his analysis of the pastoral poems of Chartist William Jones, pp. 240–51.

198. *Northern Star*, vol. 3, no. 150, Sept. 26, 1840. See also P. Pickering, *Chartism and the Chartists*, p. 119.

199. *Manchester News*, vol. 1, no. 2, May 27, 1848. For local lectures against land monopoly or for the land company, see *Northern Star*, vol. 8, no. 392, May 17, 1845; vol. 8, no. 411, Sept. 27, 1845; vol. 8, no. 400, July 12, 1845; vol. 8, no. 403, Aug. 2, 1845; *Manchester Guardian*, no. 1952, Sept. 22, 1847.

200. *Northern Star*, vol. 1, no. 45, Sept. 22, 1838; vol. 1, no. 8, Jan. 6, 1838. Lancashire Chartists had also been some of the most enthusiastic proponents of physical-force methods. See Sykes, "Physical-Force Chartism."

201. *Northern Star*, vol. 1, no. 13, Feb. 10, 1838.

202. On Salford, see Garrard, *Leadership and Power*; P. Pickering, *Chartism and the Chartists*.

On Oldham, see Sykes, "Some Aspects of Working-Class Consciousness"; J. Foster, *Class Struggle and the Industrial Revolution*; Gadian, "Class Consciousness in Oldham"; Winstanley, "Oldham Radicalism," pp. 619–43; and Gurr and Hunt, eds., *Cotton Mills of Oldham*.

On Preston, see Hewitson, *History of Preston*; K. Spence, "Social and Economic Geography of Preston," Todd, "Condition of the Working Classes in Preston"; and N. Morgan, *Deadly Dwellings*.

On Wigan, see *Public Health Act . . . Wigan*; Kirk, *Labour and Society*, vol. 1, p. 129.

On Colne, see photographs of Colne, Colne Public Library; Carr, *Annals and Stories of Colne*, p. 32; W. Cooke Taylor, *Notes of a Tour*, pp. 79–84; Napier to Phillips, Aug. 15, 1840, PRO HO 40/58, no. 359, photocopies in Colne Public Library; *Preston Guardian*, no. 129, July 25, 1846.

203. On Bolton, see P. Taylor, "Popular Politics and Labour-Capital Relations in Bolton"; Brimelow, *Political and Parliamentary History of Bolton*.

On Bury, see Waugh, *Sketches of Lancashire Life*; see also *Northern Star*, vol. 1, no. 22, Apr. 14, 1838; vol. 2, no. 61, Jan. 12, 1839.

204. *Bolton Chronicle*, vol. 15, no. 747, Feb. 16, 1839. See also vol. 16, no. 759, Feb. 15, 1840; vol. 16, no. 766, Apr. 4, 1840; *Bolton Free Press*, vol. 6, no. 279, Mar. 20, 1841. As Taylor points out, the Anti–Corn Law League petitions mustered working-class signatures in numbers which compared favorably with signatures to the Chartist petitions. See P. Taylor, "Popular Politics and Labour-Capital Relations in Bolton," p. 157; *Manchester Guardian*, no. 1614, June 26, 1844.

205. *Bolton Chronicle*, vol. 22, no. 1416, Jan. 24, 1846; vol. 22, no. 1447, Aug. 1, 1846; *Manchester Guardian*, no. 1715, June 14, 1845; *Northern Star*, vol. 6, no. 310, Oct. 21, 1843; vol. 14, no. 703, Apr. 26, 1851.

206. *Preston Guardian*, no. 127, July 11, 1846.

207. On the Chartist presence in Preston, see *Preston Guardian*, no. 20, June 22, 1844; no. 31, Aug. 31, 1844; no. 83, Sept. 6, 1845; no. 145, Nov. 14, 1846; no. 154, Jan. 16, 1847; no. 163, Mar. 20, 1847.

208. On reconciliation with factory owners, see *Preston Chronicle*, no. 1704, Apr. 26, 1845; *Preston Guardian*, no. 64, Apr. 26, 1845. On the tradition of employer paternalism, see Huberman, "Economic Origins of Paternalism."

209. Out of the other side of his mouth O'Connor praised Gardner's initiative. *Preston Guardian*, no. 80, Aug. 16, 1845.

210. Garrard, *Leadership and Power*, pp. 129–31. For Livsey (also spelled Livesey) presiding over meetings of the "O'Connorites," see *Rochdale Spectator*, no. 2, Apr. 1, 1844; *Manchester Guardian*, no. 1579, Feb. 24, 1844; no. 1770, Dec. 23, 1845. Livesey was also listed, with his occupation "brassmoulder," in the list of land-company shareholders for Rochdale. The

episode with the Oddfellows is recorded in *Manchester Examiner*, vol. 2, no. 116, Nov. 13, 1847.

211. On conditions in Ashton and Stalybridge, see Harrop, "Nineteenth-Century Housing in Ashton," in Harrop and Rose, eds., *Victorian Ashton*, pp. 29–49; Coulthart, *Report on the Sanatory Conditions*. The most comprehensive recent study of radicalism and the working class in Ashton is R. Hall, "Work, Class and Politics."

212. On support for Stephens in Stalybridge and Ashton, see *Northern Star*, vol. 2, no. 53, Nov. 17, 1838; vol. 2, no. 74, Apr. 13, 1839; vol. 2, no. 79, May 18, 1839; *Manchester Examiner*, vol. 1, no. 7, Feb. 21, 1846; *Ashton Chronicle and District Advertiser*, no. 5, May 1, 1848. For the only modern full biography of Joseph Rayner Stephens, see Edwards, *Purge This Realm*.

213. On Joseph Rayner Stephens's own land plan, see *People's Magazine*, vol. 1, no. 11, Aug. 1841. Although Stephens promised his readership an editorial on the folly of "political building societies," evidently adverting to the National Land Company, it was never forthcoming. The closest the *Ashton Chronicle* came to a mention of the land company was an editorial signed "M.S.": "Now I should think the man ought to be respected who has the courage to propose a plan, and the boldness to try how it will work in the face of his own countrymen; and this has been tried in England, and if report speak correctly those who are located are in a most impoverished and famishing state." *Ashton Chronicle and Lancashire Advertiser*, no. 60, Aug. 4, 1849.

214. On Lancashire involvement in the 1842 general strike, see Jenkins, *General Strike of 1842*; Home Office Papers HO 45/249, no. 121, Robert Thompson, Schoolmaster of Howell Croft, Bolton-le-Moors, to Home Office, Aug. 15, 1842. William Nield, the mayor of Manchester, noted that original demands for reinstatement of wages had been amplified to include a call for the Charter. HO 45/249C, no. 122, letter from Nield to Home Office, Aug. 13, 1842. HO 45/249, no. 103, Campbell, postmaster of Bolton, to Home Office, Aug. 13, 1842; HO 45/249, no. 51, Oldham Magistrates to Sir James Graham, Aug. 8, 1842; HO 45/264, nos. 100–102, William Ayre to Home Office, Aug. 16, 1842; HO 45/249, no. 63, E. Hibbert and Mellors, magistrates, to Home Office; HO 45/249, no. 66, J. Fred Foster to Home Office, Aug. 11, 1842.

215. Home Office Papers HO 45/249C, no. 361, memorial dated Sept. 26, 1842; HO 45/249A, no. 40, undated poster.

216. *Manchester Guardian*, no. 1418, Aug. 10, 1842.

217. Wild Letters, Tameside Local History Library Archives, DD 178/7, Stalybridge. The emigrant, named Wild, emigrated to East Hamburg, N.Y., from Hyde in 1842, and immediately wrote back that he looked forward to the day when he and his boys could vote the Democratic ticket. DD 178/1.

218. One old Chartist, James Ramsbottom of Corporation Street, Stalybridge, remembered how he walked to one of Jones's Lancashire meetings on Blackstone Edge; so many people were present that you could practically walk on their heads. Ramsbottom was interviewed for an article published

in an unknown newspaper on Jun. 29, 1912. Born August 25, 1824, he was 88 years old at the time of the interview. Tameside Local History Library, Stalybridge, DD 13/18/7, Notebooks of Local Historian John Cassidy. Ramsbottom remembered the land company: "We had what was called 'Fergus O'Connor's Land Scheme,'" he said. "Feargus O'Connor got some land near Gloucester, and there were two who went there from Staly-bridge—William Charlesworth, a dresser at the factory, and James Green-wood, a weaver at Leech's mill. They took plots of this land. The idea was to put men upon the land in order to create freehold voters." James Ramsbot-tom appears in the list of National Land Company subscribers for Staly-bridge.

219. *Northern Star*, vol. 6, no. 306, Sept. 23, 1843; *Manchester Guard-ian*, no. 1565, Jan. 6, 1844; no. 1596, Apr. 24, 1844; *Preston Chronicle*, no. 1877, Aug. 19, 1848.

220. Tagg was also an Oddfellow. Board of Trade Papers 41/474–76; *Pres-ton Guardian*, no. 357, Dec. 28, 1850. *Manchester Guardian*, no. 151, June 28, 1843; Home Office Papers HO 45/249, no. 23, Apr. 15, 1842, letter from James Whitaker; no. 21, Apr. 27, 1842, letter from James Whitaker. *Man-chester Guardian*, no. 1510, June 28, 1843; *Manchester News*, July 17, 1848; *Preston Chronicle*, no. 1668, Aug. 17, 1844; no. 1865, May 27, 1848; no. 1844, Nov. 20, 1847.

221. *Northern Star*, vol. 8, no. 395, June 7, 1845; *Preston Chronicle*, no. 1804, Mar. 27, 1847.

222. *Northern Star*, vol. 10, no. 430, Feb. 7, 1846; vol. 10, no. 442, May 2, 1846.

223. *Northern Star*, vol. 11, no. 533, Jan. 8, 1848.

224. *Manchester News*, June 10, 1848.

225. Comparing land-plan subscribers in Middlesborough with census and rate books, Malcolm Chase found a large constituency of lodgers, in-cluding many married couples sharing homes with parents, and felt that for these subscribers, housing rather than political or economic concerns may have been foremost. Chase, "Chartist Land Plan and the Local Historian," p. 78.

226. Wilson was still somewhat positive about the principles of the land scheme in 1887: "Feargus had a great many difficulties to contend against, for he had nearly all the press in the country against him, whilst a great many got on to the land who had no knowledge of it, and what with the op-position outside and the dissatisfaction within, the company was thrown into Chancery. Two or three from Halifax went on to the land, but the scheme was before its time; yet I believe the day is not far distant which it will be successfully carried out." Wilson, "Struggles of an Old Chartist," in Vincent, ed., *Testaments of Radicalism*, p. 210.

227. The one local exception to this rule is Oldham. After Feargus O'Connor was denied access to the town hall there for a lecture, he sug-gested the workingmen raise a subscription, in shares of £1 each, to build their own workingmen's hall. Despite a severe depression, £1,000 was

raised, and a building was erected which could hold 1,200 to 1,500 people. See *Manchester Guardian*, no. 1648, Oct. 23, 1844; Bates, *Handy Book of Oldham*, p. 30.

228. See, e.g., *Manchester Examiner*, vol. 1, no. 42, Oct. 24, 1846. The Chartists of Ashton placarded the town for a meeting, to get up a petition for the Charter. Although they asked the mayor, John Mellor, to preside over it, he not only declined but also refused them the use of the town hall. In Salford the "Chartist Rooms" were in Bank St., Great George St., and the town's mayor informed the government that the room had been in use for Chartist meetings for several years prior to 1848. See Home Office Papers HO 45 OS 2410A, no. 78, letter dated Mar. 30, 1848.

229. The powerloom weavers of Stalybridge met in the Co-Operative Land Society's room to discuss strike tactics. See *Manchester Examiner*, vol. 1, no. 35, Sept. 5, 1846.

230. Philip Howell has captured the Chartist strategy of overlapping local, regional and national lecturers in "Diffusing the Light of Liberty."

231. In one week, he visited Rochdale, Ashton, and Oldham, personally enrolling members of the National Charter Association. *Northern Star*, vol. 5, no. 212, Dec. 4, 1841; vol. 7, no. 337, Apr. 27, 1844.

232. *Bolton Free Press*, vol. 6, no. 315, Nov. 27, 1841; *Northern Star*, vol. 8, no. 406, Aug. 23, 1845.

233. *Manchester Guardian*, no. 1529, Sept. 2, 1843; no.1530 Sept. 6, 1843; *Northern Star*, vol. 6, no. 287, May 13, 1843, vol. 6, no. 302, Aug. 26, 1843; vol. 7, no. 333, Mar. 30, 1844; vol. 7, no. 334, Apr. 13, 1844.

234. Ernest Jones Diary, Apr. 5, 1847.

235. *Preston Chronicle*, no. 1713, June 28, 1845.

236. *Northern Star*, vol. 7, no. 328, Feb. 24, 1844; vol. 7, no. 329, Mar. 2, 1844. Even little Bacup produced fifty members after one visit by Dixon.

237. *Manchester Examiner*, vol. 2, no. 67, Apr. 17, 1847; *Northern Star*, vol. 6, no. 291, June 10, 1843; vol. 10, no. 517, Sept. 18, 1847; King, *Richard Marsden*, p. 36; *Preston Chronicle*, no. 1804, Mar. 27, 1847.

238. The tract was titled "Letter Addressed to Odd Fellows, Foresters, Druids, etc., Calling Their Attention to the National Land and Labour Bank." *Manchester Examiner*, vol. 2, no. 118, Nov. 20, 1847; *Northern Star*, vol. 10, no. 522, Oct. 23, 1847; vol. 13, no. 640, Jan. 26, 1850. Candelet, a weaver, had also participated in the 1842 general strike. *Trial of Feargus O'Connor*, p. 171.

239. For the allegations against the land company, which appeared in the *Manchester Examiner*, see Chapter 7 *infra*.

240. Home Office Papers HO 45 OS 2410A, no. 294, letter dated July 9, 1848; no. 423, July 16, 1848; *Manchester Guardian*, Sept. 22, 1847; *Preston Guardian*, no. 154, Jan. 16, 1847.

241. *Manchester Guardian*, no. 1933, July 17, 1847; no. 2005, Mar. 25, 1848; *Manchester Times*, vol. 16, no. 875, July 26, 1845; *Northern Star*, vol. 8, no. 400, July 12, 1845; vol. 8, no. 410, Sept. 13, 1845; vol. 10, no. 475, Nov. 28, 1846. McGrath, a master dyer and former member of the Chartist

national executive, had been financial secretary of the land company since July 11, 1847. Clark and Doyle were two of the company's original promoters. Clark was an Irishman who had moved to Stockport as a small child and became a physical-force, O'Connorite Chartist in 1839, speaking regularly in 1841–42 in Cheshire and Lancashire. He was appointed to the general executive of the Chartist Association in 1843. Reid, "Thomas Clark"; S. Roberts, *Radical Politicians and Poets*, pp. 89–105. Doyle had been called from his original occupation—weaving waterproofs in Manchester for 16s to 18s per week—to become O'Connor's land-company building manager at £2 5s per week. Parliamentary Papers, *Reports from Committees*, vol. 19 (1847–48), "First Report from the Select Committee on the National Land Company," pp. 3, 40; "Second Report of the Select Committee," p. 14; "Third Report," p. 43.

242. *Preston Guardian*, no. 83, Sept. 6, 1845. As members of the company directorship, Clark, McGrath, and Doyle received a salary of 30s per week plus traveling expenses; Wheeler, as secretary, received £2 per week. These were all princely sums compared with a 10s-per-week powerloom-weaver's wage, but these salaries theoretically also paid for travel.

243. *Preston Guardian*, no. 163, Mar. 20, 1847.

244. *Preston Guardian*, no. 190, Sept. 25, 1847.

245. *Bolton Chronicle*, vol. 21, no. 1036, Sept. 6, 1845. Board of Trade Papers 41/474–76. Joseph Wood, who led another short-time meeting, reported in *Bolton Chronicle*, vol. 21, no. 10412, Dec. 20, 1845, may be Joseph Fielding Wood, another Bolton land-company subscriber.

246. "Colliers' Appeal to the Country" (1844), D/DZA 31/52, Mining Broadsides, Wigan Archives, Leigh. The best recent treatment of mining life in this period is Colls, *Pitmen of the Northern Coalfield*.

247. Roberts, born in 1806, was a middle-class attorney, the fifth son of a vicar monied enough to send him to Charterhouse. He was introduced to Chartism in Bath, where he met Henry Vincent; the two then traveled around Wiltshire spreading the gospel of Chartism and being run ignobly out of various towns. Roberts gained fame in the North for his advocacy of the miners' unions during strikes in 1843, and became treasurer of the land company in 1845. See Challinor, *Radical Lawyer in Victorian England*, pp. 29, 106.

248. *Miner's Advocate*, vol. 2, no. 24, D/DZ A31/89, Mining Broadsides, Wigan Archives, Leigh.

249. Roy Church felt the land plan would have appealed to the inherent conservatism of the miners; it also probably made few demands on their insufficient educations, something which could not have been said for pre-1842 Chartism. Church, "Chartism and the Miners."

250. *Miner's Advocate*, vol. 1, no. 22, Nov. 16, 1844.

251. Home Office Papers HO 45 OS 249, no. 29, orange placard; no. 40, placard dated June 20, 1842; no. 28, deposition of John Broadbent, May 26, 1842.

252. *Manchester Guardian*, no. 1560, Dec. 20, 1843.

253. *Manchester Guardian*, no. 1739, Sept. 8, 1845.

254. Formerly a Methodist preacher in southeastern Lancashire, Barker was so popular that, when expelled from the Methodist New Connexion in 1841, he took 29 congregations with him, all from the West Riding, Lancashire, Cheshire, and Staffordshire. He then moved to Yorkshire, where he started his own printing establishment in the hopes of making the classics available to a wider audience. In his speaking engagements, he was a proponent of emigration, of republicanism, of land reform through legal reform, and of the elimination of entail and primogeniture. Along with William James Linton, he proposed this legal reform and collaboration with the middle classes as a "third way" for disaffected Chartists. Barker also formed an important bridge between the American and British land-reform movements. His newspaper, *The People*, estimated to have sold 20,000 copies per week, abounded with firsthand accounts of emigration to America. Barker himself conducted one six-month lecture tour of the United States in 1847, and then emigrated to central Ohio in 1851, unable to resist the glowing reports of the United States which could be found in his own newspaper. He campaigned against slavery, and conducted lecture tours in Nebraska, before returning to England in 1860. For a short time, he edited a secularist newspaper, coincidentally titled *National Reformer*. Barker would end his days in the United States. Brook, "Joseph Barker and the *People*"; "Joseph Barker," in Sidney Lee, ed., *Dictionary of National Biography*, vol. 3 (New York: Macmillan, 1899), p. 204; Barker, *Cause of the Distress at Present Prevailing* and *Reformer's Almanac*; S. Roberts, "Joseph Barker and the Radical Cause." On Linton, see F. B. Smith, *Radical Artisan*.

255. *Manchester Examiner*, Oct. 21, 1848. Home Office Papers HO 45 OS 2410A, no. 283, letter from Hall and Taylor to Home Office dated June 16, 1848. Although Barker tried to be a tribune of the working classes, he was clearly traumatized by the dirty state of his prison cell after his arrest for sedition in September 1848. See "Full Account of the Arrest, Imprisonment and Liberation on Bail of Joseph Barker," bound with *The People: Their Rights and Liberties, Their Duties and Their Interests*. The account appears at the end of vol. 1.

256. Barker in fact toured America to get a sense of where his countrymen should emigrate to. *The People*, vol. 2, no. 69, p. 133; vol. 2, no. 54, p. 11; Home Office Papers HO 45 OS 2410A, no. 244, letter from Thomas Birchall, mayor of Preston, dated July 31, 1848.

257. *Rochdale Spectator*, no. 25, Mar. 1, 1846.

258. *Northern Star*, vol. 8, no. 403, Aug. 2, 1845. Not all Lancashire land-plan enrollees were Chartists, according to the *Northern Star*, vol. 10, no. 425, Jan. 3, 1846; in Ashton-under-Lyne, however, land-society members automatically paid a penny a week to the Chartist Association. *Northern Star*, vol. 9, no. 466, Oct. 17, 1846.

259. *Northern Star*, vol. 8, no. 395, June 7, 1845; vol. 10, no. 442, May 2, 1846; vol. 11, no. 530, Dec. 18, 1847; vol. 9, no. 464, Oct. 3, 1846.

260. *Northern Star*, vol. 6, no. 293, June 24, 1843.

261. *Northern Star*, vol. 8, no. 399, July 5, 1845. The branch became so large that it split into two. *Northern Star*, vol. 10, no. 508, June 17, 1847.

262. *Preston Guardian*, no. 190, Sept. 25, 1847

263. *Northern Star*, vol. 10, no. 520, Oct. 9, 1847; vol. 11, no. 543, Mar. 18, 1848.

264. *Northern Star*, vol. 10, no. 502, June 5, 1847; see also vol. 10, no. 430, Feb. 7, 1846; vol. 10, no. 496, Apr. 26, 1847.

265. *Manchester Examiner*, vol. 2, no. 69, May 1, 1847; *Northern Star*, vol. 10 [sic], no. 497, May 1, 1847. Of allottees chosen for four of the allotments (Great Dodford being excepted), 15.78 percent were from southeastern Lancashire or nearby areas of Cheshire. Four of the original Herringsgate (O'Connorville) tenants hailed from Ashton-under-Lyne. Hadfield, *Chartist Land Company*, app. 3. For the tea parties, see *Preston Chronicle*, no. 1854, Mar. 11, 1848; *Preston Guardian*, no. 214, Mar. 11, 1848.

266. Cornwall, "Heronsgate and the Chartists."

267. On the difficulties inherent in local leadership, and on the relative importance of the Lancashire regional Chartist meetings, see Gadian, "Comparative Study," pp. 281–95.

268. R. Gregory, "Chartism in Bolton, " p. 123; *Northern Star*, vol. 10, no. 424, Dec. 27, 1845; *Bolton Free Press*, vol. 9, no. 435, Mar. 16, 1844.

269. He won a writing prize by urging workmen to visit the 1851 exhibition not to humor their employers but because a visit would "do more towards completing you in your several trades and callings than two or three years spent at your occupations. You can examine the different way of working, the tools and materials from nearly every town in Great Britain and from different parts of the continent of Europe." Pickvance, *Prize Essay*, p. 2.

270. *Bolton Free Press*, vol. 11, no. 533, Feb. 7, 1846.

271. *Bolton Times and Lancashire Advertiser*, vol. 1, no. 2, Jan. 8, 1848.

272. *Northern Star*, vol. 8, no. 401, July 19, 1845.

273. *Bolton Free Press*, vol. 11, no. 529, Jan. 10, 1846; vol. 11, no. 530, Jan. 17, 1846.

274. *Bolton Times and Lancashire Advertiser*, vol. 1, no. 12, Apr. 1, 1848; *Bolton Chronicle*, vol. 24, no. 1221, Apr. 1, 1848. By 1849, however, Pickvance was described in the newspaper as "late Chartist secretary"; it is unclear whether the Chartists there had disbanded or whether Pickvance had simply left his post. *Bolton Chronicle*, vol. 24, no. 1269, Mar. 17, 1849.

275. As *Northern Star*, vol. 8, no. 406, Aug. 23, 1845, reported, O'Connor discovered two separate land organizations in Preston on his visit there. King, *Richard Marsden*, p. 37.

276. See his letters to the *Preston Chronicle*, no. 1699, Mar. 22, 1845; no. 1701, Apr. 5, 1845; *The People*, vol. 1, no. 16, p. 127. See also King, *Richard Marsden*, pp. 22–37.

277. Brown fended off attacks on O'Connor and the land plan by the press. *Preston Guardian*, no. 209, Feb. 5, 1848; no. 303, Nov. 24, 1849; no. 304, Dec. 1, 1849.

278. *Northern Star*, vol. 10, no. 489, Mar. 6, 1847; vol. 10, no. 507, July

10, 1847. After reversing his position, he was unanimously chosen as the Preston delegate to the 1848 convention. *Preston Chronicle*, no. 1856, Mar. 25, 1848.

279. The correspondent went on to acknowledge the reverence for O'Connor in Rochdale: "Sum on yo ur olis to reddy fur to beleeve o us Fergus ses, un aw welly thynk us sum on yo ud subscroibe yor bras iv e sed it wur fur to buy lond i'th moon we." *Rochdale Spectator*, no. 23, Jan. 1, 1846.

280. *Rochdale Spectator*, new series, Feb. 1847. See *infra*, Chap. 7.

281. *Preston Chronicle*, no. 1723, Sept. 6, 1845. The newspaper became even more condemnatory as time passed; see no. 1725, Sept. 20, 1845.

282. *Preston Guardian*, no. 239, Sept. 2, 1848.

283. *Public Entry of John Fielden*, p. 4.

284. *Manchester Guardian*, no. 1670, Jan. 8, 1845. The ballot problem was pointed out by Richard Haslam, a local Chartist, during the question-and-answer period. Cobden was touring southern Lancashire during this period, visiting most of the larger cotton towns.

285. On freehold land societies as a nexus between working-class self-help and radical agrarian traditions, see Chase, "Out of Radicalism."

286. *National*, no. 4, Apr. 4, 1846.

287. Butterworth, *Historical Sketches of Oldham*, p. 238.

288. *Bolton Advertiser*, July and Nov. 1849.

289. *Potters' Examiner and Emigrants' Advocate*, vol. 9, no. 77, p. 608; vol. 9, no. 84, pp. 672–73; vol. 9, no. 86, pp. 679–80. *Preston Guardian*, no. 308, Dec. 29, 1849.

290. *Preston Guardian*, no. 242, Sept. 23, 1848.

291. *Potters' Examiner and Emigrants' Advocate*, vol. 9, no. 78, pp. 621–22.

292. *Potters' Examiner and Emigrants' Advocate*, vol. 9, no. 72, pp. 568–59.

293. *Potter's Examiner and Emigrants' Advocate*, vol. 9, no. 67, p. 537.

294. *Potters' Examiner and Emigrants' Advocate*, vol. 9, no. 73, pp. 581–82.

295. *Potters' Examiner and Emigrants' Advocate*, vol. 9, no. 74, pp. 587–89.

296. In his study of popular politics in Leicestershire, Alan Little warned that it would be wrong to equate participation in the Chartist Land Company with participation in Chartism; the activities of the National Charter Association were at their lowest ebb in Leicester while the land company was at its zenith. Moreover, none of the committee members of the Leicester branches of the land company was known to have been an active Chartist previously, and only 41 of the 172 identifiable National Charter Association Council members for 1841–43 could be confidently identified in the land-company lists. Little, "Chartism and Liberalism," p. 83.

297. Kirk, *Growth of Working-Class Reformism*, p. 59. Malcolm Chase has argued that the land plan was responsible in large part for the revival of later Chartism on Teesside. See Chase, "Chartism, 1838–1858," p. 164.

298. *Manchester Examiner*, vol. 3, no. 160, Apr. 15, 1848; *Manchester Guardian*, no. 2004, Mar. 22, 1848. On the weekly meetings, see *Northern Star*, vol. 10, no. 449, June 6, 1846.

299. Home Office Papers HO 45 OS 2410A, no. 257, 260, letters from chief constable of Preston to Home Office; no. 390, Rochdale superintendent of police (James Fowler) to Home Office, Mar. 20, 1848; HO 45 OS 2410A, nos. 282, 582, posters. Evidently feeling government pressure as a result of his participation in the events of 1848, Richard Pilling emigrated to America. *Northern Star*, vol. 12, no. 582, Dec. 16, 1848.

300. Home Office Papers HO 45 OS 2410A, no. 283, letter from Hall and Taylor at Ashton-under-Lyne dated June 16, 1848.

301. Home Office Papers HO 45 OS 2410A, no. 422, poster; no. 440, letter from John Lord dated Mar. 13 1848; no. 543, letter from J. Winder dated July 28, 1848.

302. *Manchester Guardian*, no. 2026, June 7, 1848.

303. John Lawton, a grocer, of Rassbottom Street, Stalybridge, who held shares in the land company, collected funds for the defense of William Bevan, a local man charged with training and drilling. *Truth Teller*, vol. 1, no. 3, in Home Office Papers HO 45 OS 2410A, no. 1228.

304. Home Office Papers HO 45 OS 2410A, no. 232. On the mustering of Ashton's "national guard" and the shooting of the constable, see Harrop and Rose, eds., *Victorian Ashton*, pp. 16–28.

305. An Ashton meeting was "so disgusted with a large portion of the fortunate allottees and members for their treatment and ingratitude towards Mr. O'Connor, who has devoted his life and property in their behalf, that they are of opinion the only plan in our present position is for that gentleman to apply to parliament for leave to wind up the affairs of the company, and pay off all the dissatisfied members," but only so O'Connor could then start up a new company. *Northern Star*, vol. 12, no. 614, July 28, 1849. Brown, of Preston, also stood up for O'Connor against rack-rent allegations in the *Northern Star* and the *Preston Journal*. *Northern Star*, vol. 13, no. 637, Jan. 5, 1850; vol. 13, no. 651, Apr. 13, 1850; vol. 13, no. 666, July 27, 1850; vol. 13, no. 668, Aug. 10, 1850. Of course there were exceptions, such as the Bury subscribers who, in regional newspapers rather than the working-class press, demanded their money back. See letter from John Bentley in *Manchester Examiner*, vol. 2, no. 120, Nov. 27, 1847.

CHAPTER 7: THE LAND PLANS, POLITICS,
AND THE PRESS

1. *Reynolds' Political Instructor*, vol. 1, no. 1, Nov. 10, 1849.
2. *New York Daily Tribune*, vol. 11, no. 3165, June 9, 1851.
3. Katznelson, "Working-Class Formation and the State."
4. On judicial conservatism regarding the plight of the worker in this period, see Tomlins, *Law, Labor and Ideology*; Marston, "Creation of a Common-Law Rule."
5. While there was occasional talk in Britain of opening up Crown lands

or wastelands for cultivation by the poor, such a scheme was widely recognized as quixotic. See *People's Magazine*, vol. 1, no. 11, Aug. 1841.

6. On the party reconfiguration of the 1850's, see Holt, *Political Crisis of the 1850's*; E. Foner, *Free Soil*; Gienapp, *Origins of the Republican Party, 1852–1856*; and Bernstein, *New York City Draft Riots*, chaps. 3–5.

7. Eastwood, "Amplifying the Province of the Legislature."

8. Wheeler, *Brief Memoir of the Late Mr. Feargus O'Connor*, p. 8. For another evocation of newspaper opposition, see Wilson's "Struggles of an Old Chartist," in Vincent, ed., *Testaments of Radicalism*, p. 210.

9. *Young America*, reprinted in *Albany Freeholder*, vol. 3, no. 32, Nov. 10, 1847. See also *Northern Star*, vol. 7, no. 361, Oct. 12, 1844.

10. Somerville, *Cobdenic Policy*, pp. 39–40. Somerville (1811–85) was born in Lothian, and served as a cowherd and a sawyer in early life before joining the Scots Greys in 1832. In that year he took the lead in protesting to headquarters against the order to march on London, and to sharpen swords in preparation for combat with the reform rioters there. For this he received 100 lashes. He became a celebrity after winning an official inquiry into the flogging; those who had ordered the flogging were reprimanded. In 1842, Somerville began a new career as a journalist, writing letters to the *Morning Chronicle* on the Corn Laws, and Cobden sent him around the country gathering information for the league. He became a correspondent for the *Manchester Examiner* in 1844. "Alexander Somerville," in Sidney Lee, ed., *Dictionary of National Biography*, vol. 18 (New York: Macmillan, 1899), p. 656; Somerville, *Autobiography of a Working Man*.

11. The league owed Somerville £65, which went unpaid 1846–52; he was subsequently imprisoned for another debt, which he could have covered had the league paid him. See Somerville, *Cobdenic Policy*, pp. 61, 72.

12. Ibid., p. 80.

13. Cobden to John Bright, Nov. 4, 1849, in Morley, *Life of Richard Cobden*, vol. 2, p. 54. In the *Manchester Examiner*, vol. 1, no. 50, Dec. 26, 1846, Somerville described some of his expenses related to research on the land plan: he spent half a crown for O'Connor's book, a shilling to have a look at the registration of the company at Chancery Lane, and another 1s 3d to buy a copy of the Joint-Stock Company Registration Act. Clearly, someone was paying him for his diligence.

14. *Northern Star*, vol. 13, no. 667, Aug. 3, 1850.

15. The *Examiner* was not a paper for the working classes; according to one Chartist correspondent, its constant criticism of the land scheme estranged any working people who might have read it. Nonetheless, it was very influential in setting a tone and in reaching those in government who could thwart the scheme. *Manchester Examiner*, vol. 3, no. 188, July 22, 1848.

16. *Manchester Examiner*, vol. 1, no. 48, Dec. 12, 1846.

17. *Manchester Examiner*, vol. 1, no. 49, Dec. 19, 1846.

18. *Manchester Examiner*, vol. 1, no. 50, Dec. 26, 1846.

19. *Manchester Examiner*, vol. 2, no. 52, Jan. 2, 1847.

20. Ibid.

21. *Manchester Examiner*, vol. 2, no. 109, Oct. 16, 1847.

22. *Manchester Examiner*, vol. 2, no. 111, Oct. 26, 1847.

23. *Hobson's Letters on the Land Scheme of Feargus O'Connor, Nov. 1849*, scrapbook, William Lovett Collection, Goldsmith's Library A.847, University of London. The letters are dated Nov. 2, 9, and 24 and Dec. 1 and 21, 1847, and Jan. 3, 13, and 21, 1848, and are clearly from a newspaper, but their provenance is unknown.

24. *Manchester Examiner*, vol. 2, no. 112, Oct. 30, 1847.

25. *Manchester Examiner*, vol. 2, no. 117, Nov. 16, 1847. George Candelet responded with a pamphlet outlining the positive investment potential in the bank for these groups in his "Letter Addressed to Odd Fellows, Foresters, Druids, etc., Calling Their Attention to the National Land and Labour Bank." See *Manchester Examiner*, vol. 2, no. 118, Nov. 20, 1847.

26. Parliamentary Papers, *Reports from Committees*, vol. 19 (1847–48), Second Report of the Select Committee, p. 35. Newspapers opposing O'Connor and his connection with the scheme included London newspapers like the *Weekly Dispatch*, *Globe*, *Lloyd's Weekly Newspaper*, and *Nonconformist*, and the *Nottingham Mercury*. See K. Marx and Engels, *Collected Works*, vol. 6, p. 359.

27. O'Connor also had an entire pamphlet printed refuting Somerville's charges. See *Reply of Feargus O'Connor, Esq., to the Charges against His Land and Labour Scheme*.

28. *Gloucester Journal*, no. 6517, Dec. 4, 1847.

29. *Bolton Chronicle*, vol. 22, no. 1435, May 9, 1846.

30. *National Reformer*, vol. 1, no. 15, Jan. 9, 1847.

31. *Poor Man's Guardian and Repealer's Friend* (1843), vol. 7, pp. 50–54.

32. This was a common criticism; see also *Manchester Examiner*, vol. 3, no. 182, June 27, 1848.

33. *Lloyd's Weekly London News*, no. 134, June 15, 1845.

34. See the "independent" rebuttal to Alexander Somerville: Robinson, *Letter Addressed to the Trades*.

35. K. Marx and Engels, *Collected Works*, vol. 6, pp. 358–60, 686. On the transition in Engels's thought, see Claeys, "Political Ideas of the Young Engels."

36. It cost 6d and carried as evidence of its prosperity seven pages of ads in every issue. Among its regular features were columns on Scottish, Irish, and foreign events, "town talk," and information on what was in the theaters. *Jerrold's Weekly Newspaper*, no. 1, July 18, 1846, p. 13; no. 54, July 24, 1847, p. 908.

37. *Spirit of the Age*, no. 4, Aug. 19, 1848. See also the letter of "Cromwell" (William Lloyd Jones) to *Spirit of the Times*, no. 27, Sept. 15, 1849; no. 28, Sept. 22, 1849.

38. *Weekly Tribune*, vol. 2, no. 54, enlarged series, no. 4, Mar. 2, 1850.

39. *Reynolds' Political Instructor*, vol. 1, no. 18, Mar. 9. 1850.

40. *Journal: Odd Fellows and Friendly Societies' Advocate/London Journal*, no. 77, n.s., no. 9, Aug. 28, 1846; no. 79, n.s., no. 11, Sept. 12, 1846.

41. *London Journal*, n.s., no. 10, Sept. 5, 1846; n.s., no. 12, Sept. 19, 1846; n.s., no. 13, Sept. 26, 1846; n.s., no. 14, Oct. 3, 1846. For further communication on this subject, see *London Journal*, n.s., no. 5, Oct. 10, 1846; n.s., no. 17, Oct. 24, 1846.

42. *London Journal*, no. 77, n.s., no. 9, Aug. 28, 1846.

43. Unknown writer, quoted in Foreman, "Settlement of English Potters in Wisconsin," p. 394.

44. *Spirit of the Times*, no. 6, Apr. 14, 1849.

45. *Potters' Examiner and Emigrants' Advocate*, vol. 9, no. 73, p. 582.

46. *Potters' Examiner and Emigrants' Advocate*, vol. 9, no. 95, p. 756.

47. Commons, "Horace Greeley"; Norman Ware rightly characterized Greeley as an editor first, a Whig second, and a friend of labor third. N. Ware, *Industrial Worker*, p. 21.

48. He continued to support National Reform because it promoted the cause of Association. See Greeley to James Kay, Dec. 1, 1847, box 1, Horace Greeley Papers, New York Public Library. Greeley worked with Lewis Ryckman as late as 1852 to design an Associative boarding house; see Greeley to William E. Geociner(?), Jan. 15, 1852, box 1, Horace Greeley Papers, New York Public Library.

49. *New York Daily Tribune*, vol. 5, no. 141, Sept. 22, 1845.

50. Commons, *Documentary History of American Industrial Society*, vol. 8, p. 42.

51. Robbins, "Horace Greeley: Land Reform and Unemployment."

52. *Nineteenth Century*, vol. 1, no. 1 (Jan. 1848), pp. 13–17.

53. National Reform in its most oppositional (capital-vs.-labor) form, and the type of reform which Greeley advocated, represent two ends of a rhetorical spectrum, but they should not be considered mutually exclusive. As I have emphasized throughout, working people could combine the desire to be provided for economically with the willingness to improve themselves morally; they could also combine an understanding of the safety-valve principle with an attraction to the romance of the great West and of O'Sullivan's "manifest destiny." I am not suggesting that Greeley's views, inasmuch as they were probably espoused by some of the many homestead petitioners, lie outside the realm of National Reform—after all, even Greeley saw himself as a National Reformer at the time. Rather, his employer status led him, then and since, to be given more credit for innovation on the homestead idea than he merited.

54. Greeley to Colfax, Apr. 22, 1846, box 6, folder 4, Horace Greeley Papers, New York Public Library.

55. "I am going to vote for Gen. Taylor—at least, I think I am—and I am not clear that this is right. If I could make Van Buren president tomorrow, I would. I don't like the man, but I DO like the principles he now embodies— Free Soil and Land Reform. And, very briefly, the Free Soil Party is the only

live party around us. It ought to triumph, but God works out his ends by other instruments than majorities; therefore, it will fail, but fail gloriously." Greeley to Colfax, Sept. 15, 1848, box 6 folder 5, Horace Greeley Papers, New York Public Library. Greeley tried to persuade Congressman Colfax to support a free-land resolution. See Greeley to Colfax, Feb. 12, 1850, box 6, folder 6, Horace Greeley Papers.

56. Thomas Devyr, constantly striving to make land reform a Democratic Party issue, railed at the connection of Greeley's name with land reform. "I am writing out Greely's record," Devyr wrote to Gerrit Smith, "what I know of it since 1840. He poses for a Reformer and has brought after him nearly every one of the original Land Reformers. He is using and betraying them. If you help to print it good and well." Devyr hoped to publish Greeley's record as an election sheet for the benefit of Stephen Douglas. Smith may have responded with surprise at Devyr's vehemence against Greeley, because Devyr wrote back in December, "Sir you are under a great mistake if you suppose that Horace Greeley did any service to land Reform. That was outweighed a thousand times by the evil he and his predecessor Van Buren did it by their pretended friendship." Devyr to Smith, Sept. 16, 1860, and Dec. 12, 1860, Gerrit Smith Papers, Syracuse University Archive.

57. *New York Tribune*, quoted in *Albany Freeholder*, vol. 6, no. 3, Jan. 16, 1850.

58. *Albany Freeholder*, vol. 2, no. 7, May 20, 1846.

59. See Bronstein, "Under Their Own Vine and Fig Tree," pp. 387–88.

60. *Chester Reveille and Homestead Advocate*, vol. 2, no. 23, Aug. 19, 1848, vol. 1, no. 22, July 17, 1847.

61. *Northern Star*, vol. 10, no. 509, July 24, 1847.

62. *Labourer*, vol. 2 (1847), p. 154.

63. Yeo, "Some Practices and Problems of Chartist Democracy."

64. *Manchester Guardian*, no. 1975, Dec. 11, 1847. Feargus O'Connor was not the only Chartist legislative supporter whose Irish measures caused controversy in this period; Sharman Crawford's bill to legalize tenants' rights in Ireland was defeated, 112 votes to 25. See Bull, *Land, Politics and Nationalism*, p. 38.

65. *Hansard's Parliamentary Debates*, vol. 100 (July–Aug. 1848), July 22, 1848, cols. 718–19.

66. *Northern Star*, vol. 11, no. 544, Mar. 25, 1848.

67. *Journal of the House of Commons*, vol. 103, p. 442 (Apr. 13, 1848).

68. Wakley, founder of the *Lancet* and coroner for Middlesex, was also a pioneer in the attempt to secure compensation for workers injured in industrial accidents. Sidney Lee, ed., *Dictionary of National Biography*, vol. 59 (New York: Macmillan, 1899), pp. 4–8. *Journal of the House of Commons*, vol. 103, p. 335 (Mar. 16, 1848). The bill's second reading was brought up and deferred on June 10; see p. 617. The connection between the Friendly Societies Act and the Select Committee investigation is also pointed out in Read and Glasgow, *Feargus O'Connor*, p. 112.

69. *Manchester Examiner*, vol. 3, no. 172, May 27, 1848.

70. Home Office Papers HO 45 OS 2665.

71. As listed in the *Journal of the House of Commons*, vol. 103 (1847–48), O'Connor introduced petitions to the government from the Salisbury branch of the land company, Feb. 28, 1848, p. 277; from the mayor of Northampton and the Members and Friends of the National Land Company, Mar. 1, 1848, p. 280; from the chairman of a meeting of inhabitants of Bolton, Mar. 2, 1848, p. 283; from George Adams, cabinetmaker, of Kings Street, Cheltenham, Mar. 3, 1848, p. 288; from Greenock, Mar. 7, 1848, p. 298; from the inhabitants of Worksop, Mar. 16, 1848, p. 333. The introduction of O'Connor's proposed legislation is on p. 335 of the *Journal*; the second reading, p. 617.

72. *Northern Star*, vol. 11, no. 544, Mar. 25, 1848.

73. *Hansard's Parliamentary Debates*, vol. 98 (Apr.–May 1848), May 12, 1848, col. 928. Benjamin Hall, son of a Welsh iron magnate, had an extensive public career beginning with his first election to the House of Commons in 1831. He became the president of the General Board of Health and First Commissioner of Her Majesty's Works and Public Buildings in the 1850's. Although never attaining a Cabinet post, Hall was raised to the House of Lords by Palmerston, becoming the Baron of Llanover. The clock tower at Westminster was called "Big Ben" in his honor in 1856. *British Biographical Archive*, vol. 502 (London: K. G Saur, 1984), pp. 332–36. The reasons for his particular aversion to O'Connor and the land company remain inscrutable.

74. *Northern Star*, vol. 11, no. 551, May 13, 1848.

75. *Manchester and Salford Advertiser and Chronicle*, vol. 18, no. 996, May 27, 1848; *Northern Star*, vol. 11, no. 554, June 3, 1848; vol. 13, no. 684, Nov. 30, 1850.

76. The appointees were Feargus O'Connor, Hayter, Viscount Ingestre, Captain Petchell, Viscount Drumlanrig, Sullivan, Henley, the judge advocate, Langston, Stuart Wortley, George Thompson, Scholefield, Sharman Crawford, George Strickland, Monsell, and Sir Benjamin Hall.

77. *Northern Star*, vol. 13, no. 667, Aug. 3, 1850. This information supposedly came from an intercepted letter which Somerville had written to a friend in Manchester.

78. Parliamentary Papers, *Reports from Committees*, vol. 19 (1847–48), Third Report from the Select Committee on the National Land Company, p. 29.

79. Parliamentary Papers, *Reports from Committees*, vol. 19 (1847–48), Fourth Report from the Select Committee on the National Land Company, p. 34.

80. Ibid., p. 39.

81. Sillett, *Evidence of John Sillett, on His Examination before a Committee of the House of Commons*.

82. Parliamentary Papers, *Reports from Committees*, vol. 19 (1847–48), Sixth Report from the Select Committee on the National Land Company, p. iii.

83. *Manchester Examiner*, vol. 3, no. 195, Aug. 12, 1848.

84. Parliamentary Papers, *Reports from Committees*, vol. 19 (1847–48), First Report from the Select Committee on the National Land Company, p. 3. Among the founders, directors and auditors were an undertaker, a weaver, a grocer, and three journeyman tailors, including the famous black Chartist William Cuffay.

85. He also publicly blamed Richard Cobden for authoring plots against him. *Northern Star*, vol. 11, no. 563, Aug. 5, 1848; vol. 11, no. 566, Aug. 26, 1848. The proceedings of the Select Committee were reprinted with O'Connor's editorial commentary in the *Labourer*, vol. 4 (1848).

86. John Stuart Mill, *Principles of Political Economy*, bk. 2, chap. 10, sect. 7, reprinted in Saville, "Introduction," p. 53. On Mill's contribution to land reform, see Dewey, "Rehabilitation of the Peasant Proprietor"; Perkin, "Land Reform and Class Conflict in Victorian Britain."

87. *Gloucester Journal*, no. 6549, July 29, 1848; no. 6550, Aug. 5, 1848.

88. Jones was placed in solitary confinement, denied pen, paper, and visits, and seemed to have received worse treatment than Chartist prisoners arrested in the earlier period. See G. Howell, "Ernest Jones, the Chartist," chap. 35, n.p.

89. *Times* (London), Feb. 15, 1850, p. 6.

90. *Times* (London), Feb. 18, 1850, p. 7.

91. Chancery Records C121/401 contains Goodchap vs. Weaving, a court case in which the appointed manager sued the mortgage holders for the Minster Lovell estates. Among the bits of evidence are Goodchap's receivership book, illustrating his abortive attempts to collect rent between 1852 and Christmas 1855. Several allotments were empty, their renters either gone away—some as far as America—or never having taken possession. John Littlewood, who owed £43 18s, alleged he had a claim against the company for work done. W. Layt, John Hicks, and Henry Wiggins all claimed their great poverty prevented payment.

92. Local and Personal Acts 14 and 15 Victoria, cap. 139, An Act to Dissolve the National Land Company.

93. *Gloucester Journal*, vol. 127, no. 6616, Dec. 8, 1849.

94. In practice, the fellow-servant rule, "assumption of risk," and contributory negligence rendered employees in nineteenth-century England responsible for the consequences of workplace hazards until 1880.

95. Stedman Jones, "Rethinking Chartism," in *Languages of Class*, pp. 90–178, esp. pp. 177–78.

96. See Saville, *1848: The British State and the Chartist Movement*. My interpretation is closest to that of Alan Little, in "Chartism and Liberalism," pp. 207–10, 371. Little theorizes that the Chartist leadership simply ran out of usable strategies by which to obtain the Charter; this was the most significant factor in the downfall of the movement.

97. According to the *Newcastle Daily Chronicle*, "the Select Committee caused a considerable sensation by bringing forward a report. They decided that the action of the land company had been altogether illegal; that

Mr. O'Connor was entirely responsible to the depositors in the bank; and that they had sent the matter to a Master in Chancery, for adjustment, in order that any further delay or mischief might be prevented." *Newcastle Daily Chronicle*, no. 5078, Jan. 27, 1875. Between Jan. 7 and Feb. 10, 1875, the *Daily Chronicle* ran an excellent series of retrospective articles revisiting the allotments.

98. Friendly Society Records FS 1 657/607. See also Foreman, "Settlement of English Potters in Wisconsin."

99. Of course, O'Connor was not the only Chartist leader on the scene, even in 1848—but he was most closely identified with the threatening, physical-force, strain of Chartism.

100. When National Reformers addressed a letter to James K. Polk in 1844 to elicit his opinion on the freedom of the public lands, Polk simply marked the document "not worthy of an answer" and ostensibly did not answer it. Sioussat, "Andrew Johnson and the Early Phases of the Homestead Bill," p. 267.

101. Zahler, *Eastern*, p. 81.

102. On this question, see E. Foner, *Free Soil*, p. 11.

103. Holt, *Political Crisis*, pp. 101–38.

104. On the Republican construction of "free labor," see E. Foner, *Free Soil*, pp. 1–39.

105. As Paul Goodman explains, homestead exemption was possible in Massachusetts in 1851 because a coalition of Free-Soil Whigs and Democrats responsive to National Reform agitation had come to power. Robinson, who drafted the law and pushed it through, had represented Marblehead since the 1830's and had long been a proponent of labor. See "Emergence of Homestead Exemption," p. 484.

106. *Bay State*, vol. 2, no. 25, Mar. 27, 1851.

107. Between 1847 and 1852, homestead exemption laws were passed in Connecticut, Maine, Vermont, Pennsylvania, New York, New Hampshire, Massachusetts, New Jersey, Michigan, Wisconsin, Ohio, Iowa, Illinois, and Indiana—roughly the entire purview of the National Reformers. See Goodman, "Emergence of Homestead Exemption," p. 472.

108. *Journal of the Assembly of the State of New York*, 70th sess., vol. 7, Assembly Document no. 203, p. 9. Cf. *National Reform Almanac for 1848*, p. 30.

109. *Journal of the Assembly of the State of New York*, 71st sess., vol. 3, Assembly Document no. 78, p. 5.

110. *Journal of the Assembly of the State of New York*, 73d sess., vol. 5, Assembly Document no. 123, p. 6. See also Zahler, *Eastern Workingmen*, p. 91.

111. Horace Greeley to J. R. Giddings, Apr. 3, 1848, Misc. Greeley Papers, New York Historical Society.

112. *Journal of the Assembly of the State of New York*, 74th sess., vol. 4, Assembly Document no. 130, p. 1.

113. *Spirit of the Times*, no. 8, Apr. 28, 1849.

114. J. Gregory, "Land Limitation Movement," p. 95.

115. Dec. 7, 1846, reprinted in Quaife, "Convention of 1846," p. 656.

116. Quaife, "Attainment of Statehood," pp. 284–96, 747–79, 793–805, 814–22.

117. Quaife, "Convention of 1846," p. 634.

118. J. Gregory, "Land Limitation Movement," p. 110.

119. Ibid., pp. 100–102.

120. See "Memorial of the Legislature of Wisconsin in Relation to the Homestead Bill and Donations of Land for Railroads," U.S. House of Representatives, 33d Congr., 1st sess., Misc. Docs., no. 56.

121. By the preemption law, prospective farmers and speculators alike were allowed to preempt unsurveyed portions of land, and to pay the minimum price of $1.25 an acre for them once surveys had been carried out. Opponents of free homesteads sometimes proposed graduation of the price of unsold lands as a palliative measure. By this plan, the price of unsold lands would drop every few years, thus preventing the undesirable accumulation of patches of unoccupied poor lands between tracts of rich lands. Zahler, *Eastern Workingmen*, pp. 124–25.

122. For summary dismissals of memorials in favor of freedom of the public lands, see *Congressional Globe*, 29th Congr., 1st sess., p. 280, Jan. 30, 1846; p. 614, Apr. 6, 1846. Shannon, "Homestead Act and the Labor Surplus," p. 642.

123. *Congressional Globe*, 29th Congr., 1st sess., p. 1061, July 6, 1846. Robert Smith of Illinois railed against "land monopoly" during the same debate; on land as a cultural issue, see H. Smith, *Virgin Land*.

124. *Congressional Globe*, 28th Congr., 2d sess., Feb. 3, 1845, app. p. 309, quoted in Zahler, *Eastern Workingmen*, p. 124.

125. Commons, *Documentary History of American Industrial Society*, vol. 8, pp. 64–65; *Congressional Globe*, 29th Congr., 1st sess., p. 563, Mar. 27, 1846.

126. *Voice of Industry*, vol. 1, no. 41, Mar. 27, 1846; *Congressional Globe*, 29th Congr., 1st sess., p. 473, Mar. 9, 1846. McConnell's bill purported to give land to those who would testify they had not the means to purchase, and would have made the tracts inalienable. Like Johnson's bill, however, it failed to set a limitation on land acquisition, and thus was not a full National Reform measure.

127. Zahler, *Eastern Workingmen*, p. 137. Her discussion of the fate of land reform in Congress is both ample and insightful; see pp. 127–76.

128. *Albany Freeholder*, vol. 6, no. 35, Aug. 28, 1850.

129. *Albany Freeholder*, vol. 7, no. 6, Feb. 5, 1851. See also the comments of H. B. Stanton in *Albany Freeholder*, vol. 7, no. 10, Mar. 5, 1851.

130. *Congressional Guide and Appendix*, vol. 20 (1850–51), 31st Congr., 2d sess., pp. 135–38, reprinted in Douglas, *Agrarianism in American History*, pp. 42–48.

131. Zahler, *Eastern*, p. 157.

132. The land reformers railed against this device, resolving "that the

cry of the enemies to the Homestead Bill, that this measure was the scheme of agrarian demagogues, is but a trick, long ago worn out, and despised by the people." *Proceedings of the Seventh Annual Industrial Congress*, p. 6.

133. Commons, *Documentary History of American Industrial Society*, vol. 8, pp. 69–70.

134. Zahler, *Eastern Workingmen*, p. 178.

135. "Proceedings and Resolutions of the Agricultural Society of New Castle County, Delaware," U.S. Senate, 33d Congr., 1st sess., Misc. Docs., no. 47.

136. *Speech of the Hon. Timothy Jenkins of New York*, Gerrit Smith Pamphlet Collection, no. 166, Syracuse University Archives.

137. *Speech of Hon. S. H. Rogers of North Carolina*, Gerrit Smith Pamphlet Collection, no. 287, Syracuse University Archives. On the impact of nativism on the debate, see also Zahler, *Eastern Workingmen*, p. 162.

138. *Speech of the Hon. Albert G. Brown, of Mississippi*, Gerrit Smith Pamphlet Collection, no. 67, Syracuse University Archives.

139. It is possible that even his contemporaries would have found this view a little flaky. Garrison, ed., *Gerrit Smith on Land Monopoly*, pp. 14–24. On the question of environmentalism versus moral reform, see Claeys, *Citizens and Saints*, p. 76.

140. On continuities between the Brotherhood of the Union and later populist politics, see Lause, "Voting Yourself a Farm."

141. Although Lippard's politics were omnipresent in his fiction, conditioning his choice of subject matter, most of it was light and exciting reading, full of filmic images, jumping tenses, and stirring explanations for the reader. A full account of Lippard's life is available in the introduction to Reynolds, *George Lippard*. See also Butterfield, "George Lippard and His Secret Brotherhood"; Denning, *Mechanic Accents*, pp. 85–117.

142. Lippard's story "The Mechanic of Brandywine" appeared in the New York *True Sun*, no. 949, Apr. 6, 1846.

143. Lippard to William MacFarlane, Oct. 18, 1852, George Lippard Papers, American Antiquarian Society. *Quaker City Weekly*, vol. 2, no. 1, June 30, 1849.

144. A presentation paper, accompanying a medal presented to one of the brothers, depicts a robed Christ standing in a sunburst, with one hand raised, and "Truth Hope Love" above his head. The mottoes along the borders of this document are "The American Continent—The Palestine of Redeemed Labor" and "The Night Is Past, the Day Is Dawning, and the Future Is Ours." In George Lippard Papers, American Antiquarian Society. The collection is on microfilm, its contents seemingly in no particular order; there is much repetition of documents.

145. *Brotherhood of the Union* (Statement of Purpose), Seligman Collection, Columbia University.

146. In a letter to the leader of Roger Williams Circle 142, Lippard assured him that ideas of cooperation are good and practical, and that he knew

a good, honest man who would buy coal for an unnamed brother at Pottersville. George Lippard Papers, American Antiquarian Society.

147. Fourth Annual Convention, October 3, 1854, Supreme Circle of the Brotherhood of the Union, George Lippard Papers, American Antiquarian Society.

148. *Flag of Freedom*, vol. 1, no. 7, Apr. 1, 1850; "Proceedings of the Semi-Annual Grand Convocation of the Grand Circle of Ohio, B.U. H.F. (which stands for Holy Flame) C.A., Cincinnati, Mar. 7–8, 1853," George Lippard Papers, American Antiquarian Society.

149. Third Annual Convention of the Supreme Circle (1852), George Lippard Papers, American Antiquarian Society.

150. *White Banner* (Philadelphia: The Author, 1851), in George Lippard Papers, American Antiquarian Society.

151. Cincinnati, Ohio, Apr. 22, 1850, HR 31A G18.4, National Archives, is on a German-language petition form and contains about 3,000 names.

152. George Lippard Papers, American Antiquarian Society.

153. Photographs of manuscript at Philadelphia Historical Society, in George Lippard Papers, American Antiquarian Society, p. 69.

154. Letter to Congress, dated Jan. 6, 1851, received Jan. 23, 1851, Sen 31A J4. Compare with letter from New Jersey Industrial Congress, written and signed by Evans, dated Feb. 13, 1851, received Feb. 18, 1851, Sen 31A J4, National Archives.

155. *Young America* in *Quaker City Weekly*, Feb. 2, 1850, quoted in Reynolds, *George Lippard*, p. 202. George Henry Evans had at one point proposed a similar secret society. See *Voice of Industry*, vol. 1, no. 21, Nov. 7, 1845. In an even further extension of the brotherhood idea, Lewis Ryckman proposed the outfiting of uniformed Industrial Guards. See *Voice of Industry*, vol. 1, no. 23, Nov. 21, 1845.

156. Reynolds, *George Lippard*, p. 37; *Quaker City Weekly*, vol. 2, no. 20, Nov. 24, 1849; vol. 2, no. 23, Dec. 15, 1849. As Reynolds notes, the Brotherhood lingered on into the twentieth century, as the Brotherhood of America. Brotherhood of the Union, "Official Souvenir," indicates that by 1900 the Brotherhood had become a glorified friendly society, based on the teachings of the Gospel of Nazareth and the Declaration of Independence. Members still professed that America was the Palestine of redeemed labor, that the public lands should be held in trust for the actual settler, and that although nature was bountiful, inequity was the reason for hopelessness. In 1900 there were 21,278 people in the Brotherhood of the Union (in 233 Grand Circles and Homes, under 7 Grand Jurisdictions), 4,822 of them in New Jersey. By the mid-1980's the group had dwindled to only around 200 members, with an average age of 70.

157. The mere existence of a circle should not be taken as a measure of its activity, however. Diary 5, George Lippard Papers, American Antiquarian Society, records many of the circles as inactive"; on Nov. 13, 1852, Lippard noted he was having some problems with a refractory circle chief who refused to communicate or to send in his collected funds.

158. *Jubilee Harbinger*, vol. 3 (Philadelphia: 1854), p. 337.

159. *Voice of the People* (New York), no. 3, Aug. 7, 1852.

160. Bridges, *City in the Republic*, pp. 114–17. Mass meeting of the unemployed attracted crowds of up to 20,000 to City Hall Park throughout the 1850's, and land reform was often a solution mentioned.

161. Fogel, *Without Consent or Contract*, pt. 2, p. 370.

162. *Monthly Jubilee* (May 1852), p. 92.

163. *Albany Freeholder*, vol. 7, no. 23, June 4, 1851; vol. 7, no. 24, June 11, 1851.

164. *New York Daily Tribune*, vol. 11, nos. 3163–65, June 7–9, 1851; vol. 12, nos. 3474, 3476, June 5–7, 1852; vol. 14, nos. 4100–4103, June 8–12, 1854; vol. 15, no. 4411, June 8, 1855. See also *Proceedings of the Seventh Annual Industrial Congress*.

165. *New York Times*, vol. 5, no. 1473, June 7, 1856, p. 8.

166. *People's Paper* (London), no. 18, Sept. 4, 1852. Ernest Jones illustrated the continued transatlantic interest in land reform by printing this excerpt and lauding the conference as tacit acceptance of the end of private property in land. He was stretching the point.

167. *New York Daily Tribune*, Aug. 16, 1850, quoted in Commons, *History of Labor in the United States*, vol. 1, p. 520.

168. Spann, *New Metropolis*, p. 151.

169. See also Bernstein, *New York City Draft Riots*, p. 98.

170. See the open letter from Commerford and Benjamin Price to the Congress, received Jan. 31, 1859, Sen 35A J1, National Archives.

171. John Commerford to U.S. Congress (printed circular), Jan. 31, 1859, Sen 35A J1, National Archives.

172. Devyr to Andrew Johnson, Dec. 9, 1859, Andrew Johnson Papers, Library of Congress.

173. Holyoake, *Sixty Years' of an Agitator's Life*, pp. 178–79.

174. John Commerford to Andrew Johnson, Sept. 16, 1866, Andrew Johnson Papers, Library of Congress.

175. National Land Reform Association, *Land and Labor*.

176. The confluence between National Reform and the later single-tax movement was pointed out to Henry George by Frederick W. Evans, George Henry Evans's brother and an elder in the Shaker Church. F. Evans, "Shaker Land Limitation Act," p. 67: "Now, I think George Henry Evans has materialized in Henry George. If it be not so, I can no more help it than I can help seeing that you have entered into his labors. You are teaching the truths which cost George Henry his life. I have seen nothing better upon the subject of land than your article." See also F. Evans, *Elder Evans to Henry George*. For Frederick Evans's own support of National Reform, see his *Shaker's Views on the Land Limitation Scheme*, 1883.12.2, 1888.1.3, blue scrapbooks of Shaker materials, and Cat. 6164 enclosure (letter from the Land Nationalisation Society, London, Jan. 9, 1886), Shaker Museum, Old Chatham, N.Y.

177. "Land Limitation—Views of Elder Evans," 1880.2.3., blue scrap-

book of Shaker materials, Shaker Museum, Old Chatham, N.Y.; Masquerier, *Sociology*, p. 103.

178. Compare a passage from pages 338–39 of George's *Progress and Poverty*: "It is difficult to reconcile the idea of human immortality with the idea that nature wastes men by constantly bringing them into being where there is no room for them. It is impossible to reconcile the idea of an intelligent and beneficent Creator with the belief that the wastefulness and degradation which are the lot of such a large proportion of human kind result from His enactments." Quoted in Offer, *Property and Politics*, p. 344.

179. Bradshaw, "George Henry Evans," p. 188. George Henry Evans owed nearly $3,000 at his death, with assets valued at $1,038: two printing presses (one power and one hand), two type cases, some stereotype plates valued at $100, and a "lot" of bound newspapers. All his effects were sold and dispersed, and his creditors received 61 cents on the dollar for their claims. His tombstone was eventually discovered and cleaned up by a New Jersey Eagle Scout in the 1980's, but by 1996 it had disappeared again, a victim of vandalism.

EPILOGUE

1. Hideo Koga disagrees, arguing that O'Connor put a paternalistic face on the land scheme so that it might appeal to the Tories, and reserved a more political and Charter-seeking face for the working classes. See Koga, "Chartist Land Scheme." Even had O'Connor been so motivated rather than just changeable and disorganized, there is no reason why the more politically freighted version of the land scheme should have had more appeal to working people.

2. Later movements to which the working-class land reformers might be said to have contributed directly and indirectly (through their animation of the public discourse of land redistribution) include the post–Civil War quest for 40 acres and a mule for freed slaves, Henry George's single-tax movement, and the Populists in the United States; the smallholding, simple-life, "back to the land," garden-city, and land-preservation movements in Britain, and even some of the organized land policies of Joseph Chamberlain and of the Liberal Party. See Lause, "Voting Yourself a Farm"; Marsh, *Back to the Land*; Offer, *Property and Politics*.

Bibliography

MANUSCRIPT COLLECTIONS

Allsop Collection, British Library of Political and Economic Science, London School of Economics, London.

Board of Trade Papers 41/136, Name Change of the National Land Company, Public Record Office, London.

Board of Trade Papers 41/474–76, Registration of the National Land Company, Public Record Office, London.

Edwin Butterworth Manuscripts, Oldham Local History Library, Oldham.

Edward S. Carpenter Diary (1844–45), American Antiquarian Society, Worcester, Mass.

Cassidy Notebooks, Tameside Local History Library, Stalybridge.

Chancery Records C121/401, Goodchap v. Weaving, Public Record Office, London.

Evans Family Bible, Scrapbooks of Shaker Materials, and Logbooks of Shaker Settlements, Shaker Museum, Old Chatham, N.Y.

Franklin-Adams Papers, Museum of American Textile History, North Andover, Mass.

Friendly Society Records FS 1 657/607, FS 2/4, Papers Relating to the Potters' Joint-Stock Emigration Society, Public Record Office, London.

Horace Greeley Papers, New York Historical Society, New York, N.Y.

Horace Greeley Papers, New York Public Library, New York, N.Y.

G. J. Holyoake Engagement Diary, Bishopsgate Institute, London.

Home Office Papers HO 40, HO 45, Reports of Disturbances, Public Record Office (PRO), London.

Andrew Johnson Papers, Library of Congress, Washington, D.C.

Ernest Jones Diary, Manchester Central Reference Library Archives, Manchester.

Ernest Jones Papers, Chetham's Library, Manchester.

Ernest Jones Papers, Seligman/Jones Collection, Special Collections, Columbia University Library, New York, N.Y.

Ernest Jones to the Earl of Aberdeen, Additional Manuscripts, 43239, British Library, London.

George Lippard Papers, American Antiquarian Society, Worcester, Mass.

Local Government Correspondence, Bolton Local History Archives, Bolton.

M.R. 105, M.R. 641, M.R. 104, Maps of Chartist Allotments, Public Record Office, London.

Metcalf-Adams Papers, Museum of American Textile History, North Andover, Mass.

Mining Broadsides, Wigan Archives, Leigh.

Bronterre O'Brien Papers, National Museum of Labour History, Manchester.

Feargus O'Connor to Joseph Sturge, Additional Manuscripts, 43845, British Library, London.

Francis Place Collection, Additional Manuscripts, 27808, British Library, London.

Political Ephemera Collection, Rochdale Local Studies Library, Rochdale.

R. J. Richardson Scrapbook, Manchester Central Reference Library Archives, Manchester.

Gerrit Smith Papers, State Library of New York, Albany, N.Y.

Gerrit Smith Papers/Pamphlet Collection, Syracuse University Archive, Syracuse, N.Y.

Edmund Stedman Papers, Stedman Collection, Special Collections, Columbia University Library, New York, N.Y.

Robert Taylor Autobiography, Manuscript Collection, New York Public Library, New York, N.Y.

Wild Letters, Tameside Local History Library, Stalybridge.

GOVERNMENT DOCUMENTS

Congressional Globe (1840–62).

Hansard's Parliamentary Debates (1838–51).

Journal of the Assembly of the State of New York. Albany: Weed, Parsons and Co., 1849–50.

Journal of the House of Commons (1847–51).

Massachusetts Acts—1851, Chap. 340, Act to Exempt from Levy on Execution the Homestead of a Householder Having a Family, Approved May 24, 1851, Massachusetts Archive, Columbia Point, Boston.

Massachusetts House/Senate, Unpassed Legislation, Massachusetts Archive, Columbia Point, Boston.

Minutes of Evidence before the Winding-Up Act of 1851; Local and Personal Acts 14 and 15 Victoria, 1851, cap 139.

Parliamentary Papers, *Accounts and Papers.* Census Abstracts, vols. 85–88, 1852–53 (1631-32, 1691-I, 1691-II); vol. 43, 1851 (1399).

Parliamentary Papers, *Reports from Commissioners.* Assistant HandLoom Weavers' Commission, 1840 (24), Part 5.

Parliamentary Papers, *Reports from Commissioners.* Royal Commission on Agriculture, 1882 (1), vol. 14.

Parliamentary Papers, *Reports from Committees.* House of Lords Select Committee on the Poor Laws, 1830–31, vol 1.

Parliamentary Papers, *Reports from Committees.* Select Committee to Inquire into Allotment System, and Propriety of Setting Apart Portion of Waste Land for Labouring Poor, 1843 (402), vol. 7.

Parliamentary Papers, *Reports from Committees.* Select Committee on the

National Land Company, Together with the Minutes of Evidence and Appendix, 1848, vol. 19.

Petitions in Favor of a Homestead Bill, Tabled Petitions and Committee on the Public Lands:

HR 29A G17, HR 29A H1.5, HR 30A H1.3, HR 31A G18.4, HR 32A H1.6, HR 32A H1.9, HR 33A G20.2, HR 30A G19.2, HR 32A H1.6, LC HR box 227, LC HR box 232, LC HR box 237, LC HR box 243, LC HR box 246, LC Territorial Papers, Sen 28A G17.2, Sen 29A G19, Sen 29A G19.1, Sen 29A H7, Sen 30A H17.2, Sen 31A H19.5, Sen 31A H19.6, Sen 31A J4, Sen 32A H20, Sen 32A H20.2, Sen 32A H20.4, Sen 32A J2, Sen 35A J1, National Archives, Washington, D.C.

U.S. House of Representatives, 33d Congress, 1st session, Miscellaneous Documents, no. 56, "Memorial of the Legislature of Wisconsin in Relation to the Homestead Bill and Donations of Land for Railroads."

NEWSPAPERS

Albany Anti-Renter (Albany, N.Y.: 1845–46).
Albany Freeholder (Albany, N.Y.: 1845–52).
American Laborer (New York, N.Y.: 1843).
Ashton Chronicle and District Advertiser/Lancashire Advertiser (Ashton-under-Lyne: 1848–49).
Awl (Lynn, Mass.: 1844–45).
Bay State (Lynn, Mass.: 1849–50).
Bay State Farmer and Mechanic's Ledger (Worcester, Mass.: 1846).
Beehive (London: 1868).
Blue Hen's Chicken (Wilmington, Del.: 1847).
Bolton Advertiser (Bolton: 1848–49).
Bolton Chronicle (Bolton: 1839–50).
Bolton Free Press (Bolton: 1839–47).
Bolton Times and Lancashire Advertiser (Bolton: 1848).
Boston Chronotype (Boston, Mass.: 1846–50).
Boston Quarterly Review (Boston, Mass.: 1840–41).
Bronterre's National Reformer (London: 1837).
Champion of American Labor (New York, N.Y.: 1847).
Cheltenham Free Press (Cheltenham: 1847–50).
Chester Reveille and Homestead Advocate (Chester, Ill.: 1847–9).
Commonweal (London: 1845).
Democratic Review (London: 1850).
English Chartist Circular and Temperance Record for England and Wales (London: 1841–44).
English Patriot and Irish Repealer (Manchester: 1848).
Evening Star (London: 1842–43).
Farmers' and Mechanics' Weekly Journal (Worcester, Mass.: 1847–48).
The Field, the Force and the Factory (Ashton-under-Lyne: 1848–49).
Flag of Freedom (Rochester, N.Y.: 1850).
Gloucester Journal (Gloucester: 1847–50).

Harbinger (New York, N.Y.: 1845–49).
Homestead Journal (Salem, Ohio: 1853).
Howitt's Journal of Literature and Popular Progress (London: 1847).
Jerrold's Weekly Newspaper (London: 1846–47).
Journal: Odd Fellows' and Friendly Societies' Advocate (London: 1846–47).
Jubilee Harbinger (Philadelphia, Pa.: 1854).
Labourer (London: 1847–48).
Labourer's Friend (London: 1833–50).
Labourer's Friend Tracts (London: 1830–40).
Lancashire Beacon (Manchester: 1848–49).
Lloyd's Weekly London News (London: 1845).
London Democrat (London: 1839).
London Journal (London: 1846).
Lowell Courier (Lowell, Mass.: 1847).
Lowell Journal (Lowell, Mass.: 1847).
Lowell Tri-Weekly American (Lowell, Mass.: 1848–53).
Manchester and Salford Advertiser and Chronicle (Manchester: 1848).
Manchester Examiner (Manchester: 1846–48).
Manchester Guardian (Manchester: 1842–50).
Manchester News (Manchester: 1848).
Manchester Times (Manchester: 1845).
Massachusetts Cataract and Temperance Standard (Worcester, Mass.:
    1847).
McDouall's Chartist Journal and Trades Advocate (London: 1841).
Mechanic (Fall River, Mass.: 1844–45).
Miners' Advocate (Lancashire: 1844).
Monthly Jubilee (Philadelphia, Pa.: 1852–55).
*National: A Weekly Family Journal of Politics, Literature, the Fine Arts
    and Record of Building Societies* (London: 1846).
National Instructor (London, 1850–51).
National Reform Almanac for 1848 (New York, N.Y.: 1848).
National Reformer (Douglas: 1846–47).
National Reformer (Rochester, N.Y.: 1848).
National Union (London: 1858).
Newcastle Daily Chronicle (Newcastle: 1875).
New England Offering (Lowell, Mass.: 1848).
New Era of Industry (Boston, Mass.: 1848).
New York Sun (New York, N.Y.: 1847–50).
New York Daily Tribune (New York, N.Y.: 1845–55).
New York Times (New York, N.Y.: 1855–56).
Nineteenth Century (Philadelphia, Pa.: 1847–48).
Northern Liberator (Newcastle: 1839–40).
Northern Star and Leeds General Advertiser (Leeds and London: 1838–51).
Notes to the People (London: 1851–52).
Offering (Lowell, Mass.: 1845–46).
Operative (London: 1839).

The People: Their Rights and Liberties, Their Duties and Their Interests (Wortley: 1848–52).

People's Chronicle and Factory Workers' Journal (Ashton-under-Lyne: 1849).

People's Journal (London: 1846–48).

People's Magazine (London: 1841).

People's Paper (London: 1852).

People's Rights and Organ of the National Reform Association (New York, N.Y.: 1844).

Pigs' Meat (London: 1793–95).

Pilor and Rochdale Reporter (Rochdale: 1847).

Politics for the People (London: 1848).

Poor Man's Guardian and Repealer's Friend (London: 1843).

Potters' Examiner and Workman's Advocate/Emigrants' Advocate (Shelton: 1843–50).

Power of the Pence (London: 1848–49).

Preston Chronicle (Preston: 1842–50).

Preston Guardian (Preston: 1844–50).

Protest (Lowell, Mass.: 1848).

Quaker City Weekly (Philadelphia, Pa.: 1849–50).

Radical, in Continuation of the Working Man's Advocate (Granville, N.J.: 1841).

Reasoner and Herald of Progress (London: 1846).

Red Republican (London: 1850).

Reformer (London: 1845–46).

Republican (London: 1824).

Reynolds' Political Instructor (London: 1849–50).

Rochdale Spectator (Rochdale: 1844–47).

Rochester Daily Advertiser (Rochester, N.Y.: 1848).

Rochester Daily Democrat (Rochester, N.Y.: 1849).

Rochester Republican (Rochester, N.Y.: 1847).

Spirit of the Age (London: 1848–49).

Star in the East (Wisbech: 1838).

Star of Freedom (London: 1852).

State Sentinel and Worcester Reformer (Worcester, Mass.: 1845).

Stephens' Monthly Magazine (Ashton-under-Lyne: 1840).

Times (London: 1846–55).

True Sun (New York, N.Y.: 1846).

Valentine's Manual (New York, N.Y.: 1919–24).

Voice of Industry (Fitchburg, Lowell, and Boston, Mass.: 1845–48).

Voice of the People (London: 1848).

Voice of the People (New York: 1852).

Vox Populi (Lowell, Mass.: 1845).

Weekly Tribune (London: 1850).

Western Agriculturist (Columbus, Ohio: 1851).

White Banner (Philadelphia, Pa.: 1851).

Wigan Times (Wigan: 1849).
Working Man's Advocate (New York, N.Y.: 1829–36, 1844–45).
Working Men's Organ (Buffalo, N.Y.: 1847–48).
Young America (New York, N.Y.: 1845–49).

OTHER SOURCES

Adams, W. E. *Memoirs of a Social Atom*. London: Hutcheson & Co., 1903.
Adshead, Joseph. *Distress in Manchester: Evidence of the State of the La-bouring Classes, 1840–42*. London: Henry Hooper, 1842.
Aiken, John. *Labor and Wages, at Home and Abroad*. Lowell, Mass.: D. Bixby, 1849.
Aitken, William. *The Writings of a Nineteenth Century Working Man*. Ed. Robert G. Hall and Stephen Roberts. Tameside: Tameside Leisure Services, 1996 [1869].
Albion, Robert G. *The Rise of New York Port, 1825–1860*. New York, N.Y.: Charles Scribner's Sons, 1939.
Allen, William. *Colonies at Home*. London: C. Greene, 1827.
Anderson, Benedict. *Imagined Communities*. London: Verso, 1983.
Anderson, Michael. *Family Structure in Nineteenth-Century Lancashire*. Cambridge: Cambridge University Press, 1971.
Appleby, Joyce. "Republicanism and Ideology." *American Quarterly* 37:4 (1985): 461–73.
Armstrong, W. A. "The Use of Information about Occupation." In E. A. Wrigley, ed., *Nineteenth-Century Society: Essays in the Use of Quantitative Methods for the Study of Social Data*, pp. 191–253. Cambridge: Cambridge University Press, 1972.
Armytage, W. H. G. "The Chartist Land Colonies, 1846–1848." *Agricultural History* 32 (1958): 87–96.
———. *Heavens Below*. London: Routlege & Kegan Paul, 1961.
———. "Manea Fen: An Experiment in Agrarian Communitarianism, 1838–41." *Bulletin of the John Rylands Library* 38 (1956): 288–310.
———. "Technology and Utopianism: J. A. Etzler in England, 1840–44." *Annals of Science*, 11:2 (June 1955): 129–36.
Ashton, Owen. "Chartism in Gloucestershire: The Contribution of the Chartist Land Plan, 1843–1850." *Transactions of the Bristol and Gloucestershire Archaeological Society* 104 (1986): 201–9.
Ashworth, Henry. *An Inquiry into the Origin, Progress, and Results of the Strike of the Operative Cotton Spinners of Preston*. Manchester: John Harrison, 1838.
———. "Statistical Illustrations of the Past and Present State of Lancashire." *Quarterly Journal of the Statistical Society of London* 5 (Nov. 1842): 10–14.
Ashworth, John. *Agrarians and Aristocrats: Party Political Ideology in the United States, 1837–1846*. London: Royal Historical Society, 1983.
Bacon, G. W. *Bacon's Guide to America*. London: G. W. Bacon, 1870.
Baker, Jean. *Affairs of Party*. Ithaca, N.Y.: Cornell University Press, 1983.

———. "From Belief into Culture: Republicanism in the Antebellum North." *American Quarterly* 37:4 (1985): 532–50.

———. "Politics, Paradigms and Public Culture." *Journal of American History* 84 (1997): 894–99.

Bamford, Samuel. *Early Days.* New York, N.Y.: Augustus M. Kelley, 1967 [1848].

———. *Passages in the Life of a Radical.* London: Frank Cass & Co., 1967 [1842].

———. *Walks in South Lancashire and on Its Borders.* Blackley: The Author, 1844.

Barker, Joseph. *A Cause of the Distress at Present Prevailing in Great Britain and Ireland.* N.p., n.d.

———. *Life of Joseph Barker.* London: Hodder and Stoughton, 1880.

———. *Reformer's Almanac and Companion to the Almanacs.* Wortley: Joseph Barker, 1848.

Barkun, Michael. *Crucible of the Millennium: The Burned-Over District of New York in the 1840's.* Syracuse, N.Y.: Syracuse University Press, 1986.

Barnett, D. C. "Allotments and the Problem of Rural Poverty." In E. L. Jones and G. E. Mingay, eds., *Land, Labour and Population in the Industrial Revolution*, pp. 162–86. New York, N.Y.: Barnes and Noble, 1967.

Bates, William. *Handy Book of Oldham.* Oldham: Bates and Fairbourn, 1877.

Beaudry, Mary C. "The Lowell Boott Mills Complex and Its Housing: Material Expressions of Corporate Ideology." *Historical Archaeology* 23 (1989): 19–32.

———. "Public Aesthetics versus Personal Experience: Worker Health and Well-Being in Nineteenth-Century Lowell, Massachusetts." *Historical Archaeology* 27 (1993): 90–105.

Beer, Max. *Pioneers of Land Reform.* London: G. Bell, 1920.

Belchem, John. "Beyond Chartist Studies: Class, Community and Party in Early Victorian Populist Politics." In Derek Fraser, ed., *Cities, Class, and Communication*, pp. 105–26. New York, N.Y.: Harvester, 1990.

Bellamy, Edward. *Looking Backward.* New York, N.Y.: Signet Classics, 1960 [1888].

Bender, Thomas. *Toward an Urban Vision: Ideas and Institutions in Nineteenth-Century America.* Baltimore: Johns Hopkins University Press, 1975.

Berg, Maxine. *The Age of Manufactures.* Oxford: Basil Blackwell, 1985.

Berlin, Isaiah. *Four Essays on Liberty.* Oxford: Oxford University Press, 1969.

Bernstein, Iver. *The New York City Draft Riots.* New York, N.Y.: Oxford University Press, 1990.

Berrien, Hobart. *A Brief Sketch of the Origin and Rise of the Working Men's Party in the City of New York.* Washington, D.C.: n.p., n.d.

Berthoff, Roland. "Independence and Attachment, Virtue and Interest:

From Republican Citizen to Free Enterpriser, 1787–1837." In Richard L. Bushman et al., eds., *Uprooted Americans*, pp. 97–124. Boston: Little, Brown and Co., 1978.

Bestor, Arthur. "Albert Brisbane: Propagandist for Socialism in the 1840's." *New York History* 28 (Apr. 1947): 128–58.

———. "The Evolution of the Socialist Vocabulary." *Journal of the History of Ideas* 9 (1948): 259–302.

———. "Patent-Office Models of the Good Society: Some Relationships between Social Reform and Westward Expansion." *American Historical Review* 58 (1953): 505–26.

Blacker, William. *An Essay on the Improvement to Be Made in the Cultivation of Small Farms by the Introduction of Green Crops and Housefeeding*. Dublin: William Curry, n.d.

Blackmar, Elizabeth. *Manhattan for Rent, 1785–1850*. Ithaca, N.Y.: Cornell University Press, 1989.

Blewett, Mary H. *Men Women and Work: Class, Gender and Protest in the New England Shoe Industry, 1780–1910*. Urbana, Ill.: University of Illinois Press, 1988.

Boston, Ray. *British Chartists in America*. Manchester: Manchester University Press, 1971.

———. "William Evans and the Potters' Emigration Society." Research paper, University of Keele, May 1974.

Bowkett, T. E. *Freehold Property for Mechanics*. London: Cleave, 1843.

Bowman, Winifred M. *England in Ashton-under Lyne*. Ashton: John Sherratt and Co., 1960.

Bradshaw, John Stanford. "George Henry Evans." In Perry J. Ashley, ed., *American Newspaper Journalists*, Dictionary of Literary Biography, vol. 43, pp. 184–88. Detroit, Ill.: Bruccoli Clark, 1985.

Bray, John Francis. *Labour's Wrongs and Labour's Remedy*. Leeds: David Green, 1839.

Bridges, Amy. *A City in the Republic*. Cambridge: Cambridge University Press, 1984.

Brierley, Ben. *Home Memories; or, Recollections of a Life*. Manchester: Abel Heywood, 1886.

Briggs, Asa, ed. *Chartist Studies*. London: Macmillan, 1960.

Brimelow, W. *Political and Parliamentary History of Bolton*. Bolton: Tillotson and Son, 1882.

Brisbane, Albert. *A Concise Exposition of the Doctrine of Association*. New York, N.Y.: J. S. Redfield, 1843.

———. *Social Destiny of Man*. Philadelphia, Pa.: C. F. Stollmeyer, 1840.

Bronstein, Jamie L. "Land Reform, Community-Building and the Labor Press in Antebellum America and Britain." In Michael Harris and Tom O'Malley, eds., *Studies in Newspaper and Periodical History, 1995 Annual*, pp. 69–84. Westport, Conn.: Greenwood Press, 1997.

———. "Under Their Own Vine and Fig Tree: Land Reform and Working-

Class Experience in Britain and America, 1830–1860." Ph.D. dissertation, Stanford University, 1996.

Brook, Michael. "Joseph Barker and the *People*, the True Emigrants' Guide." *Publications of the Thoresby Society* 13 (1963): 331–78.

———. "Lawrence Pitkeithly, Dr. Smyles, and Canadian Revolutionaries in the United States, 1842." *Ontario History* 57 (1965): 79–84.

Brooke, John L. *The Heart of the Commonwealth: Society and Political Culture in Worcester County, Massachusetts, 1713–1861.* Cambridge: Cambridge University Press, 1989.

———. *The Refiner's Fire.* Cambridge: Cambridge University Press, 1995.

Brooks, Frank, ed. *The Individualist Anarchists: An Anthology of Liberty.* New Brunswick: Transaction Publishers, 1994.

Brotherhood of the Union. *B.C.G.* [Secret Initiation Rite]. N.p., n.d. [circa 1852].

Brotherhood of the Union. "Official Souvenir, October 7th to 11th, 1900." N.p.: Published under the Auspices of the Anniversary Committee, 1900.

Brotherhood of the Union. "One Hundreth Anniversary: Supreme Circle, Brotherhood of America, October 7, 1950." N.p., 1950.

Brotherhood of the Union. N.p., n.d. [Seligman Collection, Special Collections, Columbia University Library, New York, N.Y.]

Brown, Lucy. "The Chartists and the Anti-Corn-Law League." In Asa Briggs, ed., *Chartist Studies,* pp. 342–71. London: Macmillan, 1960.

Brownson, Orestes. *The Laboring Classes.* Boston, Mass.: Benajmin Greene, 1842.

Buckley, Peter. "To the Opera House: Culture and Society in New York City, 1820–1860." Ph.D. dissertation, SUNY Stonybrook, 1984.

Bull, Philip. *Land, Politics and Nationalism: A Study of the Irish Land Question.* Dublin: Gill and Macmillan, 1996.

Burchill, Frank, and Richard Ross. *A History of the Potters' Union.* Hanley, Stoke-on-Trent: Ceramic and Allied Trades Union, 1977.

Burke, Martin J. *The Conundrum of Class: Public Discourse on the Social Order in America.* Chicago, Ill.: University of Chicago Press, 1995.

Burn, James. *Autobiography of a Beggar Boy.* Ed. David Vincent. London: Europa Publications, 1978 [1855].

Burn, John Ilderton. *Familiar Letters on Population, Emigration, etc.* London: John W. Parker, 1841.

Bury, J. P. T. "Nationalities and Nationalism." In *New Cambridge Modern History,* vol. 10, p. 217. Cambridge: Cambridge University Press, 1964.

Butterfield, Roger. "George Lippard and His Secret Brotherhood." *Pennsylvania Magazine of History* 79 (1955): 285–309.

Butterworth, Edwin. *Historical Sketches of Oldham.* Oldham: John Hirst, 1856.

Byllesby, Langton. *Observations on the Sources and Effects of Unequal Wealth.* New York, N.Y.: Lewis Nichols, 1826.

Byrdsall, Frederick. *History of the Loco-Foco or Equal Rights Party*. New York, N.Y.: 1842.

Bythell, Duncan. *The Handloom Weavers*. Cambridge: Cambridge University Press, 1969.

Campbell, John. *A Theory of Equality; or, The Way of Making Every Man Act Honestly*. Philadelphia, Pa.: John Perry, 1848.

———. *Negro-Mania*. Philadelphia, Pa.: Campbell and Power, 1851.

Carlton, Frank T. "The Working Men's Party of New York City, 1829–31." *Political Science Quarterly* 22 (Sept. 1907): 401–15.

Carr, James. *Annals and Stories of Colne and Neighbourhood*. Manchester: Heywood, 1878.

[Carter, Thomas]. *Memoirs of a Working Man*. London: Charles Knight & Co., 1845.

Carwardine, Richard. "Evangelicals, Politics, and the Coming of the American Civil War: A Transatlantic Perspective." In Mark Noll, David Bebbington, and George Rawlyk, eds., *Evangelicalism: Comparative Studies of Popular Protestantism in North America, the British Isles, and Beyond, 1700–1990*, pp. 198–218. New York, N.Y.: Oxford University Press, 1994.

Catalogue of the Library of the Middlesex Mechanic Association. Lowell, Mass.: Leonard Huntress, 1840.

Challinor, Raymond. *A Radical Lawyer in Victorian England*. London: I. B. Tauris, 1990.

Chartist and Anti-Chartist Pamphlets. New York: Garland, 1986.

The Chartists's Friend, by the Author of "Aids to Development," "Mothers and Governesses," etc. London: B. Wertheim, 1848.

Chase, Malcolm. "Chartism, 1838–58: Responses in Two Teesside Towns." *Northern History* 24 (1987): 146–71.

———. "The Chartist Land Plan and the Local Historian." *Local Historian* 18 (May 1988): 76–79.

———. "The Land and the Working Classes: English Agrarianism circa 1775–1851," D. Phil. thesis, University of Sussex, 1984.

———. "Out of Radicalism: The Mid-Victorian Freehold Land Movement." *English Historical Review* 106 (Apr. 1991): 319–45.

———. "Paine, Spence and the 'Real Rights of Man.'" *Bulletin of the Society for the Study of Labour History* 52 (1987): 32–41.

———. *The People's Farm: English Radical Agrarianism 1775–1840*. Oxford: Oxford University Press, 1988.

———. "We Wish Only to Work for Ourselves: The Chartist Land Plan." In Malcolm Chase and Ian Dyck, eds., *Living and Learning: Essays in Honour of J. F. C. Harrison*, pp. 133–48. Aldershot: Scolar Press, 1996.

———, ed. *The Life and Literary Pursuits of Allen Davenport, with a Further Selection of the Author's Work*. Aldershot: Scolar Press, 1994.

Chase, Malcolm, and Christopher Shaw. *The Imagined Past*. Manchester: Manchester University Press, 1989.

Chevalier, Michael. *Society, Mannners and Politics in the United States.* New York, N.Y.: Burt Franklin, 1969 [1842].

Christman, Henry. *Tin Horns and Calico.* New York, N.Y.: Holt, 1945.

Church, Roy. "Chartism and the Miners: A Reinterpretation." *Labour History Review* 56 (1991): 23–36.

Claeys, Gregory. "The *Chartist Pilot*: Feminist and Socialist Chartism in Leicester, 1843–44." *Bulletin of the Society for the Study of Labour History* 45 (1982): 18.

———. *Citizens and Saints.* Cambridge: Cambridge University Press, 1989.

———. "The Example of America a Warning to England? The Transformation of America in British Radicalism and Socialism, 1790–1850." In Malcolm Chase and Ian Dyck, eds., *Living and Learning: Essays in Honour of J. F. C. Harrison*, pp. 66–80. Aldershot: Scolar Press, 1996.

———. "John Adolphus Etzler, Technological Utopianism, and British Socialism: The Tropical Emigration Society's Venezuelan Mission and Its Social Context, 1833–48." *English Historical Review* 101 (Apr. 1986): 331–75.

———. "Lewis Masquerier and the Later Development of American Owenism, 1835–45." *Labor History* 29 (1988): 230–40.

———. *Machinery, Money and the Millennium.* Cambridge: Polity Press, 1987.

———. "Paine's Agrarian Justice." *Society for the Study of Labour History Bulletin* 52:3 (1987): 21–31.

———. "The Political Ideas of the Young Engels, 1842–1845: Owenism, Chartism, and the Question of Violent Revolution in the Transition from 'Utopian' to 'Scientific' Socialism." *History of Political Thought* 6:3 (1985): 455–78.

———. *Thomas Paine.* Boston, Mass.: Unwin Hyman, 1989.

Clark, Anna. "The Rhetoric of Chartist Domesticity: Gender, Language and Class in the 1830's and 1840's." *Journal of British Studies* 31 (Jan. 1992): 62–88.

Clark, Christopher. *The Roots of Rural Capitalism: Western Massachusetts, 1780–1860.* Ithaca, N.Y.: Cornell University Press, 1989.

Clark, Thomas. *Letter Addressed to G. W. M Reynolds, Reviewing His Conduct as a Professed Chartist.* London: T. Clark, 1850.

Clegg, James. *Annals of Bolton.* Bolton: Chronicle Office, 1888.

Cobbett, William. *Cottage Economy.* Oxford: Oxford University Press, 1979 [1826].

Cole, G. D. H. *Chartist Portraits.* London: Cassell, 1989.

Cole, John. "Chartism in Rochdale." M.A. thesis, Manchester Polytechnic, 1986.

Colley, Linda. *Britons.* New Haven, Conn.: Yale University Press, 1992.

Colls, Robert. *Pitmen of the Northern Coalfield.* Manchester: Manchester University Press, 1987.

Commons, John. *Documentary History of American Industrial Society.*
Vols. 5–8. Cleveland, Oh.: Arthur H Clark, 1910.

———. *History of Labor in the United States.* Vol. 1. New York, N.Y.:
Macmillan, 1926.

———. "Horace Greeley and the Working-Class Origins of the Republican
Party." *Political Science Quarterly* 24 (1909): 468–88.

Conkin, Paul K. *Prophets of Prosperity: America's First Political Economists.* Bloomington, Ind.: Indiana University Press, 1980.

Cooke Taylor, W. *Factories and the Factory System.* London: Jeremiah
How, 1844.

———. *Notes of a Tour in the Manufacturing Districts of Lancashire.* London: Frank Cass & Co., 1968 [1842].

Cooper, Thomas. *The Land for the Labourers, and the Fraternity of Nations.* London: Effingham Wilson, 1848.

———. *Life of Thomas Cooper.* New York, N.Y.: Humanities Press, 1971
[1872].

Cooper, William Waldo. *Mr. Feargus O'Connor's Land Scheme.* London:
Francis & John Rivington, 1848.

Cornwall, Godfrey. "Heronsgate and the Chartists." *Rickmansworth Historical Society Quarterly* 2:1 (n.d.): 6–16.

Coulthart, J. R. *A Report on the Sanatory Conditions of the Town of Ashton-under-Lyne.* Ashton: Luke Swallow, 1844.

Crèvecoeur, J. Hector St. John de. *Letters from an American Farmer.* New
York, N.Y.: Penguin Books, 1986 [1781].

Crossley, James. *Ernest Jones: Who Is He? What Has He Done?* Manchester:
Abel Heywood, n.d.

Cunliffe, Marcus. *Chattel Slavery and Wage Slavery.* Athens, Ga.: University of Georgia Press, 1979.

Davenport, Allen. *The Life and Literary Pursuits of Allen Davenport.* New
York: Garland, 1986 [1845].

———. *The Life, Writings and Principles of Thomas Spence.* London:
Wakelin, 1836.

Davies, Ebeneezer. *American Scenes and Christian Slavery.* London: John
Snow, 1849.

Davis, Susan G. *Parades and Power: Street Theater in Nineteenth-Century
Philadelphia.* Philadelphia, Pa.: Temple University Press, 1986.

Dawley, Alan. *Class and Community: The Industrial Revolution in Lynn.*
Cambridge, Mass.: Harvard University Press, 1976.

Dawley, Alan, and Paul Faler. "Working-Class Culture and Politics in the
Industrial Revolution: Sources of Loyalism and Rebellion," *Journal of
Social History* 9 (June 1976): 466–80.

Dayton, A. C. *The Last Days of Knickerbocker Life in New York.* New
York: George W. Harlan, 1882.

Degler, Carl. "An Inquiry into the Locofoco Party." M.A. thesis, Columbia
University, 1947.

————. "The Locofocos; Urban Agrarians." *Journal of Economic History* 16 (1956): 322–33.

————. "The West as a Solution for Urban Unemployment." *New York History* 36 (Jan. 1955): 63–84.

Denning, Michael. *Mechanic Accents.* New York, N.Y.: Verso, 1987.

Dennis, Richard. *English Industrial Cities of the Nineteenth Century: A Social Geography.* Cambridge: Cambridge University Press, 1984.

Deverell, William F. "To Loosen the Safety Valve: Eastern Workers and Western Lands." *Western Historical Quarterly* 19 (1988): 269–85.

Devyr, Thomas. *A War of Classes and How to Avert It.* New York: n.p., 1878.

————. *Odd Book of the Nineteenth Century.* New York: The Author, 1882.

————. *Our Natural Rights: A Pamphlet for People by One of Themselves.* Williamsburg, N.Y.: The Author, 1882.

————. *Statement of Facts.* Williamsburg, N.Y.: n.p., 1860.

Dewey, Clive J. "The Rehabilitation of the Peasant Proprietor in Nineteenth-Century Economic Thought." *History of Political Economy* 6 (1974): 17–47.

DeWitt, Francis, ed. *Statistical Information Relating to Certain Branches of Industry in Massachusetts.* Boston, Mass.: William White, 1856.

Dick, Everett. *The Lure of the Land: A Social History of the Public Lands from the Articles of Confederation to the New Deal.* Lincoln, Nebr.: University of Nebraska Press, 1970.

Dickinson, T. C. *Lancashire under Steam.* Preston: Lancashire County Council Library and Leisure Committee, 1984.

Dix, John. *Local Loiterings and Visits in the Vicinity of Boston, by a Looker-On.* Boston, Mass.: Redding & Co., 1845.

Dodd, William. *The Factory System Illustrated.* London: John Murray, 1842.

————. *Narrative of the Experience and Sufferings of William Dodd.* London: 1841.

Dorfman, Joseph. *The Economic Mind in American Civilization, 1606–1865.* Vol. 2. London: George Harrap, 1947.

————. "The Jackson Wage-Earner Thesis." *American Historical Review* 54 (Jan. 1949): 296–306.

Douglas, Louis H. *Agrarianism in American History.* Lexington, Mass.: D.C. Heath, 1969.

Drescher, Seymour. "Cart Whip and Billy Roller; or, Antislavery and Reform Symbolism in Industrializing Britain." *Journal of Social History* 15 (1981): 3–24.

Driver, Felix. "Tory Radicalism? Ideology, Strategy and Locality in Popular Politics during the 1830's." *Northern History* 27 (1991): 120–38.

Dublin, Thomas, ed. *Farm to Factory: Women's Letters, 1840–1860.* New York, N.Y.: Columbia University Press, 1981.

————. *Women at Work: The Transformation of Work and Community in Lowell, Massachusetts, 1826–1860.* New York, N.Y.: Columbia University Press, 1979.

Dwight, Marianne. *Letters from Brook Farm, 1844–1847.* Ed. Amy L. Reed. Poughkeepsie, N.Y.: Vassar College, 1928.

Dyck, Ian. *William Cobbett and Rural Popular Culture.* Cambridge: Cambridge University Press, 1992.

Earle, Jonathan Halperin. "The Undaunted Democracy: Jacksonian Antislavery and Free Soil, 1828–1848." Ph.D. dissertation, Princeton University, 1996.

Eastwood, David. "Amplifying the Province of the Legislature: The Flow of Information and the English State in the Early Nineteenth Century." *Historical Research* 62 (1989): 276–94.

Eayrs, James. "Political Ideas of the English Agrarians." *Canadian Journal of Economics and Political Science* 18 (1952): 287–302.

Edwards, Michael S. *Purge This Realm: A Life of Joseph Rayner Stephens.* London: Epworth, 1994.

Ensor, George. *Of Property, and of Its Equal Distribution.* London: Effingham Wilson, 1844.

Epstein, James. "The Constitutional Idiom: Radical Reasoning, Rhetoric and Action in Early Nineteenth-Century England." *Journal of Social History* 23 (1990): 553–74.

————. *The Lion of Freedom.* London: Croom Helm, 1982.

————. *Radical Expression: Political Language, Ritual and Symbol in England, 1790–1850.* New York, N.Y.: Oxford University Press, 1994.

Erickson, Charlotte J. "Immigration from the British Isles to the U.S.A. in 1841, Part 1: Emigration from the British Isles." *Population Studies* 43 (1989): 347–67.

————. "Emigration from the British Isles to the USA in 1841, Part II: Who Were the English Immigrants?" *Population Studies* 44 (1990): 21–40.

————. *Invisible Immigrants.* Ithaca, N.Y.: Cornell University Press, 1972.

Ernst, Robert. *Immigrant Life in New York City, 1835–63.* New York, N.Y.: Kings Crown Press, 1949.

————. "The One and Only Mike Walsh." *New York Historical Society Quarterly* 26 (1952): 43–65.

Evans, Frederick W. *Elder Evans to Henry George.* Mt. Lebanon, N.Y.: n.p., 1886.

————. "Land Limitation." *The Shaker* 7 (Oct. 1877): 74–75.

————. "Shaker Land Limitation Act." *The Manifesto* 17:3 (n.d.): 67.

————. *A Shaker's Views on the Land Limitation Scheme and Land Monopoly, and Mormon Prosecution.* Mt. Lebanon, N.Y.: n.p., 1887.

Evans, William. *Art and History of the Potting Business.* Shelton: Examiner Office, 1846.

"The Factory System." *Chartist Tracts for the Times.* Wortley: Joseph Barker, 1849.

Factory Tracts, no. 1. Lowell, Mass.: Lowell Female Labor Reform League, 1845.

Faler, Paul G. *Mechanics and Manufacturers in the Early Industrial Revolution: Lynn, Massachusetts, 1780–1860*. Albany, N.Y.: State University of New York Press, 1981.

Fallas, T. *The People's Rights and How to Get Them*. N.p., 1844.

Faragher, John Mack. "Open-Country Community: Sugar Creek, Illinois, 1820–1850." In Jonathan Prude and Stephen Hahn, eds., *The Countryside in the Age of Capitalist Transformation*, pp. 233–58. Chapel Hill, N.C.: University of North Carolina Press, 1985.

———. *Women and Men on the Overland Trail*. New Haven, Conn.: Yale University Press, 1979.

Faucher, M. Leon. *Manchester in 1844*. Manchester: Abel Heywood, 1844.

Feller, Daniel. *The Public Lands in Jacksonian Politics*. Madison, Wisc.: University of Wisconsin Press, 1984.

Fellman, Michael. *The Unbounded Frame: Freedom and Community in Nineteenth-Century American Utopianism*. Westport, Conn.: Greenwood Press, 1972.

Field, Alexander James. "Sectoral Shift in Antebellum Massachusetts: A Reconsideration." *Explorations in Economic History* 15 (1978): 146–71.

Finn, Margot. *After Chartism: Class and Nation in English Radical Politics, 1848–1874*. Cambridge: Cambridge University Press, 1993.

Fitzhugh, George. *Cannibals All! or, Slaves Without Masters*, ed. C. Vann Woodward. Cambridge, Mass.: Harvard University Press, 1960 [1857].

Fladeland, Betty. *Abolitionists and Working Class Problems in the Age of Industrialization*. Baton Rouge, La.: Louisiana State University Press, 1984.

Fleischman, Richard K., Jr. *Conditions of Life among the Cotton Workers of Southeastern Lancashire, 1780–1850*. New York, N.Y.: Garland, 1985.

Flett, Keith. "To Make That Future Now: The Land Question in 19th Century Radical Politics." *The Raven: An Anarchist Quarterly* 17 (1991): 63–70.

Flint, David. *Rebel Against Authority: William Lyon Mackenzie*. Toronto: Oxford University Press, 1971.

Fogel, Robert. *Without Consent or Contract*. New York, N.Y.: W. W. Norton & Co., 1989.

Foner, Eric. "Abolitionism and the Labor Movement in Antebellum America." In Christine Bolt and Seymour Drescher, eds., *Anti-Slavery, Religion and Reform*, pp. 254–71. Folkestone: Wm. Dawson & Sons, 1980.

———. *Free Soil, Free Labor, Free Men: The Ideology of the Republican Party before the Civil War*. London: Oxford University Press, 1970.

———. *A Short History of Reconstruction*. New York, N.Y.: Harper & Row, 1990.

———. *Tom Paine and Revolutionary America*. New York, N.Y.: New York University Press, 1976.

Foner, Philip S., ed. *American Labor Songs of the Nineteenth Century*. Urbana, Ill.: University of Illinois Press, 1975.

———. *The Factory Girls*. Urbana, Ill.: University of Illinois Press, 1977.

Foreman, Grant "Settlement of English Potters in Wisconsin." *Wisconsin Magazine of History* 21 (June 1938): 375–96.

Foster, George. *New York in Slices*. New York, N.Y.: Tribune Office, 1849.

Foster, George F. *Ashton Under Lyne: Its Story through the Ages*. Rochdale: Edwards and Bryning, 1947.

Foster, John. *Class Struggle and the Industrial Revolution*. London: Weidenfeld and Nicolson, 1974.

Fredrickson, George M. "From Exceptionalism to Varliability: Recent Developments in Cross-National Comparative History." *Journal of American History* 80 (Sept. 1995): 587–604.

Frost, Thomas. *Forty Years' Recollections*. New York, N.Y.: Garland, 1986 [1880].

Frothingham, Octavius Brooks. *Gerrit Smith*. New York, N.Y.: G. P. Putnam's Sons, 1878.

Frow, Edmund and Ruth. *Radical Salford*. Swinton: Neil Richardson, 1984.

Gadian, D. S. "Class Consciousness in Oldham and Other Northwest Industrial Towns, 1830–1850." *Historical Journal* 21 (1978): 161–72.

———. "A Comparative Study of Popular Movements in North-West Industrial Towns 1830–1850." Ph.D. dissertation, Lancaster University, 1976.

Gallop, G. I., ed. *Pigs' Meat: The Selected Writings of Thomas Spence, Radical and Pioneer Land Reformer*. Nottingham: Spokesman Press, 1982.

Gammage, R. G. *History of the Chartist Movement*. John Saville, ed. London: Merlin Press, 1976 [1854].

Garrard, John. *Leadership and Power in Victorian Industrial Towns, 1830–1880*. Manchester: Manchester University Press, 1983.

Garrison, William Lloyd Jr., ed. *Gerrit Smith on Land Monopoly*. Chicago: Public Publishing Co., 1905.

Gaskell, Peter. *Artisans and Machinery: The Moral and Physical Condition of the Manufacturing Population*. London: John W. Parker, 1836.

Gienapp, William E. *The Origins of the Republican Party, 1852–1856*. New York, N.Y.: Oxford University Press, 1987.

Gilbert, Amos. "A Sketch of the Life of Thomas Skidmore." *Free Enquirer* (New York), Mar. 30, Apr. 6, and 13, 1834.

Gilje, Paul. "The Rise of Capitalism in the Early Republic." *Journal of the Early Republic* 16 (1996): 159–82.

Ginswick, J. *Labour and the Poor in England and Wales, 1849–51*. London: Frank Cass, 1983.

Gladstone Pottery Museum, Longton, Stoke-on-Trent. Museum Displays of 19th-Century Pottery Production Process. May 1994.

Glickstein, Jonathan. "Poverty Is Not Slavery: American Abolitionists and the American Labor Market." Lewis Perry and Michael Fellman, eds., *Antislavery Reconsidered*. Baton Rouge, La.: Louisiana State University Press, 1979, pp. 119–43.

Godwin, William. *Godwin's Political Justice, A Reprint of the "Essay on Property,"* ed. H. S. Salt. London: George Allen & Unwin, 1929.

Goodman, Paul. "The Emergence of Homestead Exemption in the United States: Accommodation and Resistance to the Market Revolution, 1840–1880." *Journal of American History*. 80:2 (Sept. 1993): 471–98.

———. *The Politics of Industrialism: Massachusetts, 1830–1870*. In Richard L. Bushman et al., eds., *Uprooted Americans*, pp. 161–207. Boston, Mass.: Little, Brown and Co., 1978.

Goodwyn, Lawrence. *The Populist Moment*. Oxford: Oxford University Press, 1978.

Gray, Robert Q. *The Factory Question and Industrial England, 1830–1860*. New York, N.Y.: Cambridge University Press, 1996.

Green, David. *The Claims of the Redemption Society Considered . . . A Lecture Delivered before the Members of the Odd-Fellows' Literary Institution, Trinity-Street, Leeds, on the 7th of December, 1848*. London: James Watson, 1848.

———. *The Claims of the Redemption Society Considered*. London: Berger, 1849.

Gregory, John Goadby. "The Land Limitation Movement." *Parkman Club Publications* 14. Milwaukee, Wisc.: Edward Keough, 1897.

Gregory, Rita. "Chartism in Bolton." B.A. thesis, Manchester University, 1969.

Griswold, A. Whitney. *Farming and Democracy*. New York, N.Y.: Harcourt Brace, 1948.

Gronowicz, Anthony. "Revising the Concept of Jacksonian Democracy." Ph.D. dissertation, University of Pennsylvania, 1981.

Guarneri, Carl J. "Reconstructing the Antebellum Communitarian Movement: Oneida and Fourierism." *Journal of the Early Republic* 16 (1996): 463–88.

———. *The Utopian Alternative: Fourierism in Nineteenth-Century America*. Ithaca, N.Y.: Cornell University Press, 1991.

Gurr, Duncan, and Julian Hunt, eds. *The Cotton Mills of Oldham*. Oldham: Oldham Cultural and Information Services, 1989.

Hackett, Nan. *19th-Century British Working Class Autogiographies: An Annotated Bibliography*. New York, N.Y.: AMS Press, 1985.

Hadfield, Mary Alice. *The Chartist Land Company*. Newton Abbott: David and Charles, 1970.

Hall, Charles. *The Effects of Civilization on the People in European States*. London: Charles Gilpin, 1850 [1805].

Hall, Robert G. "Work, Class and Politics in Ashton Under Lyne, 1830–1850." Ph.D. dissertation, Vanderbilt University, 1991.

Hambrick, Margaret. *A Chartist's Library*. London: Mansell Publishing, 1986.

Hamilton, Robert. *The Progress of Society.* New York, N.Y.: Augustus Kelley, 1969 [1830].

Hammond, Jabez D. *A History of the Political Parties of the State of New York.* Vol. 2. Albany, N.Y.: C. Van Benthuysen, 1842.

Hannavy, John. *Historic Wigan.* Preston: Carnegie Publishing, 1990.

————, and Chris Ryan. *Working in Wigan Mills: One Hundred Years of Photographs.* Wigan: Smith's Books, 1987.

Hardwick, Charles. *History of the Borough of Preston.* Preston: Worthington and Co., 1857.

Hardy, Dennis. *Alternative Communities in the Nineteenth Century.* London: Longman, 1979.

Harrington, James. *The Commonwealth of Oceana and a System of Politics,* J. G. A. Pocock, ed. Cambridge: Cambridge University Press, 1992 [1656].

Harrison, Brian, and Patricia Hollis, eds. *Robert Lowery, Radical and Chartist.* London: Europa Publications, 1979.

Harrison, J. F. C. *Robert Owen and the Owenites in Britain and America: The Quest for the New Moral World.* London: Routlege and Kegan Paul, 1969.

Harrop, Sylvia, and E. A. Rose, eds. *Victorian Ashton.* Ashton: Tameide Libraries and Arts Committee, 1974.

Hartz, Louis. "Seth Luther: The Story of a Working Class Rebel." *New England Quarterly* 13 (Sept. 1940): 401–18.

Haswell, Charles H. *Reminiscences of an Octogenarian of the City of New York.* New York, N.Y.: Harper & Bros., 1897.

Hattam, Victoria. *Labor Visions and State Power: The Origins of Business Unionism in the United States.* Princeton: Princeton University Press, 1993.

Haynes, Ian. *Cotton in Ashton.* Tameside Metropolitan Borough Libraries and Arts Committee, 1987.

————. *Stalybridge Cotton Mills.* Neil Richardson, 1990.

Health of Towns Commission. *Report on the Sanitary Condition of Large Towns in Lancashire.* London: W. Clowes and Sons, 1845.

Helton, Leonard L. "George Henry Evans: Anti-Monopolist." M.A. thesis, University of Tennessee, 1952.

Hermit of Pimlico. *An Appeal to the Chartists Proper.* London: McGowan, 1849.

Hewitson, Anthony. *History of Preston.* Preston: Chronicle Office, 1883.

Hibbard, Benjamin Horace. *A History of the Public Land Policies.* New York, N.Y.: Macmillan, 1924.

Hill, James. *Life Boat: A Weekly Political Pamphlet.* London: n.p., 1843.

Hill, William. *A Scabbard for Mr. O'Connor's Sword.* Hull: R. Johnson, 1844.

Himmelfarb, Gertrude. *The Idea of Poverty.* London: Faber and Faber, 1984.

Historical Sketch of the Worcester County Mechanics Association, with the Charter and By-Laws, a List of Members, and Catalogue of the Library. Worcester, Mass.: Henry J. Howland, 1854.

Hobsbawm, Eric. "Man and Woman: Images on the Left." in *Workers: Worlds of Labor.* New York, N.Y.: Pantheon Books, 1984, pp. 82–102.

————. and Joan Scott. "Political Shoemakers," in *Workers: Worlds of Labor,* pp. 103–30. New York, N.Y.: Pantheon Books, 1984.

Hobson's Letters on the Land Scheme of Feargus O'Connor, Nov. 1849, William Lovett Collection, Goldsmith's Library, University of London.

Hodgskin, Thomas. *The Natural and Artificial Rights of Property Contrasted.* London: B. Steil, 1832.

Holt, Michael. *The Political Crisis of the 1850's.* New York, N.Y.: John Wiley and Sons, 1978.

Holyoake, George Jacob. *Sixty Years of an Agitator's Life.* London: T. Fisher Unwin, 1900.

Home Colonization Company. *Prospectus.* London: Ostell, 1842.

The Homestead. New York, N.Y.: National Reform Association, n.d.

Horn, Pamela. "The Chartist Land Company." *Cake and Cockhorse* (Banbury Historical Society) 4 (Winter 1968): 19–24.

Howell, George. "Ernest Jones, The Chartist: Poet and Orator, Patriot and Politician." Unpaginated, undated scrapbook of articles orignally from the *Newcastle Weekly Chronicle,* 1898. Bishopsgate Institute Library, item no. 4039.

Howell, Philip. "Diffusing the Light of Liberty: The Geography of Political Lecturing in the Chartist Movement." *Journal of Historical Geography* 21 (1995): 23–28.

Huberman, Michael. "The Economic Origins of Paternalism: Lancashire Cotton Spinning in the First Half of the Nineteenth Century." *Social History* 12 (2) May 1988: 177–92.

Hugins, Walter. "Ely Moore: The Case of a Jacksonian Labor Leader." *Political Science Quarterly* 65 (1950): 105–25.

————. *Jacksonian Democracy and the Working Class.* Stanford: Stanford University Press, 1960.

Hunt, David. *A History of Preston.* Preston: Carnegie Publishing, 1992.

Huston, John Reeve. "Land and Freedom: The Anti-Rent Wars, Jacksonian Politics and the Contest over Free Labor in New York, 1765–1865." Ph.D. dissertation, Yale University, 1994.

Huxhorn, Sieglinde. "United We Stand, Divided We Fall! Chartist Celebrations in Ashton Under Lyne in the 1840's." Typescript, Tameside Local History Library, L322.

Ignatiev, Noel. *How the Irish Became White.* New York, N.Y.: Routledge, 1995.

Ingalls, J. K. *Reminiscences of an Octogenarian in the Fields of Industrial and Social Reform.* Elmira: Gazette Company, 1897.

Jackson, John. *The Demagogue Done Up.* Bradford: The Author, 1844.

Jebb, L. *Smallholdings.* London: John Murray, 1907.

Jefferson, Thomas. *Notes on the State of Virginia*. Chapel Hill, N.C.: University of North Carolina Press, 1955 [1785].

Jeffrey, Newman. "The Social Origins of George Henry Evans, Workingman's Advocate." M.A. thesis, Wayne State University, 1960.

Jenkins, Mick. *The General Strike of 1842*. London: Lawrence and Wishart, 1980.

Jentz, John B. "Artisans, Evangelicals, and the City: A Social History of Abolitionism and Labor Reform in Jacksonian New York." Ph.D. dissertation, City University of New York, 1977.

Jeremy, David J. "British and American Entrepreneurial Values in the Early Nineteenth Century: a Parting of the Ways?" In R. A. Burchell, ed., *The End of Anglo-America*, pp. 24–59. Manchester: Manchester University Press, 1991.

Johnson, Curtis D. *Redeeming America: Evangelicals and the Road to Civil War*. Chicago, Ill.: Ivan R. Dee, 1993.

Johnson, David N. *Sketches of Lynn: The Changes of Fifty Years*. Westport, Conn.: Greenwood Press, 1970 [1880].

Johnson, Hildegard Binder. *Order upon the Land: The U.S. Rectangular Land Survey and the Upper Mississippi Country*. New York, N.Y.: Oxford University Press, 1976.

Johnson, Paul. *A Shopkeeper's Millennium: Society and Revivals in Rochester, New York, 1815–1837*. New York, N.Y.: Hill and Wang, 1978.

Johnson, Samuel A. "The Genesis of the New England Emigrant Aid Company." *New England Quarterly* 3 (1930): 95–122.

Jones, David. *Chartism and the Chartists*. London: Penguin, 1975.

Jones, Ebeneezer. *The Land Monopoly: The Suffering and Demoralization Caused by It, and the Justice and Expediency of Its Abolition*. London: Charles Fox, 1849.

Jones, Ernest. *Chartist Songs and Fugitive Pieces*. N.p., n.d.

———. *Evenings with the People, an Address Delivered at St Martin's Hall*. London: Ernest Jones, 1856.

Josephson, Hannah. *Golden Threads*. New York, N.Y.: Duell, Sloan and Pearce, 1949.

Joyce, Patrick. *Democratic Subjects: The Self and the Social in Nineteenth Century England*. Cambridge: Cambridge University Press, 1994.

———. *Visions of the People: Industrial England and the Question of Class, 1848–1914*. Cambridge: Cambridge University Press, 1991.

The Jubilee. New York, N.Y.: Young America, n.d.

Katznelson, Ira. "Working-Class Formation and the State: Nineteenth-Century England in American Perspective." In Dietrich Rueschemeyer, Theda Skocpol, and Peter B. Evans, eds., *Bringing the State Back In*, pp. 257–84. Cambridge: Cambridge University Press, 1985.

Kemp-Ashraf, P. M. "Introduction" and "A Selection from the Works of Thomas Spence." In *Life and Literature of the Working Class: Essays in Honour of William Gallacher*, pp. 271–350. Berlin: Humboldt-Universitat, 1966.

Kilbourn, William. *The Firebrand*. London: Jonathan Cape, 1956.

King, J. E. *Richard Marsden and the Preston Chartists*. University of Lancaster: Center for North-West Regional Studies, Occasional Paper no. 10, 1981.

Kirk, Neville. "In Defense of Class." *International Review of Social History* 31 (1987): 2–47.

———. *The Growth of Working-Class Reformism in Mid-Victorian England*. London: Croom Helm, 1985.

———. *Labour and Society in Britain and the USA*. Vol. 1. Aldershot: Scolar Press, 1994.

Kirkdale Chartist Prisoners. *Chartist Tracts for the Times*. Wortley: Joseph Barker, 1849.

Knight, Charles. *The British Mechanic's and Labourer's Handbook and Guide to the United States*. London: Charles Knight & Co., 1843.

Knox, Thomas R. "Thomas Spence: The Trumpet of Jubilee." *Past and Present* 76 (1977): 75–98.

Koga, Hideo. "The Chartist Land Scheme." *Journal of the Faculty of Liberal Arts of Yamaguchi University* 10 (1976): 29–49.

Kohl, J. G. *Ireland, Scotland and England*. London: Chapman and Hall, 1844.

Kraut, Alan Morton. "The Liberty Men of New York: Political Abolitionism in New York State, 1840–1848." Ph.D. dissertation, Cornell University, 1975.

Kulik, Gary, Roger Parks, and Theodore Z. Penn, eds. *The New England Mill Village*. Cambridge: MIT Press, 1982.

Labourer's Friend Society. *Facts and Illustrations*. London: The Society, 1830.

The Land of England Belongs to the People of England. N.p., 1848?

Laurie, Bruce. *Artisans into Workers*. New York, N.Y.: Hill and Wang, 1989.

Lause, Mark A. "Progress Impoverished: Origin of Henry George's Single Tax." *Historian* 52 (1990): 394–410.

———. "Voting Yourself a Farm in Antebellum Iowa: Towards an Urban, Working-Class Prehistory of the Post–Civil War Agrarian Insurgency." *Annals of Iowa* 49 (1988): 169–86.

Lazerow, Jama. "Religion and Labor Reform in Antebellum America: The World of William Field Young." *American Quarterly* 38 (1986): 265–86.

———. "Religion and the New England Mill Girl: A New Perspective on an Old Theme." *New England Quarterly* 60 (1987): 429–53.

Leach, James. *Stubborn Facts from the Factories*. London: John Ollivier, 1844.

Letters from the United States on the Workings of Democracy. London: James Gilbert, 1844.

Leys, Colin. "Petitioning in the Nineteenth and Twentieth Centuries." *Political Studies* 3 (1955): 45–64.

Lillibridge, G. C. *Beacon of Freedom: The Impact of American Democracy upon Great Britain 1830–1870*. University of Pennsylvania Press, 1954.

Lindsay, Jack. "Ebeneezer Jones, 1820–1860: An English Symbolist." In Maurice Cornforth, ed., *Rebels and Their Causes*, pp. 151–76. London: Lawrence and Wishart, 1978.

Linton, W. J. *Memoirs* in *Literacy and Society*, ed., Victor Neuberg. London: Woburn Press, 1971 [1879].

———. *The People's Land: And an Easy Way to Recover It*. London: J. Watson, 1850.

———. *Three Score Years and Ten*. New York, N.Y.: Charles Scribner's Sons, 1894.

Little, Alan. "Chartism and Liberalism: Popular Politics in Leicershire, 1842–72." Ph.D. dissertation, Manchester University, 1991.

———. "Liverpool Chartists: Subscribers to the National Land Company, 1847–8." In John Belchem, ed., *Popular Politics, Riot, and Labour: Essays in Liverpool History*, pp. 247–51. Liverpool: Liverpool University Press, 1992.

Lockwood, Carol A. "Capturing the Rural Myth? The Land Settlement Scheme in East Sussex." Paper presented at the North American Conference on British Studies, Washington D.C., Oct. 6, 1995.

London Health of Towns Association, *Address to the Inhabitants of Manchester and Salford: Why Are Towns Unhealthy?* N.p., n.d.

Longmate, Norman. *The Breadstealers*. London: St. Martin's Press, 1984.

Longworth, James. *The Cotton Mills of Bolton: A Historical Directory*. Bolton: Bolton Museum and Art Gallery, 1986.

Lott, Eric. *Love and Theft: Blackface Minstrelsy and the American Working Class*. Oxford: Oxford University Press, 1993.

Loudon, J. C. *A Manual of Cottage Gardening, Husbandry and Architecture*. London: A and R. Spottiswoode, 1830.

Lovett, William. *Life and Struggles of William Lovett*. London: MacGibbon & Kee, 1967 [1876].

Lowe, R. A. "Mutual Improvement in the Potteries." *North Staffordshire Journal of Field Studies* 12 (1972): 75–82.

Lowe, W. J. *The Irish in Mid-Victorian Lancashire*. New York, N.Y.: Peter Lang, 1989.

Lowell Directory. Boston, Mass.: Sampson and Murdock, 1851.

Lowell State/National Park, Lowell, Massachusetts. Museum Displays of 19th-Century Cotton Production and Workers' Experiences, Aug. 1994.

Luther, Seth. *Address to the Working Men of New England on the State of Education and on the Condition of the Producing Classes in Europe and America*. New York, N.Y.: George H. Evans, 1833.

MacAskill, Joy. "The Chartist Land Plan." In Asa Briggs., ed., *Chartist Studies*, pp. 302–41. London: Macmillan, 1960.

Magdol, Edward. *The Antislavery Rank and File*. Westport, Conn.: Greenwood Press, 1986.

Marsden, Richard. *Cotton Weaving: Its Development, Principles and Practice*. London: George Bell and Sons, 1895.

Marsh, Jan. *Back to the Land: The Pastoral Impulse in Victorian England from 1880 to 1914*. London: Quartet Books, 1982.

Marston, Jerrilyn. "The Creation of a Common-Law Rule: The Fellow Servant Rule, 1837–1860," *University of Pennsylvania Law Review* 32 (1984): 579–620.

Martin, David. "Land Reform." In Patricia Hollis, ed., *Pressure from Without*, pp. 131–58. London: Edward Arnold, 1974.

Martineau, Harriet. *Society in America*. Gloucester: Peter Smith, 1968 [1837].

Marx, Karl, and Frederick Engels. *Collected Works*. Vol. 6. London: Lawrence and Wishart, 1976.

Marx, Leo. *The Machine in the Garden*. New York, N.Y.: Oxford University Press, 1964.

Masquerier, Lewis. *Scientific Division and Nomenclature of the Earth, and Particularly the Territory of the United States, into States, Counties, Townships, Farms and Lots . . .* New York, N.Y.: L. Masquerier, 1847.

———. *Sociology*. Westport, Conn.: Greenwood Press, 1970 [1877].

Mather, F. C., ed. *Chartism and Society: An Anthology of Documents*. London: Ball & Hyman, 1980.

McCalman, Iain. *The Horrors of Slavery and Other Writings by Robert Wedderburn*. New York, N.Y.: Markus Wiener, 1991.

———. *Radical Underworld: Prophets, Revolutionaries and Pornographers in London, 1795–1840*. Cambridge: Cambridge University Press, 1988.

McCord, Norman. *The Anti–Corn Law League*. London: Allen and Unwin, 1968.

McElroy, J. L. "Social Reform in the Burned-Over District: Rochester, New York as a Test Case, 1830–1854." Ph.D. dissertation, SUNY-Binghamton, 1974.

McFarland, C. K., and Robert L. Thistlethwaite. "20 Years of a Successful Labor Paper: The Working Man's Advocate, 1829–49." *Journalism Quarterly* 59 (1983): 35–39.

Miles, Rev. Henry A. *Lowell as It Is and as It Was*. Lowell: Powers and Bagley and N. L. Dayton, 1845.

Mind Amongst the Spindles: A Selection from the Lowell Offering. London: Charles Knight & Co., 1844–45.

Minor, Jodie. "The Not-So-Friendly Societies: Benefit Societies, Radicalism and the British State, 1832–1867." Paper presented at the North American Conference on British Studies, Washington, D.C., Oct. 6, 1995.

Montgomery, David. *Citizen Worker: The Experience of Workers in the United States with Democracy and the Free Market during the Nineteenth Century*. Cambridge: Cambridge University Press, 1993.

Moore, Ely. *Address on Civil Government, Given before the New York Typographical Society, Society Library Lecture Room, Feb 25, 1847*. New York, N.Y.: B. R. Barlow, 1847.

————. *Oration Delivered before the Mechanics and Workingmen of the City of New York on the Fourth of July 1843*. New York, N.Y.: John Windt, 1843.

Moore, Kevin. "This Whig and Tory-Ridden Town: Popular Politics in Liverpool in the Chartist Era." In John Belchem, ed., *Popular Politics, Riot and Labour*, pp. 38–67. Liverpool: Liverpool University Press, 1992.

Morgan, John Minter. *The Christian Commonwealth*. London: Chapman and Hall, 1845.

Morgan, Nigel. *Deadly Dwellings: Housing and Health in a Lancashire Cotton Town: Preston from 1840 to 1914*. Preston: Mullion Books, 1993.

Morley, John. *Life of Richard Cobden*. London: T. Fisher Unwin, n.d.

Murphy, Theresa. *Ten Hours' Labor: Religion, Reform and Gender in Early New England*. Ithaca: Cornell University Press, 1992.

Nadel, Stanley. "From the Barricades of Paris to the Sidewalks of New York: German Artisans and the European Roots of Amerian Labor Radicalism." *Labor History* 30 (1989): 47–75.

Nadworny, Milton. "New Jersey Workingmen and the Jacksonians." *Proceedings of the New Jersey Historical Society* 67 (July 1949): 185–89.

National Land Reform Association. *Land and Labor: Their Relation in Nature—How Violated by Monopoly*. New York, N.Y.: National Land Reform Association, n.d.

National Land-Draining Company for England, Ireland and Scotland, *Thoughts Upon Supplying Food and Employment for the Working Population of the United Kingdom*. London: William Clowes and Sons, 1845.

National Reform Almanac for 1848. New York, N.Y.: n.p., 1848.

Nevins, Allan, ed. *The Diary of Phillip Hone*. New York, N.Y.: Dodd, Mead & Co., 1927.

New York Association for Improving the Condition of the Poor. *Annual Report*. New York, N.Y.: John F. Trow, 1852.

Newbould, T. Palmer, *Pages from a Life of Strife*. London: Frank Palmer, 1910.

Noakes, John. *The Right of the Aristocracy to the Soil Considered*. London: Effingham Wilson, 1848.

Norris, Joe L. "The Land Reform Movement." In *Papers in Illinois History, Transactions for the Year 1937*, pp. 73–82. Springfield, Ill.: The Society, 1939.

O'Brien, James Bronterre. *Bronterre's Letters*. Scrapbook, British Library.

O'Connor, Feargus. *The Employer and the Employed: Chambers' Philosophy Refuted*. N.p., 1844.

————. *The Land and Its Capabilities: A Lecture by Feargus O'Connor at the Hall of Science, Camp Field, Manchester on Monday, March 7, 1842*. Manchester: Abel Heywood, 1842.

————. *A Letter from Feargus O'Connor to John Humphreys Parry, Barrister-at-Law, But Neither Farmer Nor Lawyer*. London: John Cleave, 1843.

————. *A Letter from Feargus O'Connor, Esq. to the Reverend William Hill*. London: John Cleave, 1843.

————. *A Practical Work on the Management of Small Farms*. Manchester: Abel Heywood, 1846.

————. *The Remedy for National Poverty and Impending National Ruin*. Leeds: Joshua Hobson, 1841.

————. *Reply of Feargus O'Connor, Esq., to the Charges against His Land and Labour Scheme ... on Tuesday Evening, October 26, 1847, in the Hall of Science, Camp Field, Manchester*. Manchester: Abel Heywood, 1847.

————. *The Speech of Feargus O'Connor Esq. on the Day of Nomination, Nottingham, July 28, 1847*. Halifax, Nicholson and Wilson, 1847.

————. *What May Be Done with Three Acres of Land*. N.p., n.d.

Offer, Avner. *Property and Politics, 1970–1914: Landownership, Law, Ideology and Urban Development in England*. Cambridge: Cambridge University Press, 1981.

Ogilvie, William. *An Essay on the Right of Property in Land*. London: J. Walter, 1781.

Orwell, George. *The Road to Wigan Pier*. London: V. Gollancz, 1937.

Owen, Harold. *The Staffordshire Potter*. Bath: Kingsmead Reprints, 1970 [1901].

Paine, Thomas. *Agrarian Justice Opposed to Agrarian Law and to Agrarian Monopoly*. In Max Beer, ed., *Pioneers of Land Reform*, pp. 182–95. Colne: Colne Public Library, n.d.

Parker, K. *Chartism in Colne, 1839–42*. Colne: Colne Public Library, n.d.

Parnissen, T. M. "Thomas Spence and the Origins of English Land Nationalization." *Journal of the History of Ideas* 34 (1973): 135–41.

Parry, J. H. *A Letter to Feargus O'Connor, Esq*. London: H. Hetherington, 1843.

Paul, W. *History of the Origin and Progress of Operative Conservative Societies*. Leeds, 1838.

Perkin, Harold. "Land Reform and Class Conflict in Victorian Britain." In J. Butt and I. F. Clarke, eds., *The Victorians and Social Protest*. Newton Abbott: Archon Books, 1973, pp. 177–217.

Pessen, Edward. "Thomas Skidmore: Agrarian Reformer in the Early American Labor Movement." *New York State Historical Association Proceedings* 25 (1954): 280–96.

————. "The Ideology of Stephen Simpson, Upperclass Champion of the Early Philadelphia Workingmen's Movement." *Pennsylvania History* 22 (Oct. 1955): 328–40.

————. *Most Uncommon Jacksonians: The Radical Leaders of the Early Labor Movement*. Albany, N.Y.: State University of New York Press, 1967.

————. "The Working Men's Movement of the Jacksonian Era." *Mississippi Valley Historical Review* 43 (Dec. 1956): 428–43.

Pettit, Richard Norman. "Albert Brisbane: Aspostle of Fourierism in the United States, 1834–1898." Ph.D. dissertation, Miami University, 1982.

Phythian-Adams, Charles. "Ceremony and the Communal Year at Coventry, 1450–1550." In Richard Hold and Gervase Rosser, eds., *The English Medieval Town: A Reader in English Urban History, 1200–1540*, pp. 238–64. London: Longman, 1990.

Pickering, John. *The Working Man's Political Economy*. New York, N.Y.: Arno/ The New York Times, 1971 [1847].

Pickering, Paul. *Chartism and the Chartists in Manchester and Salford*. London: Macmillan, 1995.

Pickvance, William W. *Prize Essay on the Advantages Working Men Will Derive by Visiting the Exhibition of 1851*. Manchester: J. Leach, 1851.

Pierson, Michael D. "'Guard the Foundation Well': Antebellum New York Democrats and the Defense of Patriarchy." *Gender and History* 7 (1995): 25–40.

Platt, Daniel W. "Horace Greeley." In Perry J. Ashley, ed., *American Newspaper Journalists, Dictionary of Literary Biography*, vol. 43, pp. 256–72. Detroit, Ill.: Bruccoli Clark, 1985.

Plummer, Alfred. *Bronterre*. London: George Allen & Unwin, 1971.

———. "Spade Husbandry during the Industrial Revolution." *Journal of the South-West Essex Technical College and School of Art* 1:2 (1942): 84–96.

Post, Albert. *Popular Freethought in America, 1815–1860*. New York, N.Y.: Columbia University Press, 1943.

Prentice, Archibald. *A Tour of the United States, with Two Lectures on Emigration*. London: John Johnson, 1849.

Proceedings of the Seventh Annual Industrial Congress. Philadelphia, Pa.: John Sailer, 1852.

Propositions of the National Reform League for the Regeneration of Society. London: Working Printers' Co-operative Association, n.d.

Prude, Jonathan. *The Coming of Industrial Order: A Study of Town and Factory Life in Rural Massachusetts, 1813–1860*. Cambridge: Cambridge University Press, 1983.

———. "Town-Factory Conflicts in Rural Massachusetts." In Stephen Hahn and Jonathan Prude, eds., *The Countryside in the Age of Capitalist Transformation*, pp. 71–102. Chapel Hill, N.C.: University of North Carolina Press, 1985.

Public Entry of John Fielden, Esq., MP and General Johnson, MP into Oldham. Manchester: Grant and Co., 1847.

Public Health Act, 11 & 12 Victoria, Cap. 63. *Report to the General Board of Health on a Preliminary Inquiry into the Sewerage, Drainage and Supply of Water, and the Sanitary Condition of the Inhabitants, of the Chapelry District of Bacup, in the County of Lancaster*. London: W. Clowes, 1849.

Public Health Act, 11 & 12 Victoria, Cap. 63. *Report to the General Board of Health on a Preliminary Inquiry into the Sewerage, Drainage and Supply of Water, and the Sanitary Condition of the Inhabitants, of the Borough of Preston*. London: W. Clowes, 1849.

Public Health Act, 11 & 12 Victoria, Cap. 63. *Report to the General Board of Health on a Preliminary Inquiry into the Sewerage, Drainage and*

Supply of Water, and the Sanitary Condition of the Inhabitants, of the Borough of Wigan. London: W. Clowes, 1849.

Public Health Act, 11th and 12 Vict Cap. 63. *Report to the General Board of Health on a Preliminary Inquiry into the Sewerage, Drainage and Supply of Water, and the Sanitary Condition of the Inhabitants of the Township of Pendleton.* London: W. Clowes and Son, 1851.

Quaife, Milo M. "The Attainment of Statehood." *Publications of the State Historical Society of Wisconsin* 29. Evansville: Antes Press, 1928.

———. "The Convention of 1846." *Publications of the State Historical Society of Wisconsin* 27. Evansville: Antes Press, 1919.

Rayback, Joseph G. "The Industrial Workman and the Antislavery Crusade." *Journal of Economic History* 3 (1943): 152–63.

Reach, A. B. *Manchester and the Textile Districts in 1849.* Rossendale: Helmshore Local History Society, 1972.

Read, Donald. "Chartism in Manchester." In Asa Briggs, ed., *Chartist Studies*, pp. 29–64. London: Macmillan, 1960.

Read, Donald, and Eric Glasgow. *Feargus O'Connor, Irishman and Chartist.* London: Edward Arnold, 1961.

Reed, Amy L., ed. *Letters from Brook Farm, 1844–1847.* Poughkeepsie, N.Y.: Vassar College, 1928.

Reid, Naomi. "Richard Pilling." In Joyce M. Bellamy and John Saville, eds., *Dictionary of Labour Biography*, vol. 6, pp. 216–23. London: Macmillan Press, 1982.

———. "Thomas Clark." In Joyce M. Bellamy and John Saville, eds. *Dictionary of Labour Biography*, vol. 6, pp. 55–59. London: Macmillan Press, 1982.

Reynolds, David S. *George Lippard, Prophet of Protest.* New York, N.Y.: Peter Lang, 1986.

Ritchie, J. Ewing. *Freehold Land Societies: Their History, Present Position and Claims.* London: Woodfall and Kinder, 1853.

Robbins, Roy. "Horace Greeley, Land Reform and Unemployment, 1837–1862." *Agricultural History* 7 (1933): 18–41.

Roberts, David. *Paternalism in Early Victorian England.* New Brunswick: Rutgers University Press, 1979.

Roberts, Stephen. "Joseph Barker and the Radical Cause, 1848–1851." In *Publications of the Thoresby Society, vol 1 for 1990*, pp. 59–71. Oxford: Clarendon Press, 1991.

———. *Radical Politicians and Poets in Early Victorian Britain: The Voices of Six Chartist Leaders.* Lewiston: Edwin Mellen, 1993.

Robinson, William B. *A Letter Addressed to the Trades, Orders and the Public on the Principles of the Charter, the National Land Company, and the National Land and Labour Bank.* Manchester: C. Jacques, 1847.

Rodgers, Daniel T. "Republicanism: The Career of a Concept." *Journal of American History* 79 (June 1992): 11–38.

Roediger, David R., and Phillip S. Foner. *Our Own Time.* New York, N.Y.: Verso, 1989.

Rogers, Frank. "Mike Walsh, a Voice of Protest," M.A. thesis, Columbia University, 1952.

Rose, Anne C. *Transcendentalism as a Social Movement*. New Haven, Conn.: Yale University Press, 1981.

Rozwenc, Edwin C. *Cooperatives Come to America: The History of the Protective Union Movement, 1845–1867*. Mt. Vernon, N.Y.: Hawkeye-Record, 1941.

Rudkin, Olive. *Thomas Spence and His Connections*. London: George Allen and Unwin, 1927.

"Rules to Be Observed by the Hands Employed in This Mill." Haslingden: J. Read, 1851.

Russell, R. W. *America Compared with England*. London: J. Watson, 1849.

Ryckman, L. W. *The Largest Liberty Defined: A Treatise on the Inherent Rights and Obligations of Man*. New York, N.Y.: W. Applegate, 1840.

Savage, Michael. *The Dynamics of Working-Class Politics: The Labour Movement in Preston, 1880–1940*. Cambridge: Cambridge University Press, 1987.

Savetsky, Seymour. "The New York Working Men's Party." M.A. thesis, Columbia University, 1948.

Saville, John. *1848: The British State and the Chartist Movement*. Cambridge: Cambridge Unversity Press, 1987.

———. *Ernest Jones, Chartist*. London: Lawrence and Wishart, 1952.

———. "Introduction." In R. G. Gammage, ed., *History of the Chartist Movement*, pp. 1–61. New York, N.Y.: Augustus M. Kelley, 1969 [1854].

Saxton, Alexander. "Problems of Class and Race in the Origins of the Mass Circulation Press." *American Quarterly* 36 (1984): 211–34.

———. *The Rise and Fall of the White Republic*. London: Verso, 1990.

Schlesinger, Arthur. *Age of Jackson*. Boston: Little, Brown and Company, 1945.

Schlueter, Hermann. *Lincoln, Labor and Slavery: A Chapter from the Social History of America*. New York, N.Y.: Socialist Literature Co., 1913.

Scholes, John Christopher. *History of Bolton: With Memorials of the Old Parish Church*. Bolton: Daily Chronicle Office, 1892.

Schwartzkopf, Jutta. *Women in the Chartist Movement*. New York, N.Y.: St. Martin's Press, 1991.

Schwarzlose, Richard. "The Foreign Connection: Transatlantic Newspapers in the 1840's." *Journalism History* 10 (1983): 44–49.

Scoresby, Henry. *American Factories and their Female Operatives*. London: Longman, 1845.

Scott, Joan. "On Language, Gender and Working-Class History." In *Gender and the Politics of History*, pp. 53–67. New York, N.Y.: Columbia University Press, 1988.

Sellers, Charles. *The Market Revolution: Jacksonian America, 1815–1846*. New York, N.Y.: Oxford University Press, 1991.

Shannon, Fred. "The Homestead Act and the Labor Surplus." *American Historical Review* 41 (1936): 637–51.

Shepperson, Wilbur. *Emigration and Disenchantment: Portraits of Englishmen Repatriated from the United States.* Norman, Okla.: University of Oklahoma Press, 1965.

Shlakman, Vera. "Economic History of a Factory Town: A Study of Chicopee, Massachusetts." *Smith College Studies in History* 20 (1934–35): 1–264.

Sillett, John. *The Evidence of John Sillett, on His Examination before a Committee of the House of Commons ... [on the] National Land Company, Clearly Proving That a Man May Live Well and Save Money on Two Acres of Land.* London: J. Watson, 1848.

———. *A Practical System of Fork and Spade Husbandry.* London: M'Gowan &Co., 1848.

Simpson, Stephen. *The Working Man's Manual: A New Theory of Political Economy.* Philadelphia, Pa.: n.p., 1831.

Sioussat, St. George L. "Andrew Johnson and the Early Phases of the Homestead Bill." *Mississippi Valley Historical Review* 5 (Dec. 1918): 253–87.

Skidmore, Thomas. *The Rights of Man to Property!* New York, N.Y.: Alexander Ming, 1829.

Smith, Charles Manby. *The Working Man's Way in the World.* London: Printing Historical Society, 1967.

Smith, F. B. *Radical Artisan: William James Linton, 1812–97.* Manchester: Manchester University Press, 1973.

Smith, Henry Nash. *Virgin Land: The American West as Symbol and Myth.* Cambridge, Mass.: Harvard University Press, 1950.

Smyles, John. *A Letter Addressed to Mr. Pitkeithly.* London: J. Watson, 1842.

Solly, Henry. *James Woodford, Carpenter and Chartist.* London: S. Low, Searle and Rivington, 1881.

———. *Re-Housing of the Industrial Classes: Village Communities versus Town Rookeries.* London: W. Swan Sonnenschein, 1884.

Somerville, Alexander. *Autobiography of a Working Man.* London: Charles Gilpin, 1848.

———. *Cobdenic Policy the Internal Enemy of England.* London: Robert Hardwicke, 1854.

———. *A Letter to the Farmers of England.* London: James Ridgway, 1843.

Spann, Edward K. *The New Metropolis: New York, 1840–1857.* New York, N.Y.: Columbia University Press, 1981.

Speech of Hon. S. H. Rogers of North Carolina, April 28, 1854. N.p., 1854.

Speech of the Hon. Albert G. Brown, of Mississippi, on the Homestead Bill. Washington(?): Donelson and Armstrong, 1852.

Speech of the Hon. H. B. Stanton in the Senate, on the Subject of the Distribution of the Public Lands. N.p., 1854.

Speech of the Hon. John Pettit of Indiana on the Homestead Bill, Delivered in the Senate, April 18, 1854. N.p., 1854.

Spence, Kenneth M. "Social and Economic Geography of Preston." M.A. thesis, University of Liverpool, 1968.

Spence, Thomas. *The End of Oppression, or a Quartern Loaf for Two Pence.* London: T. Spence, n.d.

———. *Pigs' Meat: The Selected Writings of Thomas Spence, Radical and Pioneer Land Reformer,* ed. G. I. Gallop. Nottingham: Spokesman Press, 1982.

———. "Selected Writings of Thomas Spence." In P. M. Kemp-Ashraf, ed., *Life and Literature of the Working Class: Essays in Honour of William Gallacher,* pp. 271–350. Berlin: Humboldt-Universitat, 1966.

———. *Spence's Recantation of the End of Oppression.* London: T. Spence, n.d.

———. *Trial of Thomas Spence in 1801,* ed. Arthur Waters. Leamington Spa: Courier Press, 1917.

Stansell, Christine. *City of Women: Sex and Class in New York, 1789–1860.* Chicago, Ill.: University of Illinois Press, 1987.

Stedman Jones, Gareth. "Rethinking Chartism." In *Languages of Class,* pp. 90–178. Cambridge: Cambridge University Press, 1983.

———. "The Language of Chartism." In James Epstein and Dorothy Thompson, eds., *The Chartist Experience: Studies in Working-Class Radicalism and Culture, 1830–1860,* pp. 3-58. New York, N.Y.: Macmillan, 1982.

Stephens, Joseph Rayner. *People's Magazine.* London: John Cleave, 1841.

———. *The Political Pulpit.* Ashton-Under-Lyne: n.p., 1839.

Stephenson, George. *The Political History of the Public Lands from 1840 to 1862.* Boston: R. G. Badger, 1917.

Stevens, William. *A Memoir of Thomas Martin Wheeler.* In *Chartist Biographies and Autobiographies.* New York, N.Y.: Garland, 1986 [1862].

Stokes, Melvyn, and Stephen Conway, eds. *The Market Revolution in America: Social, Political and Religious Expressions, 1800–1880.* Charlottesville, Va.: University Press of Virginia, 1996.

Stott, Richard. *Workers in the Metropolis.* Ithaca, N.Y.: Cornell University Press, 1990.

Styal Mill, Styal, Cheshire. Museum Displays of Working Cotton Mill and Apprentice House, Mar. 1994.

Swajkowski, Cynthia Anne Paul. "Chartist Contributions to the American Workers." Ph.D. dissertation, George Washington University, 1996.

Sweeney, Kevin. "Rum, Romanism and Reform: Coalition Politics in Massachusetts, 1847–1853." *Civil War History* 12 (1976): 116–37.

Sykes, Robert. "Early Chartism and Trade Unionism in Southeast Lancashire." In James Epstein and Dorothy Thompson, eds., *The Chartist Experience,* pp. 152–93. London: Macmillan, 1982.

———. "Physical Force Chartism: The Cotton District and the Chartist Crisis of 1839." *International Review of Social History* 30 (1985): 207–36.

———. "Some Aspects of Working-Class Consciousness in Oldham, 1830–1842." *Historical Journal* 23 (1980): 167–79.

Taylor, Peter Forbes. "Popular Politics and Labour-Capital Relations in Bolton, 1825–1850." Ph.D. dissertation, University of Lancaster, 1991.

Texan Emigration and Land Company. *Texas: Being a Prospectus of the Advantages Offiered to Emigrants*. London: Richardson, 1843.

Thistlethwaite, Frank. *America and the Atlantic Community: Anglo-American Aspects, 1790–1850*. New York, N.Y.: Harper & Row, 1959.

Thom, William. *Rhymes and Recollections of a Hand-Loom Weaver*. London: Smith, Elder & Co., 1845.

Thomason, A. *Men and Things in America, Being the Experience of a Year's Residence in the United States*. London: William Smith, 1838.

Thomason, William. *O'Connorism and Democracy Inconsistent with Each Other*. Newcastle: Tyne Mercury Office, 1844.

Thompson, Dorothy. *The Chartists: Popular Politics in the Industrial Revolution*. London: Maurice Temple Smith, 1984.

Thompson, E. P. *The Making of the English Working Class*. London: Penguin Books, 1980.

———. "The Moral Economy of the English Crowd in the Eighteenth Century." *Past and Present* 50 (1971): 76–136.

———. "Time, Work-Discipline, and Industrial Capitalism." *Past and Present* 38 (1967): 56–97.

Thornton, William Thomas. *Overpopulation and Its Remedy*. London: Longmans Green. 1845.

———. *A Plea for Peasant Proprietors*. London: John Murray, 1848.

Tiller, Kate. "Charterville and the Chartist Land Company." *Oxoniensia* 50 (1985): 251–66.

Todd, Franciscus Allen. "The Condition of the Working Classes in Preston, 1790–1855." M.Litt. thesis, University of Lancaster, 1972.

Tomlins, Christopher. *Law, Labor and Ideology in the Early American Republic*. Cambridge: Cambridge University Press, 1993.

Trash! Museum Exhibition, New York Public Library, Dec. 23, 1994.

The Trial of Feargus O'Connor, Esq., and Fifty-Eight Others. London: John Cleave, 1843.

Ure, Andrew. *Dictionary of Arts, Manufactures and Mines*. London: Longman, 1843.

Van Amringe, Harry Hamlin. *Association and Christianity*. Pittsburgh: J. W. Cook, 1845.

Vernon, James. *Politics and the People: A Study in English Political Culture, 1815–1867*. Cambridge: Cambridge University Press, 1993.

View of Rochdale from Broadfield (lithograph). Rochdale: E. Wrigley, n.d.

Vincent, David, ed. *Testaments of Radicalism*. London: Europa, 1977.

Walsh, Elizabeth O'Neil. "Leisure for the Operatives in Nineteenth-Century Fall River, Massachusetts." M.A. thesis, Boston College, 1989.

Walsh, Mike. *Sketches of the Speeches and Writings of Michael Walsh*. New York, N.Y.: Thomas McSpedon, 1843.

Warburton, W. H. *The History of Trade Union Organization in the North Staffordshire Potteries*. London: George Allen and Unwin, 1931.

Ware, Caroline F. *The Early New England Cotton Manufacture*. Boston, Mass.: Houghton Mifflin, 1931.

Ware, Norman. *The Industrial Worker: 1840–1860*. Boston, Mass.: Houghton Mifflin, 1924.

Warnes, A. M. "Early Separation of Homes from Workplaces and the Urban Structure of Chorley, 1780 to 1850," *Transactions of the Historial Society of Lancashire and Cheshire* 122 (1970): 105–35.

Warren, Josiah. *Equitable Commerce*. New York, N.Y.: n.p., 1852.

Watson, Harry L. *Liberty and Power: The Politics of Jacksonian America*. New York, N.Y.: Hill and Wang, 1990.

Waugh, Edwin. *Sketches of Lancashire Life and Localities*. London: Whittaker and Co., 1855.

Webb, Beatrice. *My Apprenticeship*. Bath: Pitman Press, 1979 [1926].

Wellwood, Samuel. *A Letter to Feargus O'Connor, Esq., against His Plan of Dividing the Land*. London: James Young, 1842.

Wennersten, John Raymond. "Parke Godwin, Utopian Socialism, and the Politics of Antislavery." *New York Historical Society Quarterly* 60 (1976): 107–27.

———. "A Reformer's Odyssey: The Public Career of Parke Godwin of the New York *Evening Post*." Ph.D. dissertation, University of Maryland, 1979.

Wheeler, Thomas Martin. *A Brief Memoir of the Late Mr. Feargus O'Connor, M.P.* London: Holyoake & Co., 1855.

White, George. *An Answer to John Humphreys Parry*. London: T. Stutter, 1843.

Whitehead, Andrew. "The *New World* and the O'Brienite Colony in Kansas." *Bulletin of the Society for the Study of Labour History* 53 (1988): 40–43.

Whittle, D. *History of the Borough of Preston*. Preston: P. and H. Whittle, 1837,

Wiener, Joel H. *Radicalism and Freethought in Nineteenth-Century Britain: The Life of Richard Carlile*. Westport, Conn.: Greenwood Press, 1983.

Wiener, Martin. *Reconstructing the Criminal: Culture, Law and Policy in England, 1830–1914*. Cambridge: Cambridge University Press, 1990.

Wigan Operatives' Reform Association. Wigan: J. Brown, 1836.

Wigan Record Office. *Those Dark Satanic Mills: An Illustrated Record of the Industrial Revolution in South Lancashire*. Wigan: Wigan Metropolitan Borough Council, 1981.

Wilentz, Sean. *Chants Democratic: New York City and the Rise of the American Working Class 1788–1850*. New York, N.Y.: Oxford University Press, 1984.

———. *The Kingdom of Matthias*. New York, N.Y.: Oxford University Press, 1994.

Williams, Mike, with D. A. Farnie. *Cotton Mills in Greater Manchester*. Preston: Carnegie Publishing, 1992.

Winstanley, Michael. "Oldham Radicalism and the Origins of Popular Liberalism." *Historical Journal* 36 (1993): 619–43.

Wittke, Carl. *The Utopian Communist: A Biography of Wilhelm Weitling, Nineteenth-Century Reformer.* Baton Rouge, La.: Louisiana State University Press, 1950.

Wood, Marcus. *Radical Satire and Print Culture, 1790–1822.* Oxford: Clarendon Press, 1994.

Worcester Almanac, Directory and Business Advertiser for 1851. Worcester, Mass.: Henry J. Howland, 1851.

Wright, Benjamin. "The Philosopher of Jeffersonian Democracy." *American Political Science Review* 22 (Nov. 1928): 870–92.

Wright, T. *A Short Address to the Public on the Monpoly of Small Farms: A Great Cause of the Present Scarcity and Dearness of Provisions.* London: H. L. Galabin, 1795.

Yeo, Eileen. "Some Practices and Problems of Chartist Democracy." In James Epstein and Dorothy Thompson, eds., *The Chartist Experience: Studies in Working-Clas Radicalism and Culture, 1830–1860,* pp. 345–80. London: Macmillan, 1982.

Young America. New York, N.Y.: Young America, n.d.

Young, Arthur. *An Inquiry into the Propriety of Applying Wastes to the Better Maintenance and Support of the Poor.* Bury: J. Backham, 1801.

Zahler, Helene Sara. *Eastern Workingmen and National Land Policy, 1829–1862.* New York, N.Y.: Columbia University Press, 1941.

Zboray, Ronald J. "Technology and the Character of Community Life in Antebellum America: The Role of Story Papers." In Leonard I. Sweet, ed., *Communication and Change in American Religious History,* pp. 185–215. Grand Rapids, Mich.: William B. Eerdmans, 1993.

Zboray, Ronald J., and Mary Saracino Zboray. "Political News and Female Readership in Antebellum Boston and Its Region." *Journalism History* 22 (1996): 2–14.

Zonderman, David. *Aspirations and Anxieties: New England Workers and the Mechanized Factory System, 1815–1850.* New York, N.Y.: Oxford University Press, 1992.

Index

In this index an "f" after a number indicates a separate reference on the next page, and an "ff" indicates separate references on the next two pages. A continuous discussion over two or more pages is indicated by a span of page numbers, e.g., "57-59." *Passim* is used for a cluster of references in close but not consecutive sequence.

Library of Congress Cataloging-in-Publication Data
Bronstein, Jamie L.
    Land reform and working-class experience in Britain and the United States,
1800–1862 / Jamie L. Bronstein
        p.   cm.
    Includes bibliographical references and index.
    ISBN 0-8047-3451-8 (cloth : alk. paper)
        1. Land reform—Great Britain—History—19th century.   2. Land reform—
United States—History—19th century.   3. Working class—Great Britain—
History—19th century   4. Working class—United States—History—19th century.
5. Right of property—United States—History—19th century.   6. Right of
property—Great Britain—History—19th century.   I. Title.

HD1333.G7B76   1999
333.3'142—dc21
98-28068   CIP

This book is printed on acid-free, recycled paper.

Original printing 1999
Last figure below indicates year of this printing:
08   07   06   05   04   03   02   01   00   99